images, heroes, and self-perceptions

images, heroes,

prentice-hall, inc., englewood cliffs, new jersey

LOU BENSON

Los Angeles Valley College

photographs by
Charles, Larry, and Steve Cline

and
self-perceptions

the struggle for identity—
from mask-wearing to authenticity

Library of Congress Cataloging in Publication Data

BENSON, LOU
    Images, heroes, and self-perceptions.

    Bibliography: p.
      1. Identity (Psychology)   2. Self-perception.
  I. Title.
BF697.B4   155.2   73-17134
ISBN 0-13-451187-5

images, heroes, and self-perceptions

the struggle for identity— from mask-wearing to authenticity

LOU BENSON

Printed in the United States of America.

10   9   8   7   6   5   4   3   2   1

Photographs by Charles, Larry, and Steve Cline, except for the following: page 15, by Herbert, from Frederic Lewis; page 76, Bettman Archives, Inc.; pages 143 and 178, courtesy of Trans World Airlines; page 251, Department of Interior; page 306, Photo Researchers, Inc.; page 328, National Institute of Mental Health; page 400, Department of Interior, National Park Service; page 406, National Aeronautics and Space Administration.

PRENTICE-HALL INTERNATIONAL, INC., *London*
PRENTICE-HALL OF AUSTRALIA, PTY. LTD., *Sydney*
PRENTICE-HALL OF CANADA, LTD., *Toronto*
PRENTICE-HALL OF INDIA PRIVATE LIMITED, *New Delhi*
PRENTICE-HALL OF JAPAN, INC., *Tokyo*

for nancy, kathy, and bob

contents

vii

man, nature, and psychopathology

ix

x

prologue

There are a few moments in an individual's life when he has a fleeting glimpse of who he is and what he might become. These are moments in which certain authentic portions of himself are struggling to be recognized. But such occasions are rare and not easily recognized for what they are. And so, for most of us, they pass into the stream of memory as unimportant items in that huge accumulation of past events to which we hardly pay heed.

Thus occurs one of the least heralded tragedies of our lives. For these are momentous events. They are the critical moments in which our lives might change—they are the opportunities when we might discover those things that could give our existence meaning and fulfillment. They are brief illuminations of inner realities that could bring to our lives excitement and richness beyond our fondest dreams.

These moments pass without notice because we have somehow learned to distrust them—to devalue them—to disqualify them from serious consideration. We live in a world that is saturated with information about who we are and who we must be. And most of that information runs contrary to the promptings of these impulses, which are in fact our real selves striving for expression. We therefore respond to the outer influences and ignore the inner ones. The tragic nature of this choice will, it is hoped, become clear shortly.

A large number of human beings live their lives in a kind of apathetic resignation. The world, they feel, is an unhappy place. And the lot of human beings is not much better. To seek happiness is to reach for the impossible. So they settle for a kind of empty, uniform, vegetative existence.

The assumptions underlying the communication in this book is that this outlook is neither true nor necessary. It is my contention and the contention of those upon whose work I have depended for support that human beings are capable of great joy and a large measure of fulfillment; that life is largely an exciting adventure for those who are willing to give up the safety of compulsive self-concealment and risk living in a way that opens them up to their own unfolding.

The two conditions necessary for this process are self-understanding and self-love. Self-understanding, in this sense, means more than simply being intellectually knowledgeable about oneself. It means being in intimate contact with one's deepest emotions. And self-love means being uncritically accepting of them. These are not easy tasks. Most of us fear that the discovery of those emotions that are darkly hidden will simply confirm what we already fear—that we are terrible, evil, sinful creatures who are not worthy of anyone's love, let alone our own. And so self-knowledge becomes anathema to us.

But it is an interesting bit of irony that those of us who resist self-knowledge because we are afraid that it might lead to self-hatred, end up hating ourselves anyway. Because on some level we know that we are concealing something (which must of course be terrible, otherwise why should we hide it) and, therefore, whatever that deep dark secret is, it is of no consequence. We need not know the specifics of our evil doing in order to realize its baseness. And so we hate ourselves anyway. Thus we have fulfilled neither of the two conditions.

The aim of this book is therefore to present reasons for the cultivation of an attitude of openness toward the self and to offer alternate ways of responding to those forces in our society that prevent it. But the very subject matter makes it important that the reader approach this material in a new way. Most academic course work can be mastered reasonably well by "standing aside," so to speak, without becoming commited in a personal sense. But it is wasteful to use this approach for the study of self-understanding. Commitment in this context, that is, exploring one's *own* self rather than an abstract self, is the whole point of such an endeavor. If it is true that American education has overwhelmingly concerned itself with developing the intellect of its charges, to the utter neglect of their emotional growth, then this book is one small attempt to begin to redress this grievance.

I would therefore like to urge each reader to consider what follows from the standpoint of his own inner experience — to think of his efforts as a journey into self-awareness. Perhaps this may become one of those moments — one of those authentic glimpses — one of those opportunities that are so often lost to us. Let us hope that this time we recognize the moment for what it is and seize it. And let us hope that we finally embrace the new self that may emerge along the way.

the presentation of the self

chapter 1
the ego trip

Most Americans don't know who they are. They don't know who they are because they mistake their egos for themselves. Like Frenchmen, Italians, Indonesians, or Eskimos, Americans wear masks in their interactions with one another. But the masks worn by Americans appear to be more rigid and more opaque, and they tend to conceal more of what lies beneath. Most Americans have some illusions about what they want for themselves, but they are deceived. They are beguiled by a part of themselves that is unreal and largely superfluous.

Americans, and perhaps human beings in general, cannot know anything about themselves because they are reluctant to take off their masks, even to themselves. This aversion gives rise to a partial blindness with regard to anything concerning themselves. And since almost everything in one's experience is related to—and altered by—one's perception of himself, this blindness is continually present. It appears that Americans conceal more of themselves from others and, at the same time, conceal more of

3

themselves from themselves. Why this should be true will become clear presently.

The masks that people wear serve certain social purposes. The teacher, the doctor, the policeman, the parent, the student, the priest, all play their roles within some generally accepted province. These roles help us to predict, with some degree of accuracy, the kinds of behavior that can be expected from others. This enables us to minimize our responses while making it unnecessary for us to learn what is expected of us from every new encounter.

But the roles people play and the masks they wear can take on strange colorations when they become greatly exaggerated in form and importance. When the need to maintain the mask becomes so crucial that the individual begins to lose sight of his real needs and desires, he has lost the ability to discriminate between his *image* and his *real self*. It is likely that the American emphasis on competitiveness, achievement, material success, and status all grow out of, and contribute to, such a state. That is, these behaviors are all manifestations of an underlying syndrome which places the focus of experience upon the *mask* rather than on the *self*.

This kind of emphasis has the effect of turning the person's attention from his *experience* to his *appearance*. That is, the individual tends to ignore his state of being, his stream of consciousness, and concentrate on his objective *image*. He comes to evaluate himself within the framework of a hierarchy chosen by his society. Moreover, since he must depend to a great extent upon the views of others for his evaluation of himself, he must surrender his autonomy. His behavior under such conditions becomes dependent upon values that are rooted *outside* himself and, instead of being "who he is," he becomes "who he thinks he *should* be."

If it is true that this is an age in which people are confused, disturbed, bewildered, and anxious, then it is likely that a good deal of this kind of feeling stems from the discrepancy between what man *is* and what he attempts to *appear to be*. Moreover, a constant concern with one's image is itself an anxiety-producing situation since there are a great number of circumstances in which the image is subjected to some kind of threat. A great deal of psychopathology can be seen to be a struggle of the individual to maintain a concept or image of the self which is continually being "disconfirmed" by his experience (Phillips, 1956). In the face of this kind of contradiction, the organism tends to distort the experience (reality) and, in so doing, to give up a part of his real self for the benefit of the image. It is easy to see that every additional distortion of reality is a further step along the continuum of pathological behavior.

The idea of being one's self is often expressed as "doing one's own thing." We can say that one is being himself when he is doing (or thinking) what he really wants to do (or think). When, however, one is acting in a way that is intended to appeal to others or to a code of behavior that does not come naturally to him, *he is not "doing his own thing"* at all. He is, in fact, *"doing someone else's thing."* And doing someone else's thing without knowing it leads to trouble. The person who says, as so many do these days, "I don't really know what my feelings are" has probably denied his real feelings somewhere along the line.

THE NEED FOR SELF-AFFIRMATION

There is a drive in the human organism for some form of self-affirmation or positive self-evaluation. This drive or need is manifested in a variety of ways. However, it sometimes takes on some subtle disguises and, if we are not alert, we may easily mistake it for something else. The fact that the need exists may be obvious, for it has been confirmed by a great deal of clinical research. But the ways in which it can be altered by circumstances can be surprisingly varied.

It must first be pointed out that this drive does not present itself in the same way in lower animals, and it may be for this reason that it has often been ignored by psychologists who study motivation. A good deal of the research in this field has attempted to find general laws that apply to most organisms, assuming a continuation from animals to man. And, of course, in such drives as hunger, thirst, sex, love, and so on, a good deal of valid work has demonstrated this continuity.

But it is naive to think that we can *really* understand human behavior by studying animals even in these areas. For when we get into the area of symbolic representation, the continuity ends. The use of words, symbols, and conceptualization takes the human organism into another kind of thought realm in which his needs can be presented in other than concrete forms. His symbolic representations come to replace physical stimuli in the external world, and he may be more strongly motivated by an *idea* or a *memory* than by a morsel of food.

But the really essential difference between man and his animal progenitors, the difference that makes almost all interpolation impossible is the fact that it is highly unlikely that animals cultivate a self-image. This means that not only are all kinds of responses altered in human behavior, but most of the stimuli are differentially perceived as well.

If animals do not have a self-image, then we may assume that animals, like children, are "existentialists." They live *in* the moment, *for* the moment, keenly aware of the ongoing experience. They see and hear and feel and are clearly conscious of what they experience because they have nothing to interfere with it. It is unlikely that they reflect upon their awareness. They simply *are*.

Human adults, on the other hand, are capable of a really remarkable feat. They can experience, and at the same time they can *know* that they are experiencing. They can analyze, categorize, memorize, and so on, all while the experience is in progress. Not only can they do all of this, but they can *picture themselves* doing it. One effect of all this extracurricular activity is to dilute the experience itself, to dampen or lower its intensity so that the awareness becomes hazy because of the superimposition of these other perceptions.

But there is a more important effect of all this. Once the human adult begins to picture himself as a separate entity, he becomes concerned about his worth. Although an animal does not in all probability think of itself as "good," "worthwhile," "adequate," "bad," "worthless," "evil," and so on, human beings do. It is in this area therefore that animal research fails to clarify man's behavior.

A great deal has been written about the things that differentiate homo sapiens from the lower animal species. The development of the hand, for example, was undoubtedly an important step in the change from animal to man since it gave man the ability to fashion tools that were to greatly augment his power over the physical world. Along with this he evolved a larger brain and the faculty of symbolic speech, by which he was able to communicate more accurately and also to think, using these symbols conceptually, in a highly sophisticated way. But one of the most important things to develop out of this capacity, and one that has not always been given the attention it deserves, has been *man's ability to see himself objectively.*

In human beings, the whole style of life depends upon a person's attitude toward himself. It is, for example, an extremely important factor in the way he relates to others. Fromm (1956) has shown that a negative self-image (that is, the inability to love one's self) is so detrimental to a person that it all but eliminates his capacity to love others.

Such a finding has enormous consequences. For if the self-image is so crucial in what is surely one of the most important areas of human development, it must indeed be of fundamental importance to any understanding of human motivation. And as we shall see, it is.

THE SEARCH FOR THE HEROIC

If we accept a roughly hedonistic point of view, we may assume that man will tend to maximize his pleasant experiences and minimize his unpleasant ones. We may then make the assumption that positive self-evaluative experience is pleasant and negative experience is decidedly unpleasant. This leads to the observation that a person will generally try to maximize those situations which lead to positive self-evaluations and minimize those of a negative kind.

The term "positive self-evaluation" must be considered in its broadest sense. It does not necessarily connote approval or even affection, although these of course are often present. Its opposite is not "hate," for example, but *disinterest*. A person does not have to be liked, but *he must not be ignored*. He must, in some sense, be considered *important*. This is not generally understood. People feel rejected more by indifference than by hostility. If you hate someone, you, at least by implication, admit that he *exists*. As one psychologist has said, it is better to be actively hated than to be treated as if one's existence was unimportant or irrelevant. It is *indifference* that is the enemy of the ego. This must be understood when we use the terms "approval" or "worthwhile" in this discussion.

If one is to have a clear idea of what is meant by positive rather than negative self-evaluations, some set of criteria should be used. Certain kinds of attributes are generally considered desirable; others are not. But the division is by no means perfectly clear. The quality "submissive" might be desirable under some conditions (for example, a "good" feminine trait in some cultures) and it may be negative in others. Hair on the chest is positive for a man in our society but hardly a source of admiration in a woman. How, then, are we to classify the qualities that are desirable in a given culture? One way is by an examination of its heroes.

The hero is the traditional idol of man. He does the things that we all wish we could do. He embodies the qualities that we wish we had. Our Walter Mitty dreams cast us in the role of the great hero and for awhile, in our imagination, we participate in his exploits. In these fantasies we perform great feats, defeat powerful foes, love and are loved by the most perfect creatures imaginable, and are envied and admired by everyone.

If it is true that the qualities that are attributed to the heroes of a culture are those qualities which are most highly regarded; and if an individual tends to aspire toward them, then an examination of the heroes of any given society will reveal what that society values most highly in its people. Moreover, from a psychological point of view, the popular versions of the hero and heroine can show the difference between what people *profess* to admire and what they *do* in fact admire. It will be these qualities with which they will identify rather than a commonly espoused list of virtues.

There are different types of heroes in American life, but one that exerts a great deal of influence is one we shall call the "primitive hero." The effect of this figure on our thought and behavior is very great because he is first presented to us when we are very young.

Even before we are able to read or write, we are exposed to the primitive hero by the mass media. He is the cartoon and storybook character whose adventures appear in comic books and on the television screen early on weekend mornings. Long before we have developed critical faculties, this character becomes a dominant figure in our lives. But the primitive hero does not disappear as we grow older. He survives in a great deal of popular literature to become the one-dimensional character of pulp fiction, movies, and radio and television drama. He is simple and primitive in all his aspects. He is the "good guy" with brawn, no mind, and simple answers to all questions: "yep," "nope."

In assessing this figure Gurko (1953) makes this observation: "The accent has been on muscle over mind, instinct instead of brain, impulsiveness at the expense of reflectiveness, producing a series of one-sided, immature personalities." This hero, incidentally, is in sharp contrast to the more sophisticated characters of mature fiction who are unfortunately ignored by the vast majority of Americans, even in this age of highly educated people. The heroes of the absurd and the antiheroes of the twentieth century are even more widely neglected.

The primitive hero, however, is one we all know. And it is he who will interest us for the moment, for his qualities throw a great deal of light on our own behavior, and a close examination of his nature will prove interesting and even surprising.

the hero and the myth

The psychologist–philosopher Carl Jung made a study of the mythologies of many different peoples. He found in the histories of almost every one certain recurring symbolic representations that have also been observed in dreams. He called these symbols archetypes and classified several different kinds. Jung noted that the archetype of the hero was prominent in all the mythologies he studied. Moreover, he observed striking similarities running through the heroic legends of people in very different parts of the world. It became apparent to him that these representations were more than mere idle tales of bravery and daring. He came to attach a great deal of importance to the heroic archetype. He felt that it revealed certain instinctive proclivities in the human being which transcended cultural differences. However, he noticed that each culture tended to impose variations of its own on its archetypal symbols and that such variations could be instrumental in understanding some of the values that were preeminent to it.

Lord Ragland (1936) also made a detailed study of the hero in literature and, like Jung, found some extremely interesting consistencies among diverse cultures. Ragland focused on ancient myths and categorized some of the common elements of classical heroic figures. He found that the mythological heroes were always of royal birth, from the union between a king and a royal virgin. The hero was the firstborn and his adventures began immediately, for an attempt was always made on his life in the cradle. He was rescued and set adrift in some kind of vessel. He drifted to a distant land, where he was raised by strangers. Nothing was known of his childhood, but upon reaching manhood he began his quest to regain his kingdom or to slay a dragon or to do battle with an evil king. He was victorious over his enemy and married a princess. He ruled for a short time, but curiously he fell out of favor either with the gods or his people and, after being driven from his kingdom, he died under mysterious circumstances. The classical hero was often lame or had some vulnerability that caused his undoing.

Vulnerability was sometimes very important to the myths. Samson had his weakness in his hair, Achilles in his heel, Adam in his weak will, and even Odysseus was easily hooked on lotus. The heroines, too, had failings. Eve, Salome, Delilah, and Cleopatra all had their faults. However, in the age of chivalry this began to change. Princesses were prim and proper and barely uttered a word for two hundred years.

The classical heroes were often immortal gods or mortal men striving for immortality. They often used magic (invisibility, aid of supernatural beings, magical weapons, and so on) to destroy their enemies. They never fought ordinary men or ordinary animals but were pitted against kings,

Heroes present models with which we try to identify.

giants, demons, or such superanimals as fire-dragons. Sometimes the victory was not merely a physical one. Oedipus won his throne by solving a riddle. Moses was successful in making rain, as were a number of other Jewish heroes (a truly heroic accomplishment in the Sinai). Theseus had to find his way out of a complex maze. Other classical heroes had to overcome similar obstacles before completing their missions.

Some writers have seen the mythological hero as the symbol of man's power to transcend the phenomenal world and to acquire religious enlightenment. In this sense the hero was seen as conveying the individual's ability to go beyond the "prison of the five senses" to experience the mystical state of being. This is an interesting point because through this version of the hero, the individual is supposed to learn how to *transcend* the ego in order to reach the enlightened stage. This idea is expressed by Campbell: "As a rising smoke of an offering through the sun door, so goes the hero, released from the ego, through the walls of the world—leaving the ego—and passing on. The hero then leaves the image of the self to gain knowledge" (1949). The American version of the hero has turned the image around and, as we shall see, runs from knowledge to gain the ego.

The ancient heroes were fighting to gain enlightenment or to achieve their rightful throne in order to give their subjects the benefits of their victories. Here again the American myths have altered the theme: the hero enjoys the fruits of his labors more or less by himself. The man who rises from the gutter to become a railroad tycoon does not, in the American version of the story, spread his fortune around. The fortune in American folklore is not for the many but for the rugged individual who acquires it.

There are other variations in the hero myths which have been added in the modern American version. Where the classical hero was a prince seeking his rightful legacy, the American hero is an ordinary man seeking a princely fortune. Where the heroes of Greece and Rome had vulnerabilities, American heroes are without any signs of weakness or defect. Where the great men of mythology were sometimes sages, American heroes are mostly anti-intellectual. And where the ancient heroes were almost always virtue personified, some of the heroes of American folklore are criminals, scoundrels, or politicians who are often both.

the heroic qualities

American heroes (and heroines) fall roughly into two categories. One is the ascetic, asexual hero presented mostly for juvenile audiences, although he occasionally survives to be transformed slightly for adult consumption. The other is the libertine who breezes through a series of escapades gratifying his gluttony as he goes. We will consider first the primitive hero as presented for children, although, as we have noted, the adult audience is also susceptible to the influences of this figure.

The heroes of the simple kind are all virtue. They are pure of spirit, clear of mind, and endowed with strength and courage. After overcoming what appear to be insuperable odds, they always defeat the forces of evil. These heroes have had many names. There are Superman, the Lone Ranger, Captain Marvel, Space Ghost, Mighty Mouse, Roy Rogers, Dick Tracy, and the incomparable Batman. These creatures share certain qualities making them almost completely interchangeable. For example, they are all supremely healthy. They are completely free of the maladies and indispositions that harass the rest of us. They know nothing of hernia, gastritis, gout, or venereal disease. And they have never been debilitated by such embarrassments as hemorrhoids. (Imagine how the latter would handicap Batman as he prepares to vault into the Batmobile.)

The hero's health and vigor are visible. One can see them in his carriage, his facial expression, in the vitality of all of his movements. He must always be in top physical condition because he is a man of action. He must be prepared to react to any threat at a moment's notice. He may occasionally be wounded (an honorable infirmity), but he has no congenital imperfections. For illness in our society is viewed with some disdain. We do not look kindly upon disability. We tolerate it and even patronize it but we are not happy about it. If it exists in our family we are ashamed of it and may even try to hide it. But it does not belong to our concept of the hero, and we do not find it in our idols.

The hero is always physically attractive. (Although we are not considering the heroine here, many of these qualities are, of course, applicable to her. There are, however, certain differences, which will be dealt with shortly.) The male hero has the conventional attributes of masculine charm. The thick wavy hair, the straight teeth, the strong jaw that sometimes pulsates with determination, and the straight flawless nose, (the hallmark of all heroes with the possible exception of Dick Tracy, who must have been careless for one moment in the distant past). The task of differentiating the hero from the villain, an extremely important discrimination in all social intercourse, is greatly facilitated by these physical signs. The hero is immediately identifiable by his cleanliness, his straightforwardness, and his good looks.

This kind of hero is always completely virtuous. His virtue consists of whatever happens to be considered desirable by a broad segment of the society. This makes some of our modern heroes abstinent almost to the point of asceticism. Such a figure raises some questions regarding his virility. In fact, a man who is overly concerned with defeating the forces of evil, and who is completely oblivious to the rather strenuous efforts of voluptuous women to seduce him, is open to a number of suspicions. On the other hand, the second type of hero, who alternately mixes sexual escapades with danger in a continual series of adventures, seems to be trying desperately to assert his masculinity in the face of some self-doubt. In either case, heterosexuality in our popular heroes is not firmly established.

Not only are the classical and juvenile heroes "virtuous" to an extreme, but the mature hero is also sometimes just as straight-laced. The good-guy Western hero may have a girl friend, but he practically never lays a hand on her. John Wayne, Matt Dillon, even Li'l Abner are not too much driven by libido. Sometimes one suspects that they have no libido at all, considering their bland indifference to feminine charm. Moreover, it is not only in the sexual sphere that they are intensely "moral". They are strong supporters of law and order. They fight to maintain the status quo. They are highly conventional and vehemently oppose crime, subversion, obscenity, intellectualism, and other evils. Moreover, they have very clear (if extremely oversimplified definitions) of these vices.

The other hero to whom we have already referred is the libertine. He is only remiss in the one area of sex. Otherwise, he is just as sterling in character as the ascetic hero. Sexually he is both unresisting and irresistible, and though there is a slight intimation of naughtiness in this feature of his personality, he is forgiven for it. After all, no one is perfect. Besides, this trait adds some spice to his life. But when it comes to fighting vice and wickedness, he is just as persistent as his counterpart.

The hero is not only healthy; he is eternally young. The very thought of a hero who is not in the prime of life is ludicrous. Who can imagine Mightyoldmouse, Batelderlyman, the Decrepit Lone Ranger, or Supersenileman? How would Tarzan look with a pot belly and a bald head? How could anyone take seriously the exploits of a doddering Matt Dillon, who shoots down his enemies in spite of the Parkinsonian tremor of his gun hand. And with regard to our outlaw heroes (about whom we will have something to say shortly), how ridiculous would be the figure of "Billy the Elder"?

If health and youth are the identifying marks of the hero, courage is the psychological trait that justifies his very existence. Courage is, of course, the prerequisite heroic quality. Our heroes have absolutely no reluctance about rushing boldly into confrontations with incredible danger. Their sense of abandon is something that we all envy. They never back down from a fight no matter what the odds. And they appear to be unaffected by any hint of fear.

In fact, the whole concept of courage is changed in our mythology. For courage is the ability to overcome fear and to do what is necessary regardless of the danger. If our heroes are incapable of experiencing fear, their behavior in the face of danger is not courageous at all, but foolhardy. But fear, although natural to most mortals, is not considered heroic and is therefore left out of the repertoire of the hero.

Although the American version of the hero has certain similarities to the classical legends, it also has its differences. And one of these differences is extremely important. The American hero has one quality that the ancient heroes lacked. He has one capability that every other historical figure would surely envy. This unique characteristic, which the American mythology finds indispensable for its hero, is *infallibility*. The American hero is a *winner*. He cannot lose. There is no set of circumstances, no obstacle, however formidable, that can prevent his ultimate triumph. He may have setbacks in minor skirmishes, but he never has defeats. (Even Superman's susceptibility to some exotic substance is only temporary.) The thought of failure is foreign to the hero. In American folklore there are winners and losers, but the losers are not admired. "He's a loser" has become an exclamation of disdain. The loser is someone to be shunned. There is even the intimation that his defect is contagious and so he is afforded the social standing of a leper.

The quality of infallibility in the American hero is often aided by the presence of a "side-kick" character who keeps his eyes out for enemies who may sneak up from "the rear."

But there is no such aversion to the winner (hero). He assures us of success from the beginning. Unlike Achilles, Samson, Caesar, and the others, the American does not fall prey to the vicissitudes of mortality. He is invulnerable. Bullets miraculously miss vital areas. Buildings fall in front or behind him. Tonto, Robin, or Gabby Hayes warn him in the nick of time if someone threatens from behind. And even his horse is capable of disarming a swarthy adversary when called upon.

The American hero cannot be defeated because when defeat threatens, he makes use of his greatest gift. He suspends the laws of nature. Who has not seen Mightymouse soar into the air pushing before him any obstacle, whether earthly or cosmic, to destroy his foe with one well-placed butt of his head. And all this from a standing start! And on how many Late Shows have we seen John Wayne or James Cagney or Edward G. Robinson (or even Mickey Rooney) fight his way through a group, or a mob, or even a regiment with his bare hands? And although our hero never draws first (he is unbelievably fair) he always *shoots* first and precisely where he aims. And one by one he eliminates his enemies. Finally after an incredible assortment of perils and pitfalls, he emerges unscathed and victorious.

VIOLENCE AS THE MODUS OPERANDI

Any study of the hero image in modern American life clearly brings out one fact. The hero in modern fiction is violent. He can knock a man senseless with one blow of his fist. And he is not reluctant to resort to such measures even if only slightly provoked. Just let anyone insult a woman in his presence (unless she happens to be a "bad" woman and then *he'll* do the insulting) and he will attack without warning. And if anyone should defame the institutions he holds dear, they will suffer a similar fate.

Violence for the hero is his modus operandi. He is often depicted with a gun in his hand on the covers of paperback books or theater billboards. He kills, he maims, he breaks noses and jaws. He even occasionally knocks women around, to the delight of sado-masochistic audiences. His solutions to every kind of problem are simple and quickly executed. He does not reason. Nor does he consider alternative courses of action. He is not likely to engage in long discussions of the pros and cons of a problem. There is no need for debates since right and wrong are clearly defined for him and anyone who disagrees is obviously a pervert, communist, antichrist, or cattle rustler. His justice is therefore simple and swift—if deficient to some extent in due process. A spate of films has recently appeared depicting black heroes of this type.

It is interesting to note that the hero's proneness to violence is one

The hero is often depicted brandishing a weapon, thus identifying violence as a heroic quality.

of his most valued characteristics. He is "always looking for a good fight" and is greatly admired for this predisposition. He is therefore sometimes depicted as a senseless brawling lug who drinks hard, fights hard, and in some cases loves (fornicates) hard. He defends such institutions as virginity with a gallantry that should have disappeared with the age of chivalry (when for all intents and purposes, virginity did). But his defense is always physical. He not only does not think too much about such matters but tends to be suspicious of anyone who does. The American hero is too "masculine" to be cerebral.

It is one of the axioms of our folklore that intellectualism is either sissyish, snobbish, or subversive. And so most American heroes are clods. The stereotype of the learned man in our culture is that of an absent-minded boob, awkward in social situations, especially where women are concerned, with thick horn-rimmed glasses that render him blind to anything but the dullest books. If this character develops into a hero at all, it is because someone rescues him from the terrible world he inhabits and takes his glasses off, gets him into a fight (after he has learned judo), teaches him the latest dance step (which he has to admit is great fun), gets him to reject his life of reflection (which he now sees as unutterably square), and in effect turns him into the vacuous, gregarious, brawling, hackneyed character of most American fiction.

There have developed in recent years two hero types who have really brought the use of violence to its most exaggerated extreme. They are the gangster and the tough guy. The gangster became a hero in the American mythology because it had always been implicit in the American success syndrome that means are irrelevant. Only the end is important. And the end for the gangster was seen by the audience as la dolce vita.

There will be objections to this statement on two counts: that the gangster is not depicted as a hero, and that his end is always either punishment or death. I believe that both objections are invalid. The gangster is rich, attractive, and violent. These are heroic qualities of the first importance. The second objection, that the gangster is always punished, is even more questionable. Since for a long while, especially in popular fiction, the code demanded that crime be punished, the gangster always came to a bad end. *But his punishment was a put-on to everyone* except the censor, who by his nature had to be the most gullible creature in the world. Here we have a gangster hero who has committed every crime in the book without running afoul of the law and then on his "last job" he manages to make a small error like leaving his birth certificate at the scene of the crime and he is caught. In some cases he is never apprehended by the police but is killed accidentally (an act of divine justice). But note two things: he would have committed the perfect crime had he not made a small mistake, and *the audience knows that he could have gotten away with it if this were real life rather than a fictional, highly contrived account.* Subconsciously what we say to ourselves is: "If it were I, I'd have made it without getting caught." Moreover, most of us know that the vast majority of crimes remain unsolved in the files of most police forces.

The gangster epitomized quick success by shortcut methods. For he was able to ignore the old restraints. He could simply take whatever he wanted. He never had to wait for gratification. He was rich and his life was exciting. If he disliked someone, he could destroy him without delay. He could act at the moment when his anger was at the flood instead of waiting until he had calmed down. Moreover, he had no conscience and we secretly envied him for that. We, too, have wanted to annihilate our enemies without feeling any pangs. We, too, have wanted to be able to satisfy our every wish at once. But the gangster's greatest attraction for us was that he appeared to make success a certainty. Once committed to his methods, he could not fail. And in America success is the name of the game.

Thirty years ago (and in some cases today as well) history books presented the story of P. T. Barnum as one of our folk heroes. This man whose watchwords were "Never give a sucker an even break" and "there's a sucker born every minute" was held up to a generation as an idol. True he was a symbol of a colorful era but he was also, by his own admission, a cheat. But he passed the test of heroic qualifications. He became rich.

It was only a short step therefore from such figures as Barnum to the "hard" gangster heroes. In the 1930s and 1940s James Cagney, Edward G. Robinson, and Humphrey Bogart filled our screens with their exciting exploits. The next step logically enough was the tough-guy detective. The main difference between him and the gangster was that he was on the "right" side of the law. This helped to give some justification for his behavior but did nothing to diminish his propensity for violence. If anything, it seems to have increased it somewhat, this time sanctioned by a feeling of "righteousness." The culmination of this kind of hero occurs in the writing of Mickey Spillane. His hero, Mike Hammer, is a brutal killer in the guise of a detective who commits mayhem in the name of law and order. He has no softness (weakness) to his nature and, like the gangster, can execute punishment (and very vicious punishment it is) at the moment he feels the need. If anyone doubts our dedication to brutality and violence in our heroes, Spillane's books can dispel their skepticism. They outsell most other titles by the millions.

These, then, are some of the versions of the hero in American mythology. The characters are violent, simple-minded, healthy, strong, magical, and invincible. If the masks that people wear are modeled on their concept of the hero, then this is the kind of figure they try to emulate. Moreover, since such heroic qualities as infallibility are impossible, a certain amount of deception (and self-deception) is necessary in order to adopt such a role. The consequences of this deception can have devastating effects on the individual and profound influences on society.

THE HEROINE

the heroine as lovee

The heroine in American folklore has fared no better than her masculine counterpart. Classically the heroine was a princess or a goddess. She was the hero's prize and was presented to him more or less the way a cup is presented to him when he wins the local country club tournament. But she symbolized all that was gentle and good in mankind. If the hero was the power of man to overcome adversity, the heroine was the embodiment of kindness and humanity beside his strength and firmness. (These, perhaps, are the real symbolic meanings of the heroic figures.) And she had a seemingly infinite capacity for love.

In the fairy tales she was portrayed as Snow White and Cinderella, the archetypes of the heroine. Phillip Wylie (1942) has traced the metamorphosis which the Cinderella myth has undergone in recent times. The true legend concerns the reward for virtue. Cinderella, unlike her sisters, is kind and unselfish, and although mistreated by her stepmother, she never attempts to return such treatment in kind. Her goodness is evidently so transparent that it makes her beautiful and irresistible to the handsome prince. She is rewarded by his love, which in the legend is the source of her happiness.

The American version, as Wylie points out, changes Cinderella completely. Her goal has changed from goodness to Goods and the means have

The American woman does not do things herself. She simply cheers her man on to achievement.

changed from virtue to guile. In fact, it is not generosity and unselfishness that are now seen as virtue, but cunning. The most important aspect of this bastardization of the myth is that the modern American heroine is not seeking love as her life-goal. She is seeking *admiration*. Put another way, the modern heroine is not interested in *giving* love, but in *getting* it. And one token of this love is material. That is, she gets her prince to give her rings, houses, furs, washing machines, and cars. The more she gets (presumably), the more she is loved.

The American heroine is depicted not as a poor girl who wins her prince through being kind and loving, but as a shrewd operator who vamps the prince by withholding her sexual "favors" from him until he has guaranteed (by legal contract) that she gets to keep the palace and the fancy coach if anything goes wrong. She is not even necessarily hung up on the prince. He just provides the groceries, furs, jewels, and other necessities by which she can impress her other admirers. The "erotic" dream of the American heroine, enacted time and time again in countless movies, shows the leading lady emerging from the stage door after a triumphant performance to be mobbed by a swarm of admirers who fawn over her, begging for a moment's attention. She bestows a few smiles on the eager throng as she wades through them to a huge limousine, which whisks her away to God knows what other triumphs. The American heroine is not a lover but a lovee. She is the recipient of so much love that she literally has to fight it off as she goes about her business.

the heroine as helpmate

Sometimes the heroine is the counterpart of the activist hero. Dale Evans, while retaining her femininity, can ride and shoot almost with the same effectiveness as her man. She too remains young and healthy and carries on the good fight against the enemies of society. This kind of heroine is rare, however. The stereotype of femininity that we have inherited from antiquity is passive. She stands by and watches in fascinated horror the climactic battle between her chosen love and his enemy. And even though one well-placed blow delivered by her to the back of the villain's head would dispatch the knave quickly, she does not act. And the reason that she does not make a move in her lover's defense is that if she did so, she would up-stage the hero. And since these stories are generally written by men, they won't let her do that. Her intervention would take the hero's victory away from him and give it to *her*. Man's ego just couldn't stand still for that. So she stands by like a clod and winces as the blows fall on the handsome face.

In this connection it is interesting to note that the heroine stories vary in certain ways depending upon whether they have been written by men for male audiences or by women for women. It is very likely that those legends that have attributed the sources of all evil to women were written by men. This is the man's cop-out. Eve and Pandora can be blamed for every act of depravity, every atrocity perpetrated by mankind on his fellows. And man's ego can remain undamaged since he rejects all responsibility. If we hadn't been tempted it never would have happened, we say. It's Eve's fault, or Circe's. This kind of heroine is therefore invented by man to absolve him of his guilt.

On the other hand, the female as mother, also probably created by men, is seen as completely free of evil or sin. She is depicted by such figures as the Virgin Mary and some of the classical goddesses. This duality of thought concerning women is curious but quite widespread. As the daughter, she embodies evil. As the mother, she is all goodness. How the daughter is purged of the devil when she becomes a mother is never explained.

Another version of the heroine is the one written by women for women. Here we find the overly romantic, sickly sentimental girl-child yearning for "romance" through thousands of novels, stories, songs, and soap operas. Her sensibilities are shallow, her ambitions childish, and her expressions maudlin. She is the fantasy figure of millions of bored housewives brought to life on page or screen who takes the role of long-suffering martyr or saccharine-sweet Pollyanna. This of course is the heroine so deplored by Wylie.

Another heroine created by women for women is the castrating bitch. She is the cannibal who devours men. She is the black widow spider in human form who fascinates and destroys every man who loves her or even tries to approach her. Legman (1949) has described her as the "bitch-heroine," who has appeared in thousands of books and stories, led, he claims, by the queen of them all, Scarlet O'Hara. But because the heroine has generally been the creation of male authors, the female in modern society has suffered a loss of status as a person. Very early in life our culture defines the female role in such a way that we discourage any spirit of individuality or adventure. Little girls are given playthings which communicate what is expected of them later on. Implied in this is the message that girls (women) are not to be anything much more than housewives and mothers. It is true that more and more women transcend these limits today. But these are the boundaries that have been set forth for them. The traditional woman has been seen by society (and unfortunately by herself as well) as an adjunct to the man who sallies forth to remake the world. When a young girl dares to show signs of being adventurous, innovative, or thoughtful, her femininity may be attacked. She is thus often forced to abandon these "vices" in favor of qualities that are more "ladylike." The male writers see these as subservience, intellectual inferiority, and complete subjugation to the male hero. Thus women are truly a suppressed group in our culture.

The heroine, like the hero, does not age. Youth is even more important for her than for him. The accent on physical attractiveness makes this essential. And of course the heroine is nothing if she is not beautiful. The old and ugly woman is despised. She is the witch or the evil queen. She is the enemy of the heroine and she must be destroyed before happiness can come to the heroine. Such figures, largely symbolic in the old legends, signifying the evil[1] within all of us, have again been changed in the American mythology. Now the figure of the witch is taken literally, and age has become woman's enemy. American women hide their age as long as possible; youth and physical attractiveness have replaced virtue in the hierarchy of feminine values.

Our culture is even more anti-intellectual with regard to the female than it is with regard to the male. The popular mythology depicts the intellectual woman as a prude and a snob. She, too, has her horn-rimmed glasses for quick identification. She is shown as a rather dull, terribly frustrated, stiff-looking woman, obviously sublimating her natural, sexual, and maternal instincts in a library or schoolroom. And the intimation is that she will never escape spinsterhood unless some man gets her to do the latest dance step while she is tipsy. He also succeeds in inducing her to throw her glasses away. (The fact that she needs them to read shows how superfluous they are in her new life. Everyone knows that reading is just for people who can't "make out.")

HEROISM AND SEXUAL ATTRACTIVENESS

One essential feature of the hero and heroine when presented for adults is sexual attractiveness. Whatever variations occur in the presentations of these characters, these qualities are dependably constant. Casanova, Don Juan, Venus, and Aphrodite represent the most effective manifestations of these forms. They are present in almost all the heroic figures and present models for identification of great variety. It is interesting in this connection

---

[1]The idea of evil will be discussed later. In this context it merely means that what one believes to be evil will be found to reside in the self if the society chooses to label certain universal impulses in that way. Such impulses cannot be successfully dismissed by denial. But they can be ascribed to others. This is what Americans have done to the myths. By splitting the characters into good guys and bad guys, we have attributed to others (bad guys) whatever we cannot accept in ourselves. This leads to the most extreme form of puritanism.

to note that many of the female sex symbols of the movies have been girls with somewhat homely features, glamorized to an extreme degree so that they give the impression of great beauty while allowing a model for identification for the plain women in the audience. The implicit idea is the feeling conveyed by the message that with a little makeup and fancy furs (toward which I am working) I can look like a movie queen.

Sexual attractiveness for the female is therefore possible, she thinks, through cosmetics and wealth. And the male can acquire it through wealth alone, which he sees as power (that is, masculinity). The man can be (and is) extremely attractive to the most beautiful women if he is known to be really loaded. And the woman wrapped in furs and decorated with jewelry has all the glamor she can ask for. One suspects, therefore, that egotism has a strong sexual basis. This is particularly true in a society where sex is treated as some sort of prize. Where the man must *win* his love's favor, and where sex itself is considered taboo before fullfilling certain requirements, it is perceived as a rare commodity. It therefore requires all kinds of striving and begets a value out of proportion to its real nature. In societies where sex is open and obtainable, the ego seldom takes this form. Where everyone is, in effect, a Don Juan, there is far less need to "prove" oneself in this way.

Identification with heroic figures occurs early in life. Later, although we may not remember them, these identifications may still affect our behavior.

These, then, are the models of our primitive heroes. They are easily recognized. They are figures with whom we can easily identify. And that of course is their purpose. The question of how much credence we give these creatures is extremely important and will be discussed later. We shall see that the extent to which such figures are taken seriously, especially on an unconscious level, will profoundly influence our self-perceptions. And these, in turn, will alter our perception of the world.

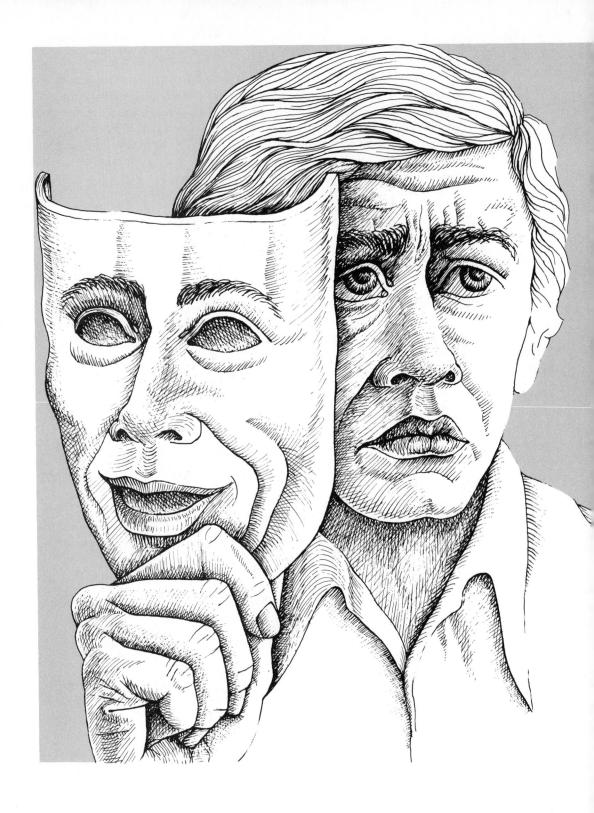

chapter 2
the two selves

The philosopher–mathematician Pascal made a very important observation about human vanity. Man, he said, is faced with a curious dilemma.

> He wishes to be great, and he sees himself small; he wishes to be happy, and he sees himself miserable; he wishes to be perfect, and he sees himself full of imperfections; he wishes to be the object of the love and esteem of men, and he sees that his defects merit only their aversion and contempt . . . he does his utmost to conceal his defects both from others and himself, and cannot bear that they should be shown to him, or that they should be seen (Robinson, 1931).

In other words, he wishes to be the hero and finds himself to be the buffoon. What a calamity! And how shall man overcome it? Pascal says, "he conceives a mortal hatred of the truth which reproves him, and convinces him of his defects. He desires to destroy it, and, not being able to destroy it in itself, he destroys it, as far as he can, in his own conscience and that of others." In other words, he does what any resourceful individual does when confronted with his own inadequacy. He lies. He denies the truth. He disguises it both from himself and others by adopting a mask. That is, he takes on the armor of the hero.

In modern terminology what Pascal is saying is that man, faced with the incontrovertible evidence of his own imperfection and fallibility, resorts to the defense mechanism of *denial*. Denial is probably the most primitive and most prevalent of all the mechanisms of defense. To some extent it is absolutely necessary to the normal functioning of everyday life. Some truths are simply too painful to face day after day, and so we refuse to acknowledge them by directing our attention to other things. This tendency is related to *perceptual defense*, which allows us not only to ignore certain aspects of the environment but also to *misperceive* them in a way that leads to gratification rather than disappointment or embarrassment. Coleman says that "we tend to avoid those aspects of a situation which are traumatic or self-devaluating or contradictory to our assumptions" (Coleman, 1964).

We not only ignore that which is self-deflating, but we alter our perceptions in order to perceive the opposite. We try to see ourselves as far as possible with heroic qualities. But this is no easy matter. If one is five foot two, dumpy, bow-legged, watery-eyed, and has pimples, how is he to picture himself as six foot four, slim, straight of limb, clear-eyed, and ruddy. Surely this appears to be an insurmountable obstacle. But of course it is no such thing. One merely needs a little ingenuity and some control over the self-image.

When we talk about the self-image we must make a very important distinction. A person is able to think of himself in two distinctly different ways. First, he can see himself as the center of his consciousness, as the viewer or perceiver of the events unfolding before him. At the same time, and superimposed upon this state of awareness, he is able to perceive himself objectively as he might appear to other observers. It is as if he could sit in the audience of a theatre and see himself as an actor on the stage. This dual aspect of the self has been described by various writers. Kant and Schopenhauer both referred to it and, as we have seen, so did Pascal. But for the most part the real importance of this phenomenon has been given little attention. The first psychologist to really recognize something of its significance was William James (1890). James called the part of the personality that is the *center* of awareness the "I." And the part that appears as the *object* of awareness he named the "me." The "I" perceives, senses, feels, knows. It is the seat or center of the "stream of consciousness." The "me," the self that is perceived objectively, is the version of the self presented for public view. It is the social self, the version that is calculated to have some effect upon others. But as we have already noted, it is also intended to have an effect on the self. We can all imagine how we appear to others, and this picture of ourselves takes on great importance for us. We ask in effect: How does this *me* appear to others? And then to convey a desired image, we strike a pose or adopt a role. Thus vanity is born.

It is necessary for an understanding of this phenomenon to consider some common assumptions about what we generally call egotism. Many people believe that the egotist is in love with himself. A person who brags about his "virtues" is thought to have a very high opinion of himself. But psychologists hold a different view. Vanity or egotism are not self-love but the *need* for a positive self-evaluation, often in its absence. *The egotist does not love himself.* He has, in fact, a good deal of dissatisfaction with regard to himself. And the pain caused by this feeling persuades him to try to do something about it. The behavior that we observe—the pompousness, bragging, arrogance, affectation—are all attempts in this direction.

The view of ourselves that we present to others therefore is not ourselves as we are, *but ourselves as we would like to have others see us.* Many psychologists feel that the reason we do not reveal our true selves to others is that we are afraid that, by so doing, we become vulnerable to attacks by others. Some writers say we may fear that if we allow others to know us truly, they will not like us. Of course there is some truth in both these statements. But perhaps there is a more important reason. Perhaps we know that if we reveal ourselves to others we *will reveal ourselves to ourselves.* And this may be the *real* fear. For if we do that, we will have to face the fact that we are not really the hero, but fallible, frightened, and mortal.

The way we avoid confronting this situation is to alter the image of the self in such a way that we do not allow the imperfections to be visible. This is what Jourard (1963) calls the "public self." The public self not only hides our imperfections from the world, but we ourselves are unable to see them. As we shall see, we are often more effective in deceiving ourselves than we are in deceiving others. But then we have a vested interest in our image.

THE PUBLIC RELATIONS PERSONALITY

It is quite clear that in general we are greatly concerned with the way we appear to others. And in our social presentations we try to create an image that will be received with approval. But the more important such approval is to a person, the more he will be concerned with his public self to the neglect of his subjective being. Martin Buber (1937) makes this distinction in discussing the difference between "essence man" and "image man." Essence man approaches life from the standpoint of *being who he is* without concern for the way he is perceived by others. Image man, on the other hand, focuses on *what he wishes to appear to be*. In reality, Buber admits that we are all a combination of both. But the tendency is to develop a life style that is dominated by one pole of this duality.

The difference between these two aspects of self-expression is crucial as regards individual freedom. The existential philosophers generally contend that man is free simply by the fact that he exists. Being-in-the-world means that man cannot escape making choices. Even if he submits to the pressures of others, he is still "choosing" such a course. This is one way to look at freedom, but let us consider another.

If we define freedom in relative terms, we can say that the number of alternatives available to an individual constitute the degrees of freedom he has. And we can see that essence man has greater freedom than image man. For essence man is not restricted by the opinions of others. He can consider all the options available to him before making a decision about a behavior or belief. He is thus able to more truly be himself when he finally makes a decision.

Image man, on the other hand, is in a straitjacket. The only choices open to him are those that he believes will elicit certain kinds of responses from others. This severely diminishes the number of alternatives available to him and tends to make him accept other people's evaluations of himself in preference to his own. *He is therefore almost completely dominated by the tastes and values of others.* Moreover, as we shall see, he comes to believe that these values and opinions are his own.

Social psychologists, sociologists, and anthropologists have been concerned with the way man presents himself to others in his daily interactions. Cooley (1902) described what he termed "the looking glass self." This is the image self as evaluated by others. Cooley says that we imagine how we must appear to another person and also imagine his judgment of us. If his judgment is favorable, we respond with a feeling of pride. If unfavorable, our response is a feeling of "mortification." One can well understand that a desire to maximize the former and minimize the latter will be quickly formed under these circumstances.

Mead (1934) describes the same phenomenon as taking on "the attitude of the other." The person comes to perceive himself as he thinks others perceive him. And this version of himself is to a great extent a fiction since it is his projection of someone else's view.

The presentation of the self for public consumption involves certain kinds of techniques. If as Adler says (1927) the individual strives for superiority but finds himself continually falling short, what action is available to him? The resourceful American as usual comes up with an ingenious solution. He invents a Madison Avenue version of himself. *This is the public relations version of his personality.* And like any public relations product, it is sold to the public by inflating it and putting it in a fancy wrapper. This PR version of the self is of course the hero or, more correctly, a modified version of it. To the extent that it is possible, we try to exhibit heroic qualities because we know that these qualities will gain for us the approval we seek.

Some people will object to the idea that we all desire heroic virtues. Many of us, it will be argued, have no such desire. We are little people who merely desire simple things. But the argument is not to be taken as literally as this. On some level we all want (need) approbation, and many of us are caused great anxiety when such approval is not forthcoming. We therefore tend to act in ways that win from others some degree of positive evaluation. To do this we must portray characteristics that are worthy of this response. And those characteristics, for lack of a better criterion, can be described as the kind displayed by heroic figures.

But the image one adopts may differ greatly from the real self. And a person may become so committed to the image aspect that he begins to mistake it for the person he really is. In such a situation his entire life is devoted to thought and action that is not his own. It is, by its very nature, dictated by someone else. However, he is unaware of this. For he has removed himself so far from his own feelings that he now believes that the motives for his actions originate in him. At this stage he no longer knows who he is.

This is extremely common in our culture. And none of us is completely free from its effects. We all have thoughts and feelings that we have been taught are wrong, sinful, useless, dirty, silly (that is, unheroic), and we decide to hide them and/or deny their existence. We behave in ways that are acceptable to the society and soon convince ourselves that this is the way we really *want* to behave. And in so doing we have given up a part of our identity. Put differently, we have given up a part of our freedom to be who we are. For when we surrender the opportunity to make our own choices (to feel our own feelings) because of the injunctions of others, we can no longer be ourselves.

This is not to say that it is possible or even desirable to try to live in the day-to-day world without playing certain roles and wearing certain masks. Societies function through the role play of their inhabitants. But if people begin to see their roles as their true selves and deny thoughts and feelings that are really present, they become estranged from themselves. And this has serious consequences.

some aspects of the public relations personality

As we have seen, the individual attempts to present some version of the hero to others. In so doing, he also tends to convince himself that he really does possess these qualities. He begins to believe that, at least in part, he really is the hero. Desire then becomes belief. And there is danger here. For there is a great difference between the desire for infallibility and the belief that one is, in fact, infallible. It is one thing to admire Superman. It is quite another to leap from a rooftop in the expectation that some profound inner quality will somehow alter the fundamental principles of aerodynamics. Figuratively we do this every day. Fortunately we do not always have to put our heroism to the test. The man, for example, who believes that he can seduce every woman he meets (playing Don Juan) simply does not have the time. He can thus entertain his fantasy without having to prove it in each instance.

The manifestations of this PR personality are many and ingenious. They can be very tricky and deceptive. And they often wear disguises, as, for example, in the case of the religious man who bragged so much of his humility that one could easily see that he was intensely proud of it. Humility had become a stance by which his PR personality could say, "See what a good man I am. See how humble I can be." The person who tries hard not to be vain, therefore, may be harboring some vanity about his modesty.

There is a good deal in the literature of modern psychology about this phenomenon. Jung gave the name *persona* to the social mask that people wear in their dealings with one another. Freud included the exclusive preoccupation with the self in his concept of narcissism. Adler saw the problem as a striving for superiority. And Karen Horney called it the ego-ideal and noted various manifestations of it as neurotic needs for such things as power, prestige, perfection, personal admiration, achievement, and so on. (Note here the marked resemblance to heroic qualities.)

It is important here to make another distinction between what is meant by the term "egotism" and what is meant by the concept of self-esteem. By egotism we mean the desire to present to others and to oneself certain qualities whether or not they exist. We want to look good, smell good, seem (not necessarily be) clever. We want respect (not necessarily deserved) and position (not necessarily earned). In short, *we want to be admired for qualities that we either have or can simulate.* The PR personality is indifferent to whether or not they are real.

Self-esteem, on the other hand, is a quiet confidence in one's own worth regardless of any shortcomings or deficiencies. Fromm describes it as the ability to love oneself, not by falsifying a version of the self, but by acceptance of what one really is. For Fromm (1956) this is an essential prerequisite to the ability to love at all. "The affirmation of one's own life, happiness, growth, freedom, is rooted in one's capacity to love, i.e. in care, respect, responsibility, and knowledge. If an individual is able to love productively he loves himself too; if he can only love others he cannot love at all."

Maslow (1968) and Rogers (1961) also stress the importance of a real sense of self-affirmation in the healthy adult. These authors see the tendency to inflate the image as a compensation for a feeling of inadequacy.

An additional observation may clarify this problem. The need for approval is ultimately the need for *self*-approval. That is, the child desires love and approbation from his parents and later from his friends, teachers, colleagues, and so on, because of a need in himself to be an object of worth. But in order to be convinced that he has filled this need, he must have evidence. This evidence comes in two forms: first in the opinions of those he respects and later in the confidence of his own judgment. The latter rests, however, upon the strength of the former and in general is directly proportional to it. When, therefore, these opinions are not strong or numerous enough to build up the needed self-assurance, the individual becomes anxious. He then tends to *create* the image that will arouse the desired approval in others. Thus is born the exaggerated, manufactured version of the self which is presented for public view. The image self or PR personality therefore grows out of a deficiency need. This is demonstrated by the fact that it is not nearly as important in the self-actualized person.

Maslow (1968) states that the self-actualized person does not present an image which society in general is likely to accept. He remains himself in spite of all kinds of pressures to "be like other people" or to "conform to the crowd." He may indeed, and often is, despised for his "unconventionality," but this does not influence him to change. He is not swayed by the fact that others disapprove. His conviction is too strong to be altered merely because of the existence of opposition. His own judgment has replaced the judgment of others in relation to his own value. But most people do not reach this stage. They are still dependent on what others think, and so their image is extremely important to them.

The essential fact about the PR personality is that it is phony. It is the polite presentation that does not "tell it like it is." It does not admit its own feelings or desires if such a revelation will cause it to suffer a loss of prestige. One cannot depend upon its pronouncements or promises since falsification is its principal mode of characterization.

The PR personality is to a great extent an American refinement. Although it is a universal phenomenon, the American way of life places a tremendous emphasis on it and continually reinforces its development. The whole of American culture is colored by this syndrome, which, to a great extent, prevents contact between people in most social situations. It leads to the superficial kinds of relationships which so characterize, not only the daily encounters between people, but even the kinds of associations between people who are ostensibly "close" to one another. (It is significant in this connection that the growth of "sensitivity" and "encounter groups" has become very important in the United States in recent years. One of the essential characteristics of these groups is the successful divestment of the masks of the participants. The group sessions offer almost the only opportunity afforded most people in our society to be themselves. In other cultures, European and Latin countries particularly, people are more apt to express their real feelings more often, and there such groups are not so numerous.)

the public relations personality and status

The achievement, success-oriented society in which we live is, to a great extent, the striving of the PR personality for a place in the hierarchy of the system. As Vance Packard (1959) has pointed out, we are a nation of status seekers. We present our images in a system of stratifications that more or less identify our place in society. But what is even more important from our point of view is that people often try to project an image which makes it appear that they are in a stratum higher than the one to which

Many of us acquire expensive "things," which are designed to enhance our public image.

they really belong. If a man is not too well off financially but can afford a high-status automobile, he may be treated while in that automobile (by people who know nothing else about him) as if he belonged to a station higher than his real one. And a person who goes to dinner in an expensive restaurant can hardly be distinguished from the millionaire at the next table (or at least so he believes).

One must not imagine that the desire for wealth, power, popularity, and so on, are motivated *only* by vanity. One could hardly defend such a view. Nor is such a defense necessary. The study of human motivation has shown that behavior is determined (and resisted) by many complex factors and that the activities we observe must often be attributed to several motives. For our purposes we may roughly divide these motives into two components. One, as we have said, is the desire to present a praiseworthy image in order to gain approval. This is the egotistical motive of the PR personality. The other is the experiential or existential component, which seeks certain experiences because they are pleasurable in themselves. Running for a touchdown to win the game may bring a great deal of adulation from the fans, but the experience of evading the tacklers, of meeting the challenge and overcoming the obstacles, has an existential component desirable in its own right.

This dualism of purpose pervades many activities. Sex used as conquest is a common example of egotistical and pleasure principles coexisting. Creativity often presents both kinds of rewards, although the existential joy of creativity is often overlooked in the avid search for glory. Success itself, and its fruits (possessions, leisure, travel, easy and immediate gratification of wants, and so on) are also rewarding in themselves. And many a businessman gets a great deal of pleasure out of the manipulations and machinations of his work. These things certainly do exist. However, they are often almost obliterated by the need for admiration and approval.

The hero needs marks of identification so that he will not be confused with other people. The symbols described by Packard provides these. It is for this reason that the symbols become ends in themselves. Moreover, it must be noted that one need not earn these symbols in a legitimate way in order to secure the benefits derived from them. People will fawn over a Rolls-Royce whether the driver is a gangster or an oil magnate. And both will be accorded the same kind of respect.

Hayakawa, in commenting on Packard's book, differentiates various kinds of status seeking. He describes a variety that he calls "status by consumption." This is the gaining of status by acquiring the commodities by which it is measured. This he believes to be a good thing since it enables people with no special talents to gain status through the things that they can acquire as consumers. But what Hayakawa does not seem to understand is that the psychological need for such a crutch is an obstacle to the development of the fully functioning person, about which he has a good deal to say elsewhere.

An analysis of American life of the kind made by Packard shows a kind of frantic concern with appearances all across the different classes. People go to tremendous lengths to impress others, even complete strangers, whom they will never see again. The pains to which people go with this kind of prepossession is reflected in the remark of one status-conscious man, who admitted: "On hot days I close all the windows of my car so that people will think I have air conditioning." It is clear from this statement that such a person is willing to put himself through a good deal of discomfort to impress people whom he does not know and who do not know him. The reinforcement that one gets from such behavior may be short-lived, but that only underlines the marked need which many people feel for positive appraisal by others.

Strangers are not the only ones who are the targets of our PR image. Anyone who has studied the kinds of disclosures which occur in psychotherapy knows that the masks that are worn, even by those closest to us, are many and varied. Many parents try to play the infallible role with their children for as long as they can get away with it. So do some teachers, psychiatrists, and ministers. And so do many husbands and wives with each other if they feel they can pull it off.

These are all merely different manifestations of what Greene (1967) has called "the hunger to be a hero" and which he believes to be a powerful motive in all of us.

This motivation has not been lost on the hucksters of the advertising business. The appeals to the ego in the public relations media are staggering. One has merely to turn on a television set or open a magazine and he is besieged by messages designed either to threaten or flatter, whichever will induce him to buy. Deodorants fall into the threatening type of message. If you don't use a particular brand, you are told, you will find people giving you a wide berth wherever you go. You will be shunned, spurned, disparaged, and humiliated. But never fear. If you merely spray, or roll, or smear a bit of the elixir in the right places (which are, incidentally, multiplying as rapidly as the brands themselves) you will be besieged by admirers the first time you go to the water cooler the next morning. However, if your deodorant stops odor but still allows even an infinitesimal amount of moisture to gather, you are doomed to spend the rest of your life in lonely isolation. Therefore, run to your drugstore tonight . . . And while you're at it, we have a product for your breath. . . .

In the same category are commercial messages for dandruff removers, teeth brighteners, hair dyes, and bleaches—cosmetics guaranteed to get you married whether you want to or not—face creams, hand lotions, hair dressings and restorers, exercise studios, massage parlors, charm schools, and success courses—all of which guarantee your popularity, desirability, irresistibility, while being absolutely essential to your continued survival. In short, all these products contribute to your *hero quotient*.

The flattering type of message works on what Packard identified as the "snob appeal" of many products. Automobiles of many kinds are in this category. So are the cigarettes that are for the chosen ones, the discriminating, intelligent smokers. Homes are of particular importance in this category. And of course the prestige that goes with a home can be enhanced by any number of things you put inside it, as well as the area in which it is built. Fashions in clothes also fall into this category. A person is depicted as "smart" or "chic" if he pays attention to the current fads. This of course affords one a simple means of presenting a good image. For he has only to consult the current "experts" through the media to be informed about what is "in" at any given time. Since this requires almost no individuality and therefore no anxiety, it is widely practiced. Fashions in art can be seen to wax and wane in a similar manner. And there is a great deal of snob appeal in having certain art works, books, records, or antiques in one's collection.

The idea is, of course, to appear knowledgeable about these things and so we find people reading articles about the current art fad, consulting authorities of various kinds about music or interior decorating, reading quick synopses of current or classical books rather than the books themselves, all in an effort to give the impression of the connoisseur while completely disregarding the *experience* afforded by these things. When these people do go to a concert or an art gallery, they are likely to be bored or at best numb. They are unable to feel anything because they have not learned how to open themselves to experience. Or, more correctly, they have unlearned what once came naturally to them as it does to all children. But they sit in a concert hall asking themselves how they are *supposed* to feel rather than merely allowing themselves to respond to what presents itself to them. They are afraid to allow themselves this freedom for they may respond "inappropriately" and thus give themselves away.

happiness and the public relations image

An interesting aspect of this phenomenon concerns the American attitude toward happiness. Since the hero always lives happily ever after, happiness is clearly one of the heroic attributes. It therefore becomes one of the necessary qualities of the PR image. But this presents a bit of a problem. Happiness is not something that is easy to come by. One cannot simply be happy on purpose. A little thought, however, shows that the difficulty can be handled like so many others that confront the ego. As Lobsenz (1962) points out, " . . . the important thing nowadays is to have fun, or to look as if you are having fun, or to think you are having fun, or at least to make believe you are having fun." The necessity to appear happy thus can become a part of the mask we wear.

It is also clearly a mark of success to have a lot of leisure time spent in the pursuit of pleasure. But Lobsenz's feeling is that this is not easily accomplished in a world where people are frantically trying to be upward-mobile. Even the women of the modern middle class are engaged in a frenetic series of activities which rob them of the leisure they might have. "What substitutes for leisure with the American female is the 'leisure look' —the little casual dress, the spike-heeled play shoes, the shorts, the care-free hairdo. She may be frazzled to a fare-thee-well internally, but on the outside, she is the very model of a modern matron-general."

The mask of happiness, like all the masks we wear, is often intended to deceive ourselves. Some people will force themselves through terribly long boring books, lectures, parties, and so on, on the grounds that they are *supposed* to be enjoyable, pleasurable, or culturally enriching. Jack Woodford (1944) believes that "millions of morons are so constituted that they will sit and drive themselves blindly through the most boring junk they can find (to read) if the *New Yorker* says it's the smart thing to do . . . ." Woodford, who advises writers about making their books salable,

A pleasure boat offers one the opportunity to wear the mask of pleasure even if he doesn't use it. Many of these boats never leave the dock.

tells them to deliberately make parts of their material dull and boring in order to convince their readership that their work has literary and intellectual merit.

Woodford makes another interesting observation. There are, he says, two kinds of writers: those who want to write and those who want "to have written." The former are, of course, those who enjoy putting words together in one form or other. The latter, however, believe that they love to write when what they really want is to be a *celebrated author*. They would like to walk into a cocktail party and have everyone fly toward them with praise and adulation, but they are generally unwilling to put in the long lonely hours of thought and effort that are necessary to create their great book. Here again we see the conflict between the desire to experience something and the desire to gain approval. Although the approval of others may be pleasant, one need not delude himself that he is happy while he is writing (or doing anything else for that matter) if in fact is not. The people who want to "have written" are often making such an error.

It is clearly the case that Americans have gone so far in denying their real natures that they do not really know if they are happy or unhappy. Put another way, they do not really enjoy many of the things they do for enjoyment. An interesting illustration of this is given by Lobsenz in a book referred to earlier (1962). He cites statistics which show that fifty million Americans spend more than $1 billion annually puttering in their gardens. One would therefore tend to believe that most of these people *enjoy* gardening. However, studies have shown that most of those questioned do not really care for it very much. But the curious thing is that they do not even realize *this*. They will say they like it if asked a direct question about it. But when asked to list the things they enjoy doing, more than half of them never mention gardening at all. Sociologist Reuel Denny believes that most people engage in gardening only because it is a high-status leisure-time behavior. He points out that gardening can be done in view of the neighbors, and so it may be used as a part of the image. But although this may be part of the reason, there may be a more subtle explanation.

Many Americans work in the garden, loll around the pool, take Sunday drives, go to parties, visit relatives, dress up in sporty clothes and lounge around their rumpus rooms, mainly because they believe that these are the things that happy successful people *are supposed* to do. They are simply playing the role that they think goes with their particular station. Somewhere just below the level of conscious awareness they feel bored and unhappy but they do not recognize the feeling because *they are convinced that these kinds of things are enjoyable*. They have so lost touch with their own feelings that they do not even recognize them when they have them.

Many of the activities which are supposed to be pleasurable are engaged in this way. We say in effect: "Look at me. I'm the successful middle-class (or upper-class or even lower-class) American "enjoying" my leisure. And we try to ignore the empty feeling that accompanies this reverie.

We are not here challenging the idea that certain kinds of activities are really enjoyable. Concerts, lectures, museums, and lounging at the pool are all genuine enjoyments at various times. The above discussion is concerned only with those other situations in which people are *really* bored or annoyed with what they are doing but disguise this fact from themselves. When these things are really rewarding, people engage in them for that reason and not because it is expected of them.

alienation and other-directedness

There is a great deal of talk today about "alienation" and the "loss of identity." Sometimes this loss is attributed to the mechanization of modern life and its effect on human beings. Some people feel that in a world of technological proliferation, the individual person is somehow lost sight of. And because of the prevailing mechanistic attitude, he is often treated like just another machine. Sometimes the loss of identity is blamed on the excessive use of numbers. In a world where numbers are increasingly used as a means of identification, some people begin to feel that they are no longer human. They feel, they say, more like a cipher than a person.

But the loss of identity seems to imply two kinds of things. One comes from the statement "I do not know who I am," the other from the phrase, "No one knows me as I would like them to." The first of these declarations is the identity problem so common in our culture. It comes, largely, from the fact that everything we do is *other-directed*. That is, we behave in ways that are dictated by an outside criterion in order to be acceptable to a certain segment of society. The term "other-directed" is used here to mean that many of the things we do are intended to secure the acceptance of others—and they therefore have their source in these other people. The opposite of this would be "self-directed"—that is, done for one-self, without being overly influenced by the demands of others. The latter concept is similar to Reisman's "autonomous man" (1950). Whether we are priests, politicians, or gangsters, our actions are determined to some extent by significant others. If this outer-directed orientation influences a great deal of our behavior, as it usually does in our society, there results a feeling of selflessness, or a sense of decentralization of the self, which creates a vacuum in the place where the self-experience would ordinarily be. In such a situation, the feeling of not knowing who one is can be very real.

The other statement, "No one knows me as I would like them to" really means, "No one believes my PR image." This is another way of saying that I have sold my PR image to myself, at least to some extent, but I cannot get others to believe it (to "buy" it). They do not appreciate my "importance." If a person believes that he is, in fact, the image he presents but also perceives the fact that he is not accepted as such by others, he is likely to feel lost and alienated. One sees therefore that these two feelings are similar. Both have the same basis: the person's life style depends upon external criteria and since these often conflict with the person's true desires (which have been denied) he is unable to make an identification with those desires. In a like manner, he is unable to identify his own behavior with himself at its source because it does not originate from his real self.

Some idea of the extent to which people have become separated from their own being is demonstrable from the following: A certain brand of sunglasses is advertised as being the favorite of celebrities. And the copy clearly suggests that if you wear these particular glasses you may very likely be mistaken for some well-known personality. In essence, what is being suggested is that you can disguise yourself as someone else and be the recipient therefore of admiration that would ordinarily be afforded *them.* Although the esteem directed toward you would not be yours, you may still, so the inference goes, enjoy the approval thus gained. The idea that one can be mistaken for someone more worthwhile is the essence of the PR personality. Any mask represents a disguise that falsifies the real self to an observer. An interesting fact about trying to wear the mask of a notable person is that we need not even admire the person in question. We may actually dislike him personally. But he has the admiration of others and that seems to be enough.

The desire to be someone else can in extreme form lead to severe psychopathology. The break with reality that is generally considered the hallmark of psychosis becomes acute when the individual is forced to separate himself so far from his own feelings that he comes to perceive them as originating in the external world. If, for example, you have homosexual feelings, but deny their existence, you are likely to perceive them in others because you are aware (on some level) that they exist, but since it is impossible that they should arise in yourself (after all the hero is supposed to be "straight"), then they must be "out there." It is easy to see how, in such a situation, one might reach a completely dissociated state.

Most of us, however, do not reach such extreme limits. Our distortions lie somewhere on a continuum between a perfectly clear perception of reality and the severely distorted world of the psychotic. But the more important the PR personality, the further along that continuum we are likely to slide. Psychopathology is therefore a relative thing.

investment of the public relations personality

An understanding of the PR personality syndrome explains behaviors which are often misunderstood or attributed to mysterious causes. Using this model we can perhaps explain some human activities in more understandable terms.

One important aspect of the PR image is that *it can be invested.* A person may identify with a group, a sect, a nation, or with another person. Psychologists say that we invest our ego in that particular thing. Once a person has invested his PR image in a cause, or group, or nation, or religion he becomes defensive about those things just as he does about the image itself. Anything that he perceives as threatening to that group, cause, religion, or nation evokes the same kind of anxiety and defensiveness as a personal threat. Moreover, he tends to distort his perception of these things in the same way that he has come to distort his perception of himself. His view of reality regarding them will therefore be faulty. Many forms of fanaticism result from this kind of identification. People who cannot bear to have their group, religion, or nation criticized are therefore often acting, not out of loyalty, devotion, or patriotism, but out of vanity. One who has no need to invest his ego in such a way is not made uncomfortable by criticism. If something in his value system is criticized, he can consider the possibility that the criticism is warranted without feeling that he personally has been attacked. Moreover, if the criticism is valid, he can make the needed correction without "losing face." If it is not valid, he can reject the criticism without rationalization or other kinds of defensiveness.

Investment of the PR image occurs in other, less obvious ways. In a society like ours in which status is admired, people tend to identify with high-status models. In terms of what we have been saying above, we invest our egos in "successful people." We make a vicarious identification with those people who have accomplished what we desire for ourselves. This often takes the form of adulation. The opposite form of this phenomenon is especially prominent in lower-status people. Here, in an attempt to elevate their own position, they must derogate that of some other group. Their victims will often be minority groups or others who may be least successful in the system. The tendency is for some of these people to look with disdain at the poor, the black, red, brown, or yellow Americans while paying homage to the wealthy, famous, successful people at the other end of the socioeconomic spectrum. These people, for example, will raise a great hue and cry about the cost of welfare (a benefit for the poor) while completely ignoring the cost of welfare in the form of federal subsidies, tax breaks, depletion allowances, farm supports, and so on (benefits for the rich). Many writers believe that the reason that people do not complain about "handouts" to the rich is that they are usually unaware of their existence. But this is not likely any longer. They do not complain because *they cannot bring themselves to condemn that in which they have invested their PR image.* One can hardly criticize someone he worships. Moreover, in his fantasy he sees himself soon becoming the successful high-status person he so admires, and he is unlikely to advocate the abolishment of one of his own future advantages. It is interesting to note that the cost of federal and state aid to the rich is enormously more burdensome to the taxpayers than aid to the poor. Nonetheless many taxpayers are extremely vocal in their opposition to such "frills" as aid to the indigent, infirm, and aged while feeling that aid to the masters of industry is justly given.

Many people do not understand the way in which the PR personality can be invested. Thus after the fall of Peron, the dictator of Argentina, the Argentine government, in a desire to expose the tyranny under which the people had been living, decided to put on display some of the personal effects of Eva Peron, wife of the deposed leader. The idea was to demonstrate to the people that while they were struggling on the verge of starvation, the Perons had spent millions on clothing and jewelry, on yachts and travel, and on every kind of extravagance for themselves, ignoring the plight of their people. The display therefore showed some of the gowns, furs, jewelry, furniture, and so on, which had been used by Mrs. Peron during her tenure as first lady. But the whole idea backfired. Instead of angering the peasants who came to view these treasures, they had the effect of dazzling them. The people were in such awe of this wealth that they came to *admire* Eva more for having it. They, in effect, invested their PR image in *her*. The government finally had to abandon the display. The fact that Peron has now returned in triumph merely underscores this fact. Heroes, no matter how tyrannical, are not easily forgotten.

The antagonism which low-status people often have for other low-status people (and the admiration for higher status ones) is one of the most important problems with which modern societies are faced. It leads, in a climate of affluence, to the kind of intolerance for the rights of minorities which has become so widespread lately. In the past, when the majority were poor or had a grievance of any kind, they were able to pull together and work for reform. But now, when only a small segment is badly off, the majority does not feel that this group is important enough for them to disturb their comfort. They will defend the wealthy minority (heroes) but not the poor one (losers). Such an attitude is of course not universal. But there are enough people who feel this way to make it a real problem in a democratic society, where the majority can exert tyrannous control over minorities.

If anyone has any doubts about this kind of invested adulation, just let him go to a hotel, for example, which is generally frequented by the wealthy. But let him somehow reveal the fact that he comes from one of the lower strata of society. Then notice with what disdain he is treated by the *help* in that hotel. Note that these people also are considered to have low status, but the snobbery of the poor is far more pernicious than that of the rich, even in a democratic society. On the other hand, if he can make

Some people invest their PR images in death itself. These are very expensive (and prestigious) tombs in which people have had themselves buried. Note the ornate decorations.

these people believe that he is one of the regular patrons, note the obsequiousness and sycophancy with which they act toward him.

The investment of the personality takes some curious forms as when people will applaud the mention of their hometown or argue about the relative merits of their state as New Yorkers and Californians did when it was becoming apparent that California's population was passing New York's. The easterners became very defensive for awhile and the westerners, no less proud. Yet no one even stopped to consider the possibility that size has nothing to do with desirability. But the ego is used to thinking in terms of hypertrophy. Texans have always expressed pride in the thousands of miles of rather inhospitable prairie in their state. And some of them were positively hostile to the idea of adding Alaska as the forty-ninth state. Somehow being the largest seems important to the ego.

Nations, like individuals, can invest their PR images in their policies. In international affairs, they must be concerned with their image. They must not "lose face" by backing down once they have taken a stand, even if that stand is disastrous. Millions of people have been killed in wars, many of which were little more than national expressions of vanity.

The investment of the ego has long been used as a tool of nationalism. Every country attempts to instill the pride of belonging into its people. If

42

the common man can become a part of the glory of the fatherland, he does not feel so insignificant. The Nazis even added another dimension to this idea. Not only do you share in the greatness of Germany, their people were told, but you are a race of Supermen. You are superior to every other group of men on earth. Although this was an extreme case, every nation tries to capture the loyalty of its people by getting them to invest their PR image in its "greatness."

There are many other manifestations of the PR personality. We invest it in our children when we insist that they excel. We demand that they be popular, superior, successful. The father who wants his son to be the star of the Little League team and who is hostile to him when he fails is not really concerned with his son at all. And when this same father says to his children, "I'm doing it all for you," it has a hollow ring, even to him.

We invest our PR image in our sexual exploits, our religion, the organizations to which we belong, and even in our death. (Undertakers have learned that by appealing to the ego, they can get us to pay for a more expensive funeral.) But the most important expression of the PR image is in our own creation of the public self. For a clear statement of the extent to which we are "compelled" by what we believe to be our role, the following quote should suffice.

> Just being male involves a lifelong struggle to be adequate, a constant striving toward toughness of fiber and toward the traditional image of manly competence. He can't let down. A man must prove himself by succeeding in a profession or business, must apply himself without stint, must be known and liked, and constantly cultivate the "right" connections. If his home is to reflect the goals he has set for himself, it must be in the proper setting, have the standard labor-saving equipment, have at least one late model car in the garage and be well maintained, usually on a modest income. By and large, the man on the way up likes to see himself and be seen as popular socially, an excellent husband, father, neighbor, host, bridge partner, sportsman, wit, competent householder, man of property and all around good fellow (Chilman, 1969).

It is obvious from this excerpt that this is the common view of a man's role in American society. But it is equally obvious that one must stop and consider whether or not these are the goals that men *really* desire. It is interesting to note in the quotation above that the obligation seems to be to *appear* to be all these things while nothing is really said about what the male would like to *be* (that is, to experience). This problem will be considered later.

Disparagement. *Painting by Judith Corona.*

chapter 3
the put-down

A mother suddenly falls into a mood of deep depression shortly after her young child misbehaves in public. A young man attempts suicide when he hears his wife expressing her love for their newborn son. A businessman has to declare bankruptcy in a certain venture and, a week later, is found in a strange city suffering from amnesia.

Although they may not appear related on the surface, all these events have something in common. Clinical analysis of these and similar cases shows that the people were the victims of what is commonly called "the put-down." The put-down as it is used in everyday speech refers to an insult, slight, humiliation, or snub. It is often said to result in "hurt feelings," "ego deflation," or "feelings of worthlessness." For our purposes we may define the put-down as *any attack upon the PR personality*. It is any statement, deed, or innuendo seen by a person as a *deflation of his public image*. It can have extremely important consequences.

An important thing to notice about this syndrome is that the put-down is a perception by the victim and may not be seen by others in the same way. A completely innocent statement, act, or event may be perceived as an insult, when in fact there was no such intent on the part of anyone. On the other hand, sometime the intent to insult may be real, but the "victim" may not perceive it as such. In that case the put-down fails to materialize.

Although this phenomenon is very important psychologically, it has not always received the attention it deserves. In fact, there is no technical term by which this syndrome is designated. The closest we come to some kind of identification of it is through the use of such terms as rejection, stigma (Goffman, 1963), ego deflation, and insult. But each of these terms has a slightly different shade of meaning.

The concept of the put-down really refers to two related things. The first is the action of one person toward another. To put someone down means to insult, humiliate, deride, ridicule, and so on. The second meaning is the feeling of the *victim* when he is belittled, derogated, spurned, and repudiated. For both of these meanings we shall use the term *disparagement*.

Disparagement, when perceived as such by the victim, always results in a feeling of self-derogation. The person comes to acknowledge the fact that some part of his PR personality has become transparent. However, this phenomenon may not always be perceived in the same light by others. This is demonstrated by the examples given above.

In the first case, the woman became depressed after her child misbehaved. Ordinarily, we might be inclined to attribute her response to disappointment in her child's behavior. But an anlysis of this particular woman's behavior showed that she had a self-image which involved a picture of herself as a good and efficient parent, whose children were "very well behaved in public." It was not the misbehavior but the fact that it occurred where her friends and others could see it that so distressed her. For it revealed, she thought, her inadequacy as a parent. Her depression was a symptomatic reaction to her feeling of inadequacy in a role that she considered important to her.

The second case concerned a young man who after observing his wife expressing her love for their newborn son, suddenly became terribly unhappy. This turned out to be the case of a very immature young man, who was generally unsure of his wife's love. They had been married only a year and had just had their first child. The girl, also immature, did not know how to express her feelings toward her husband and when she did talk about love, it was without much fervor. However, when the young man heard her talking to the infant, she was rapturous. Such phrases as "more than anyone else in the world" and "the only love of my life" stuck in his mind. He was overwhelmed by a feeling of emptiness and worthlessness and tried to end his life.

In the third example, the put-down may seem more obvious. However, here again, the surface reaction does not tell the whole story. The man did not disappear because he had lost a great deal of money but because he had lost a great deal of prestige. He was an extremely wealthy man and the money lost in this particular venture made little difference in his standing. But he had placed his reputation on the line and had publicly predicted success. When the enterprise failed, he was revealed, so he thought, as a failure (rather than as the infallible success he wanted to be) and his symptoms followed.

All these cases represent situations in which self-devaluation had a profound effect. This, of course, is not rare. Such circumstances in milder form occur every day to all of us. Our reactions, however, depend upon a great many variables. Not all of us develop neurotic symptoms when our egos come under attack. Nevertheless, the victim of a disparaging experience is always made uncomfortable (and defensive) *if he has a stake in that particular segment of his PR personality.*

DISPARAGEMENT AS DE-HERO-IZATION

If it is true that we all try to wear the mask of the hero, then disparagement has the effect of de-hero-izing us. It pierces the armor, so to speak. We are left vulnerable to the view of others and we believe that they can see our imperfections. Disparagement, therefore, reveals us to the world as someone who is unheroic. A person can, for example, be completely destroyed if someone casts an aspersion on his health. And, in fact, nurses and doctors can testify to the fact that just being ill can often be such a blow to a person's ego that it can precipitate serious emotional problems. Worse still, any derogatory allusion to one's mental health is considered a great insult. In fact, the whole family is stigmatized when one of its members is "mentally ill."

Any uncomplimentary reference about one's physical appearance is also a form of disparagement. Any statement regarding one's looks, attire, breath, body scent, hairdo, cosmetics, and so on, when negative, is a great source of humiliation. For we must remember that the hero and heroine are handsome, clean, fashionable, and sweet smelling. They are also extremely virtuous and therefore any innuendo concerning immorality or unethical behavior (except in business where such things are natural) is met with the same feeling of chagrin.

The male, of course, is put down if he cannot fight, or even worse, if he *will* not fight; if he is not good at some sports, and later in life if he can't succeed with girls. The female suffers a similar fate if she is not pretty, chic, capable of performing such "feminine" tasks as sewing or cooking, and if she is not popular with boys. Any of these "shortcomings" therefore takes a person out of the category of the hero or heroine and casts him into another role.

THE NONHERO

Since there are at least two other major types of characters in our folklore, we must fall into either of these categories. We can either be the villain or the plain guy.

The villain, as we have briefly pointed out, is not really the opposite of the hero. He has, in fact, a number of attributes of the hero. He has power; he may be wealthy. He has a certain kind of attractiveness, even fascination. He is at least the second fastest gun in the West and trying (although by foul means) to become the first. He is ambitious, violent, persuasive, strong, and healthy. Note that health is as important for the villain as for the hero. Imagine how it would look if the hero defeated a sick man. You can't chase a man who has gout, punch someone who has a toothache, run a sword through a person suffering from appendicitis, or slay a tubercular dragon. So the villain must be on a par with the hero in many areas or he is not a fit opponent for him.

The opposite of the hero, therefore, is not the villain, but the plain, ordinary, nondescript, plain guy. He is the nonhero. He is the kind of man who will whimper and beg for mercy when being tortured. He will "break" instantly even before the threat of any pain. And if he has no information, he will make some up. Sometimes he has pimples or long hair or merely skin of a different color. He is part of the supporting cast but he goes largely unnoticed as an individual. His personality is bland at best and repulsive at worst. He is the character admired and emulated by no one. If the hero is the model for the PR personality, the nonhero is the model for disparagement.

A distinction should be made here between the nonhero and what is called the "antihero" or the "hero of the absurd." In some ways the nonhero superficially resembles the antihero or the "absurd" hero of some modern fiction. Like Camus' protagonist in *The Stranger* (1946), the nonhero is an unglamorous nobody. His life is usually drab, and the events in it appear to have no meaning. He is, in effect, an unimportant person living an unimportant life. Like Sisyphus in another book by Camus (1960), he is entrapped in an endless, exhausting, and seemingly meaningless routine. He is not smooth in his endeavors. When he tries to seduce a girl, he is awkward or comical. He fails more often than he succeeds. He seldom has a "noble" mission and is sometimes childish rather than "manly."

But the similarities between the hero of the absurd and what we have been describing as the nonhero are only apparent. For in many instances the absurd hero is *really* heroic in the most profound sense. He is a man in collision with his culture. He is one who has examined his society and found it wanting. And he has decided that he will not participate in it. His heroism lies in the fact that very often it is through *his vision* (in the arts, sciences, and so on) that important new human values arise. It is true that he is an outcast. But it is often his own doing. He rejects society because of its shallowness, hypocrisy, or inhumanity and he is rejected in return for his "eccentricity."

The hero of the absurd is often cast in a humanistic mold. As Galloway says in discussing some of the most prominent American novelists, "For however unconventional the environments and 'heroes' of whom they treat, their work is part of a recognizable humanistic tradition" (Galloway, 1966). And later he clarifies the meaning of humanism for these authors. Their heroes, he explains, are rebels, but "the call to revolt is a call to humanize, to transform the inhumanity of the world."

But the nonhero is not a rebel. He is, as we shall see, an authoritarian personality and, as such, he accepts his value system without seriously questioning it. Whatever he believes, he believes because it has been enunciated for him by someone else.

The absurd hero described by Galloway is attempting to question the underlying assumptions of his society and to arrive at a system of values in which he himself can believe. Sometimes his values are in accord with the conventional wisdom, but more often they are not. When the latter is the case, he is perceived by those of a more orthodox persuasion as a troublemaker, a boat rocker, or a dangerous lunatic. It is precisely because of this fact that most of us do not have the courage to *be* the absurd hero. To do so we would "have to go it alone." We would have to disagree with the conventional wisdom where we saw it to be wrong. And we would have to suffer for our beliefs. And the price for most of us would be too dear. For we would have to face one of the most potent put-downs, ostracism.

OSTRACISM AS THE ULTIMATE FORM OF REJECTION

At West Point and the Naval Academy when someone does something that violates some part of the code of behavior, his fellow students sometimes resort to a punishment called "the silent treatment." The silent treatment means that no one may speak to the offending cadet at any time except where absolutely necessary for the performance of duty. This punishment is so harsh to some that it can have devastating consequences.

The young men who are subjected to the silent treatment vary to some extent in their reaction to it. But almost all of them feel a great deal of pressure and anxiety even from the beginning. And if the situation continues for any length of time, it becomes, for some, an agonizing ordeal. The subjective feeling for the victim of this tactic is often one of complete despair. Day after day his friends continue to go about their tasks without a word. When they pass they sometimes avert their eyes, or look right through him. People engaged in happy conversation suddenly stop when he comes into view. Their expressions become grave and their voices become muffled. He comes to perceive their sober indifference as hostility. And as a recipient of so much disdain, he begins to feel worthless. He may sometimes feel that he does not really exist. This is the ultimate rejection. Having been disregarded by everyone he sees, he becomes dubious about "being" there at all. After all, if someone exists, other people acknowledge his existence. If they don't . . . .

Such a situation is of course extreme. But it illustrates very forcefully what rejection can mean. Rejection is a powerful form of disparagement because, beside deflating the PR image, it annihilates the person's sense of self. When the rejection is universal, therefore (that is, when one is ostracized), it can have detrimental effects. But ostracism can be experienced even when it is not intended.

One girl, for example, was not invited to a social gathering by one of her friends. When she learned of the affair, she became terribly depressed and anxious. Two weeks later, she learned that the gathering had been called in secret in order to arrange a surprise party for her. She had tortured herself needlessly because she had misperceived the event.

Disparagement is one of the most destructive wounds that the ego can suffer. But it is largely a self-inflicted one. A person is only vulnerable to insults because he is sensitive in a certain area. His sensitivity is like a sore spot which feels pain at the slightest touch. It is therefore the person's own fears that lead to his devaluing himself.

DISPARAGEMENT AND THE ROLE OF WOMEN

Women are more easily disparaged than men in our society because they have been given an almost impossible role to fill. In the first place, the American woman is put into two completely contradictory positions regarding sex.[1] On the one hand, she must deny her own sexuality. ("Nice girls don't do such things. They don't even *think* about such things.") On the other hand, she is expected to be sexually attractive. That is, she is supposed to be seductive but not to be seduced; to be desirable but to have no desire. Since the primitive heroine is always a virgin with absolutely

---

[1]Although changes are beginning to occur in this area, many American women are still influenced by traditional standards.

no trace of libido until it is miraculously awakened by the hero, the American woman has often had to pretend that she has no sexual feelings. Sometimes she does this too well, and the resulting denial of her normal, natural appetites has led her to seek refuge in a world of fantasy filled with a sterile kind of romance where men bow and dance and bring gifts but never "do bad things."

But this is not all. She also has to play the subservient role without protest. She is expected to be passive, quiet, fastidious, prim, and neat. In short, she is expected to be a mannequin rather than a human being. Such demands are so flagrantly opposed to her real nature that she is forced to employ a great deal of repression in order to conform to this pattern. And this, of course, results in all kinds of defensiveness. Thus any suggestion that she is failing in any of these areas is seen as a defect and leads to anxiety, depression, or other neurotic reactions.

Another concession that she must make is that she must never be more intelligent than the man of her choice. This is the most pernicious demand of all. For in this regard she suffers either way. If she is more intelligent than the man, she is shunned and rejected. And if she is less intelligent, she comes to perceive herself as inferior to men and generally less capable and valuable to society. It is this latter image that feminist groups are so concerned with changing.

But such a change in the image of women is frightening to many men for it is seen as a threat to the male ego. The PR image of the male involves being dominant and one cannot be dominant over someone more intelligent than himself. Moreover, the male has defined the woman's role in such a way that *he* does all the interesting things in life and she gets all the routine duties that he would rather avoid. There appears to be a great deal of truth, therefore, in the complaint that women, like black people, brown people, and other "different" groups, are systematically denied opportunities that would lead them to actualize potentialities that are now suppressed.

Women also at times have the fear that they are valued by men only as objects of sexual gratification and for nothing else. And in fact, this is sometime true. But from the woman's standpoint, it presents several problems. In the first place, she perceives this as a disparagement since she is not accepted as a *person* but as a *thing*. In the second place, since she has probably been brought up to believe that sex is evil, or dirty, she sees this kind of attractiveness as "bad." To be wanted "only for one's body" is not very flattering.

A woman's perception of herself as a mere instrument of a man's desire adds to the already considerable feeling of inferiority imposed upon her by society. She is not really important to the man as a human being. Any other woman would probably do. She sees herself left out of all the things that are exciting and interesting, and she comes to feel that her presence is only tolerated because she can satisfy the man sexually.

A classic presentation of this image is the gangster's girl. She is always very flashy, sensual, somewhat gaudily made-up, wearing skintight clothing over a curvacious figure, but she is a moron. When anything serious is to be discussed, she is summarily thrown out of the room or she is sometimes given money (bribed) to spend some time elsewhere and sent on her way while the men get down to business. The girl is clearly (1) a decoration, (2) an object for ridicule or contempt, and (3) a body for sexual gratification on demand.

This image is, of course, the exaggerated version of the sex object, but it does represent the way in which women are sometimes perceived.

To be forced into such a situation is crippling to the ego of the young girl. She must always be on guard against "being used" as an object by men. She is in constant doubt about the "intentions" of the men in her life. Even when they claim that they consider her more than just a source of gratification, she must continue to be suspicious. After all, they may merely be *saying* such things for their own ulterior motives.

Women are often seen as sexually attractive servants.

Even after marriage the woman may come to feel that her husband has no use for her beyond the sexual sphere because he seldom includes her in his other pursuits. He spends time with his male friends. He prefers to watch television rather than take her places. He goes off on weekend hunting trips but would never consider taking *her* away for a weekend.

Women in our society are sometimes treated as pampered pets, sometimes as mother figures to whom we can go for comfort, sometimes as a necessary evil, but they are seldom valued as persons. They come therefore to expect such treatment and to take precautions against it. But like a person in an empty house during a storm, everything that happens tends to increase their suspicion that what they fear is actually happening. The woman perceives every incident of neglect, every inattention, every omission or oversight on the part of her man as proof of the thing she dreads. She is not a human being to him. She is a convenience. This is a humiliating experience.

Another thing that contributes still further to the conflicts in this area is the fact that a woman may also be insulted when she is *not* desired sexually. If her husband is indifferent, or attracted by other women, or is impotent with her, she may feel that she is not feminine enough. She is not a complete woman. Biologically she needs to be desired. Culturally she is afraid that she might be desired *only* biologically. The dilemma places her in constant conflict. Should she use sex to get the attention she needs, or should she use other means? If she concentrates on one, will it be to the neglect of the other?

Thus the female in American society often comes to perceive herself negatively no matter what happens. In a sense she cannot win. If she is too attractive, she may be used as an object. If she is not attractive enough, she may not be desirable at all. If she is intelligent, men may be afraid of her; if she is stupid, she will be treated like an article of furniture. If her sex drive is high, she is a tramp. If it is low, she is not a woman. It is no wonder, therefore, that women in our culture find it extremely difficult to develop their real potentialities without experiencing a great deal of emotional turmoil and stress. We will have more to say on this in Chapter Six.

PREJUDICE AND DISPARAGEMENT

The treatment of minority groups in the United States has for a long time been tinged with a particularly damaging form of disparagement. The idea, implicitly held and transmitted in many kinds of media throughout the society, that one or another group of people is evil, inferior, dirty, stupid has often been widespread. Such ideas are sometime perceived as being valid by the disparaged group itself. This results from the fact that there

is almost no information to the contrary available anywhere. Under these circumstances it is unusually difficult for anyone to disbelieve so great a mass of one-sided information.

These kinds of beliefs tend to help fulfill their predictions since people who perceive themselves as inferior come to behave and perform that way. Ideas of this kind, therefore, produce the very thing that they begin by asserting. To counteract the devastating effects of such beliefs, minority people in the United States have begun searching for new means to express their own identities. By looking at themselves in new ways, they are attempting to undo the effects of the disparagement which they have been subjected to and to develop self-images with which they can satisfactorily identify.

COMPETITIVENESS AND THE PUT-DOWN

Ten men line up at the starting blocks and take their positions for a race. The gun sounds and they burst forward, sprinting down the track at top speed. Gradually some pull ahead and some fall behind and as they approach the finish line, one of the ten takes the lead and breaks the tape a few tenths of a second before any of the others can reach it. He is the *winner*. He receives a trophy. His name gets into print. And he is generally treated as a hero.

This event is a kind of model for many endeavors which are competitive in nature. Where there are many contenders and only one winner, there must always be a large number of losers. And since only the winner is afforded any recognition or esteem, the losers may all experience disparagement. It is interesting to note that in the above situation, all the runners were almost equally as good; the difference between them was very small. Yet only the one who broke the tape received any kind of recognition for his performance.

Although this is a hypothetical situation, such occurrences are common in everyday life. The man whose business succeeds, gets all the glory (and money) while his competitor who fails gets nothing but derision. He who wins receives a distinct kind of designation; everyone else is an "also-ran." It is for this reason that the Hopi Indians, when staging a race, arrange for everyone to cross the finish line together. This establishes their spirit of cooperativeness, in stark contrast to the competitive nature of many other cultures.

It is important, therefore, to consider the consequences of competition on the people who in a competitive society are the "also-rans." It turns out that, from a psychological point of view, almost everyone in such a culture perceives himself as a loser a good part of the time. This occurs because all the methods for evaluation in competitive enterprises are stacked against everyone but a minority of winners. Let us suppose that in the race described above, the winner had been unable to compete. Then the man who finished second in that race would have been the winner and would have been the recipient of all the approval, benefits, rewards, and so on. The winner in this case is somewhat slower than in the original race. But that makes no difference at all. It does not matter how *good* one is, only *whether one is better than the others*. A number of losers are therefore necessary for the creation of a winner.

Those who are "back in the pack" may perceive themselves as inferior. This is particularly likely if they have such an experience often; and in a competitive way of life, most people do. Many people entering therapy reveal a profound sense of disappointment in themselves, which on further investigation turns out to be a feeling that was expressed by a patient as "being a champion of nothing."

It is not to be inferred that competitiveness must always lead to this kind of result. It need not do so. But the tendency will be greatest where the winners are overvalued and those who perform less well are either spurned or ignored. Competition can lead to a sense of self-esteem if the entire enterprise is viewed as an opportunity for each contestant to give his best performance. In such a case the real credo of sport becomes the watchword of the undertaking. "It matters not whether we win or lose, but how we play the game." Each person accepting the challenge and giving the best he has to give fulfills the conditions for being fully accepted. The differentiation between winners and losers becomes somewhat obscured under such conditions, and in a sense they are all perceived as champions.

SELF-DEVALUATION IN GENERAL

Human beings have always been concerned with their status in the hierarchy of nature. From the time that men became aware of their being, they

Competitive sports can be very enjoyable. But if we overvalue the winner, the loser may experience disparagement.

Our penchant for competition sometimes makes us forget that cooperation can be highly productive. The successes that occur are shared by all the participants—not just the "winner."

have looked for indications of their worth as a species wherever they could. For the most part they were able to show that they were the most important and most powerful of all God's creatures and they came to enjoy this position and to protect it.

However, certain events occurred in the history of mankind which were to shatter man's collective ego. One of the earliest and most important came out of the disclosures made by Copernicus. For many thousands of years, the view of learned men about man's place in the universe had been based on Ptolemy's astronomical theory. The earth was the fixed center of the universe and every other body revolved around it. Some bodies had rather erratic orbits; nevertheless, even these completed a revolution around the earth, thus demonstrating that no other world occupied so central a position. The implications of such uniqueness of necessity carried with it the impression of importance. For to be at the focus of things is, of course, a heroic position. The earth, and therefore the people on the earth, were the most important (that is, valuable) of all the creatures in the cosmos. This was not only a secular, but also a religious view.

Now Copernicus was a troublemaker. For one thing, he made extremely careful and accurate observations. For another, he evidently did not feel threatened by the idea that man might be moved from the center of things out somewhere to a less imposing locale. By putting the *sun* in the center of the universe, he reduced the earth's importance by an exponential factor (that is, from a winner to an also-ran) Here we were just one of several other bodies circling the "real" center, the sun. Things of course were to get worse before they got better, for we were to soon learn that even the sun held a rather unimportant position somewhat near the edge of an unimpressive galaxy.

But Copernicus's discovery caused a great deal of consternation among the learned men of the period, many of whom simply refused to accept the theory. In psychological terms, they denied the existence of facts that would give rise to a devaluation of their self-image. They simply would not believe that they were not God's reason for creating the universe in the first place. For such a belief would force them to accept a much more humble position in the scheme of things.

Man hardly recovered from one trauma before he was confronted by another. Copernicus, Kepler, Galileo, and Newton each helped to move man further away from his favored position. However, what they did to diminish man in his own eyes was nothing compared to what was done by a certain biologist named Charles Darwin.

If the astronomers had moved us away from the heart of things, we were at least divine creatures, made in God's image, and meant to have dominion over all the beasts of the earth. Or were we? Not according to the interpreters of Darwin. We were just highly developed apes. We could talk and write, but these were minor differences. We were merely a continuation of the lower life forms. Nothing unique. Perhaps not even divine. We were merely a slightly higher form of gorilla.

This was too much. We would never accept the humiliation of being a mere animal. Darwin, like Copernicus, was met with scorn and derision. When truth clashes with the ego, truth does not always fare too well.

But science was not yet through. Victorian Europe was shortly to be confronted by a bombshell delivered by one Sigmund Freud. Not only are we well-educated apes, Freud told a startled world, but we are not very nice apes at that. We are wild beasts, driven by powerful instincts for destruction and aggression which must always be held in check by the restraints of society. We are little more than dressed-up gorillas, controlling our sexual, destructive urges by a complex series of conventions that we have introjected from our parents and the rest of society. The only difference between us and the other crawling creatures is that our animal lusts are repressed.

Whether or not Freud's theories were sound is not important at the moment. Like those of Copernicus and Darwin, his ideas required a good deal of refinement as time went on. And new findings continue to shed more light on all these areas of inquiry. But the reception that all these men received was similar. Their theories were rejected not merely because they clashed with the then current orthodoxy but because they demeaned man's picture of himself in his own eyes. In a word, they were perceived as disparagement.

DISPARAGEMENT AS A WEAPON

Insults, embarrassments, humiliations, and deprecations are all used by people against one another. The aim of such treatment is usually to injure the other person by piercing the armor of his PR personality. Such conduct on the part of one person against another is an aggressive act that employs psychological weaponry. The most serious use of such a tactic occurs when it is directed against children.

The child is the crucible in which the concept of self-esteem is forged. And true self-esteem is, as we have noted earlier, a confidence in one's own worth. A child's self-esteem develops out of contacts with significant others who communicate his worth to him in many ways. But a lack of this feeling can easily be engendered in a child by parents or others who continually make derisive remarks about him.

Imagine, on the one hand, a child who is continually praised and encouraged by his parents for his many and varied efforts; and on the other hand, a child who is always berated, made fun of, and told of his stupidity.

The former is likely to develop a feeling of confidence in his own capacities, while the latter may come to perceive himself as incompetent, inept, and worthless.

The victim of these devaluing perceptions will often be subjected to what is sometimes called pathological anxiety. Brandon refers to it as "a crisis of self-esteem—any threat to a man's ego—anything which he experiences as a danger to his mind's efficacy and control—is a potential source of pathological anxiety" (Brandon, 1969).

Although disparagement is a devastating weapon when used against a child, it is also quite potent when directed against adults as well. Many of the arguments that people engage in are really exchanges of verbal barbs directed from one person to another in an attempt to undermine the other's self-image. Some cocktail parties are virtual battlegrounds for insult flinging where women can criticize one another's clothing and men can ridicule each other's romantic prowess.

Once again, it is the person with doubts about himself who is more vulnerable to these kinds of attacks. Some people are literally terrified when entering a room full of people for fear that they will say or do something that will bring shame down on them and make them the butt of ridicule. To humiliate, shame, or embarrass someone is therefore a powerful kind of disparagement, especially in front of a large number of other people.

There are many ways in which these weapons are made potent. Almost any indication that a person is not up to par in some conventionally accepted virtue is enough to evoke strong feelings of inferiority. The man who is cowardly, the girl who is promiscuous, the woman whose house is messy, the man who is impotent or the woman who is frigid, the boy who strikes out, the girl who is unpopular, the businessman who is revealed as a swindler, the sick person; all may feel that they are something less than they would like to be. And others, by calling attention to their particular shortcoming, can cause them a great deal of anguish.

Sometimes a person with the best of intentions may do something that is seen by another person as an insult. There is, for example, a very fine line drawn by many people between sympathy and pity. Although most of us will accept and appreciate sympathy from others, pity is something else. The reason for the different reactions lies in the subtle differences in the implications of the two terms.

Sympathy is an understanding or, as one dictionary puts it, "a fellow feeling or correspondence of sensation of affections." It is therefore an expression of feeling between equals. The recipient of sympathy perceives himself on the same level as the one who expresses the feeling.

Pity, on the other hand, has come to carry an intimation of derision. "I pity him" has come sometimes to be a kind of insult. This results from the fact that pity establishes the person pitied as lower in status than the pitier. It is for this reason that people often object to being helped by others, especially if that help appears to come out of a feeling of pity.

Help itself can also be perceived as a disparagement if it is offered in a condescending way. If the attitude that accompanies it seems to say, "You poor thing, I've got to help you because you are so unfortunate" (that is, helpless, unheroic, and so on), the help will more often be resented than appreciated.

Of course anything that lowers the status of another person is seen as disparagement. Therefore, any kind of treatment, from discrediting a person's reputation to taking away his key to the executive washroom, qualifies.

Some kinds of disparagement occur in industry, where certain status symbols can be dispensed or withheld. Packard (1959) describes cases where the furnishings of an office can subtly tell an executive that his status is lower or higher than another. The size of the office is one indication. So is the wood out of which the desk is made. Plush carpeting and furniture also attest to the standing of the person, as does the view from his windows. Use of the executive dining room and company paid membership in a country club are other kinds of evidence.

Sometimes there is a kind of backbiting conflict between people in industry who are all struggling to improve their status in the hierarchy of the organization. When new college-trained men and women are placed in higher positions than oldtime "managerial" people, they are viewed as "college punks" by the "regulars," who have a grand time "batting down or slyly sabotaging bright ideas staff men have for improving their own methods of operating."

Anything that can be made to puncture the facade that a person tries to present to the world is fair game. A member of the family can easily embarrass the other members by doing something in public which would cast aspersions on their "respectability," "integrity," "right-mindedness," and so on. Father coming home drunk, daughter living with a man, little Jimmy being expelled from school, Aunt Sarah being put away in a mental institution. All of these, if made public, may cause great concern among the members of the family while they may be almost ignored if they don't come to light. The concern in such cases is usually "What will the neighbors think?" Translated into therapeutic language, "What are you doing to our image in the neighborhood?"

The interesting thing to notice in this syndrome is that the other people involved who are supposed to be concerned with the welfare of the "deviant" are actually far more disturbed by the fact that whatever has tranpired will reflect badly on *themselves*. The fact that Jimmy or Aunt

Sarah have a problem which may be very difficult and distressing to them is a secondary consideration, if it is considered at all. It is the concern with the image that is paramount here, and such concern is susceptible to disparagement.

A mother much concerned with her image traveled a great deal about the country with her children. They would stop en route to have their meals in restaurants wherever they happened to be at mealtime. The mother always admonished the children to "leave some food on their plate" so that the waiters would not think "we are pigs." Even if the children were still hungry, they were not allowed to finish their food. The woman felt greatly threatened by the fact that perfect strangers might have a low opinion of her if she and her children did not conform to certain "respectable" forms of behavior. Her great fear was to be perceived as a person without breeding. This fear was greatly exaggerated because of the fact that she had come from very humble beginnings. Anything, threfore, that appeared vulgar or indecorous was extremely demeaning if it was associated with her in any way.

SEX AS A WEAPON

Sex can be used as a weapon in a number of ways. Since sexual behavior is often considered bad, dirty, or sinful in our society, people frequently come to be ashamed of their own sexual feelings or behavior. Some men use sex as a weapon of destruction against women.

J. had a pathological hatred for women because of a strong repressed hatred for a domineering, castrating mother. Sex, he believed, was degrading both to men and women, but most especially to women. (This has been a very generally held belief in America, and a clear statement of the double standard, with which we will deal later.) The way for J. to destroy women was therefore to seduce them. He was rather handsome and smooth, and so he was reasonably successful in his pursuits. He did not enjoy sex most of the time and found that he could feel respect only for those girls who refused him. He finally married a frigid woman and held her in very high esteem until, through therapy, she acquired the ability to have orgasm. This precipitated so much friction that the couple separated a number of times and were finally divorced.

Another way that sex can be used as a weapon is through the use of rejection. A woman rejecting a man's advances or a man turning down an obvious offer by a woman are both making an implicit statement to the victim about his or her sexual attractiveness. Since sex is highly valued by most people, such treatment is not always accepted graciously, although the outward behavior may attempt to conceal this fact. The rebuffed person often feels terribly depressed, because sexual attractiveness is the heroic trait that leads to the greatest rewards. The hero is, of course, never rejected completely. He may occasionally be forced to overcome some token resistance, but this is a kind of parrying in the jousting between lovers. In the end he always gets his woman. Moreover, he is desired by all women, so rejection is impossible for him. An even worse rejection is to be informed *after* intercourse that the partner did not enjoy it. This is particularly devastating, as sexual prowess is an extremely important heroic virtue.

Sex is often used by parents as a weapon against children. Adults often do not realize what damage they can do to a child in this way. The disparagement comes from the parents' vindictive attitude toward the child's normal sexuality. Their disapproval and punishment for any kind of sexually related behavior, from mere curiosity to masturbation, may stigmatize the child in his own mind. Moreover, threats of punishment (such as castration, insanity, or blindness) may produce a conditioned fear or distaste that will accompany any erotic thought or action for many years thereafter, giving rise to a feeling of self-reproach whenever sexual stimulation occurs.

Sexuality itself, high sex drive, or promiscuity in sexual behavior has been perceived as disparaging, especially for women, for a long time. A woman pointed out and whispered about was often persecuted mercilessly for her "misbehavior" and was generally considered unacceptable in the presence of "decent" people. Derogatory names (hussy, slut, tramp, harlot) were hurled at her and she was generally ostracized by all but those in the same circumstances. Nathaniel Hawthorne's novel *The Scarlet Letter* clearly depicts the attitudes of early America with regard to childbearing out of wedlock. The heroine, Hester, was forced to wear a brightly colored letter sewed to her dress so that all could see her "disgrace." She was thus stigmatized in the eyes of the community and treated as an undesirable. Although this took place in sixteenth-century Salem, the attitude toward female sexuality, although not the treatment, has endured until relatively recent times.

OTHER KINDS OF DEROGATION

People sometimes feel humiliated by certain societal conditions which are not always intended to have such an effect. People on relief during the Depression were often ashamed to let their neighbors know their plight, and those on welfare today often feel stigmatized when they have to present their food stamps in the neighborhood market. While these people are affected by their inability to earn a living, some workers feel that *they* are being taken advantage of by these very same people. The workers generally have hard, unpleasant jobs which they have held for a lifetime with little or no advancement, and they see welfare recipients doing almost as well financially without working at all. These workers therefore come to "feel like suckers," especially because their taxes are paying to "support those free-loaders."

A person who finds himself in an environment that is generally peopled by those of a "higher" station in life can also begin to feel extremely uncomfortable.

A man with little education was invited to a party where most of the guests were professional people. Their conversation was polite and often directed to him. But his discomfort continued to grow. How could he respond to such statements as: "The criteria for any kind of judgment in such an area has to be empirical." He wasn't sure about two words in the sentence and, besides that, he was not clear about what "area" they were discussing. As the evening wore on, he found himself left out of the activities more and more. First they stopped directing their words to him and finally they stopped looking at him entirely. This was not done out of malice, but merely because he continually failed to reinforce their earlier remarks by any kind of response. In the end, they came to act as if he were not there.

The same kind of feeling is reported when someone finds himself in a place where, because of his clothes, dialect, or appearance, he is shown to be "beyond his social depth." In such a situation, even though those present may try to ignore the obvious breach of decorum, their very politeness may be perceived as insulting, since there is an unspoken condescension built into the situation itself.

Mr. and Mrs. B. were invited to a country club dance by a relative somewhat more successful in the business world. Mrs. B. wore a rather fashionable party dress and her husband looked terribly uncomfortable in his rented tuxedo. Although the guests at their table were gracious and considerate, the couple could not shake the feeling of embarrassment which plagued them all evening. The more considerate the others were, the more they were made to feel like clods. The message that was communicated to them was: "You are not as polished and genteel as we, but we are generous and kind and can overlook that. We like you in spite of your poor breeding and humble origins."

The waiters and waitresses were not as kind as the other guests and continually expressed their feelings in derogatory looks and gestures, which were seen only by the unfortunate couple. Afterward the help at the country club expressed their discontent at "having the Club degraded by allowing people of low station on the premises."

THE CONSEQUENCES OF DISPARAGEMENT

The victim of any kind of disparagement undergoes a variety of unpleasant experiences. Physiologically there are a number of autonomic changes, such as sudden changes in skin color (blushing or blanching); increase or decrease in pulse and blood pressure; alteration in the respiratory rhythm;

perhaps the secretion of adrenalin or noradrenalin; increased muscular tension, especially in the gastrointestinal area; and other kinds of measurable responses, such as an increased GSR.[2]

Behaviorally there are other kinds of responses. There may be a kind of withdrawal physically, so that the person simply removes himself. Or there may be less complete withdrawal in which case the victim may merely lower his eyes, bow his head, or turn his attention to something else (Carlson, 1970). Some of his actions may be a kind of acknowledgement of his own error. He may cover his head with his hands or hit his head with the heel of his hand. He may become visibly unnerved by the incident, manifesting various kinds of discomfort by fidgeting, shaking, twisting things in his hands, wringing his (empty) hands, furtively glancing about, or he may pace back and forth. His speech may be awkward, he may stammer, begin phrases and stop abruptly, the pitch of his voice may suddenly change, he may have to swallow hard and often, or he may be completely unable to speak.

Although these behavioral changes may inform others of his plight, the subjective experiences that accompany feelings of deprecation are by far the most important as well as the most disturbing.

One of the most common responses to almost all disparaging situations is, as noted earlier, a diminution of self-esteem. Any evidence that a person is not as "good" as he thought himself to be is met with a good deal of disappointment. In such a situation, the person becomes dissatisfied with himself, feels unhappy because of his limitations, and tends to berate himself.

Such a response is particularly true of one whose PR image is extremely important to him. Since the PR image is unrealistic, such a person is continually meeting with disappointments in his expectations about himself. That is, he hopes (expects) to be "good" or "successful" at many things, but he keeps falling short of his mark. Each of these "failures" causes him to reassess his value in this new light, and every instance is met with a further lowering of his self-esteem.

The lowering of self-esteem in turn gives rise to frustration, hostility, depression, or anxiety.[3] It also often gives rise to compensatory measures intended to bolster the tottering self-image. Such measures raise the entire conflict to a higher level by attempting to further inflate the PR image. But these tactics are doomed to failure, for just as the earlier expectancies were disappointed, so will these later ones fail to materialize.

The feeling of shame is another subjective experience which accom-

---

[2]Galvanic skin response—a measure of the electrical conductivity of the skin, which tends to increase with increased tension or emotion.

[3]These reactions will be more fully treated in Chapter 9.

panies disparagement. Shame has been defined as the discrepancy between the idealized self (that is, the PR image) and the self as it is actually perceived in those moments when it is unmasked. Actually, the feeling of shame is usually associated with the fact that others can, at least potentially, see the discrepancy which the person is trying to hide. This gives one the feeling that he is literally "naked" or "undressed" and that others are witnesses to his predicament.

The experience induces a strong desire to hide, to withdraw, in order to be out of the sight of others. It is as if the actual glances of other people induce a kind of psychic pain which can only be alleviated by getting out of their presence. It is an extremely uncomfortable feeling, but it does diminish slightly as soon as the victim gets out of sight of other people.

The feeling does not disappear completely, however, for there is always one observer who cannot be avoided. That one is, of course, the self. Therefore, shame is felt when a person does not live up to the criteria which he himself has set. It is true, of course, that many of these criteria have been accepted by him because of the influence of others—parents, peers, authority figures—but it is only *his* acceptance of such standards, his belief that these criteria are valid in some sense, that affects his feelings so strongly. If a person, for example, did not believe that being poor was a disgrace, he would not feel ashamed to have this fact brought to light; in fact, there have been times when being "poor but honest" was a badge of honor for many.

A person may also experience shame when he deviates too far from the norm in an attribute that he cannot control. Goffman (1963) refers to "abominations of the body," by which he means various kinds of physical deformity. People with these kinds of problems often feel extremely uncomfortable in the presence of "ordinary" people. This occurs, he believes, because the "normals believe the person with the stigma is not quite human." One can readily see how devastating such an attitude must be on the victim. If, in fact, the disabled person believes that all normal people view him as something less than human, he may come to perceive himself in that light. His feelings of deprecation will therefore be very intense indeed.

A young girl who had been born with a clubfoot was continually made fun of by other children. She gradually began to shy away from them because she thought that she was a kind of freak who should not associate with other children. Although their taunts hurt her deeply, she became convinced that they were justified and began to perceive herself as a cursed individual who had probably done something terrible in an earlier life.

The permanently disabled person may suffer from an overwhelming feeling of depression. There is a powerful sense of futility in his life because he can do nothing about his plight and he has been led to see it as a mark of inferiority, inadequacy, abnormality, or worthlessness. Although he may try to hide his infirmity, the usual defensive techniques will not work well here. Denial, for example, is useless when one is afflicted with a defect that is clearly visible to all.

The consequences of disparagement are not always merely personal. They may be global. The feeling of disgrace suffered by the German people as a result of their defeat in World War I was never forgotten. For years they carried with them a sense of humiliation that they were anxious to overcome. They were in great need of a new philosophy which would change the image that they hated so.

Hitler was acutely aware of this feeling in the people and probably in himself also. He seized upon this great need to introduce into the thinking of the German people the new national PR image. "You are not failures," he explained. "You could have won the war, for you are more than mere men. You are Supermen. You didn't really lose to the enemy. You were betrayed from within. The Jews betrayed you and *they* are responsible for your shame."

Thus in one stroke Hitler absolved the German people of blame for their humiliating defeat, created a scapegoat, and at the same time presented the people with a new public image which they were eager to embrace. His technique was extremely successful, and he was able to win great numbers of people to his side, change the direction of an entire nation, and finally, involve most of the civilized nations of the world in a global war of massive proportions.

DISPARAGEMENT AS ANNIHILATION

The person who has made a great investment in his PR image has, of course, more to lose from attacks upon it. As was pointed out in Chapter 2, the more anxiety one feels regarding his real worth, the more he will try to inflate the value of his public self. In some cases a situation may be reached in which the person has totally lost touch with his real nature and believes himself to be, in fact, the false image that he has created. Under such circumstances, if one should suffer a severe disparagement, he may feel completely destroyed. Having no self but the one that he has invented, the disappearance of this image is the disappearance of the entire person. Extremely disturbed individuals sometimes believe that they are living in a shadow world in which nothing exists and that they themselves are unreal (Coleman, 1964). Rejection of the self, therefore, which comes as a result of rejection by others, can lead to severely painful feelings of nonbeing.

Another related kind of annihilation occurs as a result of what might be termed "existential emptiness." Experiments in sensory deprivation have shown that man needs sensory input if he is to retain his sanity (Bexton, et al., 1954). Clinical experience tends to show that emotional input is similarly essential.

If a person has lost touch with his own feelings as a result of denial, he has erected a psychological barrier against emotional input which is as real to him as any physical one. He may therefore suffer from emotional deprivation, with the result that most of his experiences reach him without having any impact. By screening out the emotional content of his awareness, his experience is impoverished. A feeling of nonbeing (existential emptiness) can easily become overwhelming under such circumstances. If, added to this, a person suffers continual rejection by people who are important to him (that is, he is ignored in situations where he feels he should be noticed), the result may be a sense of "not being there," of being a nonentity, of being invisible, lost, dead. The feeling is illustrated by the nihilistic delusions, which occur in severe form in paranoia. In these psychotic states, the person may believe that he has no brain, no insides, no feelings, or no experiencing (that is, no awareness).

Sometimes the prospect of death itself may be perceived as the ultimate form of humiliation. The idea of nonbeing, beside provoking a certain amount of fear, can also be seen as another form of valuelessness. For this and other reasons, many people refuse to face the fact that one day they will die. As May (1967) points out, by facing this (existential) fact of life one is able to experience "normal anxiety" about death. However, by repressing the normal anxiety (that is, by not dealing with the fact that one day he will no longer exist), a person is forced to project (blame) his anxiety on other things. Since this anxiety is misdirected, it is neurotic anxiety.

The need to continue to exist after "death" is, of course, reflected in many of man's myths. And as pointed out earlier, the hero, especially in American mythology, is often immortal. A belief in immortality, however, need not always be a reflection of a *need* for continued existence. It is true that in many cases it obviously is nothing more than that. But there are other reasons why men come to believe the things they believe. Psychologists must be careful in assigning the causes of all behavior to need (that is, deficiency states). As Maslow (1970) has shown, there are other kinds of motivation which may be more revealing of the nature of man. These will be discussed in Chapter 14.

If our heroes are immortal, then death is not heroic (that is, a deprecation). To some extent, our rituals with regard to death and burial are attempts to deny the finality and reality of death. We prepare the bodies of our deceased relatives in such a way as to simulate life. We are sometimes expected to be comforted in some way by the fact that so-and-so "looked so natural." The implication is, of course, that the departed person is not *completely gone*. Other ceremonial procedures intended to assure us of the continuation of the individual personality beyond the grave have similar effects. Although many of these rituals are intended to comfort the survivors, they also serve to communicate to the living that *they* will never die.

PSYCHOTHERAPY AS DISPARAGEMENT

One of the most important reasons that people seek psychotherapy is their concern with their perceptions of themselves. Almost the first complaint that one hears in the early interviews are such statements as, "I don't like myself," "I can't do anything," "I am worthless, useless—a nothing." In short, the person sees himself as an incompetent human being who is unable to manage his affairs with any kind of efficiency. He finally gives up and goes to an "expert," who he hopes will solve his problem for him. But this very action places him in the midst of a dilemma.

On the one hand, he ostensibly wants to become more competent, more useful, more autonomous, more self-sufficient. But by seeking the help of an expert, he is actually admitting that he is incapable of just such action. The feeling that one *cannot* do certain things is often a critical factor in this very inability. Moreover, in some psychotherapeutic relationships there may be a subtle communication from the therapist to the client which runs something like the following: "You are disturbed, ill, unbalanced, unlucky, and unfit (that is, you are unheroic). I, who am healthy, well, competent, and heroic, will put you on the right track."

Such a communication, although not intended, can be very clearly implied in the relationship, especially to one who is insecure about his capabilities anyway. The result can be one more bit of evidence confirming the suspicions which the client has had about himself all along. Perhaps one reason for the great success of group therapy is that it all but eliminates this problem. In a group setting, the client is more likely to perceive the others as people like himself, who help him with his problems, and *whom he helps with theirs*. The importance of helping others toward the development of a positive self-image cannot be overestimated. To be the "psychiatrist" instead of the "patient" is proof of one's worth and capability. No amount of advice or encouragement by another person is as helpful in aiding a person to gain a sense of mastery.

DEALING WITH DISPARAGEMENT

The feelings that have been described in connection with this syndrome are powerful, painful, and difficult to annul. The nature of the self-image is such that it is peculiarly vulnerable to disparaging attacks. In a sense, the self-image is perhaps the most valuable "possession" a person has. It is for *its* benefit that other "valuable" commodities are sought. A person seeks riches, fame, status, respect, and so on, to gain a view of himself that *he* can value. Some of these things may be worthwhile in themselves, but they are particularly useless if they do not also help a person develop a real feeling of self-esteem. Disparaging attacks, intended or not, have the effect of undermining this very important feeling.

What, then, can a person do to minimize or entirely eliminate the damage that disparagement can do? There are a number of things. Some kinds of responses are more effective than others.

defensive responses

A usual attempt to deal with threats against the ego (self-image) is to become very defensive about the particular trait. If someone attacks our intelligence, we may try to make a great show of erudition in order to disprove their allegation. Responses of this kind are unsatisfactory since they merely increase the falsity of the PR image and lead to greater problems later.

Another attempt to handle this kind of attack is to withdraw. In this situation we may feel that if we take ourselves out of the situation, we are no longer vulnerable. Although this may be the case, it is really avoiding the question rather than facing it. To leave the scene either physically or psychologically is a temporary palliative measure at best. It does not help a person's perception of himself to know that he had to run away from the threat of being insulted or humiliated. It merely confirms his own suspicion that he in fact deserves such treatment.

Another way to deal with the effects of disparagement is to try to build a kind of shell which says in effect, "I am invulnerable, I cannot be hurt by others." The difficulty with such a stance, however, is that there is a tendency under such conditions for the person to deny his real feelings. And in so doing, as noted earlier, he becomes alienated from himself. Health, whether physical or psychological, demands that one be in tune with all the vital functions of his body. Denial of feeling is hardly a step in that direction.

There are a number of therapies that attempt to deal with disparagement. Most of these will be considered in Chapter 13. For our purposes in this chapter we shall consider one therapeutic approach to altering one's evaluation of himself.

the rational method

Albert Ellis (1958) has tackled head-on the problem of disparagement. His approach is really quite simple. Ellis feels that most people base their beliefs and behaviors upon assumptions that in many cases are "irrational." These irrational beliefs lead to contradictions between thought and feelings. And such contradictions lead to various maladaptive kinds of behavior. To break this pattern, Ellis suggests that we reexamine our assumptions and consider more rational alternatives in their place.

For Ellis the very first irrational assumption is "the idea that it is a dire necessity for an adult to be loved or approved by almost everyone for virtually everything he does." Another assumption is related to the first. It is "the idea that one should be thoroughly competent, adequate, intelligent and achieving in all possible respects. . . ." These two assumptions, taken together, are the essential elements underlying most negative feelings about the self. Such attitudes practically guarantee disaster, for they ask the impossible. They demand infallibility and they are satisfied with nothing less. A person accepting these assumptions (and they are extremely widespread in our society) can permit nothing short of perfection in himself. And such impossible (unrealistic) ambitions must lead to serious disappointments.

an altered approach to obligation

Mrs. A., a young mother, sought help at a nearby clinic because she had been having extremely severe anxiety attacks. She was an intelligent woman of twenty-three who had been taught to believe that a woman's place is "taking care of her home and family without complaint." "A woman," her mother had always said, "should not want other things in life." But Mrs. A. *did* want other things. Moreover, she could not accept the things she thought she *should* want. She hated housework and wanted to go back to school to study law. As a result, she developed an image of herself as a worthless human being. In her mind, a woman who could not be happy in the role of wife and mother was "no good." Her anxiety attacks reflected her feelings of inadequacy.

The idea that one *ought* to want certain things is a prevailing one in our culture. Moreover, we are indoctrinated with these "oughts" at an extremely early age before we are able to develop critical judgment. But a person cannot *will* the feelings that he has. He cannot love someone simply because he *ought* to. Nor can he love the style of life that someone else has set for him. As a result, the person who cannot be what he has been told he *should* be feels that he has failed.

A solution to some of these kinds of problems lies in an altered view of what a person is *obligated* to do. As Ellis points out, most of our ideas about the things we should be and do are based upon irrational assumptions about the nature of man, the nature of woman, the nature of the universe, and so on. A reconsideration of some of these ideas may lead to a better way of being who we are instead of who we are supposed to be.

Psychotherapists of whatever persuasion generally agree that a person must be true to his own nature before he can become "well." What this means in terms of obligation is that one is obligated to acknowledge his own feelings without fearing their consequences. We must know how we feel. And we must accept our feelings without prejudging them by someone else's standards. If psychologists have discovered anything of which they can be reasonably certain, it is the fact that individual differences exist on any measure we wish to use. Each human being (and probably each animal as well) is separate and unique and can be compared to others only by ignoring these differences. *It is therefore irrational to make any general statement about all women, all children, all boys, and so on.*

To return to the problem of Mrs. A.: had she not believed that women *must* accept their role as prescribed by her mother and others, she would have had no problem. It was her acceptance of an irrational idea about the obligation of women that made her feel so worthless. Her obligation was *not* to acquiesce in her role but to *acknowledge her own nature and then strive to fulfill it.* When in the course of therapy she began to do this, her self-image began to change and her anxieties largely disappeared.

an altered approach to self-evaluation

The notion that one must be competent and achieving in all things and that he must also be loved and approved by everyone with whom he comes in contact is the underlying assumption of the PR personality. Along with this idea goes the belief that happiness is only possible when these requirements are met. In order to fulfill these demands, a person will have to play the role of the hero or suffer the humiliation of being the ordinary guy. But beside the fact that demands of this type lead to certain failure, the idea that happiness is only achievable when one is universally admired and/or completely expert in everything is an illusion. It is therefore an irrational belief. Happiness has very little to do with how *others* experience you, but *how you experience you.*

We are taught from childhood that we must excel, we must compete, we must be liked, admired, sought after, and respected. And we come to believe that our happiness, even our very psychological existence, depends upon such things. These beliefs can be shown to be false by empirical procedures: the incidence of unhappiness, suicide, and the like, is just as high among those who have great abilities and popularity as it is among those who apparently do not. But, more importantly, such beliefs are self-defeating. They can lead to only one result—destruction of one's evaluation of himself.

These kinds of beliefs therefore do not bring about the results for which they are originally adopted. Their purpose is to increase the happiness of the organism, but the adoption of these beliefs actually has the opposite effect. It increases the misery of the organism by presenting it with impossible goals.

It is not necessary to accept an idea simply because it happens to be commonplace. Most people once accepted the idea that the earth was flat. If the beliefs that we have been exploring subvert their purpose, what other beliefs might we consider that would not?

In order to understand what is about to be said, we must be prepared to jar our thinking into an unfamiliar path. We must be willing to drop all our usual assumptions and consider some very different ones. Let us see what they might be:

1. All human beings are intrinsically valuable because of the very fact that they exist.
2. Each individual is special and important because he is *unique*.
3. Each human being can and must accept his imperfections as parts of his uniqueness.
4. A person need not feel degraded, useless, worthless, because he "fails" in certain endeavors.
5. The concept of "worthiness" can exist without its opposite, "worthlessness." Every concept does not necessarily have to be countered by a contradictory one. This is simply a convention of Western civilization. But there is no law that states that all values must have negative counterparts.
6. There need be no rank ordering of value among human beings. All individuals are appraised as universally valuable.

The last assumption is a particularly difficult one for Americans. We have been conditioned to make most of our evaluations by comparisons. Our only criteria for judging ourselves and others is whether or not we are bigger, stronger, taller, prettier than someone else. And because there are superficial differences of these types which can be observed, we make the mistake that the taller, stronger, or prettier one is somehow more worthwhile. If, however, we can come to realize that each of us, no matter what his attributes, has an intrinsic, unchangeable worth, then our self-esteem need never be shaken by any external event.

We can approach this problem from another point of view. If a human being is to be valued for what he *is*, then it is necessary for us to redefine his *is-ness*. As we have seen, we can view an individual objectively, as a collection of *attributes*, or existentially as a center of awareness. But viewing a person in terms of his attributes forces us to *compare* him with others. This leads to differing evaluations of individuals. The person who has more heroic attributes becomes more valuable than those who are less well endowed. But is it rational to make such appraisals in terms of human beings? Do we really want to say that someone who is younger, or taller,

*Each human being responds to his world in his own unique
way. Each person's value lies in this uniqueness.*

or prettier, or stronger, or healthier, or even kinder than someone else is
therefore really more worthwhile in a real sense?

It is irrational to evaluate human beings in this way for two reasons.
In the first place, it is unlikely that anyone really believes that handsome
people, for example, are really more valuable than homely ones. In the
second place, if we use such criteria, every one of us will find ourselves
inadequate, and therefore experience disparagement, in any number of
areas. This makes the use of such a criterion self-defeating.

There is another problem related to the person-as-collection-of-
attributes model. Since no two people perceive an individual in exactly the
same way, *there is no real person-as-object.* There are as many different
perceptions of an individual as there are observers, so the attributes we like
or dislike in ourselves may not even exist for someone else. But if the self-
as-object is unreal, what self *is* real?

The one reality that we can all accept, is the reality of our own existence. Descartes said, "I think, therefore I am." Our own experience is the proof of our being. We are the ongoing process which informs us of the fact that *anything* exists at all. We may not be the center of the universe in the way that Ptolemy believed, but we are certainly the center of the only universe that we will ever know.

Each of us is *a vortex of awareness, a focus of experience, a center of consciousness.* This is what we are most certainly, and if we think of ourselves in this way, how can we ever say that one individual consciousness is in any way more or less valuable than any other? Although my attributal self may be compared with others, my existential self is beyond all comparison. Its value is in its very existence. It cannot be disparaged because it is void of any qualities that can be compared with any other consciousness.

One young man was asked by a solicitous questioner what he could do better than anyone else. It was the assumption of the person who asked the question that everyone has some attribute at which he excels. Thus the question was intended to help the young man discover this attribute in order to increase his self-esteem. But the answer that the questioner received was one that he was probably not prepared for. For the young man, who seemed very comfortable and self-assured, replied, "I can be *me* better than anyone else in the world."

This is the real answer to the question. Each one of us can be the unique individual self that we are, better than anyone else. And it is impossible to compare such individuals because it is like comparing apples and oranges. *We are all best at being different and unique.* If we can come to perceive ourselves this way, we cannot be disparaged. And the feelings that accompany that experience will largely disappear from our lives.

This is, of course, an ideal statement of what our aims might be. Although we may never reach the state in which we are completely invulnerable to derisive attacks, from a practical standpoint all we need do is to make progress in approaching this goal. A clear vision of a person's intrinsic worth makes him almost impervious to disparagement of any kind. Moreover, this vision dispenses with the necessity for an exaggerated PR image. Once a person perceives himself as worthwhile, he has no need to continue to present falsified versions of himself to himself and the world.

disparagement and the healthy individual

A person with a firm idea of who he is is free to experience his own feelings. Insults and disparaging situations do not touch him very deeply. He knows who he is and he likes who he is. Or if there is something about himself that he does not like, he can face that fact and perhaps try to change it. But he can only change something about himself when he admits it exists. If he denies it because it is "bad," then he can do nothing about it.

The authentic person is in touch with his own being in a very intimate sense. And he comes to admire himself partly because of this intimacy. But the essential fact about the healthy person is that he can explore his own experience without fear that it may betray him as a worthless individual. He can also feel comfortable with other people because he knows that revealing his true nature to others will bring them closer to him.

In Chapter 4 we shall see how the interpersonal relationships and early experiences in a person's life lead either to authenticity and love or to defensiveness and a perception of others as the enemy.

chapter 4
evil and the need for an enemy

THE PERCEPTION OF EVIL

From the beginning of his history, man has wrestled with the problem of evil in the world. His early attempts to escape from danger or to defend himself against the hardships of nature led him to perceive certain parts of the environment as hostile and dangerous. Disease, death, and disaster were constant visitors in the ancient world. Hunger, cold, pain, and sadness dogged man's existence. It is not surprising, therefore, that early man perceived such things as frightening. Anything that was harmful or dangerous became "bad"; that which was helpful was seen as "good." This perhaps was the most primitive idea of good and evil. But as time went on, man's perceptions of the world grew broader and so his concept of good and evil came to involve other areas of life.

Through the ages, the concept of evil has come to refer to several kinds of phenomena.

77

The first of these concerns the idea that evil exists; that there are forces in the universe that are destructive or malicious. These forces are antagonistic to man's well-being. They are pernicious. They threaten his survival and appear to be working toward his destruction.

The second idea concerns itself with good and evil in the abstract. It explores the possibility that right and wrong can be formulated in such a way that anyone can learn to discriminate one from the other. This is the special province of philosophy called "ethics."

The third problem deals with man's nature. It asks the question: Is man innately good or evil? These problems are not easy to separate from one another and, as we deal with them, we will see that each kind of evil is intimately connected with the others.

THE BIRTH OF EVIL

Prehistoric man lived in a world of complete mystery. The universe he inhabited was totally unintelligible to him. He looked out upon the elements; he saw the night sky, he observed death, but he did not understand. There were things and events that frightened him, things that seemed to be beyond his control. It was these that would come to be seen as evil. It was with these that sooner or later he would have to come to terms.

To explain or counteract the forces of evil in the world, primitive man resorted to magic. Priests would cast spells to drive out the spirit of evil from the land. Ceremonies would be presented that would assure the safety and fertility of the people. The violent forces of nature, it was thought, could be subdued by performing certain rites under appropriate conditions.

The tendency to personify evil was natural for ancient man, who often perceived all of nature in animistic terms. For him, all things had some kind of soul or will. And many of these beings were believed to be un-friendly to man. Priests often warned of spirits who could wreak destruction on the world, either as punishment for some wrongdoing or simply as some arbitrary whim to cause havoc. Angry gods could materialize from anywhere, bringing misfortune down on the populace.

The advent of collective behavior was partly an attempt to deal with the forces of destruction in the world by mobilizing the efforts of larger numbers of people. But with the creation of larger groups, there came the necessity for the improvisation of crude sets of rules that would govern the behavior of individuals. It is likely that the most primitive of these kinds of rules were taboos (Freud, 1913). Many of the taboos of primitive people were simply expressions of superstitious belief and as such did not imply any kind of moral imperative. The early "codes" of behavior, if we may call them such, were little more than injunctions to observe these taboos or to expose oneself to great dangers.

The rise of more complex civilizations created the need for somewhat more complex rules, and as the classes began to differentiate, "laws" appeared that were mainly edicts handed down by the powerful in order to protect their power. Such codes of conduct rarely concerned themselves with general rules that were valid for all men. The early "morality" considered evil in strictly personal terms. If it was bad for "our group" or "our clan," it was evil. The idea that there could be rules of behavior that might be "good" or "bad" for all had not yet appeared.

Since man personified all his ideas, he saw the forces of good and evil in terms of tangible enemies. There were hostile creatures everywhere, some of whom were real predators and true dangers to his safety, and others who were imaginary but nonetheless fearful and threatening.

Many ancient peoples worshipped the sun. The sun not only gave them light and warmth but also comfort. For primitive man the night was fearful and the sun drove it away and brought the day. This was man's

Ancient man worshipped the sun. That is not surprising, since it is the source of all life. Modern man is still awed by its beauty.

time to grow things and to hunt. Sometimes the Sun-God was a hunter who accompanied men on their expedition and aided them in finding game. When sailing in canoes on the rivers, the Sun-God could be seen beneath the waters accompanying the fishermen wherever they might go. The peasants of the Nile who predated the Egyptian civilization saw the Sun-God as a falcon who soared across the sky with his wings outstretched (Breasted, 1933).

Rain, clouds, and storms were the enemies of the Sun-God, who in one ancient myth was believed to have lost his eye to these evil gods. Anything that interfered with the sun's light was generally thought of as an enemy to the sun worshippers, whose disciples are believed to have spread across Europe to Asia and to have appeared somewhat later in the Western Hemisphere as well.

The sky naturally became the sphere of heaven, for therein dwelt the sun, and it was there that ancient man believed that his spirit would live after this life on earth was ended.

With the development of more complex civilizations, the mantle of divinity passed from the world of nature to noblemen and kings. The ruler of the city-state became the all-powerful benefactor and judge. He nurtured, but he also punished evil doers. To be his loyal subject, therefore, became good and to disobey his wishes became evil.

The most pervasive force in the life of ancient man was his religion. At first, his beliefs were simply naive attempts to explain the world about him. Most of his interpretations were highly imaginative and fantastic. His hopes and fears became his legends. His religious expression became his art. The trees, rocks, rivers, and mountains were his gods. But as his communities evolved, so did his religious outlook, and when the idea of divinity passed from the inanimate world to the kings, it ushered in a new era in which man for the first time began to think about good and evil in human affairs.

EXISTENTIAL CONSIDERATIONS

The fact that man is subject to certain kinds of misfortunes is not very startling. The Four Horsemen of the Apocalypse—death, war, famine, and pestilence—are still abroad in the world. But the way man deals with this fact is of crucial importance to his well being. As we saw in the previous chapter, there is a great tendency for most of us to deny the existence of this form of evil in our lives. We try not to face the fact that a great portion of our lives is governed by chance; that we are subject to contingency and cannot predict our fate. We avoid a direct encounter with the reality of death or we try to cling to beliefs that are designed to prove that death is not real. Such efforts to avoid *feeling* the anxiety that is normal in such circumstances leads, according to the existentialist's view, to the incapacity to *feel* at all. Or it leads to a kind of numbness that can only be overcome by the most *intense* emotional states. Perhaps it is for this reason that people seek sensation: rush to the scenes of accidents, fires, and other kinds of spectacles. Rollo May (1969) believes that violence itself may be a response to a need for contact on the part of people whose inner feelings have been turned off: "When inward life dries up, when feeling decreases and apathy increases, when one cannot affect or even genuinely touch another person, violence flares up as a daimonic necessity for contact, a mad drive forcing touch in the most direct way possible."

While there are physical evils such as death and disease, there are also psychological evils such as anxiety and depersonalization, guilt, shame, and alienation. In order to avoid these evils we sometimes develop complicated systems of defenses which have the short-term advantage of warding off the undesirable feelings. But the price we pay in the long run is to forfeit a portion of our authentic self. When we deny our anxiety, we deny a part of our being.

Authenticity is preferable to the avoidance of anxiety, but *at the time we make the choice, we do not realize this.* At the moment we choose to hide a part of ourselves, we do not see the consequences of the act. We feel the discomfort of the moment and take steps to alleviate it. Perhaps if someone at that moment could show us what our choice is leading to, we might be disuaded. But there is no one available at such moments. So we opt to avoid the present pain while we unknowingly lay the groundwork for future disaster.

One of the rewards of authenticity is that it "fits," it "feels right." It is worth the anxieties that we must face in order to obtain it. The myths of all lands have told us correctly that we must face the dragon (evil), conquer our fear, and, by so doing, slay the evil creature and find our freedom. What the myths say symbolically is that *the evil* (the dragon, the giant, the sea monster) *is really our own fear.* Conquer that and we are free.

Another form of evil that we must acknowledge is our love for horror. We are fascinated by the tales of monsters and devils. We are attracted to the morbid, the ugly, the diabolic. Stories of murder, treachery, cruelty, and torture bring us to the edge of our seats with excitement. We thrill to the exploits of fiends, ghouls, vampires, and demons. We are obsessed with death, decay, excreta, and blood. We shrink from these things but spread our fingers as we cover our eyes.

We must come to understand our preoccupation with horror. It is useless to play the game that respectable people have no interest in such things. These things frighten us and we are fascinated by our own terror.

We understand this as children but attempt to avoid it in maturity. Only when we accept the existence of such diabolical pleasures can they become an unimportant part of our past.

There are also *emotions* that are sometimes considered evil. Hate, anger, jealousy, desire for revenge, envy, and in some cases fear are believed to be "bad" emotions. When we feel any of these, we may think that we are "being bad." Such an idea will often lead to our repressing the emotion.

Mr. D. was fired for attacking his supervisor with a claw hammer. On being referred for psychiatric care, it was learned that he had lived for many years with his very strict, authoritarian father, against whom he was unable to express any anger. To feel hatred for one's father was a terrible sin, and as a boy he had only felt a gnawing sense of guilt whenever his father punished him. The outburst of anger against his supervisor was out of proportion to his superior's deed and Mr. D. himself realized that the attack was really the result of a long, smoldering hatred for his father which was "taken out" on the supervisor.

We cannot satisfactorily avoid "evil" by repressing it. Ignoring it will not make it go away. The existential facts of life, death, contingency, evil, and anxiety must be acknowledged and accepted as real. The alternative is illness. The search for health is also the search for truth.

THE BIRTH OF ETHICAL THOUGHT

Man's concern with evil in his own nature leads us to ethical considerations. There are a number of reasons why psychologists are interested in the study of ethics. First, psychologists want to understand the processes by which men come to adopt conceptual systems of various kinds. Second, psychologists would like to discover ways of encouraging "good" behavior in people if a truly ethical system could be discovered. But the most important reason for this interest is that it is the province of psychology to ascertain the kinds of behavior that are in harmony with man's nature. It is this latter function which has not been dealt with by psychologists until recently. Ethics for the last six thousand years has been the exclusive domain of theologists and philosophers. And the ethical systems that have emerged from these disciplines have had little or no relevance to the real nature of man. As a consequence, the kinds of systems that have arisen have often been inimicable to man's best interest. The task for psychology is therefore to find out not only what is *good*, but also what is good for *man*.

historical roots

The history of right and wrong is a long one. According to Breasted (1933) the earliest known religious beliefs that included any kind of moral mandate occurred about 4000 B.C., in Memphis, the capital of ancient Egypt. The concept of right and wrong, which was the concern of priests in the temples, was not at that time part of the life of the masses of people of Egypt. But gradually such ideas began to filter down from the palace aristocrats and the temple priests to the nobility who administered the provinces and, after many generations, these ideas reached down to the people themselves.

But morality, like other infants of the ancient world, did not have a smooth development. With the fall of a stable dynasty that had ruled for a thousand years, there came a period of upheaval and corruption in which the ideas of good and evil almost vanished from the earth. A few optimistic sages, however, kept the hope for social justice alive until a new era might arise which would put the idea of justice back into the thought of mankind. This optimism was to become extremely important to the subsequent development of Western man.

Since the society of that period was in a state of disarray, it was the hope of those concerned with reestablishing stability that someone might soon come who would be capable of redirecting the people into the "paths of righteousness." He who would come, therefore, would be a savior, for his task would be to save man from his wickedness. Thus the Messianic concept was born. This idea was of course later incorporated into the thinking of the Hebrews. The impact of Messianism upon the thought of Western civilization would be enormous. For the idea of the coming of a savior was to shake the foundations of the civilized world for the next several millennia.

Until this time, morality had little to do with the prevailing religions throughout the civilized world. But with the advent of the Egyptian and Hebrew notions of "righteousness," the questions of moral and ethical behavior were infused into religion for the first time. The Hebrew tradition went a step further in making ethical thought a religious issue, for it was the first system to propose a single deity who was the authority for all behavior. The idea of one God who was "just" necessitated the formulation of abstract concepts that applied to all men everywhere. If God was a moral creature, there had to be some general framework within which He worked. Evil, then, became the rejection of divine command. Although the beginning of ethical thought may be said to date from this time, there would be centuries of disagreement and violence over the "true" nature of good and evil. For it is one thing to say that man must act in an ethical manner, but it is another to determine what that manner may be.

A just God, in some ways, created more problems than He solved. For if God was all good, how could man account for the existence of evil in the world? The answer was obvious. Evil was, of course, the work of some other deity. Evil was therefore the set of beliefs of those others who did not share the commandments of *our* deity. Now we had two gods: ours the good one, and theirs the bad one. The bad god was the devil.

With the emergence of demonology, man became the center of a great conflict. The forces of good and evil were engaged in a stupendous battle for the souls of all men. Sometimes the devil got the upper hand. At other times, God was victorious. But no victory was final. The battle raged on. And man believed himself to be in the grip of one or the other of these great forces with very little ability to choose his own fate. Thus the responsibility for one's actions was seen to be outside the person himself, residing in the supernatural being who had possession of him.

Christianty sought to change this view. The devil could tempt man but could not compel him to misbehave. The choice was man's. If he was to be virtuous, he had to resist the efforts of evil, which were always at work. Only through his own will could man avoid the pitfalls that lay in wait for him.

WHAT IS GOOD?

Great men of all ages have wrestled with the question of good and evil. Some have held that good, like beauty, is in the eye of the beholder, that what we deem good is merely our *own* private way of looking at things. The terms right and wrong, according to this theory, do not have absolute meanings. They are relative terms and can only be judged by a particular person in a particular situation. Moreover, they are relative in another sense. For what may be considered good or right for one man may be evil for another.

But other theories hold that right and wrong can be objectively defined. There are, according to this kind of thinking, values which exist at all times, for all people. One of the problems with this kind of statement, however, is that there are a great number of differing "objective" theories of how men ought to behave.

One of the earliest ethical systems was Stoicism. It was a philosophy of rigid austerity, of self-denial, and quiet acquiescence to one's fate. The Stoics greatly admired Socrates for his incorruptibility, his calmness in the face of death, and his strong belief that he who commits an injustice suffers more than his victim.

Contrasted to this view of good and evil was the Epicurean philosophy. Epicurus, born about 342 B.C., began the study of philosophy at the age of fourteen, according to his own report. Although he was greatly influenced by Democritus and others, he never acknowledged this debt. His philosophy dealt with the value of pleasure. Pleasure for Epicurus was the overriding good in life. Everything that was worthwhile stemmed from this basic assumption. Virtue, justice, the quest for tranquility, were all meaningless without the infusion of pleasure. But he differed from some of the hedonists who preceded him in that he considered pleasure to be a kind of moderate response to mild stimuli (for example, hunger) rather than a passionate expression of a powerful need like sex (Russell, 1945). He saw the absence of pain as perhaps the truest pleasure, and he included in the concept of pain any strong drive based on deficency needs. He therefore anticipated by more than 2,000 years a modern theory of motivation called homeostasis (to be discussed later).

These two philosophical systems tend to set the outer boundaries for most of the ethical principles that have been advocated through the years. From asceticism to self-indulgence they present the extreme ends of the continuum of ethical ideas. In the area between are the ideas of such thinkers as Aristotle, who prescribed moderation in all things; Spinoza, who warned that the passions distract us from our real task, becoming one with God; Kant, who advocated that we act through reason in such a way that our action should constitute a universal law; and Karl Marx, who believed that the dialectical process of change was a necessary condition for progress and, in that sense, an ultimate good.

Most of these formulations have had an influence of some kind on the thought of Western man. But, as noted earlier, they generally evolved without support from an adequate understanding of man's nature. To be valid, any ethic must take into consideration those things that man's constitution and character make necessary. Is there, then, an ethical system that is consistent with man's nature? There is some evidence that one is emerging, but we will have to postpone its exposition until we have more fully explored the scientific theories of man.

GOOD, EVIL, AND THE NATURE OF MAN

The third question with regard to the problem of evil revolves around man's moral nature. Beside their concern for what is right and what is wrong, ethicists have also been interested in learning whether man himself is innately good or evil. Or perhaps it may be that he is neither of these things but simply so malleable that he can become anything under the appropriate environmental conditions.

Ancient peoples had many myths about the nature of man. Most of these stories attempted to explain the undeniable fact that men do not always act toward one another with charity. Often these myths described a godlike creature who had committed a great sin and been banished forever from the kingdom of the good god(s). He thus became an evil god—a devil.

Even in the ancient world, selfishness was seen as one of the cardinal sins. A myth concerning Ahriman, the devil of ancient Persia, describes him bursting out of the womb because he has heard his father vow that his first-born son would inherit his kingdom. Ahriman, whose twin is still in the womb, becomes the god of death and destruction. But it is his *selfishness* which is his underlying vice. His breaking out of the womb early is seen as his first evil deed. For it has as its purpose the usurpation of the throne from its rightful heir, his brother.

The concept of evil changes from time to time, for if in one case the greatest sin is avarice, in another it might be disobedience, gluttony, murder, sexuality, or sloth. Whatever its nature, evil in the ancient world is almost always presented in the form of a god who is its champion. He has somehow become separated from the good gods and has become the lord of all that is destructive in the world.

One point about the nature of evil is made in many of the myths. It concerns the fact that the god of evil *chooses* his particular path. The idea that one can choose good or evil and is not *condemned* to evil, is a central one in many religions.

The belief that human nature is inherently evil has gotten a great deal of "support" from many areas of inquiry. A simple look at the history of man since his appearance on the planet may seem to substantiate the hypothesis that human nature is intrinsically evil. Violence, cruelty, destructiveness, and selfishness have been apparent from the most ancient times to the present. Moreover, as civilization has evolved, the cruelty has become more refined and more efficient; it has not diminished or disappeared.

Darwin's revelations have also been seen by many as substantiation of man's innate cruelty. If man is merely a higher form of animal, then he has an animal nature. Since most people believe that animals are amoral at best and cruel and vicious at worst, these qualities must also be present in man. The Darwinian struggle for survival has often been seen as the basis for all behavior. And in this struggle, only the strongest and most ruthless succeed. Man's ruthlessness is seen therefore as a biological necessity of his evolutionary development.

Freud's perception of man's nature was, of course, derived at least partly from Darwin's discoveries. Man was simply a predatory beast trying to control his aggressive instincts. But his murderous tendencies periodically broke loose under certain circumstances. These tendencies took the form of murder and rape, war, pillage, or any other kind of aggression by one person against another or by one group toward another group. These actions, Freud thought, grew out of the very nature of human beings who had "a powerful measure of desire for aggressiveness . . . as part of their instinctual endowment."

Freud's view of man was even more pessimistic after World War I.

The appalling savagery of that conflict and the evident delight of some of his contemporaries with the unbelievable carnage persuaded him that men were even more depraved than he had imagined. Other people who lived through that era were similarly horrified by the slaughter. The war and its inordinate barbarity was a disillusioning experience for many and appeared on the surface to support the pessimistic views of man's nature.

Such views contributed to the long tradition in the history of thought which has seen man as a creature in need of some kind of restraint. Man has been perceived in this tradition as basically selfish, violent, and destructive. He has had to be kept from expressing his "real" nature by some kind of coercion (law), backed when possible by the application of force. Another important source of "evidence" for this idea has come from the Judeo-Christian view of man.

The religious tradition in the Western world has generally tended to view man as a sinner. Although created by God, man has rejected His commandment and fallen from grace. As a sinner, he must continually be on his guard against the tendencies within him to commit evil. When he has such desires or commits such deeds, he must confess his sins and seek repentance. According to this view, man is continually in need of some kind of redemption. Without this, he is doomed to everlasting punishment.

This Judeo-Christian idea of sin is somewhat more extreme than the one from which it grew. The Greek, Irenaeus, and other early theologians saw Adam as a childlike creature, not yet a mature man, who had been created in the "image" of God. But the Greeks differentiated the idea of "image" and "likeness." Although created in God's *image*, man was striving to gain his *likeness*. It was man's task to continue to develop until this latter stage had been reached. His "fall" during this developmental period was seen by the Greeks as a setback of *limited* importance and not as a complete transformation from a "good" to an "evil" being. The interpretations of Augustine and others seem to have altered this view radically.

St. Augustine spent the greater part of his life in preoccupation with evil. The problem which he set for himself is one that has already been alluded to. Since he believed in a God who was absolutely good, he had to somehow account for the existence of evil in the world and especially in man. How could an infinitely good being allow evil to exist? Augustine answered this question by positing the concept of corruptibility. All things created by God were good, but they could be corrupted by beings who turned away from the higher good to a lower good. This turning from the higher good (that is, God) was the evil act. It is not the lower thing that is to be considered evil but the *choosing* of it. And such behavior occurs because of man's free will. Because man is free, he sometimes chooses "wrongly." If he always chose only the good, he would not be free. For that would mean that his choices were *predetermined*. If one is *always* right, it must be because he *has* to be. In a sense, what Augustine was saying is that a free agent sometimes makes mistakes; only a predetermined one never will.

This may account for the evil in man, but it does not resolve the problem of the evil that does not have its origin in man. Augustine was aware of this fact and he had an explanation for this form of evil as well. The perception of evil in the universe was, he held, a result of a too limited view of reality. By seeing only a small portion of the total context, one may believe that what he is observing is evil. But viewed in its totality, the isolated segments can be appreciated as necessary components of the harmonious whole. God, who can perceive the entire panorama of infinite being, knows that it is infinitely good. What appears as evil is therefore only a result of a myopic view of the world. Even death contributes to the beauty of the universe by providing for the ever-changing variety of living creatures.

This latter explanation in a sense obviates the need for the former. For if evil is only *apparent*, then it would seem that man's misdeeds are themselves unreal. Augustine, however, is not willing to go this far. Man's fall is real. But the punishment which man endures as an atonement for his sins restores the equilibrium that is necessary for the whole. As long as the punishment is exactly proportional to the offense, the moral balance of the universe remains intact.

A philosophy that differs somewhat from this concept is Vedanta. These teachings are based upon the Vedas, the oldest written religious scriptures. They originated in India and are sometimes mistakenly thought to be identical with Hinduism. There is a great deal in common between the two, but the term "Vedanta" refers to all the religious beliefs, including Hinduism, which are based on a monistic world outlook.

The world, according to Vedanta, is a unity of being. All separation of persons and things is illusion, *maya*. Good, evil, and all the values in between are also *maya*. Underneath the appearance of the everyday world perceived by the senses is the real world, *Brahman*. This unchanging, eternal reality is Existence, God, the One. If one penetrates the curtain of the phenomenal world and perceives the real essence beneath, he sees that God is all things and that he himself is God. The idea of evil has no place in such a scheme (Isherwood, 1945).

A world without evil has not always enjoyed a great vogue. It is extremely difficult to defend those views which say that evil is only an illusion in the face of suffering and pain which are all too real to the victims. The German philosopher, Leibniz, perceived this fact. He agreed to some extent with the Augustinean idea of an absolutely good deity, but he also felt that evil was a necessary part of existence. God might be absolutely good, but he nevertheless presides over a world in which evil exists. But, for Leibniz, this was the best of all possible worlds. Since there are only a finite number of worlds possible, God has chosen the best of these. Any other world would have more evil than the one chosen. God, having considered all the other possibilities, has seen their disadvantages and chosen to bring this one into being. So that in Leibniz's view, a world without evil is simply impossible.

SIN, GUILT, AND REDEMPTION

The version of human nature which sees man as a creature who has fallen (that is, sinned) is an extremely pervasive one in Western society. But a concept of that sort does not spring full blown into being. Religious ideas, like other ideas, tend to evolve with time. As they are passed from one generation to another, or from one people to another, they are altered in countless, sometimes subtle ways. It is likely that some of the earliest ideas about religion referred not to God with a capital G, but to nature. For nature was a god to primitive men. Moreover, it is a reasonable assumption that some of the early priests perceived the danger inherent in man's straying too far from his natural state, and these priests probably began to preach against it. Their sermons might have sounded like this: "You must heed the message of nature. For if you fail to follow her dictates, you will surely suffer."

As originally intended, such a statement probably meant that man as a natural creature must try to undertstand what his place in nature is. He must *listen* to nature's urging. And, once understood, he must live within the boundaries of his natural self.

This admonition was an extremely important one. For man was the first innovator. Only *he* created artificial portions of his environment. Only *he* altered the instinctual rituals of living. In so doing, he ran the risk of error. He might, by his newly found creativity, take a turn that would lead him away from what he *really* was. He might create things that would stunt the development of his real potential.

Of course, the primitive priest did not put the problem in such terms. But he felt intuitively that man must remain in touch with that part of him that was atuned to the natural world. And his sermon indicated that.

There is a great deal of research demonstrating that any communication which is passed through a number of "interpreters" undergoes a variety of alterations in its meaning. These alterations depend to a great extent upon several factors. Generally speaking, the longer the time from a communication's inception to its final form, and the greater the number of individuals involved in passing the material on, the greater the degree of distortion. Moreover, the form of the distortion will depend directly upon the biases that are brought to the situation by each listener. Allport and Postman (1947), in describing the manner in which rumors change as they pass from person to person, describe what they call the phenomenon of *assimilation*. "The rumor will become assimilated with the cognitive and emotional context that the listener brings to the hearing of the rumor. The rumor is made to fit the individual's idea of a good story, is twisted so that it fits his own expectation." These writers also point out that the rumor will be changed somewhat by the listener's "linguistic habits," so that in the process of translating the communication into his own words, there may be a great deal of alteration.

Another very powerful influence on information that is handed from person to person is the personal prejudice or self-interest of the listener. In passing the story on, each person unknowingly adds a certain element based upon his own wishes or needs, so that as time goes on, the actual intent of the original can be substantially changed. Finally the communication may have no resemblance to the original one.

In all likelihood, many religious communications have undergone this kind of process. We must be aware of this when we interpret the religious literature of antiquity. In light of this, it might be interesting to examine the historical development of an idea such as the one mentioned above. Let us see how such a communication might change with the passage of time.

First, the original sermon:

"You must heed the message of nature. For if you fail to follow her dictates, you will surely suffer."

With a few slight changes this becomes:

"You must comply with the dictates of the gods. For if you fail to adhere to their laws, you will surely fall from favor."

And after a few more translations over a few thousand years, it finally reads:

"You must obey the commandments of God. For if you fail to bow to His will, you must surely be punished."

In this way we can see that the intent of the initial statement has been completely turned around by the slight variations that have been made by later "disciples." The original idea was to live in harmony with nature. But by the time the final version is developed, the meaning has changed so that one is now being told that he must behave in rigidly prescribed ways even though they may be *contrary* to his true nature. The authority has passed from *nature* to a spokesman who interprets God's word for us. However, the interpreter is several times removed from the "Word." Moreover, although he may be a disciple of a great seer, he may not be one himself. And he tends to impose his own limitations upon the vision of him whom he follows. If we add the disciple's errors to the faulty interpretations of the ancient wisdom, the amount of distortion in the final message becomes immeasurable.

We have already seen how St. Augustine's version of the fall exaggerated the ideas of the Greek theologians from whom it came. And it is probable that many other misinterpretations and faulty translations have altered the meanings of earlier myths. It is, in fact, possible that the story of the fall really referred to the misuse of the natural environment. Some early scribes may have warned of the dangerous effects of making careless changes in the ecology of small areas. Even in very early times, too much hunting or too much planting in the same small plot could have serious ecological consequences. A wise man warning of such danger might have told the people that they might run the risk of losing their "garden" forever if they did not treat it with great care. They might, in fact, have to leave it (be banished) as a consequence.

And the ancient sage might have said to his people: "Beware of how you use your new discoveries (knowledge), for indiscriminate use of them

The Christian message has spread over a large part of the world. And it has been interpreted by many disciples. Here a Franciscan monk brings his message to the New World.

might despoil your place of habitation." But future priests might easily interpret this to mean that *knowledge itself* was dangerous and thus they admonished the people to abstain from eating the fruit of the tree of knowledge for which they would be banished from Eden.

There is also the possibility that some priests, realizing that knowledge was dangerous to any dogmatic code of behavior, condemned the pursuit of knowledge in order to preserve their power. Reik (1957) expresses the opinion that knowledge to the ancients was synonymous with divine power. Therefore, to seek knowledge was, to the priests of the time, to usurp the power of the Lord. To wish to be as powerful as God was the height of pridefulness and therefore a great sin. The punishment was both banishment and mortality. The later Christians, of course, added the sexual content (the nakedness and shame) to the story.

One might note here the anthropomorphized nature of a God who would be resentful of man for acquiring knowledge equal to His own. And we may suspect that the interpreters were projecting their own feelings into the narrative. It seems unnecessary to suppose that an all-powerful, all-knowing being would feel threatened by the efforts of puny men to educate themselves. In any case it is important to note that any communication that has passed through a series of translations and interpretations can be accepted only with a certain amount of reservation.

WOMAN AS THE TEMPTRESS

In the evolution of the Fall, we see the introduction of the idea that woman is the source of all evil. This concept is a prominent one in some religions (see Chapter 1). It is Eve who destroys the otherwise virtuous Adam in the story of the Creation, so the sins of man all lie on her head. Earlier myths saw the female as the temptress who could use her charms to destroy men, to turn men into swine, or to tempt them to abandon their duty. The idea of temptation is often tied to sexuality. It is sex that is seen as the "weakness" by which man is corrupted. And in symbolic language, sex is the female. Even today the idea of women as "vessels of evil" is prevalent in parts of the Western world.

Reik, however, observes that like other elements of the Fall myth, the introduction of sex as sin is absent from the earlier versions until it has been interpreted by St. Augustine and St. Paul. In fact, it is inconceivable that the Hebrew version of original sin would consider sexual desire as the greatest violation of divine law. It may be that the Fall myths (they have emerged in almost every culture throughout history) were originally meant to explain the existence of evil in general and only after a certain amount of interpretation became concerned with man's moral qualities. This seems possible since most of these stories had their birth at a time in man's history when ethical concepts had not yet appeared. Reik cites evidence to show that the story of Creation and the Fall are *really several unrelated myths* which were *later woven into one*, so that Creation and sin are not necessarily associated in the earlier narratives.

Philip Wylie (1947) explores the idea that the Fall myth has been misinterpreted entirely. Original sin is not eating the apple, gaining knowledge, or expressing one's sexuality. It is, Wylie insists, *vanity*. Man's first mistake is his view of himself as God's chosen creature. This idea of man's own importance in the universe is where he has gone astray. He has chosen to perceive himself as a kind of demigod and, in so doing, has denied one whole part of his being.

Wylie believes that man is largely a creature of instinct. Although many psychologists would argue with the term "instinct," they would certainly agree that man has certain basic drives that must be paid heed. Wylie's point is that in our egotistical desire to present ourselves in God's image, we have been unwilling or unable to accept the basic passions that run deep within our being. By denying this part of our nature, we have committed the original sin, the sin of pride. And the wages of such sin is, if not death, at least great misery. Most of man's troubles result from his basic, real nature, fighting for expression against the tyrannical forces of repression. And the repression occurs, according to Wylie's view, because we are trying to deny our "animal" nature in our egotistical desire to be godlike.

The earlier misinterpretations of the Fall story lead to guilt. In them, we are angels who have fallen. We have status with guilt. Wylie's interpretation leaves us with very little compensation. We are animals, and what we think is status is merely pride. It is no wonder that under the circumstances, the first alternative has generally been accepted. Status with guilt is evidently preferable to feelings of worthlessness with nothing to compensate the ego.

Wylie's argument has a great deal of bearing on what we have been discussing in this book. For it is, he says, the desire for self-aggrandizement that is man's original folly. It is his need to appear to be what he is not that finally alienates him from himself. The institutions of the civilized world seize upon this ego need in order to obtain the allegiance of the people in their cause, their church, their crusade. And the people robbed of their inner harmony by the deceits of "civilizing" forces seek to reestablish that harmony by entering into a partnership with the particular institution. Thus we invest our PR images into nations, churches, organizations, corporations, friends, families, clans, the home team, the local war hero, or even the hometown beauty queen to escape the feeling that we are worthless.

But the feeling of worthlessness comes from the fact that we have sometimes defined evil as that which is basic to man's nature. In an attempt to be gods instead of what we are, we have had to repress those passions which we thought unworthy of gods. Our attempts are not completely successful, however, and we keep hearing rumblings from beneath the surface which inform us that those passions still exist. We feel disparaged by this disclosure and attempt to overcome its influence by bolstering our damaged egos. We look for a way to reduce the constant sense of sinfulness (worthlessness) by some extrinsic means. The result is often an attempt to buoy up our self-images through identification with something or someone whom we perceive as virtuous.

THE VILLAIN—EVIL PERSONIFIED

As we have seen, ancient peoples personified evil in the form of unfriendly spirits who could bring harm down upon man when the situation warranted it. Later civilizations gave this power to kings, then to priests, and finally to the devil. Each of these kinds of evildoer was useful for its age. For it situated the source of evil in one place where people could locate it easily. This gave them an object on which to fix blame or a target against which to take counteraction.

But the idea of devils and spirits does not sit well with many people in the twentieth century, and therefore other kinds of evildoers have had to be developed. The modern version of Lucifer, Satan, and all the evil spirits is the villain. The primitive version of this figure, like his counterpart, the hero, is pure. That is, he is *all* bad, with no possibility of any redeeming features. He began in the myths as an evil king or as a dragon, but he has emerged in modern times as a man (or sometimes a woman) whose path crosses that of the hero.

The villain wants most of the things that the hero wants, but he is willing to ignore the local ground rules. He has the advantage of circumventing the time-consuming procedures for getting the things he wants. He simply steals, rapes, plunders, usurps, defrauds, pilfers, kidnaps, or kills. He is a heretic. He does not respect the standards of his culture. The conventions of a society, so dear to the heart of the hero, are for the villain a lot of nonsense made for suckers. The villain can be compared to the older idea of the anti-Christ. His life is not only dedicated to evil, but he appears to *love* evil. He has no conscience. He is bad. He knows it and he revels in it. He is what psychologists call the psychopathic personality.

Like the hero, he is strong, healthy, young (or when old, very powerful in other than physical ways), courageous, and violent. He is also as anti-intellectual as the hero and as brutal in his treatment of others. But he lacks two of the heroic qualities. He is *not* infallible, or, if he is, it is only until he meets the hero. And he is usually not handsome. He may also be dirty and sweaty, qualities that the hero (and heroine) find extremely repulsive. These qualities lead to his downfall.

The villain loses out for two reasons. In the first place, he is not accepted by the heroine. She sees through him and cannot love so evil a man. She is too virtuous to be taken in by anyone so obviously bad. Moreover, she is forsworn. She loves the hero, and this precludes the possibility of her having any romantic attachment to any other man. So the villain is deprived of this particular prize. This does not deter him. He simply tries to force himself on her. For to him it makes little difference what anyone else wants. It's what he wants that counts. The second reason for his failure is his fallibility. He has some vulnerability. It may be his own evilness that does him in, as when the mad scientist dies by his own instrument. Or it might simply be the fact that he is not quite as fast on the draw as his main adversary. The main point is that final victory belongs to the hero, and so the villain must lose.

The villain also serves the purpose of being the recipient of punishment in the name of justice. Since one of the consequences of evil in the tradition of Western man is retribution, the villain has been selected for that role. Generally he is used for the vicarious expression of hostility which is aroused in the audience by his misdeeds. Early in the story he does outlandishly cruel things which arouse the anger of the hero. And this anger is allowed to build for quite a while until it has reached a very high pitch. The punishment, when it comes, is swift and complete, and, in line with the Augustinean decree, it exactly balances the transgression. (Actually it sometimes clearly exceeds the nature of the offense, but at such a time, we are in no mood to quibble.) The villain gets what he deserves and we get what we've been after since the beginning. We get our revenge.

It is extremely important to understand the nature of the villain and his functions in order to appreciate the manner in which he serves society. All human desires, needs, motives, drives, or wishes have as their object immediate gratification. They are with varying degrees of urgency, desirous of achieving consumation. Needs and desires seek such ends by definition. This means that inside every organism there is a desire for complete and immediate gratification of its various needs.

Ordinarily this does not present a problem. Every organism recognizes these needs and acts to satisfy them—that is, almost every organism. Sometimes some of these needs or desires are considered bad, inappropriate, shameful, unladylike, sinful, wicked, unmanly, dirty, immoral. (Only we humans, of all the organisms, attach positive or negative values to our motives.) In such a situation, what are we to do? We have desires that require immediate gratification and our society says that we must either postpone or even forego these satisfactions completely. Moreover, if these desires are so bad, we must try to hide their existence from ourselves.

The villain, therefore, becomes the personification of the desire for immediate gratification. In this, he is very much like the gangster hero described in Chapter 1. He represents the desire and the consummation of the many drives that we do not like to acknowledge. The villain, as already noted, takes the things he wants without waiting, without going through the many intermediate steps which ordinarily legitimize many of these gratifications. If he needs money, he does not look for a job and wait till payday. He simply goes to the bank and makes a withdrawal. (He never, of course, bothers to make deposits.) He gets the money immediately. And he gets a lot of it. If he wants sex, he rapes the prettiest or sexiest girl in town. If he is angry, he hits or kills the person he hates. If he is thirsty, he gets whiskey—if bored, he starts a fight or a game for high stakes. The villain is only interested in one thing—gratification. And he means to get it at once. This, of course, is the very nature of *need* or *desire*. A need is a vector directed toward the object that will gratify it. It is unaware of any other contingency.

We can identify vicariously with the villain because he does what we would like to do. In Freudian terms, he is the *id*, the part of the psyche that seeks pleasure. He is the narcissistic infant who knows only his own desires and is completely unconcerned with the needs or feelings of others. But even while we are enjoying his exploits, we are torn with feelings of guilt. We know that he (we) cannot get away with it. We know that he (we) must be punished. The guilt we feel because of our vicarious identification with the villain, because of the enjoyment we feel at his exploits, makes it necessary that he (we) pay for it. The villain's punishment serves the purpose of allowing us to atone for having desires that we believe we should not have. When we destroy the villain, we believe that we have rid ourselves of the evil desires. But our salvation is only temporary, for those kinds of desires return again and again.

THE CRIMINAL AS VILLAIN

The villain is a fictional character and although we may hiss him heartily when he appears, we realize that his crimes and our revenge are imaginary. But we have in society a group of people who are real and whom we can punish for real transgressions—the criminals.

For most of the people in society, the criminal plays the role of villain. He breaks the rules, he scoffs at virtue, he ridicules tradition, and for these transgressions he pays a proper penalty. But in some respects, the criminal is as much a *requirement* of the society as is the doctor, teacher, policeman, or judge.

Criminality is a defined state. A person is a criminal if he has been convicted of breaking a law in a given society. If he is not caught, or if he is not convicted, he is not a criminal. This is a confusing state of affairs because most people believe that criminal behavior is any kind of "wrong-doing." If that were true, the statistics which inform us of the crime rate would be even more frightening than they now are.

Ashley Montagu (1968) has made the observation that crime is an invention of society. Society, he claims, causes its criminal and delinquent groups to commit what it calls crimes and then punishes them for what they have done. Society may have several reasons for such behavior, but one important reason is its collective guilt.

If people believe that men are innately bad, they will tend to feel guilty themselves. But guilt is a very uncomfortable emotion and a person will go to great lengths to reduce it. If we can find a group of "bad" people who can be punished for all kinds of transgressions, we can avoid the feeling ourselves.

Our Puritan heritage tells us that where there is sin, there must be punishment. And that is fine with us. We do not mind as long as the punishment is administered to others. So we have created a criminal class to be the recipient of the punishment that we think *we* deserve. We project our own guilt upon the people who commit crimes and feel self-righteous in so doing. They are evil and they must suffer.

The police provide a buffer between society and the "undesirable" people who are created by that society.

The manner in which crime is defined establishes the behavior that is considered illegal. If stealing is a crime, one would expect all kinds of stealing to be illegal. However, there are a great many practices that might qualify as stealing which are nevertheless condoned or at least ignored. If a man steals a woman's purse containing a few dollars, he may be convicted of a felony. But if a corporation takes millions from its customers through making false claims for its product, it may only receive a reprimand. If a man kills another with a gun, he may be executed. But if a drug firm knowingly markets a product that has been shown to be fatal to certain kinds of patients and if in fact a goodly number of such people die, those responsible may not even spend a day in court.

Sutherland (1949), in his book on white collar crime, points out that there is an enormous amount of law breaking among large corporations, a good deal of which goes completely undetected. The situation is so bad that one corporation executive was appalled when brought up on charges. He was only doing what was common practice throughout his industry and was at a loss to understand why *he* was being singled out. Not only are such procedures widespread, but most of the firms that commit crimes are recidivists (that is, repeaters). Moreover, the penalties for such crimes are usually fines or merely reprimands. One need only recall the action in 1969 and 1970 against the Big Three automobile makers for conspiring to ignore the order to develop a smog-reducing device. Charges were dropped on the promise that this would not occur again.

Sutherland also claims that businessmen who are convicted of white collar crimes do not usually lose status and in fact may be admired for it. Corporation heads who use illegal maneuvers to enhance their financial standing are often considered "shrewd operators" by their colleagues. It is only when they violate the business code that they might lose some prestige. But since the business code does not always coincide with the legal code, this seldom happens. Sutherland also points out that when these people do commit crimes, they are not treated like criminals by the police and other officials, so there is no stigma attached to their deeds.

It is clear that society desires punishment for some of its lawbreakers and not for others. And it also desires its criminals to fit a certain image. The purse snatcher and the passion murderer nicely fit the picture of the wrongdoer. But the corporation executive does not. He comes from the "straight" segment of society. And we do not feel that he should suffer, although his transgression in many cases is much greater than that of the petty criminal.

Crime in the United States is an extremely serious problem. The rate exceeds those of all the other industrial nations, and it has been rising at an appalling rate. Such a predicament would lead one to think that there are certain elements in American life that are somehow conducive to criminal behavior. Ashley Montagu is convinced that there are. "Crime and criminals are the inventions and the products of society, and criminals are the instruments and the victims of that invention. It is the logic of the criminal and delinquent society to blame its crimes and delinquencies upon the criminals and delinquents and then to punish them for the offenses it has, in most cases, caused them to commit" (Montagu, 1968).

Montagu is not alone in his feelings that the society creates the criminal. Many other social critics have echoed these sentiments. A very interesting observation in this regard is made by Menninger (1968). The acts of some criminals, he argues, are simply attempts to be somebody or to amount to something. On the one hand, society places a tremendous emphasis upon "being someone important"; while on the other, it treats people like numbers or, even worse, like cattle. The feeling of being a "nobody" can be very real and very painful in such a situation, particularly for a person who is only marginally adjusted. Sometimes such a person may commit a spectacular crime and even allow himself to be apprehended to avoid remaining an anonymous nobody all his life.

Once again we can see that the need for a positive self-image does not necessarily mean a commonly accepted version of that image. A person is much more interested in being taken seriously, in being perceived as important, or in existential terms in simply being, than in being virtuous according to a generally approved set of standards. The person who commits an act that brings him to the attention of the world is sometimes trying to prove to himself that he does in fact exist.

The emphasis on success in our society makes its pursuit an essential part of the motivation of most of its citizens. Since this success is measured almost exclusively in material terms, it is a very visible form of insignia. Thus the acquisition of material things is for most Americans a highly desirable goal. But the structure of the economic system is such that there are always large groups of people who for one reason or another are deprived of the opportunity to partake of the affluence that appears to be so widespread. It is inevitable that under such conditions, some of those people will resort to extralegal means in order to achieve their ends. This will occur with more frequency where they can clearly see others who have easy access to the things they themselves are unable to obtain.

For some of these people crime is the only way out of a very oppressive situation. They realize that there is no hope of ever getting out of the vicious circle of poverty without taking what appear to them to be the only reasonable steps. Moreover, they have often seen their relatives and friends spend a lifetime at some backbreaking work with no rewards. Such a fate does not appeal to them.

At the same time, they see people who seem to have an easy time of it, getting most of the things that they want and enjoying the things they do. And it seems unfair. They begin to feel that a person has to be a sucker to work like a slave and barely get by when there is so much "easy" money around. Moreover, there is a certain amount of status and glamour to being a successful "operator," which is more than one can say about working in a mine or building a road.

Thus the disinherited individuals in American society find themselves on the one hand with the delights of affluence dangled before their eyes, and on the other with no legitimate opportunity to obtain them. At the same time, they see the tremendous emphasis placed on the acquisition of material things and come to feel that getting these things is worth the risk of going to jail because the life they now lead is not much better than jail anyway. In some cases it is even worse. If we give a man a choice between two such options, should we be surprised that he chooses the one that gives him some hope of happiness, no matter how fleeting?

It is probably no accident that such a situation exists in almost all Western countries, especially in the United States. For in a society in which guilt is so prevalent, there is a need for a class on which to vent the product of that guilt. The criminal class serves the purpose of being the recipient of the collective need for punishment which we turn outward. It is the scapegoat upon whom we seek our revenge for the misdeeds that we would like to have committed but for which we lacked the courage. Now we have someone whom we can punish, incarcerate, even kill with the sanction of law.

This, of course, is one of the most important aspects of the villain's role. He is the one against whom any kind of violent act is justified. He is the enemy we must have in order to express our hatred, release our pent-up hostility. But our feelings for him are contradictory. We do not completely despise him. We both hate and envy him. He gets the things he wants so easily that we identify with him at one moment and want to punish him the next. We feel guilty for identifying with him, but we project the guilt toward him. Thus we relieve *our* guilt by punishing him. Our feelings toward him seem to change from one time to another. We perceive him as a free spirit whom we admire and as an enemy against whom we must retaliate.

Our entire attitude toward crime and criminals is colored by this contradiction. We are repelled by it. We fear it. We vote for people who say they will control it. But we are fascinated by it and secretly (sometimes unconsciously but at other times quite openly) wish we had the guts to try it. Sometimes, in fact, we do try it. It isn't anything very big, of course.

The criminal serves the purpose of assuaging collective guilt by being punished for doing things that many of us would like to do.

But we get a little kick out of it, even if it is only cheating a little on an expense account.

The mass media know of our obsession with crime. They understand that we are attracted to the most sordid, the most barbaric, the bloodiest acts of men, and they give us surfeit of it. They keep us informed of the cruelties and atrocities of our times as religiously as they tell us of the weather. They describe the intimate details of every "sensational" trial with great relish. And we read with no less enthusiasm.

Fiction writers, too, know of our love of the morbid and they fill thousands of volumes and articles yearly describing the exploits of imaginary murderers, rapists, thugs, and cutthroats. And we buy these books and run to these films and then we shout for "law and order."

It makes no sense to say that everyone is against crime or against war. It is simply not so. Unless we understand that on some level, the most respectable citizen has larceny and murder on his mind, we will get nowhere. It is because we deny this fact that we seek enemies outside ourselves. If we cannot accept the fact that some of the things we label "evil" exist in ourselves, we will tend to see them everywhere else. We will see them in the villains of the world. They will appear in criminals, in foreigners, in people of different races, in people of different religions, in people with different ideologies. And when we see them, we will have to destroy them. For they are the things we have learned to dislike about *ourselves*. And we want to purge ourselves of them.

We will give our actions many names. We will allude to "justice," to "the defense of freedom," to "holy war." We will invoke various documents, scriptures, judgments from high tribunals. We will feel noble, generous, even humanistic as we go about our vindictive way, saving the world from all those evils *out there*, while never acknowledging the inhumanity within.

EVIL AS OTHER

It is axiomatic that each person sees himself, at least on a conscious level, as a hero of sorts. "I am the good guy. The bad guys are out there." The delinquent is not too different from the rest of us. He behaves the way he does because he has a different set of values, or different heroic models than we have. The delinquent often justifies his behavior as "the only smart way to go." Frustrated and denied opportunities at every turn, he soon sees the futility (for him) of ever "making it" in the approved ways. He decides, or it is decided for him, that the only road open is to seek economic or social advancement in deviant ways (Cloward and Ohlin, 1960). But once committed to this way of life, the delinquent perceives it as the "good" way. The "straight" world is seen as stupid, naive, a place for weaklings, losers, jerks. His models become criminals who "have made it." His ethic becomes the ethic of the criminal subculture.

To be worthwhile in this particular group, one must gain the respect of his peers. The delinquent impresses his peers by his toughness. He tries to be as callous and brutal as possible. The more ruthless he is in his dealing with other people, the more he is admired. And he is usually proud to display his cruelty whenever the opportunity presents itself. He sees love or compassion as "weakness" and disdains such feelings. Moreover, he is likely to hate anyone who shows such emotions. These youngsters place daring and bravery high on the list of virtuous qualities. And the one who will take the greatest risks and expose himself to the greatest dangers, especially in defiance of the law or other agency of conventional society, is usually the one most highly regarded.

It is difficult for most people to realize that those they perceive as the "enemy" feel self-righteous about their own motives. Some Americans were appalled when in World War II they heard German soldiers defending their country's actions with the use of such terms as "freedom," "liberty," "humanity," and the like. It was even more shocking to hear them invoking God's name, implying that He was on *their* side. After all, *we* knew that He was on *our* side.

Such naiveté about others often makes us misunderstand those we oppose. For example, we tend to attribute very dark motives to any person or group who has a value system different from our own. We believe that these people "know" that our system is the "true" one, but since they are "bad" people, they desire to destroy it. Such an attitude explains why we sometimes see dark conspiracies here and there which are bent on our destruction. Some people, therefore, have claimed that the expressed aim of the Communists is to "corrupt the youth" (Moyers, 1970).[1] What these people do not understand is that Communists or anyone else do not see their cause as *corruption* but as *liberation*. They would no more use such a word to describe their procedures than we would if we tried to convert a Communist to *our* cause. In fact, they see such activities on our part as attempts to "corrupt" the Communist mind with "evil capitalist falsehoods."

PARANOID PERCEPTION OF THE ENEMY

Failure to understand this fact leads many people to take a "we" versus "they" attitude about the world. It also tends to encourage various kinds of simple solutions to problems that are really much more complex than they seem. But the most crucial effect that such a view has upon a person or a society is that it leads to a paranoid vision of the world which is both disabling and dangerous.

The tendency to perceive one's own desires or aims in others is called *projection*. And projection is the most prominent symptom of paranoia.[2] The paranoid person comes to suspect almost everyone. He perceives the world as intensely hostile and believes that people are conspiring to do terrible things to him. He lives in a fantasy world in which he misconstrues many daily events as threatening and dangerous. He may "hear" voices talking about him or even talking *to* him advising him as to what action he must take to avoid being overwhelmed by his enemies. If he is religious,

---

[1]In an article in *Harper's* magazine, Bill Moyers cites a pamphlet that was being circulated in 1970 around Richmond, Indiana, by an American Legion Post Commander. It purported to give the "Communist Rules for Revolution," which were supposed to have been created in Dusseldorf, Germany, in 1910. Among the "rules" were the following: "Corrupt the young; get them away from religion. Get them interested in sex. Make them superficial; destroy their ruggedness." The pamphlet had been exposed as a hoax by the columnist James J. Kilpatrick, but that did not bother those who circulated it. For them it was a perfect example of the enemy's evil intent.

[2]Both projection and paranoia will be discussed more fully in Chapter Ten.

he may believe that he has a holy mission to "expose" and destroy his enemies and save mankind from their wickedness.

Paranoia is a psychosis. It is an extreme form of psychological disability. But it also occurs at times in milder forms in everyone. We all occasionally have feelings that "the world is against us" or that "people have it in for us." Such feelings are normal as a rule. But sometimes even these feelings become exaggerated enough to distort our perception of the world. In such cases they become dangerous to us and also to those whom we perceive as our enemies.

Some Americans have always viewed the world in black and white categories. These people believe that there are dark and sinister forces abroad in the world which are bent on our destruction. These forces not only exist within some foreign ideology outside our country, but they exist within our own citizenry and even in high government positions. Hofstadter (1965) cites these kinds of beliefs in his analysis of paranoid patterns in American politics. He presents the views of ultrarightists who perceive the entire fabric of American life to be infiltrated by Communist agents bent on selling capitalism down the river.

These people believe that all the institutions of society have been taken over by "subversive elements" and that at least in one case, a President of the United States (President Eisenhower) was a "dedicated, conscious agent of the Communist conspiracy" (Welch, 1963). This conspiracy is so vast, according to these thinkers, that so conservative a public figure as John Foster Dulles was branded a Communist agent by them.

The late Senator Joseph McCarthy also made such accusations against the institutions of the United States. He saw the twenty years of Democrat-controlled politics as "treason." Nor did he feel that anything had changed under the Republican administration of Eisenhower, for he believed that the "conspiracy" existed "on a scale so immense as to dwarf any previous such venture in the history of man" (McCarthy, 1951). He accused General George C. Marshall of completely betraying the interests of the United States to the Soviet Union in an attempt to bring about the moral, economic, and military ruin of his own country.

Such beliefs are clearly paranoid. They are badly distorted perceptions of the world based partly on fear and partly on projection. They seek to place the "blame" for the evil in the world on outside agents. The way in which the "enemy" is perceived is closely allied to the primitive version of the villain.

The paranoic believes that he himself is one of the few who have been able to see through the conspiratorial veil of secrecy. And it is now his task to reveal what he has learned to the world. The opponent is believed to be extremely clever and extremely powerful (as are all villains). He has developed a tremendous organization that affects every facet of contemporary life. His pernicious schemes reach into the very cradles of the community (for example, one claim states that fluoridation rots out the brain to make it accept the evil ideology). It is in control or gaining control of every major agency of business and government. In the meantime, every event in foreign affairs is viewed through these distorting lenses and interpreted as a vast international network of intrigue and espionage.

The paranoid person sees his fight as the eternal struggle between absolute good and absolute evil. The "enemy," therefore, is a completely malevolent agency whose very presence on the planet is a threat to the existence of "decent" people. He must be totally annihilated. This is seen as a defensive maneuver since the enemy is in the process of destroying *us*. He is believed at this moment to be poised to strike. And it is only a matter of time until his position is completely consolidated. (Sometimes the actual date has been prophesied. Welch predicted that Russia would attack in October 1952.)

The urgency of the situation is always apparent in the thinking of such people. They live in a constant crisis situation in which time is of the essence. The implication is that we must act in order to save ourselves and we must act *now*. (Peremptory strikes against the nuclear capabilities of the Soviet Union and China were common "defensive measures" that were advocated.)

The paranoid person makes impossible demands upon himself or his society. The measures he advocates are so bizarre that they are never really possible. This leads to a great deal of frustration and to the continuous escalation of the "danger" as he perceives it. While the "good guys" are procrastinating, the conspirators are taking advantage of the confusion and disorganization to make greater strides in their insidious plans.

Such escalations of the projected ideation leads to an even more fantastic view of the enemy and his influence: ". . . he is a perfect model of malice, a kind of amoral superman; sinister, ubiquitous, powerful, cruel, sensual, luxury-loving . . . he is a free, active, demonic agent" (Hofstadter, 1965, pp. 31–32). Note in this quote the clear descriptive similarity to the character of the villain in primitive literature. This is one of the major symptoms of paranoia. The world has been broken into two completely separable parts, each clearly differentiated from one another. One part is all evil, completely degenerate, beyond redemption. The other is all good, totally virtuous, absolutely irreproachable. The former is the enemy and the latter, of course, is ourselves.

ACKNOWLEDGING OUR NATURE

The paranoid view of the world is but a highly exaggerated mode of perception which to a lesser extent we all share. (It is not, of course, restricted to right-wing philosophies. It exists in all ideological camps.) The tendency to externalize that which we do not wish to acknowledge in ourselves is constantly present. For as long as we label some qualities of human nature unacceptable, we will project those qualities onto others.

Man cannot escape his nature. But he need not feel disparaged by it. Man is sometimes violent, selfish, and brutal. But he is also often kind, generous, and self-sacrificing. He cannot know himself unless he accepts *both* kinds of qualities as parts of his nature. *And he cannot clearly perceive the world if he does not.* It is not really necessary for man to think of himself as evil. But it is necessary for him to think of himself as *human.* And to be human is to be, not evil, but imperfect.

Perhaps this is what the religious leaders of all time have been saying. Jesus said, "Know thyself." Did he not mean that we must know our nature? Others have warned us that we must accept those qualities in our nature that we would prefer to deny. Did they not mean that to deny one part of our being was to do violence to the rest of it? If to confess (that is, admit) our sins means to realize our shortcomings, does this not mean that man cannot function through self-delusion?

The beginning of maturity and health is therefore the acknowledgment of our humanity with all that this implies. But if this is a beginning, it is not the totality. For there are many other pitfalls along the way. We shall explore some of them in the following chapters.

the
success
syndrome

Ho Tai, Chinese god of wealth.

chapter 5
money

If we were to ask a person in a civilized country what he means when he uses the term "money," we would usually get some such answer as: "Money is a medium of exchange" or "Money is what we use to get the things we need" or even "Money is a measure of value and a means by which we can give a guaranteed promise of payment."

Although all these are reasonable definitions, psychologists would not generally consider them adequate. For money, more than merely being a token of exchange for goods and services is an enormously important psychological commodity whose implications reach down into the deepest level of man's psychological life. We are not therefore interested in what money *is* but in what it *means* to the human beings who use it, seek it, work for it, save it, spend it, even steal and kill for it.

Nevertheless, to understand money psychologically it is necessary to have some conception of its role in the life of mankind. For money, like everything in man's psychological environment, has a developmental record of its own. And the manner in which we view it at any moment depends to some extent upon what it has meant to people in the past. We do not come upon our values full blown in one generation. They are the products of a long evolution in much the same way that we ourselves are. It will therefore be valuable to look briefly at the development of the monetary concept.

MONEY: SUBSTANCE OR SYMBOL

There have been some stable and sophisticated civilizations that never used a monetary medium of exchange. Large parts of Europe during the Middle Ages and China, for much of her history, were without money. In medieval times, the manors did not use a medium of exchange, nor did the monasteries or feudal estates (Angell, 1929). In Egypt there was no coin of the realm for 3,000 years. Although ingots of precious metals are believed to have been exchanged occasionally among kings and nobles, such transactions did not occur among the general populace so that money was unknown to the common man.

It is worthwhile noting that although money is an important commodity to a civilized nation, it is not a *necessary* one. Economists have generally referred to the moneyless societies of the past as "natural" economies, in contrast to "money" economies. They were, in fact, really run more like family units than like nations. Some did not even have a barter system in the usual sense of that term. Goods were distributed by paternal figures to those who were not in possession of them, for one of the functions of a father is to keep his "offspring" alive. Besides, in feudal times, the offspring were serfs who did the work that the lord of the manor would have had to do if they suddenly disappeared.

In the late 1920s in France there was a breakdown in the nation's currency and people in the cities were dying of starvation while those on the farms were well fed and had surpluses that they fed to their livestock. In this situation, as in Germany during the collapse of the mark after World War I, having money was useless. What was important was to be in a position to obtain the necessities of life, and this was not possible for everyone in such chaotic times.

Some modern writers have expressed these ideas in more radical terms (Watts, 1971; Theobald, 1963). They believe that modern man has made a colossal mistake in his understanding of economic processes because of traditional attitudes toward money. These writers believe that modern economists make a fatal psychological error with regard to the nature of money. *Money*, they say, is not *wealth*. Money is only a *symbol* of wealth. Precious metals are not intrinsically precious. They are worth *nothing* by themselves.

McLuhan (1964) also makes this point when he refers to a passage in Robinson Crusoe in which the shipwrecked sailor finds a cache of coins on the ship. Crusoe laughs at the thought of their intrinsic worthlessness in a place where a man needs such things as knives, clothes, and food staples. This is *real wealth* and money is like a tape measure that simply informs us of how much wealth (raw materials, labor, machinery, fertile land) we have.

Watts believes that we often confuse symbols with the things for which they stand. And this confusion exists in the realm of money (symbol) and wealth (useful commodities, labor, and so on). Like the primitive, we have imbued certain metals with magic. But gold or silver or paper currency are like inches, feet, gallons, pounds. They are ways to keep score. They only tell us how much of something we have but they are *not* to be confused with the real commodity itself.

Watts explains the problem this way:

> Remember the Great Depression of the Thirties? One day there was a flourishing consumer economy, with everyone on the up-and-up; and next, unemployment, poverty, and bread lines. What happened? The physical resources of the country—the brain, brawn, and raw materials— were in no way depleted, but there was a sudden absence of money, a so-called financial slump. Complex reasons for this kind of disaster can be elaborated at length by experts on banking and high finance who cannot see the forest for the trees. But it was just as if someone had come to work on building a house and, on the morning of the Depression, the boss had said, "Sorry, baby, but we can't build today. No inches." "Whaddya mean, no inches? We got wood. We got metal. We even got tape measures." "Yeah, but you don't understand business. We been using too many inches and there's just no more to go around." (Watts, 1971, p. 6)

There was no diminution of the wealth of the nation, only the money. If this is an accurate assessment of the situation, and there seems no reason to doubt that it is, then, the consequences of such an insight are enormous. It means that there is no need for depressions or poverty or starvation or any of the other evils that man has the ability to eradicate. (For a better understanding of this problem, see Theobald, 1963.) All we need is the commitment to attack these problems. The resources already exist. The man and machine power already exist. In other words, the real wealth is already present on the planet just as it was during the Depression. But the psychological mistake of believing that we cannot *pay* for what we already have (potentially) prevents us from this undertaking.

Watts believes that with a more realistic understanding of money, what we now call the national "debt" would really be seen as a national "credit" and instead of being distressed by "deficit spending" we would realize that we are merely using this credit to develop the wealth that we already possess.

It is clear, therefore, that money is *not* in itself essential to life, although modern man has come to perceive it that way. In its essence money is a token which can be exchanged for the commodities that *are* essential to our survival. Experiments have shown that even animals can learn to work for tokens (for example, poker chips) which can thereafter be exchanged for more tangible rewards (Cowles, 1937). However, although such behavior is perfectly understandable in explaining how money acts as an incentive, it is of no help whatsoever in explaining why money becomes an end in itself for human beings. No self-respecting chimpanzee would keep working for tokens if he could not exchange them for something he needs or desires, but human beings will. The reason lies not in the economic meaning of money as a substitute for goods, property, and services, but in the numerous psychological meanings that are associated with it.

THE ANTHROPOLOGY OF MONEY

Although, as we have noted, there have been stable societies without money, there have also been societies as old as these which did utilize some form of money. In fact, there have been records of cultures that utilized money for a time, gave it up for centuries, only to go back to it in a new form at a later time. Economists have sometimes been puzzled by such facts. Why should money have been important to some people and not to others? Why did some countries give up the use of money after having developed and used it for centuries?

In part, the answer to these questions appears to be the fact that the vital needs of these societies were filled in ways that did not impart to money the kinds of psychological meanings that we have come to attribute to it. But there are other reasons why money was not essential to some groups. One of these has to do with individual freedom. If some of the social units were completely self-sufficient, and if they had all their basic needs supplied by an authority or religious group, then both barter and monetary exchange served no purpose. Moreover, the people in these groups were generally unwilling or unable to demand a greater degree of individual freedom for themselves. And it is this freedom which makes the need for a monetary system more urgent. For money enables a person to choose certain options that would otherwise not be available to him.

Money has become stable in the modern world, therefore, because it has enabled both nations and individuals to go their own way. The comforts of paternalism may be inviting, but they exist at the expense of freedom. The serfs were taken care of, but they could never leave or try to change the prevailing structure too drastically. Innovation was almost impossible without an exchange system. Technological advance would suffer seriously in such circumstances. How could one, for example, decide how many cows are worth a Saturn rocket? Problems such as these have been solved in modern life by finding a way to compare cows and rockets and anything else against a third object which, as we have seen, is a kind of measuring device. We call it "money," and it can tell us precisely how many cows are equivalent in value to a rocket, battleship, skyscraper, or even a week's work by an automobile mechanic. It is as this measuring instrument that money enables us to trade things with each other and keep some kind of score.

Early man went through a period of communal living in which exchange was not necessary. The period lasted for a long time and, during that interval, money had no function. If everyone in the tribe shared all possessions equally, they had no need to keep any accounts when they exchanged things. In fact, not to share the possessions one had was considered deviant. The beginning of the monetary idea, therefore, came about when one tribe wanted to make exchanges with another tribe. The early intercourse between primitive people concerned the exchange of gifts. But there was a tacit agreement in such trades that the exchanges be fair (that is, that each side be satisfied). Such trades were simply part of the tradition of hospitality among primitive peoples and appear to have occurred with great regularity in the development of groups in very different parts of the world.

From these beginnings the next logical step was the development of a crude system of barter. However, even when the exchange became more businesslike, the old traditions still had their effect and, after consummating a "deal," there were sometimes gifts or extras "thrown in." Such customs still exist today, as when one gets a "bonus" of some kind with a purchase or when a salesman takes a client to dinner.

One of the earliest forms of trade was carried out by neighboring tribes who avoided direct contact with one another during the transaction. For this reason, the practice has sometimes been called "the silent trade." In carrying out the exchange, members of one group would lay out the possessions which they desired to trade in some predetermined spot and then they would withdraw. The people with whom they wanted to do business would then appear and place their offerings alongside the objects they wished to "purchase." Then these people would leave, and the original group would reappear to assess the "offer." If they did not consider the "payment" sufficient, they would remove some of their goods and retire once more to wait for a "counteroffer." Such behavior continued until both groups felt that they had made as good a deal as possible and then the bargaining session was over (Morgan, 1965).

In many areas of the world, cattle began to be used as a crude measure of value. It was an awkward arrangement because a cow could not be divided. They could, of course, be used to barter only for large or important items like slaves. Our language still shows this old influence. The term *pecuniary* is derived from the Latin word *pecus*, which means cattle. The word that came to denote money in ancient Rome was *pecunia*. Although cattle were used as a standard of value for large things, small exchanges still had to be accomplished by the old system of barter.

Barter served its purpose well where the measuring of value was extremely crude or where the kinds of exchanges made were reasonably simple. But as time went on there was a need for substituting an item of value for a commodity. By this time, people had taken to wearing precious metals as ornamental decoration, and it was a natural step to begin to use these objects in the bartering process. This in turn made the trading of more complex materials possible. Thus the use of precious metals (coins) in the economic life of the society was established and one might say that money was born. Some people used other items of decoration beside precious metals. Such things as sea shells, whale and porpoise teeth, boar tusks have all been used at times. Most of these, however, had their origin as decorative ornaments before they became important as articles of exchange.

It is interesting to note that money grew out of objects that were designed to adorn the human body and to invest it with value. We can see, therefore, that even at its inception, money was more than just a tool of commerce. It was not simply a means by which to acquire other things. It had much more personal meaning. It had a "value" of its own.

It is enlightening for the psychologist to learn that money has always been perceived as if it had its own intrinsic value. For this fact demonstrates that the acquisition of money has not merely been a survival mechanism. If people were willing to give up their *useful* possessions to obtain these decorative objects, they must have felt that the possession of such objects had some effect of its own. Thus the measure of one's value by the amount of money he has must have originated in primitive times.

PSYCHOLOGY OF MONEY

money in the modern world

It is quite clear that money in the modern civilized world is something far removed from the exchanges of goods or ornaments among primitive people. Today the complexity of the world of finance is so great that there are very few (perhaps none) who can completely understand it. Renowned economists disagree on many things about money, from what it is to how to prevent it from losing its value. The whole theory of money, credit, economics, cost accounting, capital, monetary policies of nations, and so on, is extremely complicated and, in general, too much for the average layman to grasp. But it is not really necessary for him to have an understanding of such things. For he has a conception of money that is very different from its real nature. For him, money has some strange and important meanings.

the need for security

Every human being has a need to feel safe. To live in constant fear is intolerable. A person cannot exist in a continual state of stress (Selye, 1956). In order to feel safe in the modern world, it is necessary to have food and shelter and to know that these things will be available with some degree of certainty and regularity. For such things to be available, money is essential. There is, therefore, a certain amount of anxiety about money which is both normal and understandable. In such circumstances, money is viewed as a means to an end. When, however, the anxiety about money becomes great enough, money may become an end in itself. It is in such situations that money comes to take on strange, even magical meaning.

American society tends to put so much emphasis upon competition that people sometimes come to feel that they must acquire more money than their neighbors at almost any cost. Such a goal, although it is intended to alleviate anxiety, actually has the effect of increasing it. For there is no end to the amount of money that a person can aspire to accumulate. And every small gain seems insufficient, especially since there are always people who have more. The desire to surpass others is almost insatiable. Once caught in this vicious circle, a person is hard-pressed to escape. Competition for money is therefore often an over-exaggerated attempt to find security.

One very strong statement about competition has been voiced by Beecher and Beecher (1966). "Competition enslaves and degrades the mind. It is one of the most prevalent and certainly the most destructive of all the many forms of psychological dependence. Eventually, if not overcome, it produces a dull, imitative, insensitive, mediocre, burned out, stereotyped individual who is devoid of initiative, imagination, originality and spontaneity. He is humanly dead. Competition produces zombies! Nonentities!"

It is interesting to notice that Beecher is condemning competition on the very grounds upon which many people in our society praise it. Competition is believed by many to lead to initiative, to bring out originality, to be a proof of a person's independence. But these, according to Beecher, are errors of interpretation about the real meanings of such terms. His rebuttal is quite emphatic. "Initiative is the opposite of competition, and *one is the death of the other*. Initiative is a natural quality of a *free mind*. It is wholly spontaneous and intuitive in its response to confronting situations as they arise like the thrusts of a swordsman. The free mind allows one to be an *inner-directed* person whose responses in action are automatic" (Beecher and Beecher, 1966).

The implication here is that the person who competes allows someone else to set the limits, define the arena, and be the "pacemaker." By so doing he has locked himself into a situation that forces him to follow the lead of others. Even if he becomes the pacemaker himself, it still must be in the area that has been defined by others. He is thus an imitator rather than an innovator. In terms of our discussion, money becomes the way to keep score in the competitive marketplace. If one observes the kinds of products our society "creates" and the types of techniques utilized by advertisers to market them, Beecher's admonition about real originality being almost wholly absent must be taken seriously.

One of the most important sources of security, as we have noted, is related to self-esteem. Money is often viewed by people in our society as a substitute for self-esteem. They believe that they need nothing but wealth in order to change the feelings that they hold with regard to themselves. And so they set out to acquire this wealth. This quest leads to two possible consequences. Sometimes they fail and continue to strive all their lives. But there are other times when a few succeed. In both these situations, the results can be disastrous. For those who fail may continue to berate themselves for their shortcomings. But those who succeed often have a very

Money and jewelry as well as other "valuables" are sometimes used to try to increase self-esteem.

different experience. Having finally accomplished what they set out to do, they now find to their astonishment that they like themselves no better than they did before. This is a terribly disheartening experience. For the feeling that one can *buy* self-esteem is deeply embedded in our folklore. When the falsity of this myth becomes evident, it is often a very painful realization indeed.

the depression syndrome

People who lived through the Depression of the 1930s often have a different attitude toward money than those who did not. Moreover, it is sometimes difficult for young people to realize what that particular period in our country's history could do to the people who suffered through it. But often the effect was profound, and the reactions to it have sometimes been extreme.

It is difficult now for many people to understand the anguish and fear that gripped the people who found themselves without jobs, without money, and without food. Many had small children who needed to be fed. And many were being dispossessed, put out of their homes, because they had no money for rent. Those who were lucky enough to get on "relief" were often humiliated by the experience. It was a desperate time. People wandered the streets aimlessly. They stood in long lines in the bitter cold just to get small handouts of food and sometimes found that nothing was left when they got to the front of the line. When sickness struck there was no money for a doctor, and if one donated his services, there was no way of obtaining the medicine he prescribed. There was an overriding feeling of helplessness in the hearts of many and, with it, a sense of impending doom.

It is not surprising that some people after undergoing such an experience should come to value money in very special ways. One reaction, of course, was to try to save every possible penny and *to buy nothing that was not absolutely necessary for survival*. Even after the Depression had passed and these people were doing quite well, it was still impossible for them to spend money frivolously. There was always the underlying feeling that they did not know when disaster would strike again and to waste money would be like trading away their security. This behavior was not realistic because the amount they might be able to save was not large and it could not carry them very long in the event of another crash. But it had a psychological meaning. To buy things that were not needed made them feel guilty and they may have unconsciously felt that they would be punished for such behavior by being visited once again by hard times.

Such an attitude cannot be readily understood by the younger people growing up in an age of affluence. They take the availability of money for granted. To make money one's major concern seems senseless to them.

After all, there are other things in life. Money is only a way of getting the things we want and need but it should not hang a person up completely. That just spoils the enjoyment of the things we do buy.

There were other reactions to the Depression that were equally incomprehensible to the young. Some who experienced the humiliation of poverty vowed that they would never again allow themselves to be caught in such a situation. For them recovery meant a long and intense drive to move upward through the social structure, to climb in the strata of society in order to compensate for the terrible feelings of shame which they had endured for so long. Again, their children sometimes found it hard to understand this pattern. It seemed as if their parents had misplaced their values. They saw them sacrifice their lives to status. They watched them struggle, always under pressure. They saw them become ill. They saw them die, and all for the sake of appearances. It was difficult to make any sense out of it. It is still difficult for young people to understand these kinds of preoccupations by their parents. For them the Depression is only an old event in a history book. How can anyone be afraid of that? But to their mothers and fathers, it is still real. In that sense one might say that the Depression is one great contributor to the gap existing today between young and old.

MONEY AND HAPPINESS

Money has many meanings for those who use it. Some of these meanings are realistic; but some are imaginary. However, imaginary meanings often have a grain of truth in them. To most Americans money is the ticket to happiness. We tend to believe that if we have money, we can go anywhere and do anything we like. There is, of course, some truth to such a statement. Wealthy people do have more freedom to choose the things that they would like to do at any given time. But a person who is uncomfortable with himself does not escape this feeling by acquiring wealth. The fantasies we have about wealth do not realistically take into consideration the problems of living from moment to moment with our own inner experiences. These problems do not necessarily change or go away because we become rich.

We often have the idea that with enough money, we can buy the kinds of entertainments and diversions to allow us to ignore those feelings that bother us. But wealthy people know only too well that this is not the case. When the things that trouble us are within ourselves, they cannot be bought off, ignored, or run away from. They go with us everywhere and they insist upon being heard even when we try to ignore them. It is difficult for most Americans to understand that money will not make them happy by itself. Like new toys, the things that we can buy with money look extremely attractive, especially when we do not have them. But after using them for a while, they start to lose their attraction and, as with the toy, we turn to something different. A proof of this statement lies in the fact that most Americans now have objects of value that kings could not have imagined a few generations ago. But it is unlikely that there is any more happiness among people today than there was in earlier times.

Although money may not buy us happiness, we do not intend to give the impression that it does not make life better in many ways. Given a reasonable kind of emotional stability, a rich man is generally better off than a poor one. He may not, however, be as much better off as the poor man thinks. But more to the point, the idea that money will do away with our unhappiness is, like many other ideas about happiness, based on an illusion. Changing external circumstances very seldom leads to satisfactory results in that area. Only through changing that which resides *within* ourselves can we influence our enjoyment of life. (Happiness will be more fully discussed in Chapter 15.)

MONEY AND THE SELF-IMAGE

Our perceptions of ourselves depend upon a great many things. We are greatly influenced during the developmental years by the attitudes of those close to us. Attitudes toward money are often extremely influential in the way we come to view human beings. If our parents and the rest of society tend to evaluate people by their wealth, we may use such a measure to appraise our own value. The manner in which we present ourselves to the world will therefore be affected by such considerations. If we have money, we will expect (and probably receive) a certain amount of respect and subsurvience from others. If we do not, we may expect very different kinds of treatment.

Money, therefore, and the things that it can buy help to create the image that we present to the world. In order to present a very favorable image, the accumulation of a great deal of money may become our most pressing motive. Money in this sense does not necessarily mean actual cash. It refers to wealth and *possession*. The important thing is to have the things that money can buy, especially those things that can be seen by others. An image gets its value by its effect on others. If others are impressed by our possessions, we are, too.

In some cases money becomes an expanded portion of the self (Knight, 1968). The person literally comes to identify himself with his goods. Sometimes the money refers to parts of the body, like limbs, that could be lost. And if the money has come to be extremely important in the identification, the man and his fortune become one. Certain people are referred to as "the millionaire, Mr. So-and-So," as if the word "millionaire" were part of his name. Such an identification of the man with what he owns is precarious, for there is always the danger that one may lose his fortune, and this can be tantamount to losing himself. It is perhaps not an accident that many of the people who lost their fortunes as a result of the Depression considered suicide the only thing left to them.

Some psychoanalysts believe that the fear of bodily injury as symbolized by the loss of money may refer to the "castration anxiety" described by Freud. Fear of genital injury (castration) was believed by Freud to arise because of the repression of forbidden sexual fantasies in childhood. Such a fear, it is believed, might be expressed symbolically in later life by the loss of one's *most cherished possession*, his money. Although the castration complex was related in Freud's thinking to Oedipal striving, it need not always be. If a person harbors fears of genital injury for whatever reason, he may in adult life come to symbolize these feelings in terms of money. Loss of his fortune would then be a serious threat to his self-image.

MONEY AND POTENCY

There seems to be no question that money is important to the male in Western societies in ways that go beyond the mere ability to purchase particular commodities. The man presents his purchasing power to the female in an obvious attempt to impress her. He believes, often correctly, that many women will be more attracted to the man with a great deal of money. For him, therefore, money is equivalent to sexual attractiveness, and for the woman it is often a sign of masculinity.

Money becomes a symbol of potency when it has the same effect as potency on the male ego. If both are attractive to and arouse the female, they have a certain kind of identity. Moreover, since money helps in various ways to break down the barriers to sexual responsiveness in the female, it has a value similar to potency. The threat of the loss of one's money can therefore be feared in the same way as the loss of sexual power.

The woman is often excited by the man who has lots of money. To her he represents things and places which she can only barely imagine but which seem exotic and glamorous. Since sexual excitement frequently accompanies and is even aroused by general excitement, she often finds herself stimulated by the rich man in a way that seems different and important. She may also feel protected by the man with money, a feeling that may enable her to relax more in his company. Both relaxation and the feeling of safety are helpful in encouraging sexual responsiveness.

Related etymologically to potency is omnipotence. Infants often develop a feeling of omnipotence because it appears to them that they have control over the world. If they need something they cry and the need is filled. Such experience, coupled with the infant's impression of being one continuous with his environment, gives the child the sense of being and affecting everything at will. Some psychologists believe that this feeling may become fixated and continue in repressed form into adult life. The experience is so gratifying that the person may often try to do whatever is necessary to prolong it. Money may be a symbolic representation of omnipotence since it is expected to make all things possible. The accumulation of money would therefore be an attempt to continue into adulthood the infantile feeling of omnipotence.

Omnipotence is infinite power, and to many people money is symbolic of such power. In sociological terms, power is the capacity by which a person can make others do his bidding. All adults, at least occasionally, get the opportunity to use some power, and such an experience is intrinsically rewarding. The reward comes in two forms. It is experiential; that is, it is enjoyable as an experience. And it is ego-involving—satisfying to one's self-image. The general presumption is that the greater the power, the greater the rewards (this is not always true although most people who seek power believe it). The tendency, therefore, is to try to accumulate as much power (that is, money) as possible.

It is almost impossible to foresee the effect of power or money upon any particular person (Berle, 1967). Some people cannot tolerate a great deal of power, especially if it comes upon them suddenly. Sometimes they simply collapse under the responsibility. If a person's wealth brings with it a responsibility to which the holder is unaccustomed, he may be unable to enjoy either the money or the power.

MONEY AS A SYMBOL OF RELATEDNESS

Man is an affiliative animal. One of the most essential of his needs is to be included within the life space of other human beings. When this need is denied satisfaction, severe personality deterioration can result. Inclusion with others involves giving and receiving. And these interactions further involve such intangibles as feelings (love, for example) as well as more substantial things. Money has often been equated with love and belonging. It represents a way of giving or receiving that which is valued. In childhood the mother and father are the sources of love and affiliation. They are also the dispensers of money, and in this role they are sometimes perceived as bestowing their favors in monetary ways. In the life of a child, therefore, the feeling of belonging often is associated with money.

Sharing that which is valuable is, of course, one of the ways in which we verify our love for others. Concern for another means that we are willing to forego something for their benefit. This is a special relationship. For it involves a kind of commitment that is not present in more superficial affiliations. The giving of money can be the tangible expression of relatedness, and the withholding of money can be the withdrawal of love.

There is an unfortunate consequence of such perceptions, however. Some parents, believing that money is a *substitute* rather than a *symbol* of love, try to "buy their children off." They give them all the material things that they can afford in an attempt to prove their love, but they neglect to transmit the real warmth and feeling that must always be communicated as love. As a result, the children of such parents are deprived of the sense of belonging so necessary to their development. Money may signify love, but it can never take its place. If parents forget this, they will usually be reminded of it by their children.

Some people equate money with the idea of "mother." Since mother always provided comfort and security when these were needed in childhood, there is a great desire, especially in times of stress, to return to such a state. In adult life, money can serve the same purpose. It is comforting and reliable and we turn toward it in moments of crisis. Money thus assumes the role of the comforting parent, allowing us to enjoy once again the contentment of dependence.

The belonging needs are closely tied to the need for acceptance. This drive, when denied in childhood, often becomes an exaggerated desire to be admired, looked up to, envied, etc. (see Chapter 1). Such desires become irrational when the demands made by the individual upon himself become so exaggerated that they are insatiable (Ellis, 1962). When a person develops a powerful need to be liked and admired by everyone with whom he comes into contact, he creates for himself a very difficult task. For there are very few methods by which he may succeed. But since money is universally respected and admired in our society, he believes that the accumulation of money will help him to fulfill his wish.

In a superficial way, he may, if he succeeds in his quest, achieve the apparent result. If he becomes wealthy, he will find that people show him great consideration and courtesy and that they treat him *as if* they did, in fact, like and admire him. On a lower level of awareness, however, he realizes that it is the money and not himself toward which the respect is directed. If he loses his money, he is acutely aware that the respect and attention to which he has become accustomed will vanish completely. Such a realization is extremely disturbing and therefore he will tend to deny it. As a result, he will have to strive continually to increase his wealth to guard against the possibility of losing it (and his own worth), and his need will now have grown to a point where it can never be satisfied.

Some studies of the attitudes of prostitutes reveal that they often see the money that they receive from men as representing the warmth and love they may have been deprived of in childhood. That money is a token of love for these women can be seen from the fact that they willingly give all of it to their pimp–lover. Evidently a strong feeling of belonging is tied to this transaction, for without it the only close relationship in their lives would vanish.

In a study by Hollender (1961), psychiatric evidence tended to confirm a need among prostitutes for some kind of relatedness, on the one hand, combined with an emotional difficulty in maintaining such feeling, on the other. The girls generally came from homes where there was a great lack of warmth and feeling, so they had been unable to form deep, lasting attachments. However, there still lived within them a need for some kind of affiliation with others, no matter how superficial. And this need found some satisfaction in the contacts with their "clients." The "gift" of money and perhaps other kinds of things confirmed the relationship for them while eliminating the need for the kind of personal commitment which they were incapable of maintaining.

MONEY AND STATUS

We are all familiar with the ways in which money affects a person's standing in the hierarchy of his society. Although there are quite a few other kinds of status symbols, money is the most vital one. Moreover, it is frequently the source of most of the others. Status is almost entirely measured in economic terms in the United States. (This may not be true in other countries, where, for example, a scientist or fine craftsman would be ranked higher than, say, a wealthy athlete.) And as we have mentioned previously, the manner in which the money is obtained is almost irrelevant. Such an attitude encourages us to value certain kinds of behavior that may not always be admirable. Lord Keynes (1932) has expressed the hope that after the need for wealth has lost its social value, we will be able to change the standards

> by which we have exalted some of the most distasteful of human qualities into the position of the highest virtues. We shall be able to afford to dare to assess the money-motive at its true value. The love of money as a possession—as distinguished from the love of money as a means to the enjoyments and realities of life—will be recognized for what it is, a somewhat disgusting morbidity, one of those semi-criminal, semi-pathological propensities which one hands over with a shudder to the specialists in mental diseases.

These are harsh words, but Lord Keynes is condemning money when it is used as an ego-enhancer. Moreover, he is concerned with the fact that this money-as-possession worship distorts our values. We come to admire guile, trickery, selfishness, even thievery, since these are often successful methods in the pursuit of wealth.[1] Whether one agrees that such behavior denotes a form of mental illness depends to a great degree upon how he defines that term. But certainly any pattern of life that is dominated by a compulsive need to enhance the PR image at almost any cost must be viewed with some concern.

This kind of perception of money makes it an important part of the ego. It may in many instances be identical with it. The fact that money can be precisely measured in quantitative terms makes this particular kind of status symbol (ego evaluator) unique. For there is an implicit assumption (although an unconscious one) that we can accurately assess each person's value by using this "instrument." On an unconscious level, therefore, the desire to acquire twice as much or three times as much value as someone else appears as a real possibility.

MONEY AND IMMORTALITY

There are many ways in which money is used to ward off the reality of death or to try to buy time against the inevitable event. Aldous Huxley (1940), in his novel *After Many a Summer Dies the Swan*, describes a man's attempts to find a way to live forever. Anthony Beavis, a very wealthy but brutish man, gives a great deal of money to a doctor who is working on the prolongation of life. Beavis, fearing death, is willing to give his whole fortune in order to escape, only to find in the end that to go beyond one's life span is to move backward in evolution.

Buying one's way into eternity is, of course, not a new idea. It is an essential part of many of the world's organized religions, although it is not usually expressed in just those terms. The implication is that immortality is given to those who themselves give when the plate comes around. Since the religious institution usually promises immortality, the money is merely a down payment on the "future." At some Jewish funerals in Europe, coins are collected and the mourners are assured that "charity saves one from death."

Another way to avoid death is to build death-defying monuments. From the pyramids to the simplest gravestones, the idea of continuity and the attack on mortality are clear. Again, there is the simplistic notion that the larger the monument, the better chance one will have to buy his ticket to eternity. If monuments are somewhat out of date, the building of a business dynasty to leave to one's heirs is not. At least part of the drive for a large estate is that it gives a person a feeling that he does not die com-

---

[1]Watergate is a perfect illustration of where such values can lead.

pletely. Some part of him, preferably a part bearing his name, continues. The desire for a son to carry on the family name is also an attempt to continue one's influence beyond the grave. Such a desire is generally more important to the rich; the poor often feel that they have nothing to leave. The money mystique is so powerful that people actually behave as if immortality is related to each person's monetary value.

MONEY, GIFTS, AND ATONEMENT

There is no doubt that, in spite of the Biblical declarations against it, most people believe that a rich man can find his way into the kingdom of heaven. Moreover, they feel that his chances are generally better than those of a poor man. The person who goes to the house of worship to confess his sins almost always drops a few coins into the collection box. It is never stated in so many words, but the implication is clearly present that the more one donates to the church, the more likely he is to be forgiven for his sins. Admitting one's sins is not, in itself, atonement for them. To be forgiven, one must also *make restitution*. But if one has already seduced his neighbor's wife, there is no way that he can unseduce her. Restitution can only be made by giving up something of value. And the greater the sacrifice, the better the chance for redemption.

Gift giving also has a similar function. To give a gift to someone carries with it the implication that that person is beholden to the giver. Such a "contract" is not conscious. In fact, most people who give something to others would deny that they want or expect anything in return. But unconsciously they do. Sometimes all they require in return is to be remembered. In some European countries, giving things to children guarantees that one will live on in their memory, a kind of watered-down immortality. But large gifts to one's religious group have a more serious aim. Like money, they are unconscious attempts to buy one's way into God's good graces. Gifts to the poor, to charity, or even to one's own family and friends can serve the same purpose.

Gift giving is also a means of seeking the approval of others. Some people give gifts to a large number of people at Christmas or on their birthdays and become extremely anxious about choosing things that will be appreciated. Very often these people are concerned about being liked and have found that this is a dependable way to ensure acceptance by others. At times there may be some guilt involved in this situation, as in the case of a young woman who avoided her mother's invitations by continually making excuses. She never failed, however, to send something on every birthday, holiday, or anniversary. Her gifts were intended to make up for her obvious neglect.

Many gifts attempt to assuage feelings of guilt. The ethic that has

Expensive gifts can be used to impress people other than the recipient. This is especially true with such highly visible commodities as jewelry.

developed in Western societies demands that a person "pay his debts" in some material way. When one has committed some wrong, he believes that he can undo it (atone) by "paying" for it. (It is interesting to note that we use the word *pay* to denote restitution. We also talk about a person's *debt* to society.) It is easier to write a check for a charity than to do something about the conditions that make the charity necessary. If we do not do the latter, we will often feel guilty enough to do the former.

On the other hand, some people feel guilty when *receiving* money under certain circumstances. Many parents who lose their sons in war find it impossible to spend the insurance money they receive. They feel that to use it would give a kind of tacit approval of the money as payment for their son, as if spending the money carries with it the implication that they *approve* of the exchange. Such a reaction might result from the fact that these parents feel some guilt about letting their son down at an earlier time in his life, and the guilt might easily transfer to the money.

Some gifts have a dual purpose. Status-conscious husbands will often shower expensive gifts on their wives with the hope that the proper people will be impressed. Such gifts will generally be highly visible commodities such as jewelry, cars, mink coats, ornate furnishings for the home. In addition to being admired for his generosity, the husband also has the bonus of being perceived as rich or powerful. Although the gifts are intended to be expressions of the man's love for his wife, that is not their real purpose.

126

They are often intended to make points for the husband with his friends and associates.

MONEY AND LOVE

People overly concerned with status tend to view other people and things in terms of how they enhance or debase their image. A wife looked at in these terms becomes an important "possession." The right kind of wife, presented in the right way, can be very helpful to a young man on the way up. And there is, therefore, the tendency for such a man to "shop" for the particular qualities that are important to his career, or prestige position, rather than to find a person with whom he can have a genuine feeling of relatedness. In these circumstances the woman is just another "mass-produced" product that he can "buy" if he has the means. Unfortunately, the woman may see herself in the same way. Her "shopping" may take the form of an "auction." She considers all the offers available to her and finally accepts the best "deal."

Fromm (1956) has used the term "personality package" to describe the marketing aspect of "love" in American society. People, he says, present themselves to one another in the same way that consumable products are presented by Madison Avenue to the purchasing public. Each person then looks the market over in an attempt to obtain the best "bargain" available. The man with more money can generally get a better "package" (that is, a more beautiful, better educated, socially more acceptable wife) than the other fellow. This may then further enhance his movement upward through the social structure since it represents an increase in his "assets."

The woman, too, enters the marketplace with an eye to bettering herself in the social hierarchy. She "wraps" herself carefully in order to make the best possible impression. If she is, or can appear to be beautiful, cultured, sexually desirable, even rich, her chances are improved. She, too, can benefit from "snaring" a high-status husband. She therefore "sells" her charm and beauty for a particular "price." Although this form of prostitution is culturally acceptable, it is not terribly different from the forms that are not. The major difference is that this kind of prostitution usually involves only one man at a time and is therefore considered respectable.

There are, of course, other kinds of love that are occasionally bought and paid for. We have already mentioned the way in which some parents try to buy the love of their children by providing them with "things" rather than with the real expressions of love. And we have also noted the transaction between the prostitute and the man who pays for a brief moment or even a lifetime of "love" from her. But there are other attempts to purchase love for a price. Nations sometimes believe that they can buy the respect and loyalty of other nations by paying for it. Politicians try to buy the votes of citizens with promises of lower taxes. Some people even try to buy the love of animals by giving them expensive gifts.

Such strategies generally fail. Love does not come with a price tag. It does not come as a duty. It is a spontaneous emotional expression of one person for the well-being of the other, and it cannot be exchanged for money because there is no way to measure it in pints, bushels, liters, or truckloads.

A particular kind of distortion of this attitude is worth noting. Some people feel that they must have evidence of their "lovability" to show to others. They therefore make a great show of the gifts that they receive from various quarters. And they obtain the respect and admiration of their friends in this way. But there are times when those who should give something fail to do so. One family found an ingenious solution to this problem. Since their son never sent them anything on the various holidays and birthdays, the parents themselves purchased expensive gifts for all these occasions which they passed off to others as having come from their son. In this way they were able to "demonstrate" their son's devotion without losing face in the eyes of their friends. Moreover, they kept close account of the amount spent over the years and planned to deduct just this amount from the inheritance that they left him in their will. Thus they not only received the gifts they so badly wanted, but they got their son to pay for them as well.

MONEY AND PERCEPTION

Social psychologists have demonstrated that we tend to perceive objects of value or importance as larger than neutral objects of the same size. In an interesting experiment on the subject, (Ashley, Harper, and Runyon, 1951) people were hypnotized and they were alternately told that they were either rich or poor. When asked to judge the size of coins under these conditions, the subjects perceived all coins as larger when they were "poor." Another experiment using poker chips which could be exchanged for objects of differing value produced similar results. The subjects in this case perceived the "more valuable" chips as larger (Lambert, Solomon, and Watson, 1949).

These findings throw some light on the psychological meaning of money to the individual. The tendency to project importance on to different aspects of the environment is directly related to our needs. The way in which we perceive objects and events has more to do with our own biases and predispositions than with any set of "objective" facts. The importance of money or any similar commodity will therefore depend more upon the person viewing it than upon any estimate of its intrinsic value.

If we perceive things of higher "value" as larger, it is likely that we also perceive wealthy people as larger or more important. This may account in part for the deference with which rich and powerful people are treated. There is often a sense of awe bordering on fear in the way some people react to those of wealth and prestige, and it seems likely that they feel that "here is no ordinary person." We even use the word "giant" to describe some extremely successful people.

HEAVY SPENDERS

Many people spend money beyond their means or their needs. Such spending becomes pathological when it creates problems that are more serious than the ones it was intended to solve. With some people, spending may even become a compulsion. In any case excessive spending is a serious problem, just as is any other kind of excess.

The heavy spender seldom has a real need for the things he buys. Often he is trying to overcome a feeling of inadequacy, or he feels that he can improve his reputation if he is seen spending a great deal of money. Sometimes he spends because of an unconscious desire to punish himself by leaving himself in debt to others. Such a person often suffers from guilt which he has denied and which he can only assuage by playing a "victim." Other spenders may desire to make a great show of their generosity in order to demonstrate their "good nature" to someone who has rejected them. For some the spending is an overcompensation for something they missed in their childhood. It might have been money itself, but more often it was a lack of love, especially where money was used as a substitute. In such a case, the person may be trying to give himself love by showering himself with the things that money can buy.

Compulsive spending can be very like alcoholism for some. They literally go on binges until all their money runs out and then they borrow or save until they have enough for the next binge. Once they start they go until they have exhausted their money, and during the spree they enjoy themselves immensely. When it is over, they have some regrets and may even swear off, but very soon they accumulate enough money and they are unable to resist the temptation to do it again. And so the vicious circle is not easily broken.

Knight (1968) refers to narcissistic compulsive spenders of several kinds. One is the *showoff*, who "enjoys astonishing people by the lavishness or unusualness of his spending." The *competitive spender* is one who "retains his social prestige by outspending others in his social group." And there is the *affection buyer*, who "tries to buy love from almost any source to bolster his feelings of inferiority." These individuals use money as a major part of their PR image. They have found a way to make an impression, to be noticed, or to gain friends. They overlook the fact that this is a temporary kind of friendship that can disappear when the money does. They try desperately to prevent this from happening by spending at every possible opportunity.

THE MISER

The miser is the opposite of the heavy spender. He is unable to part with anything of value, particularly his money. He acts as if his safety, even his life, depends upon keeping his fortune safe from others. He will often appear very poor and, in fact, live in utter poverty, although he has a great deal of wealth salted away. It is unlikely that anyone will know of his money since he guards his secret very well. He is afraid to let others know of his holdings, as he believes they would attack or rob him to get it.

The miser is an obsessive-compulsive person. He is obsessed by the idea of putting money away and spends most of his waking moments thinking about how much he has and how he can get more. He finds it extremely difficult to spend any of it and, when he does, the thought that he may have wasted it haunts him for days. He deprives himself of all but the most essential things for survival, and even these are often in short supply. When other people take an interest in him, he will usually become very suspicious about their motives, believing that they are only interested in getting their hands on his money. (See paranoid reactions, Chapter 12.)

Such people are often emotional isolates. They live like hermits, partly because they are afraid to let others get near them but also perhaps because they have never been able to form a real relationship with another human being. In many cases the devotion to money serves as a substitute for the devotion to others which has been impossible in the miser's life. Money becomes the symbol of love, but it is a love that he can depend upon because if he is careful with it, it will not run out on him. As long as he has his money, he does not need anyone. He has company enough.

Psychoanalytic theory relates excessive saving to the period of toilet training. It is believed that during this period the child becomes concerned with "saving" of his feces. He resents his parents insistence on flushing away something that he considers very valuable. If the parents are extremely rigid in their treatment of the child, the experience is likely to be traumatic for him. And the result can be a fixation, an arrested development at the anal stage. Under these circumstances, the child is said to become overly concerned with holding on to whatever possessions he has. This tendency then generalizes in later life to money or other kinds of valuable objects, and the person becomes very stingy and cautious with his possessions.

Since this kind of attitude tends to alienate one from others, it is not long before this person finds himself alone—and the pattern of the miser has now fully emerged.

MONEY GAMES

Knight believes that narcissistic spenders are generally immature and have a great need for acceptance. "Their all-consuming goal in life is to enhance their appearance and thereby to attract the admiration of others" (Knight, 1968). There are, however, other kinds of spenders who are not as interested in getting others to like them as in beating them in a game of "bargaining." The idea of this game is, of course, to get the best of a deal in a transaction. And the player does everything he can to outdo his opponent. Of course, he sometimes falls prey to a smooth operator and loses. But such is the nature of games. The person interested in bargains, however, is not above deluding himself that he has really "scored" when, in fact, he has been taken. Once again we see that the simple mechanism of denial can be useful when self-delusion becomes necessary.

Other money games that are quite widespread have been described by Berne (1964). One game is called "Debtor." In this game, the young couple, usually just married, take on the obligations of family life in the United States. This means that they go into debt in such a way that it will generally take all their productive years to discharge the debt, if, in fact, they ever do. They borrow money for a house, car, various kinds of insurance, and for their children's education. The game ends if and when all the debts are paid off. By this time the people are generally too old to do anything besides retire to a community for senior citizens.

A related game cited by Berne is called "Try and Collect" (TAC). This game is also played by young married couples, but in this version the idea is to *not* pay for the things purchased. The couple proceeds to purchase a great number of goods and services on credit. They ignore the first few notices and the several final notices in the hope that the creditor will simply find it unprofitable to pursue the matter further. This does happen occasionally, and in such a case the buyers have "won" the game easily. Sometimes, however, the creditors are not so easily discouraged and a battle of sorts ensues. The buyers have the enjoyment of "the chase" while they have the use of the products. When the creditor cannot be dissuaded, the game gets nasty. To collect, the creditor is forced to turn to rather drastic measures. He may inform the buyer's employer or try to ruin his credit rating. Such measures, however, give the buyer a feeling of justification for what he has done. His thinking runs somewhat as follows: "Since all creditors are really greedy usurers, I am right in feeling that I might as well try to get all that I can out of them." Although in this situation he may have to pay, he still "wins" in the sense that he has "proved" his case that "all creditors are selfish, grasping, insensitive creeps."

gambling—the biggest money game of all

Every time a human being makes a conscious choice about anything, he is making a wager that *his* choice will have a favorable outcome for him. He may be wrong and in such a case, he "loses." And of course if he is right, he "wins." In most life situations there are a large number of variables working in any choice situation. We have some idea of the probabilities involved with some of these variables. But there are a great many others about which we have no knowledge. For example, when we choose a wife or husband, we have no way of knowing whether they will become ill, or meet with an accident, or fall in love with someone else, or die. We do know (or think we do) certain things about their personality which enables us to make predictions about our future lives together. However, even in this area, our knowledge is badly limited. The statistics on divorce make this observation quite obvious. It is quite clear, therefore, that every choice we make in life is a gamble *because we cannot know what the outcome will be in advance.*

Gambling for money is somewhat different. In most cases, the probabilities of a favorable outcome can be accurately determined and are known or can be learned by those playing. Whether the player goes to the trouble of learning what those probabilities are is another matter. For the actual odds have very little to do with the way those odds are perceived psychologically by those engaged in the game.

There are two ways in which we strive to deal with contingency in our lives. In the first method, we employ science as a tool. Through science we try to make sense out of the world and to gain some control over it. With this method we try to eliminate, as far as possible, the effects of chance so that we may predict events with a fair degree of accuracy. By the use of this control over the forces of nature, we can try to direct them for our own benefit. This is a comforting feeling. For the impression that one is impotent in the face of powerful forces gives rise to great anxiety.

In the second method, we are not interested in knowing the outcome of certain events in advance. We prefer to remain ignorant of the outcome because the excitement resides in the *expectancy* generated by the anticipated event. We are stimulated by *not knowing* the outcome. The kind of person interested in the second method would, for example, prefer not to know the ending of a murder mystery until he has read the entire thing and comes to that point himself. The advocate of the former might take a peek at the back of the book before beginning the story.

Most people have trouble understanding the thrill of gambling because they focus on the payoff (that is, whether one wins or loses). This, of course, is important, but it is not the essential part of the game. The gambler is looking for excitement, for thrills. And the thrill occurs at that moment *just before* the result becomes known, before the last card is turned over, or the dice have stopped rolling, or the final whistle blows. The excitement is really all over by the time the payoff comes. The heart is pounding and the head throbbing as the horses approach the wire, *regardless of whether one wins or loses*. And by the time one gets to the window to collect, he is relatively calm.

The excitement occurs because there are two possible outcomes, one favorable and one unfavorable. It is the anticipation of the favorable outcome that keeps the gambler going. But if the outcome were certain, that is, if the person knew that he would always win (or always lose), he would lose interest in the game. Work is a "game" in which the outcome is known. We do a certain amount of work and we get a certain payoff. It may even be a fairly good payoff. But it is not very exciting as a rule, partly because there is no doubt about the outcome. Work on an assembly line is rather routine, even though the payoff may be high. But a person will sit at a blackjack table all day, also a routine task, making far less for his efforts, and never feel bored for a moment.

The kind of excitement we have been describing exists for anyone who gambles. It is far more enjoyable to go to a football game than to read the final score in the newspaper. This is particularly true if we have a bet on the game. Part of the reason is, of course, because football itself is exciting. But there is another factor. If we were interested *only* in winning our bet, the game itself would be simply a long period of waiting. But winning is not all we want. The thing we really desire is *to be present while the outcome is still in doubt*. This is the existential moment of truth for the gambler.

Most of us can enjoy such excitement when it is available and simply forget about it when it is not. However, there are some people who cannot forget about it ever. Gambling for these people is an all-consuming need. They cannot live from day to day without betting some money (usually a substantial amount) on something. These kinds of people are called *compulsive gamblers*.

It has been estimated that there are some 6 million compulsive gamblers in the United States. Their losses run to 20 billion dollars a year. Although there has not been a great deal of research on this problem, some studies have attempted to establish the personality traits that seem to be predominant in people who gamble compulsively. A number of writers have held that this kind of person is immature, hostile, rebellious, somewhat unconventional, and magical in his thinking (Coleman, 1964; Goldenson, 1970). In this as in so many other psychological phenomena, however, the determinants of the behavior appear to be complex and numerous.

The compulsive gambler is often a person trying to prove his power and potency by playing with reckless abandon. He enjoys the admiration of the onlookers as he pushes big stakes onto the board again and again. Said one young man in his twenties, "I can't baby the dice. I've got to go all out. That's the only time I feel like somebody." This man lost his salary every week and had to borrow from his friends simply to survive. An interesting insight into the gambler's personality may be gained by another trait of this person. He was continually cited for speeding and was generally reckless in his driving. His explanation for this was similar to the one for his gambling. "I can't baby the road. I feel like a fool just plugging along." The desire to feel powerful and the need for excitement seem quite strong in this man's personality.

Although the compulsive gambler knows that the odds are against him, this knowledge exists only on a conscious level. Unconsciously he believes that he "is lucky." He feels that he is the "chosen one" and that very shortly Lady Luck will smile on him. He is a contradictory person, pompous and aggressive on the outside, but driven by doubts and fears about his capabilities on the inside. He keeps trying to obtain from fate the sign that he is the one she prizes above all others. And no matter how much he loses, he is convinced that his day is coming. "The neurotic gambler seeks a sign from Fate that he is omnipotent" (Knight, 1968).

Rosten (1961) found compulsive gamblers to be very easily bored with life when they didn't have any "action." Their whole approach to living was completely egocentric. They had a great need to have excitement in their lives. They looked for anything that was stimulating and were fascinated by risk. When these elements were lacking, they felt terribly unsatisfied and frustrated.

Many psychoanalysts believe that compulsive gamblers have an unconscious desire to *lose*. They are believed to be guilt-ridden people who have strong masochistic tendencies. And their gambling represents a repressed desire to suffer in order to relieve their guilt. Since the guilt in this situation is related to childhood experiences, it is usually unconscious and the person does not understand his behavior as being self-destructive.

Although gambling often carries with it a kind of stigma of illegality and underworld influence, it is really an important part of American business. The people who speculate on the stock market are doing very nearly the same thing as the person putting his money on the line in a crap game. They are betting that they are right, that the stock will go up, and that they will be able to sell at a profit. And there are a good number of these "respectable" gamblers who are driven by the same kinds of motives as those people we have been describing. It is quite clear, therefore, that gambling is not confined to a particular segment of the society, but that it is part of the very sinews of modern American life.

We have traced the ways in which money influences people in modern life. And we have tried to show that money has psychological meanings that are very different from those usually ascribed to it. Money is one of the more important symbols of the success syndrome. We shall consider the others in the next several chapters.

chapter 6
sex:
the biological imperative

No subject elicits more interest or brings about more controversy than human sexuality. It is at once the most provocative of human tendencies and at the same time the area of greatest misunderstanding. Reams are written about the subject and advice about it comes from many quarters, yet we are more ignorant of our own sexual natures than we are of almost any quality we label human. It is likely that we know more about the sex life of the flea, the ant, the mosquito, the dog, the horse, the ring-tailed dove, or even the hairy-nosed porcupine than we do about our own species. However, the subject is enormously important, for there is no doubt, the detractors of Freud notwithstanding, that this is an area of man's life which can give rise to a great amount of emotional pain and torment.

DOES MAN HAVE A SEXUAL NATURE?

Questions about what man is in the absence of culture are extremely difficult to answer. In the area of sex they are even more difficult because they are confounded by the fears, prejudices, and misinformation that is so

137

prevalent in regard to that subject matter. Any statement, therefore, about the nature of the sex drive or appetite in man must be made with great caution. In fact, we may find that sexuality differs so much from one individual to another that assumptions about a "drive" which is the same for each of us may be unsound.

There is, nevertheless, a need for some concept of the role of sex in the life of man before it has been radically altered by the societies of which he is a part. It is for this reason that we look to animal and tribal human societies for some clues. By noting that sexuality is expressed in greatly differing ways in different places, we can at least establish the fact that many of the "truths" about sex in any society are merely prejudiced cultural perceptions.

It is important to note at this point that these cultural biases have until very recently colored a great number of the anthropological studies of primitive societies. With a very few exceptions, American and European scholars went into their field studies with the very preconceptions that such investigations might otherwise dispel. As a result they often badly misinterpreted or distorted what they observed and, in so doing, revealed their own puritanistic parochialism. In some cases these investigators simply gave sex a very cursory mention, as if it had very little importance to the society in question; in others, they showed their own uptightness with regard to sex by using disparaging words or innuendos to describe practices that differed markedly from their own.

> The basic prudery implicit in such works is manifest by occasional slips of the pen—undetailed references to "licentiousness" or "promiscuity". (Marshall and Suggs, 1971)

It is unfortunate that the majority of anthropologists allowed their own preconceptions to influence their observations, for it has contributed to the ignorance about human sexuality from which we all continue to be affected.

One assumption made by many of the more conservative anthropologists was that there was an "upward" evolution of human societies from the extremely primitive to the highly "civilized" (that is, industrialized). This was perhaps a natural extension of the then newly formulated theory of the evolution of life forms. If species developed from more primitive to "higher" forms, it seemed reasonable that societies similarly evolved. And European and American investigators made the somewhat chauvinistic assumption that their own societies represented "higher" cultural forms.

Warranted or not, such an assumption carried with it the implication that the sexual practices in the cultures from which the anthropologists had come were more "civilized," "correct," "moral," or even more "normal" than those they were studying.

Such attitudes unfortunately prevented these investigators from entertaining the possibility that their own cultures had perhaps made some fundamental errors in understanding and dealing with human sexuality. It also interfered with their learning one of anthropology's most important lessons; the ways in which culture can affect human behavior, perception, and philosophy. This influence is in fact so pervasive that it contributed to this very oversight. The process of enculturation had done its work so well that even these learned men believed that their own culture was the "proper" one and that all others were deviations from this norm.

Having made note of these earlier inaccuracies, modern scholars have hurried to make amends. Most anthropologists begin today from a different premise. Human babies having almost no instincts, are at the mercy of their elders and other members of their group for instruction in the methods considered proper for dealing with the problems of day-to-day living. Each society makes an effort to find reasonable ways to handle such problems. And each group finds its *own* solution to them. These attempts account for the range of differences seen from one part of the globe to another. Probably none of them is perfect. But it is both pompous and naive to believe that a society advanced in one area of endeavor is necessarily advanced in all. The attitudes toward sex are, like other forms of behavior, learned by the inhabitants of a culture. And the fact that they differ merely proves that man is both malleable and innovative. It does not reflect upon the moral or intellectual superiority of one group or another.

The relativity of behavior among different cultures should demonstrate a need for caution in assigning such terms of evaluation as "right" or "wrong," "good" or "bad," to customs or beliefs with which we disagree. All these cultural traditions are merely experiments in living. They are attempts to solve the many problems that man creates for himself in the process of changing from an animal ruled completely by instincts to an organism, relatively free to alter his environment and his mode of living, who in the process may make a large number of mistakes. The more freedom, of course, the more opportunity for error. And since man is among the freest of organisms on this planet, perhaps he may be forgiven if he has made a large number of miscalculations.

If we are to understand human sexuality, we must make some effort to lay to rest a number of myths that man has concocted about himself so that we can view our own behavior without the usual biases that prevent a clear understanding of its nature. As we noted earlier, man's vanity prompted him to adopt the idea that he was a godlike creature, very different and far removed from the lower animals. And the Darwinian revelations gave rise to a kind of panic when this lofty position came under threat. However, the reaction was unnecessary. Man's discovery of his "animal" nature need not be a cause for concern. There is great beauty and dignity in the life of a healthy animal and man loses none of his nobility by such an identification.

It will therefore be instructive to examine sexuality in man's nearest relatives in the hope that some clues to our own erotic natures can thus be gained. It is not likely that we can make too many inferences about ourselves from the study of lower forms, but it is possible that we can get some idea of what sex is in a natural environment before any cultural influences are brought to bear on it.

SEX AND THE SINGLE GORILLA

Until recently most studies of animals have been done in the artificial environments of zoos or laboratories, and for that reason they are of little use. The kinds of reactions that occur in such situations do not give us a genuine look at the *real* nature of the organism. Restraints of any kind sometimes have drastic effects on behavior, and this is particularly true of sex, because unlike hunger or thirst, it is extremely susceptible to disruptions of the environment.

In recent years a number of investigators have gone into the jungles to study various primates in their natural habitat. One study (Schaller, 1964) has been rather enlightening. Schaller was able to build blinds and hide himself reasonably well in order to study the mountain gorillas of Albert National Park in the Congo. He studied several troops of animals who wander through the rain forest, and among his observations there were a few that are pertinent to our discussion here.

Schaller noted that sexual episodes were quite rare in the wild, contrary to some popular views. He was able to observe only two of them in approximately two years of observation. He also reports that he saw no episodes of homosexuality or masturbation in the natural setting, although these do occur fairly often in zoos. There were other surprises in the sexual behavior of the gorillas. There did not appear to be intense rivalry among the males for access to the females. Any male might mate with one of the females in the troop and the others would practically ignore them. This was so even though there is a hierarchy in the gorilla troop and one male is usually the dominant one in this structure. But Schaller observed one animal copulating with a female right next to the dominant male of the group, who sat there ignoring the episode.

Gorillas, like many primates, live in a communal society. They move through the jungle together, the large males generally protecting the rest of the group from any dangers. The sexual life of the adults is both polygamous and polyandrous. There is no pairing off in permanent male–female dyads, and the young are often cared for by the entire group.

Other studies demonstrate other kinds of behavior in primates. And it is certainly not clear that homosexuality and masturbation are completely absent, even in the wild. But since most of the studies on gorillas previous to Schaller's had been done on animals in captivity, his findings appear significant.

Although we do not intend to make any close comparisons between man and these other species, it may be informative to note two things. There are a few primitive human societies in which the social structure is strikingly similar to that of some of the other primates, and there are experiments now afoot in which communal living patterns of various kinds are being attempted in highly civilized countries.

SEX AS A SOCIAL ENCOUNTER

In humans there is a social component to sex which may be more important to some people than the physical one. In some ways this may be an unfortunate situation, for it complicates an otherwise delightful physical experience.

The actual physical encounter with the organism of the opposite sex has not always been necessary during the evolutionary development of the animal kingdom. Some fishes simply deposit their eggs and move on, leaving them for the male, who comes along afterward to fertilize them. In such a situation, it is hardly necessary for the individuals to be properly introduced, for there is no direct communication between them. And it may be that some human beings envy the asocial sex life of these animals because of this very fact.

But somewhere along the evolutionary line it became necessary for the eggs of the female to be fertilized *inside* her body instead of outside and some form of communication became necessary. (It may be interesting to note that it is in this area of *communication* that the troubles regarding human sexuality occur—*not* in the biology of the organism.) At first the form of the communication was quite simple and very impersonal. In the plant kingdom, for example, the communication is carried on by a third party, a sort of marriage broker, usually an insect, who carries the spermatozoa from the male organs of one plant to the female organs of another.

Fertilization takes place with a minimum of interaction between the organisms and, one might suspect, with a minimum of "trouble."

As the organisms become more complex, so, of course, does the communication. The information that must be transmitted generally takes the form of the female letting the male know of her "receptive period." This is a crucial disclosure, as any rebuffed male knows. For sexual behavior is to a great extent a female prerogative. The degree to which the female's disclosure of her readiness is critical can be seen by the example of the porcupine. The sex life of this little creature is confined to only one day a year and to only a few hours of that particular day. Some may feel that considering the hazards inherent in mating with a porcupine, that is quite enough. Nevertheless, the message conveyed by the female must be perfectly clear, since an attempt by the male at any other time of year could result in a dangerous miscalculation. Fortunately, the male usually understands the signal and the act of mating occurs during the three to five hours in the whole year when the female is fertile (Carrighar, 1965).

The means of communication in the lower animals takes the form of dancing and caressing. These activities are fairly stereotyped until we get into the more highly evolved organisms. Finally, when we get to man, one notices that the changes that have occurred are more apparent than real. *The major part of the communication from the female to the male is still nonverbal.* And the dancing and caressing is still present (although the music has certainly undergone a good deal of modification). But the greatest difference in the human sexual sphere comes from the fact that the male may very often misread the communication from the female about her receptivity. There are a number of reasons for this.

In the first place, unlike almost all other animals, the human female does not have specific periods of readiness. She is, generally speaking, always ready. However, this is a biological, not a psychological state. And from a practical standpoint, there are many times when she is not receptive. This is confusing to the male because these periods are largely unpredictable. Moreover, even worse confusion grows out of still another situation. Sexual communication among humans is often deliberately misleading. For example, when the woman says "no," she often means "yes." But there are also many times when she says "no" and means "no." And again there are times when she says "yes" and means "no" and when she says "yes" and means "yes" and even when she says one or the other and means "maybe." Added to this is the nonverbal part of the message, which is also often contradictory. It is not surprising, therefore, that human beings are bewildered about sex.

For his own part, the male also presents some of his messages in forms that are not easily deciphered by the female. He may, for example, be very shy, and although desiring a certain female very much, his behavior may not show it. His reticence may, in fact, be read by her to mean that he has absolutely no interest in her. Thus we have the paradoxical predicament of two people having strong mutual feelings for one another and never giving expression to them. This could never happen to a pair of healthy animals.

Sometimes the male communicates interest of a sexual and/or romantic nature when he actually has no such interest. His motives may be something *other* than sexual. He may be interested in a woman's money or some

Much sexual communication can be nonverbal. These people are enjoying themselves in the lounge of one of today's modern airplanes.

other assets. Or he may have a need to make a *conquest* and the particular girl may be of no consequence to him. His message would therefore carry false information about his real sexual feelings, which in this situation might be negligible. And he might succeed in performing the sex act in spite of the fact that he had little or no desire for it.

If communication is essential to the successful commission of the sex act, it is clear that the human being is severely handicapped. But there are other even more compelling reasons for man's sexual difficulties. To understand them, we must go back to sexuality in nature.

Some psychologists call sex a drive. Some call it an appetite. In either case the arousal of the feeling or desire appears to be natural and universal. Animals in nature and human beings in some primitive societies can act upon their feelings with some degree of freedom, and they are not punished or reprimanded for so behaving. But civilized people cannot always give way to their biological needs for a variety of reasons. Some of these may be sensible reasons. A fireman, for example, cannot walk away in the middle of his job simply because he sees a beautiful girl down the block. But some of the other reasons are not very sensible. Among these the most dangerous from a psychological point of view are the ones branding sex as immoral, dirty, sinful, or bestial. *Most of the problems that arise in the sphere of human sexuality result not from sex itself but from the beliefs that have been associated with it in civilized societies.*

SEX AND GUILT

There are undoubtedly a great number of reasons for the sexual taboos that have evolved in various cultures. Some were no doubt intended to prevent incest (Freud, 1913). Others probably had the prevention of venereal disease and unwanted pregnancy as their concerns. Whatever their original intentions, these became lost. Remaining were (and still are) a series of superstitions, half-truths, prohibitions, condemnations, pontifications, obstructions, restraints, and commandments which are perhaps the most destructive of all of man's beliefs. Let us see why.

ANIMALS, INSTINCT, AND HUMAN INNOVATION

Like much of their behavior, the sex life of animals is governed by instinct. Nature sets out a complicated series of responses to particular stimuli and the animals almost never deviate from this pattern. There is, therefore, almost no margin of freedom to alter the specific pattern of behavior. They are always the same, and they are universal within the species. This, in effect, is what psychologists mean by the term *instinct*.

In the human sphere, however, the pattern is different. Man does not respond in fixed, predetermined sequences which are laid out by the genetic makeup of his species. But he does have drives and appetites which have instinctive bases. The great difference in man lies not so much in the need or drive but in the variety of responses from which he may choose. The responses available to him have a greater degree of flexibility than those of his animal forebears. For this reason we may speak of man's sexual behavior as *instinctoid* (instinctlike) rather than instinctive. Man's ability to choose among a number of alternative modes of behavior in order to satisfy basic needs leads to a certain degree of *innovation* which is absent in the life of most animals.

In man, therefore, there is a *gap* between the *instinctoid drives or appetites* and the *mode of responding* in order to satisfy them. The criteria that man uses to make his decisions about how to deal with such needs are many. They may be based on tradition, superstition, arbitrary whim, or even on reason. But the distance between the originally instinctive mode of behavior and the one that has been altered by the process of innovation has a great effect upon him. It can have consequences for the ultimate well-being of the organism. For in the human being, the way in which he comes to *perceive* these instinctoid needs can be crucial to his emotional stability.

Human societies, often because of a lack of understanding about man's instinctoid nature, have evolved ways of dealing with his basic needs which have often been contrary to those needs. The most flagrant miscalculation of this sort probably occurs in the area of sex. Civilized man does not understand sex, partly because of his concept of "civilization." He has evolved a number of beliefs and superstitions about what the cultured person *should be*, how he or she *should feel*, and how they *should act*. Most of these beliefs have little or nothing to do with who in fact instinctoid man is.

Human innovation is the beginning of man's freedom. But it is also paradoxically sometimes the cause of his greatest imprisonment. There is a price for freedom. It is the possibility of choosing incorrectly. We often do. In the realm of sex our poor choices have often been disastrous. *Man's problems stem not from his animality but from a distorted conception of what the civilized person should be.*

THE SEX DRIVE: HOW STRONG IS IT?

Most people, if asked, would say that the sex drive is one of the most powerful in the animal kingdom, and anyone observing human behavior in the twentieth century would no doubt agree. But most studies show that among animals in their natural environment, or in some human primitive cultures where sex is not greatly inhibited, it does not appear to be much different from the other basic drives. Sex attains its importance in many human societies because of its repression. It may be true, as Desmond Morris (1967) contends, that man is the sexiest animal extant. Nevertheless, primitive people do not generally show the kind of *obsessive* concern about the subject as is evidenced in civilized societies.

There seem to be two factors that increase the importance of sex in the life of civilized men. One is the hiding of the body and the other is the "forbidden fruit" attitude. People who practice nudity, whether primitive or modern, find that sexual arousal is far greater when the body is covered or partially covered than when it is nude. This should not really be too surprising. Any appetite increases when its object is partially removed from view. Clothes act to cover and at the same time to enhance the "mystery" of the body. Some kinds of attire are made deliberately enticing by covering only certain parts or accentuating others. In these instances the imagination of the viewer plays as much a part as the clothing itself. The total effect of covering the body, therefore, is to make sex more mysterious, exotic, and exciting, and it tends to increase our preoccupation with it. Nudity itself, however, can also be exciting sexually in a repressive atmosphere, as we shall see shortly. It is only where nudity is a way of life that it actually has the effect of diminishing sexual interest.

The "forbidden fruit" syndrome has an even greater effect on the sexual consciousness of civilized people than has the wearing of clothing. Anything that is prohibited is bound to arouse the curiosity and desire of those who are denied it. Sex, being a particularly suggestible kind of drive, is extremely susceptible to such treatment. It is interesting to note in this respect that those people who show so much concern about "not acting like animals" should really be concerned about acting more like animals and less like humans, if they want to diminish our fanatical preoccupation with sexuality. It is the human being who as a result of the prohibitions and taboos regarding sex has become what these people generally believe the animal to be.

The ingredients necessary to make sex an obsessive preoccupation are present in modern American life. Although the attitudes have been changing, the greatest change has come in the focus of attention rather than in the severity of the preoccupation. Americans are obsessed with sex because they have been putting out two contradictory messages regarding it for a long time. The first message is that "sex is dirty or evil or beneath the dignity of civilized men." And the second message is a "come-on." It presents the male and female to one another in such a way as to exaggerate their sexual desirability. It would be possible to make anything seem fascinating with this technique.

Although the new sexual freedom may be an attempt to change some of these conditions, it does not always succeed. Most of what is now occurring is not really sexual freedom in a real sense. It is a reaction against the repressive atmosphere of the recent past. As such, the tendency is for the pendulum to swing quickly and far to the opposite end of the spectrum. What we are witnessing now is the obsession being given its head. It will take a little time for it to ventilate itself, and then it may come to take its place as a more normal part of our lives.

The question of how strong the sex drive is cannot be answered in an unequivocal fashion. It appears to vary greatly from person to person. It is also extremely susceptible to cultural variations, and it is related in complex ways to the amount of repression that a society exerts upon its expression. We can agree, however, that it is a very strong motivating factor in human life despite these variations. It is not so much that the drive itself varies, but that the arousal of it is so complicated by the particular society in which it is studied that it is difficult to decide just how much of it is innate and how much is cultivated.

ATTITUDES, ANTHROPOLOGY, AND LIBIDO

It is almost impossible for most of us to realize (or perhaps to accept the fact) that most of the attitudes we hold about ourselves and the world are inculcated (often arbitrarily) by the society in which we live. Many of the things that we consider "the facts of life" or "laws of nature" are in actuality local, sometimes very naive ideas concerning the nature of the world. It is true, of course, that many of the differences to be seen between one culture and another are obvious enough for anyone to acknowledge. Clothes, for example. Anyone will admit that the costumes of people differ from one another because of tradition. That is surely simple to all of us. But how about beauty? How about disgust? Does it ever occur to most of us that what we call beautiful, in the feminine figure, for example, is largely defined by our society? Or would anyone suspect that the response of vomiting, which is obviously a reflex, can be culturally determined; or, more incredible yet, culturally inhibited? Again, would not most Americans argue that the "problems" of adolescence are universal and therefore an inevitable part of the process of growing up?

Contrary to the expectations of most people, all these things are learned. They exist in some societies under certain conditions and are absent in others. Sometimes, as in the problems of adolescence, they are nonexistent (Mead, 1928). The concept of beauty or sexual attractiveness is so subject to cultural influence that it changes radically within the same society every few years. Remember the "flapper"? And Rudolph Valentino? Look at Reubens' paintings of women. Do we perceive them as "stacked"? He probably did. Do we become disgusted at the idea of eating spiders, or snails, or worms, or at the sight of blood, or at the smell of feces? Others do not. Ah, but they are primitive. They are mere savages, we think. They just don't know any better. But it is not true. We had to *learn* to be repelled by such things. We were conditioned to respond with disgust to certain kinds of cues. And even now, we would respond differently under the right conditions. If we become doctors or nurses, our responses to blood changes almost immediately. We may be repelled by saliva, but not in the Pavlovian experiments. And a very finicky mother can examine the contents of her baby's diaper without the slightest compunction.

Among the things to which we have learned to respond with disgust are our eliminative functions. Along with the functions, we have developed an intense repugnance for the organs involved in elimination. But very closely allied to these (sometimes they are identical) are the organs of sex and reproduction. So that for modern man, especially modern Americans, the sexual organs have acquired the same kind of connotations as the eliminative organs. It is partly for this reason that sex and sexuality are regarded by many in our society as "dirty." *But this is a learned attitude. It is* not *a fact of life. It is* not *a law of nature. It is a cultural bias.*

Civilized people are so divorced from the functions of their bodies that they cannot possibly make clear judgments concerning them. In this area we Americans are even more alienated than many others. Perhaps it is an outgrowth of Puritanism, but the fact is that we act *as if* certain human functions do not exist. When we are in "polite company," many of the vital functions of the body are never mentioned—and they are certainly never indulged in. Moreover, the miracle of modern plumbing makes it possible for us to immediately separate ourselves from the products of elimination in such a way that that area of our lives has become quite foreign to us. Added to this, the enterprising masters of industry have concocted a great number of deodorants and lotions so that we move through a perfumed haze that all but obliterates the stark realities of our life functions.

There are certain obvious advantages to all of this. But there is also a very subtle bit of subterfuge which leads to a great deal of misunderstanding. Because we are able to separate ourselves from those functions—because we do not particularly like to identify them with ourselves, we come to perceive ourselves without them. We simply fail to acknowledge them. We put a great premium on cleanliness. We dress in fine clothes. We make ourselves neat and sanitary. We spray ourselves with things that will prevent us from perspiring. We cover every part of our bodies that might give some hint of our "indelicate" functions. We mask every possible area of offense with perfumes and then we act for all intents and purposes as if we are in fact these sweet-smelling creatures. In short, we pretend that we are delicate and immaculate, but in reality we are hung up about our *real* bodies.

The net result of such attitudes is reflected in our feelings about sex. Even among those of us who believe that there is nothing dirty about sex, there is likely to be a residual feeling about it based on the idea that the body is an evil-smelling, filth-creating organism. Along with this there is often the underlying wish that it could be otherwise. Such an attitude is related to the desire to present a faultless image, for we must remember the hero and heroine are as perfect in this area as they are in others. The psychic damage done by this separation from the real life functions is not always obvious; but it is serious, nonetheless. For in the area of sex, this state of mind leads to a great conflict. There is, on the one hand, the feeling of attraction, and on the other, the sense of disgust, both with the body and with one's own behavior toward the body of the other. These feelings are not always clearly conscious, but they are instrumental in many of the kinds of sexual problems with which many of us are affected.

There is a relationship between one's feelings about the body and his manifest sex drive. But it is a complicated one. There are undoubtedly many people in our society who because of their distorted perception of bodily processes have blunted sexual feelings. Their libido is simply "turned off" (that is, repressed) by this repugnance for anything that is involved with the physical side of their functioning. But there are others whose sexual energy is altered in a different way. For these people there is both disgust and fascination with the organs of the body, and they may become sexually attracted to people or behaviors that are actually repulsive to them. It is as if they have become conditioned to two things, one attractive and the other repellent, by a process of continual association. Such a feeling may generalize so that other kinds of distasteful experiences may take on erotic coloring.

It is quite obvious that these attitudes concerning the body can and often do severely restrict or distort the enjoyment of sex for many people in our society. Perhaps the degree to which attitudes can affect the enjoyment of sex can be shown by a comparison between two extremely different cultures.

Two anthropological studies (Messenger, 1971; Marshall and Suggs, 1971) present very interesting contrasts in the sexual activities of people who are at opposite polls with regard to their acceptance of man's sexual nature. One study (Messenger) concerns the sexual puritanism of a group of people on a small island off the coast of Ireland. The other (Marshall and Suggs) describes the erotic life of the completely uninhibited Polynesians on the island of Mangaia in the Cook chain.

The life of the Irish people of the island in Messenger's study is marked by a complete denial of sex in any kind of social situation that includes the young. There is no discussion or instruction about such things as menstruation, pregnancy, or intercourse. Sex is considered a "duty" that must be "endured" by women. Young girls are often horrified at their first menstrual flow because they have not been prepared by their mothers for this inevitable event. It seems likely that the women of this community never or very seldom experience orgasm. Nudity is strenuously shunned even during intercourse, which is done quickly and surreptitiously by married couples. Even bathing is done by sponging arms, legs, and faces and necks without undressing. It appears that other parts of the body never get a real bath. The "good" woman does not like sex. And any woman that shows any kind of interest or capability is "bad." Children are taught to repress any kind of sexual behavior by covering their bodies even in the presence of their siblings and by punishment for any kind of erotic behavior. Sex on this island is a hidden, shame-filled, quickly performed, joyless thing.

The attitude of the people on the Polynesian island of Mangaia is completely different. There is an almost totally uninhibited approach to sex among these islanders from the beginning of adolescence. The approach to intercourse is matter of fact. A man is sometimes berated for *not* taking part in coitus often enough. Coitus occurs without any feeling of shame or misgiving. An interesting fact about these people is that there is little or no social contact between the sexes except for copulation. Sometimes without a word passing between them, a young adolescent boy and girl will simply look at one another and go off together, have intercourse, and then go their own ways. Every meeting of any kind between the two sexes leads to intercourse whenever possible.

> There is no social contact between the sexes, no rendezvous, no equivalent of our "necking," that does not culminate directly and immediately in copulation. Coitus is the only imaginable end for any kind of sexual contact among Mangaians. (Marshall and Suggs, 1971)

A Mangaian boy will often steal into the family sleeping room and have intercourse with the daughter of the family while the parents feign sleep. The parents' real concern is their hope that their daughter is happy with her new-found partner. A girl may also initiate the contact by slipping into the boy's sleeping room. The main emphasis on Mangaia is orgasm. The boy learns how to excite the woman and to bring her to orgasm a number of times during intercourse. Moreover, he learns how to hold back so that the final climax is mutual.

Young people on Mangaia like variety. They have many different partners during their early youth. The parents encourage their daughters to have sex with a number of different men in order to find those who are best suited for her. An interesting sidelight to this radical kind of sexual freedom is that there is no homosexuality on the island. There is no taboo against it and the islanders know of its existence on Tahiti and some of the other islands where the French have had a great influence, but there appears to be no need for such behavior where sexual freedom of a heterosexual kind exists.

The Mangaians are easily aroused. The sounds of others engaged in intercourse, music of various kinds, the nude body of one of the opposite sex are all said to excite the sexual appetite. But whereas the genitalia can arouse the partner, Mangaian men cannot understand the Westerner's preoccupation with the female breast. For them, this has no particular sexual significance.

In the Mangaian culture as in many others throughout the world, sex and love are not necessarily combined.

> Sexual intimacy is *not* achieved by first demonstrating personal affection; the reverse is true. The Mangaian or Polynesian girl takes an immediate demonstration of sexual virility and masculinity as the first test of her partner's desire for her and as the reflection of her own desirability. Personal affection may or may not result from acts of sexual intimacy, but the latter are requisite to the former—exactly the reverse of the ideals of Western society. (Marshall and Suggs, 1971)

There are other societies in many parts of the world which lie somewhere between these two on the continuum of repression–expression with regard to sexuality. But what is at once clear from the anthropological evidence is that there are great differences in human sexual attitudes and that these differences make it obvious that there is no "correct" attitude toward human sexuality. Moreover, it seems reasonable to acknowledge that some societies deal with sex in ways which from a psychological point of view are more satisfactory than others.

It is also clear from these two studies that it is extremely difficult to ascertain the real strength of the human sex drive. One reason for this is that it can very easily be masked, on a conscious level at least, especially where there is a great deal of repression. The women in the Irish study, for example, show very little desire for sex and very few, if any, ever reached orgasm. To most of them, as to many American women of the last generation, sex is an unpleasant duty. The Mangaian women, on the other hand, are frankly and openly sexual. They enjoy sex greatly and appear to feel no shame concerning it. According to Marshall and Suggs, every woman on the island achieves orgasm. This, they believe, is a capability that must be learned. If this is true, such learning must be enhanced by an atmosphere of freedom. Where a woman feels restrained by guilt, fear, or disgust, she is not likely to allow herself this kind of feeling. Marshall makes one final observation which should be of interest to anyone in a society where one sex outnumbers the other. He says, "no man—or woman—is so maimed, so ugly, so poor, or so abberrant that he—or she—cannot find a sexual partner" (Marshall and Suggs, 1971). It might be that we in our highly civilized, technologized nations have lost sight of the importance of this simple fact with regard to human happiness.

Sexual attitudes of the kind described by Marshall and Suggs are not unique. Life, for the young of Samoa, another Polynesian people, is similar to that of the Mangaians. From adolescence on, young men and women are expected to engage in a number of sexual escapades with various partners. These escapades are permitted and even encouraged by the elders. They do not stigmatize promiscuity in the way that most Westerners do and for the most part they seem to feel that sex is an end to be enjoyed for itself rather than a means to other ends such as the production of children or the establishment of lasting personal relationships. It is tacitly accepted, for example, that a woman whose husband is absent for any great length of time will engage in sexual behavior with someone else during his absence. This practice is not disparaged by the Samoans, who do not perceive sexual activity as the exclusive "possession" of one person by another (Mead, 1928).

These attitudes have certain kinds of effects upon the people of Samoa which are of interest to us. These people experience no guilt or shame regarding their bodies. They are therefore relatively free of the kinds of neurotic tendencies with regard to sex that are so common in our own society.

> The wider range which these practices give prevents the development of obsessions of guilt which are so frequent a cause of maladjustment among us. (Mead, 1928)

The freedom of action among the young of Samoa has another bonus. Adolescents are not as easily deceived about their feelings for members of the opposite sex as are youngsters in more repressive societies. As Mead explains it:

The Samoan girl who shrugs her shoulder over the excellent technique of some young Lothario is nearer to recognition of sex as an impersonal force without any intrinsic validity, than is the sheltered American girl who falls in love with the first man who kisses her.

Among the Masai of Kenya, East Africa, there is an even more explicit arrangement for premarital sexual activity than those on Mangaia or Samoa. The Masai warrior spends from ten to fifteen years during which he is not permitted to marry. But during this period of his life, young unmarried girls live in the same complex as the warriors and become their sexual partners.

> These matings are explicitly transitory and solely for the purpose of sexual gratification; the men and girls involved are not considered married. Living with the warriors places no stigma on the girl, for every normal Masai girl has this experience in her youth. Should a girl become pregnant, she returns to the village to be married. Having a child out of wedlock stigmatizes neither the girl nor the child. Indeed, it aids a girl to secure a husband, for the Masai welcome children and regard barrenness as a principal cause for divorce. (Beals and Hoijer, 1965)

Literally thousands of different ways of dealing with sexuality exist throughout the world. Not all tribal societies are as free and permissive as Mangaia and Samoa. In some, chastity before marriage is held to be a virtue and there are sanctions against those who violate these taboos. Malinowski (1962) claims that a number of "the lowest savages, such as the Veddas, Fuegians, Kubu of Sumatra, Senoi and other Malayan negritos, do not tolerate sexual intercourse before marriage." In such cultures, however, marriage generally occurs very early, in most cases very shortly after puberty, so that sexual desire does not have to be inhibited for very long.

There are other tribal groups throughout the world where some degree of continence is expected from unmarried people, although in many cases the sanctions against "offenders" are so slight as to be almost ineffectual. In other places, although there is a tacit prohibition against premarital intercourse, most everyone makes a public show of complying while secretly defying the decree. This is also often true with regard to extramarital sex. In some societies the husband who is being cuckolded is aware of the fact that his wife is having an affair with another man. But he saves face by acting as if he does not know about it. And the other members of the community, who are also aware of the subterfuge, do not embarrass him by speaking of the arrangement in his presence.

Tribal societies in which chastity is expected before marriage are definitely in the minority. In a great many, special arrangements are made by the adults for bachelors and young girls to live together in "mixed houses." The Trobriand Islanders from puberty on are free to have intercourse with many partners, and this practice is encouraged by the elders, for it is a period of experimentation which is expected to lead in time to the development of highly stable relationships. And, in fact, they do develop.

> As time goes on and the boys and girls grow older, their intrigues naturally and without any outer pressure extend in length and depth; the ties between lovers become stronger and more permanent. One decided preference as a rule develops and stands out against the lesser love affairs. It is important to note that such preferences are clearly based on genuine attachments resulting from real affinity of character. The protracted intrigue becomes a matter of public notice as well as a test of mutual compatibility, the girl's family signify their consent and marriage is finally concluded between the two lovers. (Malinowski, 1962, pp. 5–6)

It seems clear that such accounts can be multiplied many times over. The modes developed by man to deal with his sexuality are as varied as the societies that he has evolved. If one were to try to make deductions about the sexual nature of man from such findings, his task would be a difficult one indeed. Choosing between so many differing patterns of behavior in order to find the "right" one seems almost futile. However, certain observations can be made with regard to man's sexuality as it relates to our modern notions of emotional health.

It seems apparent from studying man in various kinds of social situations that sex is an important and pervasive part of his nature. Attempts to repress this part of his personality have generally led to emotional problems of a very serious nature, general unhappiness, and the emergence of sexual activity which is often considered less desirable than the so-called "natural" expression of this important drive. Moreover, it now seems reasonably certain that when sexuality is driven underground, it may give rise to other kinds of behaviors which are more dangerous and destructive to the social fabric of a society than that which is being repressed. Studies of frustration have frequently demonstrated that hostility and aggression are very often its immediate consequences (Miller, 1941). The aggressiveness need not always be expressed overtly. It may also be repressed, creating even more hostility, or it may be turned inward so that the person becomes self-punitive or suicidal. There are other kinds of reactions to frustration, as we shall see in Chapter 9.

The conclusions that might be drawn from these considerations are that many, perhaps most, civilized societies have failed to deal in a realistic way with human sexuality. Sex is a "problem" in the modern world because we have not really decided what we want to do about it, because we have adopted rather arbitrary kinds of attitudes toward it, and because we have failed to understand and accept the human body as it functions in nature. Moreover, as with many other psychological processes, we believe that if we turn away from a human problem and forget or ignore it, it will disappear. There is little question that the current interest in sex is a result of the failure of earlier approaches to handle it. Man is a sexual animal. He is a passionate creature. No amount of hiding or denying this fact can change it. We must, therefore, meet this question on its real terms. Only then will we be able to have an erotic existence that remains in balance with the other parts of man's being.

HUMAN AND ANIMAL SEXUALITY COMPARED

The major dimension along which humans are differentiated from "lower" animals is, as we have noted, the one that describes instinct. Most of the behavior engaged in by animals is dictated by instincts which make their lives generally similar to other animals of the same species the world over. Quite the opposite is true of man. The task of ordering the instinctoid tendencies, in this case sex, is one that man must do in his own way through some decision which he or one of his kind makes somewhere along his developmental way. The result is a wide and diverse pattern of sexual customs throughout the world.

We have observed therefore that it is very difficult to point to any one group or culture and say that this is the way man must deal with sexuality. Some ways are obviously better than others and some ways are clearly destructive to the organism, but no way is perfect. And it is certain that what works in one society may be completely impossible or impractical elsewhere. Yet there are valuable lessons to be learned from the ways in which other peoples deal with this important human function. And it is essential that we profit from the information which anthropology contributes to our knowledge of man so that our behavior in this area will be more rational that it has been in the past. Let us therefore see what we have learned.

ANTHROPOLOGY AND MAN'S SEXUAL NATURE

One of the most important things that we have gained from our survey of the erotic life of other people is the realization that what we have often taken to be *truth* with regard to sexuality is simply a narrow provincialism on our part. It seems quite clear that very few, if any, societies reflect the *real* nature of human sexuality by themselves. And it is only through a consideration of the many different life styles in various parts of the world that we can begin to perceive a pattern with regard to this extremely complicated problem.

Certain facts emerge from the studies of these varied cultures which should be considered in any science of man. The problems that arise in societies which do not adequately understand man's sexual nature are mainly psychological. But these in turn give rise to others, which may be sociological, religious, economic, and political. Sex is so pervasive that no area of human endeavor is unaffected by it.

There are a number of questions about man's sexual nature that our anthropological studies have tried to answer. Is man naturally monogamous? It seems unlikely. Although many societies do provide for monogamous marriage, a good number practice polygamy (one man with two or more wives) or polyandry (one woman with two or more husbands). Schusky and Culbert (1967) report that there are more polygamous societies than there are monogamous ones. Moreover, in almost all societies in which monogamy is the rule, there are some kinds of extramarital sexual encounters (either sanctioned or condemned) practiced by a large part of the population. In addition, there are in some cultures careful provisions for premarital sex as well as such varied customs as wife lending, concubinage, *composite family*, in which two or more nuclear families share a common husband or wife, and in more "civilized" cultures the practice of the "double standard," which winks at promiscuity in the male while condemning it fiercely in the female.

Generally speaking, monogamy and polygamy seem to be related to two particular situations. One is the ratio of male to female inhabitants; the other is the legitimization and preservation of a family line. In societies in which the number of males and females is almost equal monogamy is usually maintained in the name of fairness. Given the fact that some individuals are more attractive than others, without some form of control these would have a large number of mates while others would have none at all. Incidentally, our society does not qualify in this regard since there are at any given time several million more women than men. As a result, the practice of monogamy in the United States forces a large number of women into spinsterhood.

Monogamous marriage in many societies grows out of a desire on the part of the inhabitants to identify their progeny. And, in fact, the particular marriage customs of most cultures are related more to this issue than the sexual one. In a number of societies, including our own, the marriage contract rather than the sexual behavior of the parents determines who the *legal* father of the children of that marriage is. This is the case regardless of whether or not he is actually the biological one.

The establishment of the family unit by some kind of marriage agreement appears to be more or less universal. This is true of polygamous societies as well as monogamous ones. But the family unit, whatever its ratio of husbands to wives or wives to husbands, is generally set up for the rearing of children and may have very little to do with the sexual life of its members.

> Marriage on the whole is rather a contract for the production and maintenance of children than an authorization for sexual intercourse. The main reason why marriage has not been regarded as establishing an exclusive sexual relationship lies in the fact that in many human societies sexual relations have been allowed under certain conditions before marriage, while marriage did not necessarily exclude the continuance of similar relations. (Malinowski, 1962)

It may be that although man is sometimes monogamous in regard to his offspring, he nevertheless desires a number of sexual partners. He is often exclusive in the choice of the parent of his children but not necessarily in his choice of sexual partners. This is somewhat confusing to Americans because we have always made a public display of the myth that marriage implies sexual exclusiveness. Yet in everyday living, most people do not observe this practice.

There is no doubt that people can be attracted to one another on a purely sexual basis. This is obvious from the behavior of the young in many of the cultures mentioned. But it is also evident in our own society. Since we do not generally allow such desires free expression, they must often show themselves in indirect ways. The "crushes" on movie stars, the increased interest in entertainment with overt sexual content, the altered attitudes toward "swinging," all testify to this kind of attraction. Although it has been fashionable for women to deny such interests, their preoccupation with "romance" and their dreams (sexual experiences with strange men, for example) tend to give them away.

The question of whether homosexuality is "natural" or not is a difficult one to answer. Although in some very free societies there is no homosexuality, in others almost as free, there is some. However, there is a higher incidence of homosexuality in more industrialized nations. Since these are usually more repressed societies, it may be inferred that homosexuality is less frequent where repression is low. Moreover, the testimony of observers of animal behavior with regard to the rarity of homosexual behavior in the wild as compared to its prevalence in zoos tends to support an environmental view. Although there are some observers who believe that at least some kinds of homosexuality are congenital (Oliven, 1965), it is difficult to understand why these kinds of individuals are absent from societies in which heterosexual unions are more available. Homosexuality in modern civilized societies is a separate issue and requires some comment, which will be given in Chapter 7.

SEXUAL JEALOUSY

The feeling of jealousy appears to be so common and so natural that most Americans have a difficult time understanding that it is not universal. Yet this is the case. The sense of hurt and discomfort that we feel when our loved one "cheats" on us is so pervasive and instantaneous for most people in our culture that it never occurs to us that it might be learned. Our feelings of jealousy are related to certain assumptions about the world which are deeply ingrained in Western traditions and which seem self-evident to most of us and therefore beyond the realm of conjecture. Among these assumptions are the concepts of quantity and property.

SEX AND QUANTITY

Western science teaches us that everything is finite. There is only a limited supply of any commodity and when a given measure of some commodity is "used up," it is generally gone. Machines, for example, can only function for a certain period of time. When they wear out, or use up their source of energy, they fail. Each organism has only a finite amount of energy, and when this is discharged, the organism "runs down."

This concept of quantity is carried over into our life functions and is reflected in our feelings about sex. Many of our slang expressions reveal this quantitative orientation. "I want to get a little." "I'd rather sell it than give it away." "Will she get up off of some?" Such statements are clearly indicative of the feeling of an *amount* of sex which is used up or lost in some kind of transaction.

SEX AND PROPERTY

Along with our ideas of quantity, we Westerners are extremely materialistic. We have a conception of the world that is profoundly physical. Our sciences are founded upon the proposition that the universe can be completely described in terms of matter and energy and we believe that mathematical expressions can be formulated that will someday completely describe all natural phenomena. Our picture of the world is therefore finite and physical. But we are also possessive. If the universe is material, we believe that there is a share of this universe which should be ours. We think that each man should have whatever portion he is capable of obtaining. And many of us work diligently to increase our allocations.

Our assumptions about the universe are extended to other areas of our thinking. We believe that sex, like everything else, can be allocated. We act as if there is only a finite amount of sex in a given partner and, if we have chosen that partner for ourselves, we believe that all of his/her sex *belongs* to us. Our partner may have other friends, other acquaintances, business relationships, various kinds of contacts with other human beings, but they must *save* their sex for us. We own that in the same way that we own our cars. We act toward it like we act toward money. We are *cheated* if we find that it has been *spent* on someone else. We may even feel justified in killing someone who steals it.

If we feel possessive about sex, then we feel the same way about the person who is the source of it. Our sexual partner, be it wife, lover, concubine, husband, *belongs* to us. They are part of our portion of the universe. And we treat them accordingly. We often go so far as to treat them like *things* instead of people. We cannot *own* people. But if we perceive them as material objects, we make the error of believing that we can. Such an error leads to a sense of possessiveness in our personal (that is, sexual) affairs.

Jealousy is related to our feelings of possession. We feel an intense emotion toward those who take that which we believe is ours. As a result, we are jealous when our chosen sex partner engages in even a mild flirtation with someone else. Moreover, if he or she dares to enjoy a real or imagined relationship with someone else, we are furious. We believe that we have been robbed of a portion of our allocation of sexual property. We are therefore justified in our anger and even, in many cases, in taking some drastic action to right the wrong.

We are generally convinced that this feeling is natural and universal. And we would expect to find it in all cultures at all times. Imagine, therefore, the astonishment the early anthropologists must have felt when they discovered societies in which people did not exhibit this quality. Imagine further their wonder when a member of the local tribe offered his wife to a perfect stranger as a sign of hospitality. And how surprised they must have been to see a man sharing his wife with a number of other men, while he himself may have divided his time among two or three wives. The complete absence of jealousy in such circumstances must have seemed incredible.

Sexual jealousy is not necessary. Some people in our society claim that it is an expression of the intensity of their love. But it is not. It is a defense against feelings of rejection. By accepting someone else, our partner appears to be rejecting us. Since we believe that no one else must "use this particular sexual property," we become angry. But our anger, far from being a measure of our love, is a measure of our insecurity. We have suffered a disparagement, with the inevitable accompaniment of self-devaluation.

Possessive love makes it impossible for us to be generous about our loved one's pleasures. We desire his/her happiness but only under special circumstances. We are angered that our paramour can be happy with anyone else. We would rather see him unhappy than have him find happiness with another. If love is concern for the happiness and well-being of the other, it may be that sexual jealousy is really an extremely poor measure of it.

Sexual jealousy is generally greater in men than in women in American society. The idea that a man's wife can be "unfaithful" is a devastating blow to many a man. This, of course, is related to the double standard, which accepts a certain amount of male, but not female, promiscuity. In contrast, the French, for example, do not make as big a fuss over an occasional extramarital affair for either sex, although again the woman is expected to show more restraint.

It is likely that the feeling of sexual jealousy is related to the way the rest of the society views the cuckold. The humiliation a Westerner suffers when his partner goes off with someone else is almost unbearable. He is utterly shattered. He may be laughed at and ridiculed, and if this is not done openly, it is done covertly. Sometimes, instead of being ridiculed, he is pitied by his friends. This is even worse.

It is a simple matter to feel great hatred for the person who has caused one such pain. What we call jealousy is therefore this hatred. It is related to the destruction of our PR personality. The "unfaithful" partner has exposed our vulnerability. Our mask is gone. We are laid naked before the world.

If this is the reason for our jealousy, then it is unnecessary in places where other people do not perceive the situation in this way. And that, in fact, is the case. In societies in which "infidelity" is acceptable, sexual jealousy is practically nonexistent.

CONCLUSIONS

In considering the anthropological data concerning human sexuality, we have tried to show the diverse nature of human erotic expression. The main value in such an exposition should be a loosening of the ethnocentrism which prevents an understanding of man's nature, especially in the highly emotional area of sexuality. Human unhappiness in highly industrialized, technologized societies is related in important ways to our lack of understanding of this important area of functioning. In Chapter 7 we shall explore the changing nature of sexuality in modern societies. We shall see that the "sexual revolution" is influenced in many ways by the knowledge gained from other cultures.

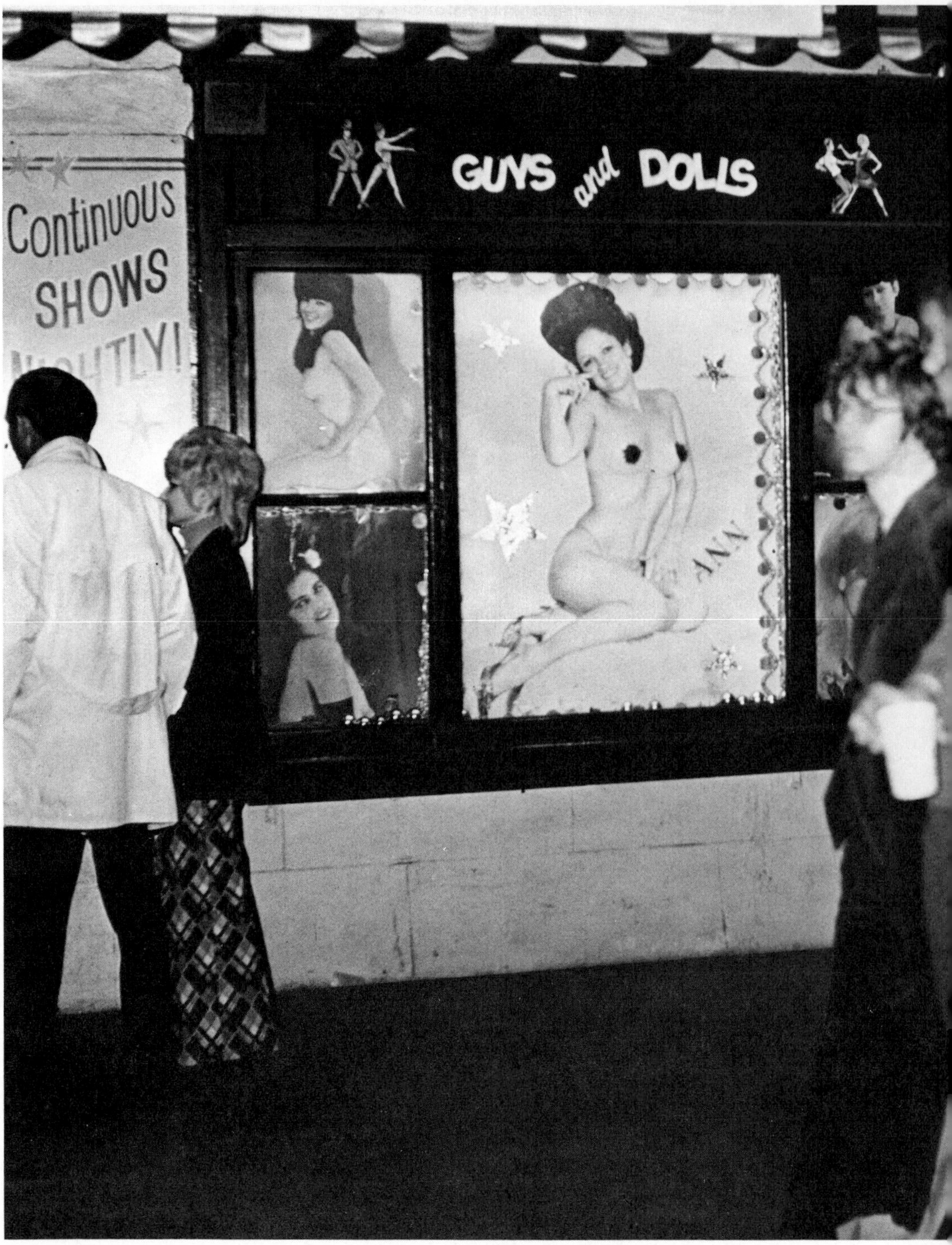
Continuous
SHOWS
GUYS and DOLLS

chapter 7
sex:
the human imperative

SEX IN THE CIVILIZED WORLD

Sex, whether accompanied by love or not, is a natural physical activity. It is not an intellectual pursuit and it cannot be improved by intellectual means. Yet many Americans think that they can learn to enjoy sex by reading about it in books. Literally thousands of books have been written that purport to teach the reader how to increase his potency, prolong the sex act, or maximize the enjoyment to a point beyond his fondest dreams.

It is not impossible to gain valuable knowledge from books. And it is not even impossible to do so in the sexual sphere. But the approach taken on this subject in many books may do more harm than good. In fact, most of the information provided concerning sex and its ramifications is likely to confuse people rather than inform them. In one sense, learning how to enjoy sex through a book is something like trying to learn to ride a bicycle by the same means. A person can have all kinds of theoretical

163

and conceptual understanding about the dynamics of bicycle riding but he will never succeed in balancing himself on one until he sits on it and obtains the feedback from his muscles, until that is, he gets the "feel" of it. This is true of the sex act as well. But in this case there is another complication.

Ideas about how sex is supposed to feel, how it must be done, with whom, under what circumstances, what meaning we should attach to it, how we should feel toward our partner, at what age we should begin, whether it is expected by our peers, whether we should feel guilty if we do or whether we should feel guilty if we don't, what we can do to become better lovers, how we can impress our partners or give them greater enjoyment—all these questions are discussed and argued at great length. And "experts" present their opinions and techniques for the eager public who read and devour the millions of words or attend the thousands of lectures in a vain attempt to find the answers to questions about human sexuality. But most of this advice is self-defeating, for one of the worst things we can do to the erotic experience is to have intellectualized expectations about what we should do or how we should feel.

Just the simple idea that a woman *must* achieve orgasm can prevent her from so doing. Any attempt to *force* the experience to be pleasurable can kill all the feeling in it. The reason that sex is pleasurable and enjoyable for the Samoans, the Trobrianders, the Mangaians is that they have very few preconceived notions about how they *should* act or *should* feel. They merely allow sex to happen to them rather than trying to control it, as many civilized people do. They give themselves to the act and allow the experience to unfold, but they do not try to *steer* the experience in any prescribed direction.

Other kinds of intellectualization also can have the effect of inhibiting the sexual experience. Concern over the morality of the act can be as destructive as any other preconceived attitude. Since in our society sex has usually been made a moral issue, this problem is quite widespread. And for many it is not a simple matter to resolve. Whether or not sex should be a moral question will be discussed shortly. However, the fact is that in many situations, people do believe that sex is permissible only under certain specified conditions. If they find themselves engaged in intercourse when these conditions are not met, the episode is likely to be extremely trying for them. In such a situation, sex is likely to be more painful than pleasurable.

America is in the midst of a revolution in many areas of its life, and sex is certainly one of the more prominent of these. But a revolution is a response to a particular standard which has outlived its usefulness, and in order to understand the dynamics of the revolution, one must understand the tradition against which it is reacting. It is necessary, therefore, to examine the traditional attitudes toward sexuality in American life and attempt by so doing to gain a clearer understanding of those changes which are now sweeping through the society with regard to this very important human function.

Modern American society came out of a puritan tradition which made sex a secret, sinful, almost inhuman thing. From the earliest times, Americans have been even more repressive about sex than their European forebears. Children have been brought up without any understanding of the erotic life and with a great many fears and repressions about the functions of their bodies. Even up to the present generation, children have been taught to believe that sex is evil and that to desire sex too greatly is a serious fault.

The modern attempt to change this view is really only a change on the surface. People so deeply imbued with an idea do not change it easily, and although some Americans try to view sex in a more realistic light, most are still deeply influenced by the traditional views and find themselves appalled and repelled by the "new freedom." The tradition is so strong that people equate morality with the old view and consider the modern attitudes toward sex to be signs of moral decay. The new freedom that is so much a part of the current scene appears to most people in our society to be a regression to a more primitive and therefore less moral period. Sexual laxity becomes for them a letting down of standards or a relaxation of moral control. Such feelings lead to confusion about this basic drive.

Confusion over sexuality and one's sex role is of course another intellectualized area of concern that can have a detrimental effect upon an individual's freedom to enjoy sex. We have already mentioned the problems of women in American society (see Chapter 1), but it would be remiss of us not to consider the specific area of sex with regard to women, for it is in this area that many psychologists and psychiatrists believe that they have been dealt an impossible hand.

Women in American society have until recently been given two communications which are completely contradictory concerning their sexual roles. On the one hand, they have been told that sex is evil, or dirty, or lustful, fit only for animals, and so on. They have been made to believe that "nice" girls don't enjoy sex, don't have fantasies about it, are rather indifferent to the physical side of love, that girls who are easily aroused sexually are "bad," "harlots," "sluts." On the other hand, they have been told that they must be sexually attractive, exciting, stimulating, and sensual. Like the naive heroine they must be sexy but not too sexy. They must not cross the invisible line between being provocative and provoking too much. They must *act* as if they feel aroused, but they must not *really* feel that way.

From the standpoint of the young girl, especially until recently, there was a large no man's land between these two areas which was not clearly defined. She could not discriminate between what was acceptable and what was not. She would often begin to suspect her own feelings. Are they *too* strong? Is she a "Jezebel"? On the other hand, is she too indifferent? Is she frigid? There was no point between these areas where she could feel comfortable. Moreover, she could not discuss this problem with anyone. If she mentioned it to her mother, there was often a terrible kind of embarrassed stammering. And she dared not mention it to her friends for fear of what they would think of her. She felt alone and helpless and somewhat unsure of her sanity.

To add to this problem, the young girl was often deceived by the outward calm and assurance of her friends, practically all of whom were suffering in a similar manner. But the need to present an image of a competent, well-adjusted young adult was so strongly inculcated in the young that each one succeeded in hiding from the other the fact that she, too, had these same doubts and fears. As a result, each youngster felt that only *she* had these concerns, a belief that tended to further isolate her and to increase her fears.

Such preoccupations do not necessarily disappear with age, so that by the time these young women began to engage in sexual activity, whether in marriage or not, they were still beset by a great number of intellectualized notions about what they should or should not feel, what degree of passion they should respond with, how active or passive they should be, and so on. Such considerations could only have a detrimental effect upon the sexual experience because they try to place it under voluntary conscious control. And passion is really an emotion that grows out of a *loss* of control. We will have more to say on this subject presently.

What has been said here in regard to girls is also true, but usually to a lesser extent, of boys. The boy has also been told how he should feel, how he should act, how much guilt he should feel. These concerns have affected him in the same way those of the girl affected her. The difference, of course, is that for the male there are fewer indeterminate areas with which to deal, so that he has never been under the same kind of pressures as the girl. Nevertheless, the stresses have been great enough to give rise to a tremendous number of sexual problems among men as well as women in the modern world.

CONTROLLING THE EXPERIENCE

Americans are particularly concerned about being in control of their feelings. Such phrases as "letting our emotions get out of hand" or "letting go" are used to denote the kinds of behavior we dislike. We are often quite proud of our ability to keep our feelings in check, especially in situations where their free expression would be embarrassing or inappropriate. The open expression of emotion is not generally acceptable in our culture, and we tend to cover the feelings we have so that others do not see what they are.

But there is a certain amount of confusion about what we really mean by the phrase "controlling the emotions." If I am angry at my boss but do not show it for obvious reasons, I may be said to be controlling my emotions. In this sense I am simply *concealing* a feeling from the views of others. This is certainly one thing that we all do at various times. We do not express a particular emotion in spite of the fact that we are clearly aware of its existence. But another meaning of the word "control" has to do with "steering the emotions." And this is something quite different. For this is an attempt by the will to force the emotion to *be* what we desire it to be. For example, if a young child is told that he should love his brother, he may *try* to do so. If a woman believes that she should love her husband, she may make a great effort to bring such a feeling about. If a person is told how he should feel during intercourse, he may make an effort to experience that feeling. Such attempts will usually result in failure.

We cannot love someone simply because we have been told that we must. We cannot love someone *on purpose*. And we cannot steer the sexual experience without destroying it. The very nature of the sexual climacteric requires that one "let go" of his feelings and literally "lose control." The orgasm is a kind of convulsion and *it is patently absurd for anyone to be in control of his own convulsions*. It is for this reason that preconceived notions about how one must feel during the sex act are likely to act as dampers to the experience.

There are, of course, certain kinds of limited control which can be exercised during coitus in order, for example, to prolong or shorten the length of time before orgasm. But the intent here is not to alter the sensation so much as to either heighten or lower it temporarily. Such techniques are not intended to steer the experience in a preconceived direction and, although they may not always be efficient, they are at least not destructive to the enjoyment of sex.

SEX ROLES OF HEROES AND VILLAINS

We have already made reference to the fact that the hero always gets the heroine at the end of the movie and we see them arm in arm heading into a brilliant sunset as the scene fades. This act of touching at the final curtain may often be the first and only time that the two principals have made physical contact with one another in the entire story. The reason for this is partly the result of the traditional attitude toward sex, which holds that the hero must not make physical contact with a woman unless (1) it is his mother, or (2) his intentions are honorable. The hero is not sexy. He is cool. He does not try to seduce women because he knows that this is beneath the dignity of any red-blooded hero. This function is reserved for the villain.

The villain does all the things the hero cannot do. He paws the heroine, grabs her, rapes her if he can. He forces his will on her (to the extent that the meddling hero will let him) and generally demonstrates the identity between villainy and sexuality.

A similar situation occurs on the feminine side. The heroine is almost asexual. She is all but unarousable. She has no physical desire at all. But the villainous, bitch-heroine is something else again. She is oversexed. She has "evil" desires. She would sleep with King Kong if she could get him alone. Her very desire is the quality that makes her evil. There is no doubt about this. How many films were made in the heyday of Hollywood depicting these characters? The clean-cut, smooth-haired heroes and the nice-as-apple-pie heroines going through five reels not doing their thing, while the bad guys and girls were having all the fun.

The end result was only too clear. People with any normal sex drive, and this of course included everyone, came to view themselves as fiends. There were only two possible solutions to this dilemma. One was to deny the existence of the libido and to try to play the role of ascetic hero or heroine. The other was to acknowledge the existence of one's sexuality and feel dirty and guilty about it for life.

It is literally impossible for one to feel guilty about sex and still enter the sexual situation with the kind of abandon necessary to enjoy it freely. This also holds true for those who feel that the body, particularly with regard to the organs of elimination and/or sex, is dirty. Most American men and practically all American women have been brought up to believe one or both of these things. It is no wonder that we have extraordinary sexual problems. And these problems are not diminished by the fact that a great many things in our society are aimed at increasing the sex drive. As we shall see, this only adds to the difficulty.

There is another interesting problem rearing its head in the new climate. In the wake of the sexual liberation of women, men have begun to be much more concerned with their performance. Since, according to the old tradition, women were not supposed to be "experienced" sexually, it hardly mattered how "well" a man performed. In fact, many men never concerned themselves with their partners' enjoyment but were interested only in their own. Now, however, when a woman may have other partners with whom one may be compared, a lot of men become so anxious about how they will be rated that they become impotent or have other kinds of performance failures.

The PR image is, of course, extremely sensitive to sexual disparagement, and the fear of being "graded" lower than some other individual is a real threat to it. One can almost hear the man asking, "Honey, how did I do?" And she answers, "You got a C minus." The PR image would collapse under such a report. Once again, we can see how concern with the image rather than with the experience can lead to unnecessary problems.

THE CONTRADICTORY COMMUNICATION

Psychologists use the term "double bind" to describe a situation in which a person is a victim of two conflicting messages, both of which lead to self-devaluation. Sometimes a mother reprimands her youngster for not showing enough affection for her, and the child, desiring to please her, may respond in an affectionate manner. When he does, however, she will often reject his advances, thus punishing him for the very thing she had obliged him to do.

In some ways society puts people into a double bind regarding sex. Everything we read, the movies we see, the way we dress, the atmosphere of many of our places of leisure are frankly sexy. But the communication that we get from religious and moral leaders, from the traditional roots of our society, carry an opposite message. Everything about sex is all right except sexual intercourse. That is definitely bad. Although sex within marriage was traditionally considered allowable, the implication was that even here it was simply tolerated, but that it was not something that really "nice" people liked very much.

The traditional view of sexuality clashes with the real nature of man who, as we have seen, is a sexy animal. It is impossible for man to really be the creature that he has created out of his puritanical background. He cannot be indifferent to sex and he cannot be disinterested in it. His attempts to play such a role are doomed to failure and have, in fact, caused a great deal of trouble for him in his attempt to make a healthy adjustment to his world. The revolution which is now in progress has observed these facts and has attempted to do something about the problem. One of its aims has been to change one part of the communication. The new view of human sexuality has tried to divorce sex completely from the moral sphere. Sex, it claims, cannot be judged as "good" or "evil" in any moral sense. It is a human function like hunger and thirst, and it has no ethical dimensions.

But the traditional view dies hard. It is deeply ingrained in our people. In spite of their intellectualized sense of freedom, they may often carry doubts because of their early indoctrination. And psychiatrists and psychologists report that the patients they now see appear to have emotional inhibitions regarding sex in spite of these intellectualized feelings of freedom. It is in this sense that the revolution may only be skin deep. For most of

the young people who are rebelling against the tradition had parents who held the old view of sex, and they instructed their children in that way. Such instruction is very persuasive because it is given to the very young long before there is any kind of critical faculty with which one may challenge the conventional wisdom. As any psychologist can attest, early conditioning is the most difficult to extinguish. It is not clear, therefore, that the young people who are trying to change the existing attitudes toward sex have as yet accomplished their ends. The communications are still contradictory but perhaps less so than in the past.

Young people also have other kinds of problems with the new freedom. The current attitude is so pro sex that people who do not want to indulge are liable to the same kind of ostracism as those who did indulge in the past. Some college students complain that they cannot go out on a date without the expectation that they will have sex with their partner whether they really want to or not. This again can be very disturbing to some, especially those brought up in the old tradition who have not yet become comfortable with the new attitudes. Where the students of an earlier day felt inadequate because they *did* give in to their sexual desires, some of today's students have guilt feelings for the opposite reasons. They may also begin to wonder about their mental health if they find that they have less libido than is currently considered adequate. Such problems are simply the other side of the coin.

170

Although monogamy has always been the nominal arrangement in the Western civilized countries, almost nowhere is it universally the *real* practice. Extramarital affairs have occurred with such regularity that one might say that this "custom" is the norm rather than the exception. Kinsey (1948, 1953) estimated that even during the period of the traditional morality, 50 percent of males and 27 percent of females had extramarital affairs at one time or another. And such figures could be spuriously low since Kinsey's work was done by asking people for self-reports about their sexual behavior. People who believe that such behavior is terribly wrong (as would be true of the vast majority of his sample) would be likely to deny this kind of activity more often than not. Moreover, this kind of questioning does not give any indication of the number of people who *would* indulge in extramarital affairs but never get the opportunity for a variety of reasons.

From such considerations it becomes clear that the "new" attitudes are not complete breaks with the past, but simply continuations of behaviors that have been widespread for a long time. In fact, one of the major complaints of young people is that the old morality was simply a great hypocrisy. If we are going to act in certain ways they say, let us at least acknowledge them. It may be true that there is little more extramarital sex than there used to be. But at least now there may be a bit more honesty about it. That is one of the aims of the new approaches toward sexuality.

THE USES AND ABUSES OF SEX

procreation

Human sex, like all other sex, is the act that ensures the continuation of the species. Its biological function is to bring new individuals into the world and thereby increase the probabilities of the survival of the species. This function of sex is not part of the motivation of the individual who seeks and engages in sexual activity. Nature is evidently too wise to entrust so important a function to each individual. For in a certain sense, the birth of offspring signals the future demise of the parent. The earth has only a finite capacity to support life, and the emergence of new individuals is the death knell of those already present. (In some cases, as with the black widow spider, the male dies immediately after completing his sexual mission, even *before* the young are born.) It is not likely that organisms would be too anxious to have young if they realized this fact on a conscious level. In fact, if procreation were left to the whim of the individual, most species might disappear in a generation or so.

But nature makes certain that we will have offspring whether we want to or not. She accomplishes this by making the sex drive practically irresistible. (It may be that no adult goes through life without a sexual experience, for even the ascetic cannot control his dreams. St. Theresa, for example, recounts a dream in which her abdomen is pierced by the spear of the Lord and she feels the fiery point inside her body producing both pain and ecstasy. The sexual symbolism of such a dream is quite apparent.) Nature takes the responsibility for the continuation of the species by literally making sex so powerful as to overcome almost all obstacles.

However, in her overall "strategy," nature sometimes goes too far in one direction. For example, in responding to a brain injury, the swelling (edema), which is part of the body's mobilization aimed at warding off infection, may finally become too great and kill the patient. In quite a similar way, the human species, having overcome most of its natural enemies, is now overproducing its kind. The procreative function of sex has exceeded its purpose and produced a superabundance of individuals. This condition could lead to disaster in a short time. It could even conceivably lead to the annihilation of the species. It is clear, therefore, that the procreative function of sex is now somewhat superfluous. But for human beings, sex has other, perhaps even more important functions.

sex as a physiological need

To the physical organism, sex is a biologically based need or drive which requires certain kinds of activity for its reduction. In a state of arousal, the other functions of sex will often be completely ignored. The only concern in the mature adult is the release of this tension through some kind of sexual stimulation. Although the ideal and probably most natural release occurs in heterosexual union, this is not a necessary outlet. There are, as we shall see, a great number of ways in which human beings can achieve sexual satisfaction of some kind. And from the physiological point of view, one method is approximately as good as another.

Like other physiological needs, the sex drive is related to some extent to deprivation, but the relationship is a rather complex one. There is no simple increase in sexual desire with a long period of abstinence. There may, in fact, be a decrease, at least on a conscious level during long periods without ordinary sexual opportunities. At times, the drive appears to be stronger when sexual outlets are readily available and when sexual encounters are plentiful. Some people believe, in fact, that the desire for sex increases with the frequency of sexual intercourse.

Some interesting facts about the infertility of unmarried adolescents in primitive cultures points up the physiological nature of the sex drive. A number of anthropologists have noted that in the kinds of societies described earlier where a good deal of promiscuous sexual behavior occurs during adolescence, almost no pregnancies occur until a later time, after the youngsters have matured and married. This fact is all the more remarkable because there is a complete absence of any kind of contraception. No form of abortion is practiced although there is no stigma attached to premarital pregnancy.

Ashley Montagu (1957) has made a study of the phenomenon. He notes that there are a number of societies in which marriage does not occur until some years after the establishment of menarche (the first menstruation) which, according to many, is also the beginning of female fertility. In spite of this fact, there is an almost complete absence of pregnancy during this period. "In communities of the Melanesian type, post pubertal adolescent girls indulge quite freely in sexual intercourse without, as a rule, becoming pregnant. Infertility, indeed, among the unmarried women is the rule and pregnancy the exception." The phenomenon appears to be rather widespread among primitives, and a variety of explanations have been offered. One theory held that the female Trobriand Islanders were specially endowed or gifted with ejaculatory powers by which she could, after intercourse, expel the male seed. But such a contraceptive capability is highly unlikely if not physically impossible. There is evidently a better explanation.

Some natives of the Eddystone Islands believe that the practice of certain magical rites contributes to sterility. In fact, it is believed that the rites can be practiced over the male as well as the female with the same results. For here, as elsewhere in the world where intercourse begins early, there are almost no pregnancies until marriage. Some investigators have even felt that although the magic may not be effective, the concoctions used by the participants might have some detrimental effect upon conception. Such a view, however, has little to recommend it. It appears highly unlikely that these people long ago discovered "the pill."

A more likely explanation lies in the fact that the arrival of menarche is not coincident with the beginning of fertility. Montagu (1957) has noticed that among people where intercourse begins with puberty, and where it is freely indulged in for years, pregnancy rarely occurs, even where marriage occurs in adolescence. The young girl seldom conceives until she reaches a fuller maturity. The inference that Montagu draws from this is that puberty is *not* the beginning of fertility and that a certain further maturity is necessary before conception can occur.

If this is true, it tends to support the contention that sex is, at least at times, a physiological function only. For if, as most psychologists believe, the sexual appetite is at its height during adolescence and, if during this period there is little or no chance of conception, then the intercourse which occurs during this period can have no reproductive function. During this period, at least, the function of sexual union must be mainly one of drive reduction.

Another fact which contributes to the idea that human sex in particular is sometimes a physiological rather than a reproductive function relates to the female cycle. In the lower animals, females are generally unreceptive to sexual approaches except at specific times of their periodic cycles. The period of receptivity is called estrus, and it coincides very closely to the process of ovulation, so most acts of coitus end in conception. In the human female there is continuous receptivity regardless of the stage of the cycle. The period of fertility is not marked by any special increase in libido and, in fact, usually passes without a woman's knowledge. (This is sometimes lamented by those who would like to have children but seem to fail in their "timing.")

The actual period of fertility is a small proportion of the entire monthly cycle. The ovum is in the correct position for only a short time, perhaps only a few hours of one day in the entire month. If it is not fertilized at this time, it is carried out shortly thereafter by the menstrual flow. This short period of fecundity is the only time that coitus can result in pregnancy. However, intercourse can and does occur throughout the cycle. The greater part of it must therefore serve a different function.

Another period during which sex is not effective as a reproductive act is during pregnancy. The woman during most of this nine-month period may have a great deal of libido, and coitus may occur quite often, but, again, there is no chance that any of these encounters can lead to conception.

Attributing sex to a purely physiological need evokes a certain amount of criticism from some quarters. Sex, it is said, cannot be divorced from the human contact, the love, the intimacy between people. Moreover, it also cannot be divorced from the participant's ethical values. For sex, this view holds, is tied up with all these things.

Such arguments may have some validity at times and under certain conditions. But they do not change the fact that the sex *drive* is a form of human energy that seeks a mode of release. Our remarks about some of the primitive people who have sexual encounters with practically no "personal" involvement, plus the evidence that the release of sexual energy occurs in various situations in the absence of other living organisms (for example, in masturbation and dreams), seem to support the physiological function some of the time. This is not to say that sex is *only* physiological. It is certainly other things as well. But if we do not understand its biological nature, we will make the kinds of mistakes about it which have been made for centuries. It is just as hazardous to ascribe meanings and qualities to a human function which are superfluous as it is to neglect such meanings. For example, sex sometimes occurs with some kind of *personal* involvement, but it also occurs *without* such involvement. We should be prepared to examine both sorts of sexuality and attribute to each the importance it deserves.

sex as pleasure

Sigmund Freud, the great Viennese physician and father of psycho-analysis, was one of the first men in modern times to establish the importance of human sexuality in the civilized world. Freud believed that man's basic drives came out of a part of the psyche called the *id*. The id was the storehouse of animal instincts which acted on only one basis, the *pleasure principle*. The human organism, he felt, was driven by the desire for pleasure. The energy of the id was the libido or sexual drive. But sex for Freud was a very broad area of human craving. And practically every form of pleasure had sexual content. Almost any part of the body could be stimulated and result in some kind of sexual gratification. For Freud, pleasure and sex were practically synonomous.

Many people disagreed with the view that the libido had such broad parameters. As a result, a reaction against the Freudian view of sex was inevitable. Although the reaction might have been warranted, the tendency has sometimes been to overlook the role of pleasure in the sexual life of man.

In many of the books and scholarly discussions about why sex is so important to human beings, the idea of pleasure is often passed over so lightly that one would think that sex is not a highly enjoyable experience. Perhaps because of our puritan background, we are loath to admit too much enjoyment in "pleasures of the flesh." Some psychiatric studies, in attempting to explain promiscuity, for example, look for all kinds of hidden reasons to explain the behavior without ever weighing the pleasure component as an important part of the motivation. Nevertheless, sex is one of the most intensely pleasurable experiences in life.

Psychologists have done a good deal of research on pleasure as an incentive for behavior. And it is quite clear that although pleasure acts as a reward for certain activities, it also acts as an incentive for the future recurrence of these same activities. The intensity of the pleasure associated with sex guarantees that this will act as a very powerful incentive toward action throughout a person's life. But it is not only the promise of future pleasure that activates the organism, for the drive is so constituted that each small satisfaction of a sexual nature produces an increment in the pleasure of the moment and a higher level of desire. For example, one of the earlier desires in the sexual encounter is usually to touch. This touching brings pleasure and at the same time increases desire for more touching. In other words, the appetite increases up to a point by what it feeds on; and the pleasure does as well.

It is because of the intense pleasure associated with sex that it receives so much attention in our lives. Any discussion can be immediately enlivened by it. Most routine activities can be made attractive by its presence. Movies, theatres, books, magazines, television shows all make use of the pleasure factor in sex in order to gain interest.

The pleasure of sex is so powerful a feeling that during orgasm the higher centers of the brain may actually lose control to the more primitive ones and the body is literally racked by spasms of intense feeling. *The concentration of the sensation may become so pronounced that the person literally forgets where he is as he focuses on the feeling.* Such an experience is both a satisfaction and an incentive, for the anticipation of repeating this pleasurable episode acts as a powerful reinforcer for future sexual pursuits.

SEX AND THE PUBLIC RELATIONS PERSONALITY

Even in societies where sex is relatively free and where everyone can have some kind of sexual relationship whenever he chooses, there is sometimes a kind of prestige attached to sexual prowess or outstanding ability or endurance. For example, in the Polynesian islands it is often considered important that the man satisfy the woman a number of times before he himself reaches orgasm and those who can do so are admired and those who cannot may be ridiculed. But since most people in such cultures generally have a number of sexual partners, there is no particular honor in "conquest." (Or if there is, it is very slight.)

In American society the situation has usually been quite different. Since seduction here is indirect and requires a great deal of finesse and even cunning, it is often looked upon as an achievement rather than as an experience or relationship. This has been especially true in the case of the young adolescent male because he has had to try to overcome the traditional restraints with which the adolescent female has been reared. For the male in our society, therefore, it has often been considered a great accomplishment when he could seduce the most desirable (or perhaps the most unapproachable) girl. It may not have even been necessary to really do so if he could make others believe that he had. Alternatively, the same kind of impression could be made by simply being seen in public with a particular girl who was considered by others to be important or desirable.

Sex is therefore used, especially in restrictive societies, to enhance the PR image. The person adds to his prestige, gains admiration, affection, or even envy from others and feels that he is, in fact, a better person. This situation gives sex and sexual attractiveness a somewhat exaggerated value. People come to measure themselves according to the responses they elicit from members of the opposite sex, and a great deal of anxiety can thereby be aroused. Moreover, it is not only attractiveness that comes to be considered important, for there is also a great emphasis placed on *performance*.

This accent on physical capability is carried to its extreme in what is sometimes called "sexual acrobatics." In an effort to excel in the sexual sphere, some people make extravagant claims about their accomplishments which are intended to impress others with their prowess. Whether such claims are true or not is beside the point. Their effect is to enhance the image of the person making them. But they may also result in raising some serious anxieties in people who do not come up to the "standards." For it becomes necessary not only to become successful in seducing certain people, but in performing certain kinds of acts that reflect favorably upon one's capabilities.

The demands placed on young people by these "requirements" can be tremendous. Since sex is a relatively new experience for them, they are at a loss to know what to do and how to do it. Yet they have heard all of the claims and boasts and their concern that they may not live up to expectations can be so great that it may undermine their own feeling of adequacy. Concerns of this type, as we have already mentioned, can lead to the very things we fear—impotency, frigidity, premature ejaculation and so on. Yet a person's sexual status, his PR personality, rides on these kinds of criteria.

Both sexes are to some extent affected by these kinds of problems regarding status and prestige. But the problems of women are once again somewhat more complex. For the woman, the use of sex to gain status, self-esteem, and so on, is extremely touchy. Since the traditional view of womanhood equates virtue with an absence of libido, a large number of "conquests" will not generally enhance a woman's self-image.

Since it is a good deal easier for a woman to seduce a man than vice versa, there is no particular advantage to simply having intercourse with a variety of men. The woman has to get more of a commitment from a man. As a result, she may hold back her sexual "favors" until a certain kind of promise is made (marriage, going steady, love). If the man is a high-status person, especially if he is higher than she is, she enhances her own PR personality by such a maneuver. It must be stated that in both these cases, and in fact in any situation where sex is used to gain status or enhance the self-image, the relationship is exploitive and manipulative and very often people who engage in such behavior do not enjoy sex very much. Their motivation is not really sexual in the main. It is largely egotistical.

It is also very often seen as status-enhancing to *turn down* an offer for sex. This is more true for the man than the woman because of the difference in availability of partners. There is an unwritten agreement among us that the man who is *cool* is somehow superior to the one who is not. Moreover, by turning down an offer, a man demonstrates both *coolness and abundance*. He is really saying, "I don't need what you offer. I have enough already." He is also saying, "I am too good for you." This is particularly advantageous if the person he turns down has high status. For such an action enhances his image. There is no particular value in refusing an undesirable or low-status person because this is expected. It is when the one refused is considered worthwhile to others that it leads to status enhancement. It is also necessary that others *know* of the event, for if they are ignorant of it, it fails to serve its purpose. For this reason, the rejection may have to be made publicly or at least advertised in some way in order to have the desired result.

Anything that can raise one's status or increase the value of the PR image can also, under other circumstances, have the opposite effect. It can lower the status or devalue the PR personality. Anyone who is spurned by a person having a lower sexual status loses a certain amount of prestige. This is also true of any relationship where the sexual status

There is a great deal of nonverbal sexual communication in dancing. This scene is from County Cork, Ireland.

has not been clearly established. This condition leads to a kind of "game" (Berne, 1964) in which we do not always show our sexual interest in someone until they have committed themselves in some way. But even here their communication may be veiled in such a manner that one cannot be sure that it is really sexual. "Let's have a cup of coffee" can be a simple statement of a desire for coffee or it may be an introductory stage in seduction. The reply is also complicated by ambiguity. Agreement may mean acceptance of the coffee only, but it may also imply an acceptance of the underlying sexual invitation. Refusal may also imply either possibility. Moreover, there is always the possibility that one of the participants does not recognize the underlying message and simply construes the invitation as nothing more than what it is on the surface.

All such possibilities have an effect on the self-image. If we offer such an invitation and it is refused, we can comfort ourselves by believing that only the coffee has been turned down. This, in fact, is the function of the game. It enables us to probe the responses of others without exposing ourselves to the danger of losing status.

Once having committed ourselves sexually to another person, the game is usually over. We can no longer use the disguised forms of communications in the same way. One person in such a situation will often openly pursue another without attempting to cover up his or her intentions. This, of course, increases one's vulnerability, for in such a situation if there is a rejection there is no way to soften the blow.

As we have noted, a woman may feel disparaged by two quite contradictory responses by men. She is insulted if a man desires her *only* physically. "He only wants me for my body." And she is also hurt when a man shows her that she is undesirable sexually. Although these two responses may appear antagonistic, they make a certain kind of sense. They are the result of the way women have been perceived and mistreated by men in the past.

Although men have always tried to seduce women, they have generally had very little respect for those with whom they succeeded. And they have often treated them shamefully as a result. The women, desiring a modicum of respect as persons, were literally forced by this kind of ethic to deny themselves to their suitors or suffer humiliations of all kinds if they "gave in." Moreover, by holding back sex, they were able to feel that there were other qualities for which they were valued. If a man continued to see them without sex, he must have seen some other qualities that he valued. At the same time, our culture tells us that a woman is not a woman unless she is sexually desirable. We have therefore the phenomenon of the American female being insulted by being desired and also by not being desired. This leaves her very little room for developing a feeling of self-esteem. This is part of the dilemma that American women have in the past had to face.

THE NEED FOR CONTACT

Harlow (1960) and others have established that the need for physical contact between one organism and another begins at birth. It is likely that this need never completely disappears, for it appears to be present throughout the life span of many higher animals. Children, adolescents, middle-aged and elderly people all need some form of physical, tactual communication with others. We know from the studies done on infants that deprivation of this need leads to rather dire circumstances. It appears likely that deprivation in later life, although not as critical, may nevertheless give rise to serious problems.

Sex is undoubtedly one of the most important forms of contact in adult life. Most of the preliminaries to intercourse involve some kind of physical closeness, from hand-holding and kissing, to foreplay. Even when intercourse is not the final stage, as in "petting," there is still a great deal of personal contact.

The need for physical intimacy with another human being may be far more urgent than we have thought. We have already mentioned that some theorists believe that violence is a form of reaching out to make some kind of contact when no other form is available. Such a tendency might be increased in the United States, where touching is almost taboo. Many people traveling abroad are amazed to see the way in which Europeans hold hands, put their arms around one another, link arms, and so on, even with people of the same sex. But Americans have developed a kind of distance between one another that is almost never violated. And this must add to our feeling of alienation. Perhaps part of the reason for this distance has to do with our ideas about the body. We are terribly concerned about "offending" others and we take all kinds of pains to avoid doing so by spraying and perfuming and shampooing. But this tendency also keeps before our minds the feeling that closeness can be offensive. If this is true, certainly touching, the ultimate in closeness, must be avoided.

Another reason for our tendency to keep a shield of space between ourselves and others may relate to our competitiveness. There is a tendency to keep one's competitors at a distance. We should not be too friendly with someone we are trying to beat. If we get to like him, we may lose our resolve. If we allow him to get too close, he may learn some of our secrets. We must therefore hold ourselves at a reasonable distance so as not to incur these risks. Research on this subject by Kinzel (1970) and Horowitz (1968) relates this tendency to such variables as violence and psychopathology. Violence-prone subjects have a much larger personal space (which they will protect by overt aggressive means) than control subjects. Hall (1959) has shown that the way we perceive and utilize space is very much culture-bound.

> I have observed an American backing up the entire length of a corridor while a foreigner whom he considers pushy tries to catch up with him. This scene has been enacted thousands and thousands of times—one person trying to increase the distance in order to be at ease, while the other tries to decrease it for the same reason, neither one being aware of what was going on. We have here an example of the tremendous depth to which culture can condition behavior. (Hall, 1959)

If, as we have a right to suspect, there are a great number of Americans who are literally starved for close contact with others and, if there are conventions which make such contact rare or even impossible for some of them, then one way in which these people might find some of the satisfaction they crave may be through sex. We noted earlier that Hollender (1961) has pointed to the fact that many prostitutes find a kind of relatedness in their work which satisfies a need for physical but nonpersonal contact in their lives. It is likely that this need exists in people of both sexes, and they might find promiscuity to be a simple answer to this pressing problem.

The need for contact may therefore find expression through sexual "acting out" when this is the only outlet available. Such behavior may partly explain such phenomena as nymphomania and satyriasis. These terms apply to excessive sexual behavior on the part of females and males, respectively. In these syndromes there appears to be a continuous state of arousal which is never satisfied completely, or if satisfaction occurs, it is of short duration so that almost immediately after intercourse, even with orgasm, the person is ready to begin again. This pattern continues almost endlessly, so that the sexual appetite appears to be insatiable. Although the need for contact does not completely account for this kind of behavior, it may contribute to it. There are other dynamics involved in these excessive reactions, if indeed they really are excessive, which are probably more important. We shall explore these later.

SEX AS HOSTILITY

To most people it may appear peculiar to link sex with hostility. Sex, which they believe to be an act related to love, should be the polar opposite of such things as anger, hatred, and aggression. Hostility and aggression seem to most of us as far removed from sex as it is possible to get. However, this is a superficial view of human motivation.

It is true that many of us equate sex with love, but this identity often exists only on a conscious level. On an unconscious level we may have very different attitudes. This is especially true of those of us who underwent early training in which sex was equated not with love but with evil. Although we may intellectually begin to shed such ideas as we grow to maturity, on a deeper level it is not always a simple matter to expunge them. As a result, many of us may still harbor the less-than-conscious idea that sex can be used *against* others in various ways.

It has been well established both in learning theory and in the psychiatric literature that feelings of hostility can generalize to include entire groups of stimuli (people). Some men, for example, because of an early hatred for one woman, usually their mother, transfer this hatred to all women. Such a feeling is generally unconscious and these men are seldom aware of it. But given this feeling and, along with it, the idea that by seducing a woman one can *destroy* her, such a man might very easily come to use his capabilities in this area in hostile ways. He might literally perceive his "conquests" as acts of annihilation.

The destructive aspects of sex can take other forms as well. It is believed, for example, that sadistic behavior (that is, the inflicting of physical pain on the sex partner) is sometimes associated with intense feeling about sex as degrading. The cruelty becomes a cover-up for real sexual desire while affording the opportunity to "punish" one's partner for his or her sexuality. Since in this instance the intense emotion accompanying the sadistic behavior has become associated with sex, the result is an erotic experience. For the sadist, sexual gratification has become impossible without the inflicting of pain or humiliation (Oliven, 1965).

The sadist as well as the masochist (one who obtains sexual satisfaction by being the recipient of pain) often has had pain associated with erotic experience as, for example, when parents discovered some sort of sexual experimentation which they immediately punished physically. Sadism or masochism may also be the result of reading or hearing about violent crimes, sometimes of a sexual nature. Coleman (1964) observes that almost any strong emotional experience can acquire a sexual component, particularly during the adolescent period. For some masochists orgasm is impossible unless accompanied by intense pain.

There is also some evidence that the Protestant ethic, which exalts deprivation and suffering as a kind of atonement for sin, might contribute to these syndromes. Some people come to feel extremely self-righteous and noble when suffering, and this feeling may pave the way for the sado-masochistic tendencies. In some cases people who feel that any sexual experience must be punished may masochistically submit to that punishment before the sex act in order to get it out of the way so that they can enjoy sex without feeling guilty. It is only possible for sex to be equated with hostility where the erotic appetite is perceived in a negative fashion. One would not believe that he was humiliating a woman by having intercourse with her unless the act itself carried an evil connotation. It is therefore only in those societies where such a connotation is stressed that we might find this kind of behavior.

SEX AND LOVE

Although sex may be an act of love and the ultimate expression of that emotion, it appears from what has been said above that love and sex do not always coexist. The question of love will be discussed later but it is pertinent here insofar as love is often believed to be the sine qua non for either sexual desire or sexual enjoyment.

There is, among Americans, a great deal of controversy concerning this problem. Is sex an appetite, based only on psychological needs—or is it an expression of an emotion that symbolizes and unifies two individuals who become one in an act of love?

It seems apparent from the study of cultures like the Mangaian and some others that sexual enjoyment does not require what we ordinarily call love. Sometimes the Mangaian couples engage in intercourse without having spoken to one another at all. There is, of course, what we might call physical attraction but hardly anything that might qualify as real commitment or even affection.

Perhaps, therefore, the question should be asked differently: Is it possible for sex to be satisfactory in the absence of love? And does love fulfill itself without sex? The evidence is that both questions can be answered in the affirmative. Sex and love are not necessary to one another. One might argue that *complete* sexual fulfillment is not possible in the absence of love, but the Mangaians would probably disagree. And certainly love, even what we call "romantic love," is possible without sex, although such a relationship might fall short of its most complete expression.

But perhaps the *real* question is why we have come to assume that sex and love are so essential to one another. If Americans, especially American women, have been taught that love is good and sex is bad, then the only way that sex can be made acceptable is when it is accompanied by love. For this reason, when the young girl and to some extent the young boy as well first begins to feel sexual desire, they may easily misinterpret its meaning. Since sex is unacceptable, they misperceive their feelings. What they feel must be the long-awaited experience of love. After all, desire is love according to the myths of our time. And desire is certainly part of the thing they feel. Many people therefore do not acknowledge their sexual feelings. Instead they experience the inner urgency that they have as being in love.

Some recent research in the area of emotions can shed some light on this important subject. Schacter and Singer (1962) have shown that the subjective experience of emotion is dependent upon at least two factors. One is physiological arousal and the other, cognitive cues that occur in connection with arousal. These researchers injected subjects with adrenalin and then placed them in a situation calculated to set a cognitive mood state. In some cases the mood was happy. In others, the mood was one of anger. Since adrenaline closely mimics the physiological arousal in human emotions, the aroused state was paired with one or the other kind of emotional setting. The mood was set by a stooge, who acted either happy or angry in the presence of the aroused subject. Schacter and Singer found that those subjects who were subjected to a happy situation became happy and euphoric, while those placed in any anger-producing environment became angry and hostile. Control subjects, by contrast, who were given a placebo injection and then placed in the two "arousing" situations, showed almost no emotional response. The writers concluded that the evidence supported the hypothesis that a person perceives his state of arousal in terms of the context of the cognitive setting in which he finds himself. His emotion is not dictated by the inner state of arousal alone, but by the inner state interacting with specific kinds of information which the subject interprets as pleasant, unpleasant, happiness, anger, sadness, fear and so on.

Walster and Bercheid (1971), impressed with Schacter's findings, have examined the notion that passionate love can be triggered by intense physiological arousal, whether pleasant or unpleasant, which under certain circumstances can be interpreted as love. Such emotional states as fear, anger, frustration, and hatred were examined in a number of experiments in which the subjects were led to label the aroused state as a powerful feeling for a person of the opposite sex. In many cases, these feelings were later perceived as affection or attraction.

The important thing about these findings for our discussion is the discovery that general arousal can be interpreted as love under the right circumstances. And, of course, sexual attraction is a state of very intense arousal. Since the interpretation of the emotional state depends upon the expectations of the person involved, and since romantic love is part of the folklore of our culture, *there is a high probability that sexual attraction will quite often be perceived as love.* This is particularly true in cases where sexual attraction itself cannot be acknowledged.

The *expectation of* "falling in love" therefore leads, especially in con-

*The expectation of "falling in love" is often encouraged by
the repression and misinterpretation of sexual feelings and a
romantic mythology which, in the U.S., has been so ably
abetted by Hollywood.*

nection with the heightened inner feelings that accompany sexual excitement, to the belief that these feelings are in fact love. Such an experience may be very common, and there is some question about its ability to sustain itself for any extended period of time. But it does seem to explain the kind of meteoric experience of romantic love which is so engrossing while it lasts and so widely sought by people in our society.

Such a feeling is not too dangerous in adolescence since it rarely involves the principals in a really permanent relationship. Unfortunately this kind of immaturity is not confined to the adolescent period, and many of us carry such misperceptions into our later years. It is in these latter situations that such misreadings of our feelings can be disasterous, for in these circumstances we may make permanent kinds of commitments.

185

Sex is not love and it generally cannot be sustained over long periods of time without love. It is likely that many marriages fail because the couples have mistaken sexual attraction for love. Sex without love may be delightful, but it is not a basis for marriage.

We can deceive ourselves about love if we believe that it is necessary to do so. And we do it in numerous ways. Parents are supposed to love their children. Children are supposed to love their parents. People in encounter groups are supposed to love (after a time) the other members. And they all do sometimes. But sometimes they don't. And sometimes people who are sexually attracted to one another don't love each other. And if they cannot or will not accept physical attraction as part of their being, they must deceive themselves about love.

Many people believe that a relationship based upon sex without love is too shallow and superficial to be meaningful. This, of course, depends upon what we mean by "meaningful." In those situations where a person enters into the relationship expecting nothing more than sex, there is not likely to be anything more to the situation. And this may be perfectly acceptable to him (or her). But the question of whether one can have a good sexual relationship with someone in the absence of love really revolves around one's acceptance or nonacceptance of the traditional beliefs of the culture. Biologically, sex does not require love. But our culture has insisted for quite a long time that without love, sex is degrading. For those who accept this idea and, even in this day of liberated people, there are a great number who do, sexual relationships in the absence of some deeper attachment are inadvisable. Such people will only feel guilty or hurt and may come to see themselves as used by the other.

On the other hand, if both parties can clearly accept sex with one another without deeper commitment, without guilt or belittlement, then as adults they may be able to approach the situation somewhat as the Mangaians do. If so, it is their decision to make. But let us make an important point. It is possible and necessary for one person to show consideration for another whether or not there is a deeper relationship between them. It is particularly necessary for a person to have respect for human beings with whom he interacts sexually. For sex is an extremely intimate, shared joy. This means that if two adults decide upon a purely sexual relationship, it can only be satisfactory for both if they do not use it to hurt or manipulate one another. It also means that they will not simply have sex with one another and ignore their responsibilities in other areas. A man who respects women will not carelessly get a girl pregnant and leave her to face the consequences. And a woman will not knowingly spread venereal disease to someone because she doesn't care about him. It would seem that a sincere respect for one another is better than a sentimentally contrived "love," which is usually a deception to both parties.

One other observation is important. Since it is extremely difficult for people in our society to relate to others in a purely sexual way, there is a danger that people will try to rationalize their feelings and insist to themselves that they are free of guilt concerning such a relationship, when in fact they have only repressed it. Such a situation is fraught with danger. Repressed guilt can lead to all kinds of problems, and the "peace of mind" bought at this price can be extremely expensive.

It is simple for the Mangaians to deal with the purely sexual encounter. It may not always be simple for us.

THE SEXUAL OBJECT

Many women have long deplored the fact that men often perceive them as playthings, to be used for sexual gratification and little less. This attitude, as we have noted, is considered by most women to be disparaging. But it appears that there is, even among some sophisticated people, the implicit acceptance of the "sex is evil" dictum. If this were not so, being desired for sex only would not be objectionable. The disinclination to being perceived as "merely a sex object" seems to imply some of the old puritanism, which such people often believe they have outgrown. They would never, for example, object to being perceived as "merely an *intellectual* object" or as "merely a *personality* object." To be desired for one's qualities of generosity or kindness is perfectly acceptable. But to be desired for one's sexual attractiveness is for most women, demeaning. Somehow it seems that we are still convinced that our sexuality is unworthy or unclean.

The use of the word "object" in this context tends to obscure the real problem. (We have already observed that treating another human being as an *object* is demeaning whether it be as a sex object or any other kind of *thing*.) It might be better if we used the term "sexual person" rather than sexual object. For if sex is not really demeaning, being desired sexually should be no less acceptable than being desired for any of our other qualities. Only if one has such an attitude can he or she enjoy a sexual relationship that does not include any long-range commitment. Sex without love is only satisfying, therefore, accompanied by *respect for the other person* and *respect for sex itself!*

It has been noted by sociologists and anthropologists that where there is no love mystique, where the concept of romantic love is absent, there is no romantic love in the sense that we know it. In societies where, for example, marriages are arranged, there is no such phenomenon as "falling in love." This is not to say that in such cultures there is no such thing as love, even love between the sexes. It is merely to state that what we have defined as "romantic love" is mainly a culturally learned concept.

We have presented a number of reasons for this. We have shown that falling in love, like other culturally defined activities, is something that is expected of everyone. And we tend to "experience" those things which are expected. Moreover, since we believe that we are less than normal and complete without this experience, we are constantly "on the lookout" for its occurrence. We are assured by every love song, by every romantic novel, movie, and play that falling in love is as inevitable as the sunset. Such powerful forms of suggestion are not easily ignored.

The *desire* for romantic love is another important reason for its appearance. Once convinced of its reality as well as its beauty, it is bound to evoke strong wishes for fulfillment. Such needs will in themselves bring about the illusion of the experience.

A third reason for the "in-love" syndrome relates to the self-image. Love is the ultimate reward of the hero and heroine. And to be in love makes each one of us heroic. It therefore becomes an essential part of one's PR personality to find someone to love. This someone, we may believe, was put on earth especially for this purpose. Since the hero and heroine always live happily ever after, this becomes the only fate possible once "the right one comes along."

The object of romantic love cannot be real. The *paramour* is an impossible dream. The perfection, the never-changing beauty, the eternal bliss of "togetherness" are impossible fancies. It is one thing to desire them. It is quite another to believe that they can come to pass. The idea that one can live in a paradise of eternal bliss is pure fantasy. It is only by projecting our desires and dreams onto the love object that we allow ourselves to be so deceived. And such deception leads to a very rude awakening when the realities of life, love, and marriage come crashing in on us.

As already noted, part of the responsibility for this illusion must be blamed on our attitude toward sex. There is little doubt that the traditional attitudes toward sex have made their contribution to the "love mystique." For in the absence of a clear experience of sexuality, an individual is bound to perceive his needs in terms acceptable to his times. Feelings that are originally sexual become altered by the process of inhibition (repression) and are experienced as "romantic" rather than sexual. This gives rise to a kind of *nongenital romantic love syndrome* in which the idealized lover is literally perceived as having no genitalia. The romantic figures of juvenile fiction, as we have already shown, are sexless insofar as intercourse and its correlates are concerned, although they play masculine and feminine roles to conventional perfection.

Romantic fiction shows heroes and heroines who are almost obsessively "clean"—not only in their crisp linens and sparkling ornaments, but in their sexless, passionless "love." These characters are depicted without bodily functions. They eat and drink, but they could never be imagined urinating or moving their bowels. They dance for hours but they never sweat. They hold hands or even kiss (somewhat coldly, without much fervor), but the lower parts of their bodies never touch. Such is the perception of romance, devoid of its sexual component.

The romantic syndrome is not really love at all. It is infatuation. It is an ecstatic but temporary state in which the person, generally too immature for a real love relationship, is in love with love. It is almost immaterial who the object of his love is, for the lover does not have anything like a real perception of that person at all. The infatuated person has so idealized the image of the "loved one" that it is entirely a creation of his own making. He attributes all kinds of impossible qualities to his paramour and in the haze and dazzle of the moment is certain of their existence. If there is a sexual component to such a feeling it is usually repressed, so that the lovers themselves are swept away by the romantic aura which blinds them to the erotic quality that underlies their feeling. Many of these attachments are short lived for, like a meteor, they burn fiercely for a few brief moments and then, having consumed all their energy, they vanish as quickly as they came.

But other infatuations never get the opportunity to burn themselves out because they remain unrequited. When this occurs, the memory of this youthful passion may go on for years since it never has to be tested by reality. Unrequited love can be carried in its pristine state for a lifetime in fantasy. We can maintain all our exaggerated ideas of how beautiful and perfect it might have been. And we may never allow anyone else to fill the place that was once occupied by this fantasy "lover."

Perhaps the main disadvantage of the romantic love myth is that it fosters a concept of love that is destructive of man's real capacity to love. The infatuation that is the core of most romantic love is extremely self-centered and narcissistic. The lover is only interested in his own needs and has no real understanding of the needs or desires of the other. Moreover, his love is not based on the actual person but on a projection which is almost a complete fiction. This projection makes the loved one appear perfect and therefore without any needs of his or her own. The lover is thus relieved of the responsibility of having to consider the other's welfare. Infatuation is therefore generally selfish. Many young people, believing that they are in love, are extremely self-centered in their dealings with those they are supposed to love and are appalled when that person does not accede to their every wish.

But human beings are capable of another kind of love, love that is centered in the other person. It is a love that perceives its object realistically. It is a love that concerns itself with the loved one's welfare. The most beautiful sexual experience is, of course, the one which is the vehicle for the expression of this love. The tender passionate caring which one person feels for another finds its greatest fulfillment in the physical union of two individuals.

This kind of love, however, is not as intense in its inception as is romantic love and for that reason it may at first not appear to be love at all. This is particularly true of people who have been told by their parents, friends, the media that they will feel fireworks go off in their heads and bells ring "when they meet the right person." Such a suggestion is doubly dangerous. In the first place, since people believe that they are abnormal if such a thing does not occur, they will try very hard to experience it. And such fantasizing leads to the illusion of the experience. But, more importantly, this idea fosters the belief that there is only one person in the world who can trigger this event. And so love becomes a very narrow kind of relationship with only one human being. Such an attitude is not conducive to a real capacity to love, as we shall see later.

SEX AND MARRIAGE

Sex within marriage is the only officially sanctioned kind of erotic activity in our society. Even within the marriage bed various kinds of activities are frowned on by the Judeo-Christian tradition. In fact, there are a number of states in which it is *illegal* to do a variety of things that almost all married couples do at one time or another. Some of these may involve nothing more than varying from the conventional position of the man prone on top of the supine woman. Nevertheless, within these narrow confinements, sex is considered legitimate and one might therefore think that it takes place freely. Nothing could be further from the truth.

People come to the marriage bed with the same set of hangups with which they approach all the aspects of their lives. The attitudes which have been deeply ingrained in children and adolescents do not suddenly disappear simply because someone has said a few words legitimizing the relationship. Inhibitions, fears, shame, disgust, guilt, and pain are still present in those who have harbored these feelings in the past. Such problems can even be intensified in marriage by the newly acquired necessity to function sexually where until this time these difficulties may have been avoided by not being tested.

THE BATTLE

What has been termed "the battle of the sexes" is not misnamed. This is true particularly in the case of people who are immature and who have mistaken need or infatuation for love. It can also be true for some people who have genuine affection for one another, for even in these relationships, there are times when one or the other party may try to use love or sex as punishment or reward. When the sexes engage in battle, sex is often the weapon.

Often it is the woman who refuses sex with her husband, for reasons which may be difficult for either party to understand. For example, the husband may forget a little courtesy, like holding a door or taking her arm while walking. Or his transgression may be something much more serious, such as looking longingly at another (perhaps younger) woman or coming home late without an explanation. Whatever the actual circumstances, the wife is piqued, often without consciously realizing it. She carries her resentment quietly under her usual demeanor throughout dinner and the rest of the evening. But then at bedtime the unsuspecting husband begins to make romantic overtures toward her and she cannot respond. Her attitude is contained in the unspoken thought, "he doesn't deserve it. And besides I can't put my heart into it feeling the way I do." The argument that often ensues does nothing to diminish the feelings of hostility, which are now mutual. It might even happen that if the wife finally agrees that having gotten everything off her chest she is now willing, the husband may be so angry that he refuses or, even if he tries, he may find himself impotent.

Of course, there are other reasons for either party refusing to engage in intercourse. They may *really* have headaches, or feel tired, or simply have no desire. There may, in fact, be a great difference in libido between the partners. These, of course, are legitimate reasons for rejecting the other person's advances and should not be perceived by that person as disparagement. Unfortunately, this is not always the case. Our PR image is conditioned to respond to such treatment with resentment and such resentment often harms an otherwise affectionate relationship.

If the woman uses sex as punishment and reward, the man has his own weapons in the battle of the sexes. If the woman withholds sex, the man can retaliate by withholding love. The behavior may or may not be a conscious effort on the part of the man to hurt his wife, who has by her action hurt him. He may, in fact, not always recognize the resentment that he harbors. Yet he acts in ways that are cooler and more distant than usual. And although there may be no verbal exchange between them which clarifies the underlying hostility, his wife begins to feel its presence. Such behavior can lead to a vicious circle in which case the hostility can escalate over a period of time until the relationship between the two partners is very badly strained.

There are, of course, other possible outcomes. The woman may begin to feel guilty, for she sees her husband sulking unhappily about the house and feels that his discontent is a result of her behavior. In this case there may be a reconciliation in which intercourse becomes the act of apology for both parties. It is likely that such a pattern of behavior can become a recurring game for many couples. It is a destructive one, however, because it bases the sexual encounter on "making up" rather than on love. It means that the relationship requires some hostility and reconciliation in order to prove satisfying. It is therefore based on immature attitudes on the part of both individuals.

Sex may be refused for another reason. Either partner, but more usually the woman in our society, may refuse sex in order to establish some kind of superiority, especially moral superiority. By refusing in a derogatory way, she may be communicating a message which says, "I am not the animal you are, and I don't want to engage in that kind of thing." It is likely that here, too, there is some underlying hostility. A woman who loves her husband and feels friendly toward him does not want to disparage him in this way. However, if she has been hurt in some way, or made to feel inferior to him, or to men in general, then she may have the need to get back at him in this manner. Once again there may be little relation between this behavior and the person's underlying sex drive. In marriage, the libido can become subservient to these other needs, which may have a greater effect upon the sex life of the partners than other more biological factors.

SUPPLY AND DEMAND IN THE SEXUAL MARKETPLACE

We have already noted that as a society of consumers, Americans "shop" for sex as they shop for other commodities (see Chapter 5). Although most people will not admit it, there is a certain kind of "bargaining" which takes place in the search for sexual partners in which each individual "purchases" whatever he can afford. The currency in this exchange may be real money, or it may be currency in another form. Value in the sexual sphere refers to desirability. A highly desirable sex partner brings a "high price" in the sexual arena. This may be in the form of a high-status partner, or in the form of a more tangible reward. Even in the world of prostitutes, there are the high-priced call girls, usually rather attractive, and the street walkers who are not too well endowed and who receive a good deal less money.

Although this kind of differing evaluation is obvious in the sphere of commercialized sex, it exists just as surely in "legitimate" circles. But in the latter situation, the "bargaining" is much more subtle. Our earlier reference to Fromm (1956) has pointed out that modern society has so alienated people in the industrialized areas of the world that it has made them slaves to the consumption-oriented colossus. They are, he says, automatons. "Automatons cannot love; they can exchange their 'personality packages' and hope for a fair bargain." The search for a fair exchange on the sexual market starts with a process of elimination. Some partners are simply out of a person's league. They are too beautiful, too rich, too powerful, or move in circles too far removed for contact. The real bargaining occurs within limits that have already eliminated these kinds of prospects.

Other possibilities are eliminated simply by the fact that individuals who might otherwise be available to one another are separated physically. They live too far apart to see each other often. Or they meet only in passing one another once and then go their separate ways. The number of available partners therefore becomes limited by a number of circumstances. Each person, however, does his or her best to maximize these potential partners by making themselves more attractive, increasing their income, moving upward through the status structure, and so on. Finally, each person must deal with the real choices available to him. He or she (sometimes rather cold-bloodedly) weighs the "benefits" offered by one or the other suitors. In some situations there is only one suitor and it appears from past experience that there will not be others, so that the final decision is more or less predetermined. In any case, a choice is finally made. Once having decided, there is only one thing left to do. That is to convince oneself that he or she has fallen in love with that person. This does not present too great a problem. For although automatons may be incapable of love in Fromm's sense, they can believe that they have fallen in love when this becomes necessary. And so the bargaining is over.

If the foregoing description sounds cynical, it is because such a practice is far more widespread than most people realize. Most of us grow up with the dream that somewhere there is one person who is right for us and that when we find that person, there will be no doubts and no hesitations. Since we hate to give up this dream, we try to force reality (the shopping and bargaining procedure) to fit the dream. Such self-deception leads to serious problems when such a relationship is used as a basis for marriage.

It must be made clear that not all people in our society are incapable of forming real attachments or feeling love. However, the capacity for mature feeling is not widespread.

> No objective observer of our Western life can doubt that love—brotherly love, motherly love, and erotic love—is a relatively rare phenomenon, and that its place is taken by a number of forms of pseudo-love which are in reality so many forms of the disintegration of love. (Fromm, 1956)

The fact that real love is very rare and that it is so very seldom a part of the relationship in marriage is a grave problem for our society. We shall deal later with the problem of love in the healthy individual.

HOMOSEXUALITY

Homosexuality is considered here as a special problem, not because it really is, but because there is so much misunderstanding about its nature. Homosexuality is defined as any erotic relationship between members of the same sex. And in order to understand it, it is necessary to understand a little about sexual attraction in general.

The sexual drive is dependent upon a number of factors, the most important from a physiological point of view being hormonal. The relationship between the various endocrine glands is extremely complex and is still incompletely understood. However, it is quite certain that both male and female hormones are present in both sexes. In lower animals, a male can be made to act like a female (and vice versa) by the administration of enough of the hormone of the opposite sex. But in human beings the situation is, as usual, more complicated. The kind of sexual response elicited in humans depends to a great extent upon social cues interacting with the physiological arousal of the organism. And it is believed by most psychologists that anyone is capable of directing his or her erotic desires in a variety of ways, especially under certain kinds of environmental conditions. This means that our sexual appetite is not perfectly specific, especially when it first appears, and that there are certain requirements for it to become so. Another way of saying the same thing is that we are all potentially bisexual and, given the necessary circumstances, anyone might exhibit such tendencies.

The statement above is perhaps one that causes more consternation among Americans than any other. We are horrified at the idea that *we* might have such leanings. But it is our denial of femininity in men and masculinity in women that leads to our perception of homosexuals as monstrous creatures who should be treated like criminals and punished or at least avoided in disgust. Such an attitude is similar to the one we have toward other "villains," and it is related to the same kind of defensiveness. But it is unfortunate for two reasons: it brands the homosexual in a way that is disparaging to him, and it gets us terribly uptight about our own natures. Fears about our own possible homosexual tendencies can lead to very serious psychopathology, especially if homosexuality itself is branded by the society as some monstrous abnormality.

It is therefore necessary to see this life style in its proper perspective. For it is more a life style than a perversion. It is, for some, the way they have come to express their sexuality, and it is as natural to them as heterosexuality is for others. It is also important to remember that many people who are considered homosexual insofar as society is concerned are actually bisexual. But since any homosexual act is considered indicative of one's sexual orientation, many such people are considered completely "queer."

etiology of homosexuality

There are a number of theories about how homosexuality occurs. And they are related in a certain way to how heterosexuality develops. To repeat something we have already mentioned, the libido is directed in a very nonspecific way, especially in the early years of childhood and adolescence. And the manner in which it finally fixates upon its permanent object depends on many factors. In a sexually repressive society, many of the factors that can give rise to homosexuality are present in both men and women.

Given the fact that each of us carries within him or her the hormonal secretions of both sexes, our erotic appetite can probably be aroused by either sex. And during our development we become attracted to one and lose our interest in the other. For most of us this attraction is toward the opposite sex. But for a number of others, it is not. Let us see why.

factors leading to homosexuality

Physiological factors by themselves do not seem to be determinants in homosexual development. The main determinant appears to be psychological. Certain environmental influences working with the hitherto undirected libido can lead to an attachment to someone of the same sex. From then on, the pattern has been set. It appears that heterosexual patterns develop in a similar way. As Coleman (1964) indicates,

> There is no *a priori* assurance that . . . heterosexual behavior will develop without specific social encouragement, and in societies which have en-

couraged homosexuality, sexual development has been found to be directed toward such homosexual patterns.

Coleman also mentions a number of conditioning experiences which tend to establish homosexual tendencies:

1. Early homosexual experiences. These alone do not set the trend but, when reinforced by continual similar experiences, they can be significant.
2. Pathogenic family background. Sometimes a domineering mother can "castrate" the males of the family so completely that a young boy cannot make an identification with his father. And he identifies instead with his mother. In the case of lesbianism the father may be the culprit. He is often puritanical and reacts very harshly to the young girl's normal heterosexual explorations. In a way, he communicates that closeness with any male except himself is distasteful and evil.
3. Traumatic social experiences. Sometimes the child is ridiculed by people of the opposite sex in such a way that he cannot overcome the feeling of humiliation. This experience, coupled with acceptance by a homosexual at just the "right time," can lead to the desire for only such a partner in the future.
4. Prolonged sexual frustration. In any situation where normal heterosexual partners are unavailable or unresponsive, the only outlet possible may be with another member of one's own sex. This situation, of course, occurs in jails, in military and naval life, and in societies where heterosexual pairings are prevented for long periods of time by social custom.

homosexuality—disease or variation on a normal theme?

The problem of how to classify homosexuality has been getting some new attention in recent years. The old idea was that homosexuality was a hideous abnormality. This view gave way about a half century ago to the newer conception of homosexuality as a disease. But there have been objections to this theory more recently because it brands as deviant a person who might otherwise be considered a normal member of society. Moreover, the normal/abnormal dichotomy has begun to lose some of its meaning, since almost every kind of pathology exists in some quantity in "normal" individuals.

Whether or not homosexuality is "normal" or "abnormal" is now beside the point. We have already pointed out that there is little real homosexuality among animals in the wild, but that it sometimes appears in zoos. This could indicate that homosexuality is a natural result of restraint. We have also seen that in places like Mangaia, where there is practically no restriction on heterosexual activity, homosexuality fails to appear. Its presence in modern industrialized society might therefore be a response to the restraints that such a society places on sexual expression.

Homosexuality might be viewed, therefore, as an adaptation by some people to the conditions under which they live. It is a mode of sexual expression and whether or not we approve is irrelevant. These people are human beings who have simply made an adjustment to their world that differs from the rest of us. They should neither be condemned nor ostracized. And the question of "treatment" becomes academic since most of these people have little or no desire to be "cured." One can imagine how he would feel if a psychologist offered to "treat" him for his heterosexual tendencies. There are, of course, a few cases of people who change from homo- to heterosexual behavior. But such individuals are generally very strongly motivated and are in all likelihood bisexual to begin with.

It seems reasonable, therefore, that any kind of sexual behavior between consenting adults should be viewed as falling within normal limits. This is particularly true of behaviors which these people themselves do not wish to change. Such life styles, when they do not interfere with the life styles of other individuals, are perhaps better dealt with by leaving them alone. This may not be a popular attitude but it is one that is growing very rapidly as people become educated about the facts. It is not necessary to emphasize our own heterosexuality by condemning and persecuting those who behave differently. This is often a defensive way of refuting our own homosexual feelings. If we simply realize that such feelings exist in all of us in an unconscious form, we need not adopt such a strategy. We might also note that the acquisition of freer attitudes toward "aberrant" sexual behaviors simplifies the legal problems that have so plagued this entire issue in recent years.

THE SEXUAL REVOLUTION

Many of the comments that have been made up to this point have referred to the traditional sexual attitudes in the United States during the last generation. These attitudes are based largely on the puritan ethic and are accepted by the large majority of people brought up prior to the 1960s. As we have already noted, these traditions are so powerfully conditioned that most people believe that they are laws of nature or of God rather than culture-bound, largely arbitrary customs. It is acknowledgment of this fact that has to a great degree led to what is called the *sexual revolution*.

Young people growing up in the world today are often perplexed by the hypocrisy of their elders. Marriage, they are told, is sacred. Fidelity is the most important ingredient in that sacred institution. But it is clear on all sides that almost no one acts as if he really believes these statements. Moreover, many young people cannot understand why a perfectly natural human function should be considered immoral whether outside marriage or within it. How, they ask, can the words of a stranger or the printing on a piece of paper change something from being immoral at one moment into something sacred the next?

There are other reasons for the changing attitudes that are part of the modern consciousness. The old morality appears to many to have failed. People have been preaching brotherly love for centuries while they have been killing one another by the millions; and now it appears that these very values have brought the world to the brink of nuclear destruction.

Another objection to the traditional morality is related to violence and sex. We have on the one hand prohibitions against children seeing any kind of sexual activity while, on the other, no restrictions are placed on their viewing the most barbarous violence. To many young people, this inconsistency seems very strange. What we seem to be communicating to children is that sex is bad but violence is all right. We do not, of course, say this openly. In fact, consciously we pay lip service to the idea that violence is bad and sex is a part of love. But the communication that underlies this pretty bit of rhetoric denies it.

Such considerations have led to a complete reassessment of the values within the entire Western civilized world. Sex is only one among these values, and the sexual revolution is merely a part of a larger revolution that the entire society appears to be undergoing.

Young people are also rebelling against the puritanical idea that anything that is pleasurable is evil. Why, they wonder, should something that brings pleasure be prohibited? If something is pleasurable, why should we not experiment with it, especially if in so doing one does not harm anyone else? The new morality has turned the priorities around. Instead of self-denial and the hope for happiness in the next world, the aim is for happiness spiced with pleasure in this one. For in the age of the existential recognition of death, planning for a world that may never be seems the height of folly.

The sexual revolution, therefore, in its most thoroughgoing form, throws away all the old codes of behavior. Marriage, monogamy, premarital chastity, sexual exclusiveness, alienation from the body—all of these are abandoned or at least diminished in importance. Freedom is the watchword. The individual is free to express his or her sexuality in a variety of ways. Such sexual expression is seen not as evil or sinful but as natural and healthy. The selection of partners is based on new criteria—not on expediency, nor on marital status or eligibility, nor on other accepted measures. Moreover, some differing forms of marriage are being explored to attempt to find alternatives to what is seen by many as the bankruptcy of monogamous marriage in the modern world.

At this end of the spectrum a great variety of experimental approaches to the expression of human sexuality are underway. We shall mention a few of them shortly. But revolutions, like other cultural phenomena, do not affect everyone in a complex society in a similar manner. As a result, there is a long continuum of patterns of behavior from one end to the other. We have, on the one hand, very "free" sexual encounters without obligation and, on the other, a variety of arrangements in which *responsibility* is the major concern.

VARIETIES OF NEW SEXUAL EXPRESSION

One major change in young people in the latter part of the twentieth century is in their attitude toward premarital sex. Although there was a great deal of premarital intercourse in other periods, it was usually considered wrong, and those who indulged generally felt a certain amount of guilt. The major difference in this area is not so much in the *amount* of premarital sex, but in the feeling that such behavior is not necessarily evil. This attitude is also carried over in some cases into marriage, so that some people feel that extramarital sex is not to be condemned either (O'Neill and O'Neill, 1972). Moreover, the double standard has ceased to apply in many such cases, so that what the man does the woman may also do if she so desires.

"Swinging" is one of the forms of this kind of sexual activity. In this kind of arrangement a couple, usually married, gets together with another couple, and they change partners for one evening. In some cases the swinging group may include more than two couples and the sexual activity may be more orgiastic and open.

> At first glance it would seem that married couples who "swing" have serious psychopathology, in view of sexual behavior so contrary to the popular belief of fidelity in marriage. While some swingers may have serious emotional problems the evidence to date would suggest that many fall into the category of "normal" persons . . . most are conventional middle-class individuals who show no social aberration other than their propensity to swing. (Auerback, 1971)

There are differences of opinion on this, however, for a number of psychologists, psychiatrists, and religious leaders believe that swinging is a sign of immaturity if not outright bestiality.

Although swinging is considered quite modern, it may not be as new as some people believe. Lipton (1965) reports that this kind of behavior has occurred again and again throughout history and that it has been prevalent in its modern form for a long time, on a far larger scale than most of us realize. The same may be said of the modern experiments in communal living.

THE COMMUNAL EXPERIMENTS

A number of young people, and a few older ones as well, have been investigating alternatives to the traditional monogamous kind of relationship that has for centuries been the cornerstone of the Judeo-Christian concept of the family. We have already noted that polygamous relationships are widespread in animal life as well as in human societies in various parts of the world. Most people, however, do not realize that communal arrangements are not new in the United States by any means. There have been a number of groups in American society who have practiced some form of multiple marriage from time to time. So the experiments now being undertaken in various parts of the country, rather than being unique, are actually continuations of these kinds of efforts.

the oneida experiment

Many of us are familiar with the polygamy of the Mormons, who until some years ago, still permitted a man to have a number of wives. But there are even more complex arrangements than this in American history. One of the most interesting was the system developed by John Humphrey Noyes in 1848 in Oneida, New York. Noyes was an extremely religious man; everything he did was related to his interpretation of the Scriptures. His unorthodoxy got him into trouble from time to time and he finally formed his own religious group (the Perfectionists) which was the basis for his theory of social conduct.

Noyes believed quite literally in the oneness of man with God. He also believed in the oneness of man with man—what one man in the community had, all men had. This was true, not only of property, for Noyes was a communist in the etymological sense of that word, but also of love. For Noyes, Christ had spoken for the unity of all believers. He supported his view by quoting scripture:

> All that believed were together and had all things common; and sold their possessions and goods, and parted them to all, as every man had need. The multitude of them that believed were of one heart and of one soul;

neither said any of them that aught of the things which he possessed was his own; but they had all things in common. Acts 2:44–45 and 4:32. (Noyes, 1966)

Noyes felt that the same law that abolishes exclusiveness in property also abolished it in terms of mates and children.

The possessive feeling which expresses itself by the possessive pronoun *mine*, is the same in essence when it relates to money or any other property. Amativeness and acquisitiveness are only different channels of one stream.

Thus the idea of sexual communism was merely an extension of the idea of property communism. The *family* of the Oneida Community was the community itself. Every man was "married" to every woman and vice versa. Moreover, the children were the responsibility of all. *All* adults were considered parents of *all* children. The institution of complex marriage meant that any man and any woman in the community were free to have intercourse whenever they chose. There was no sanction against promiscuity, which was considered a natural part of community life.

The idea that love for one person automatically precludes love for any other was challenged by Noyes:

All experience testifies (the theory of the novels to the contrary notwithstanding), that sexual love is not naturally restricted to pairs. Second marriages are contrary to the one-love theory, and yet are often the happiest marriages. Men and women find universally (however the fact may be concealed) that their susceptibility to love is not burnt out by one honey-moon, or satisfied by one lover. On the contrary, the secret history of the human heart will bear out the assertion that it is capable of loving any number of times and any number of persons, and that the more it loves the more it can love. This is the law of nature, thrust out of sight and condemned by common consent, and yet secretly known to all.

The law of marriage worketh wrath. 1. It provokes to secret adultery, actual or of the heart. 2. It ties together unmatched natures. 3. It sunders matched natures. 4. It gives sexual appetite only to a scanty and monotonous allowance, and so produces the natural vices of poverty, contraction of taste and stinginess or jealousy. 5. It makes no provision for the sexual appetite when that appetite is the strongest. By the custom of the world, marriage, in the average of cases, takes place at about the age of twenty four; whereas puberty commences at the age of fourteen. For ten years, therefore, and that in the very flush of life, the sexual appetite is starved. This law of society bears hardest on females, because they have less opportunity of choosing their time of marriage than men. This discrepancy between the marriage system and nature, is one of the principal sources of the peculiar diseases of women, of prostitution, masturbation, and licentiousness in general." (1966)

The Oneida Community, unlike many other communal groups, was very successful, for thirty years. It not only functioned well socially but also economically. But there arose a great deal of opposition from outside forces, however, especially from Protestant groups who viewed the experiment as the work of Satan. The marriage system was finally abolished, and in 1879 the Oneida Community became a joint stock company with assets of over $600,000. It is still in existence today, producing silver flatware.

One might be tempted to say that Noyes's ideas were really rationalizations for his own licentious desires. But that was not the case. Noyes believed in and practiced "male continence" because he realized that a series of pregnancies occurring one after the other was debilitating and destructive for women and, as he put it, "expensive" physiologically and economically. It appears, therefore, that his adherence to communal love was based upon his religious concepts rather than on what some of his critics would call "lust."

This examination of a nineteenth-century communal society has been undertaken because of its relevance to the modern sexual revolution. As we have already noted, it was one of the few successful attempts along these lines (that is, it did not dissolve because of internal dissatisfaction). There were before and there are now a number of such attempts at communal living that have met with varying degrees of success. Although sex is not the only issue of importance in the modern attempts at communal living, the whole movement is related to the sexual revolution because in almost every case the traditional kind of marriage is either greatly altered or completely absent.

modern community experiments

Modern experiments in group living are often, like the Oneida Community, initiated because of very powerful philosophical or religious convictions. One of the most common reasons for many of the communes that have been springing up around the country is the desire for "family life." In the modern industrial urban centers of the world, the old-fashioned family has largely disappeared. Even in the suburbs, where there is ostensibly a family group, there has been a widespread feeling of isolation among individuals. Young people especially complain that their parents are out of touch with them. The father leaves early, commutes to his work somewhere far removed from home, and comes home late and tired.

He is often busy with his own needs and has little time to devote to his children. The "rat race" of status climbing and keeping up with the Joneses leaves him little time for familial devotion.

The mother, on the other hand, has her own problems. She has her bridge clubs ("don't dirty the house, my friends will think I'm a terrible housekeeper. Can't you play at someone else's house?") or her political groups or her shopping sprees. And if the family ever gets together, it is probably to argue about something and not to feel close to one another. In fact, the modern family often does not *commune* with its members.

For this reason many people have attempted to find new "families" in which one can rediscover the feeling of closeness which seems now to be almost completely gone from the domestic American scene. Communal arrangements arising with this aim in mind serve as extended families in much the same way as did the community at Oneida. Many of the new experiments are simply attempts to find alternatives to the "plastic" monogamous life of modern urban and suburban dreariness. These groups simply reject the traditional approaches to love and sex and are making various kinds of arrangements, hoping to find something better. Sometimes they succeed but often they do not.

Kanter (1970) has studied a number of communes in operation in various parts of the country. He has tried to compare them with some of the nineteenth-century experiments in order to try to predict what kinds of organizations are most likely to be successful. He has found certain characteristics that appear to be essential to the stability of these groups.

Loneliness and dissatisfaction with suburban living can be influential in the search for alternative life styles.

Successful nineteenth-century communities used a variety of group techniques, including confession, self-criticism, and mutual criticism sessions, to solidify the group and deal with deviance and discontent before they became disruptive. The individual could bare his soul to the group, express his weaknesses, failings, doubts, problems, inner secrets. . . These T-group-like sessions also showed that the content of each person's inner world was important to the community. (Kanter, 1970)

The successful groups tended to have their own means of support and to jointly own all property. According to Kanter, these commitments made the groups extremely cohesive, thus contributing to their longevity. It seems also that the groups that stayed together had some kind of *structuring* (that is, routinized arrangements concerning such things as work, monetary handling, rituals for personal growth, and mutual criticism and support between members). Those which did not exist for too long a time seem to have lacked some or all of these ingredients. This was true in the past and appears to be true today. The interesting thing from the point of view of our present discussion is that the particular sexual arrangement of a given community seems to be irrelevant to its survival. Some of the groups practice monogamy, some various kinds of polygamy, some free love. But the important variable in the success or failure of the groups is almost always the *degree of closeness among the individuals* and the intensity of mutual caring. Communes that grow out of a need for people to simply escape some other intolerable situation but that do not offer some intimate contact among the members seem to dissolve within a short time.

SOME CONCLUSIONS ABOUT SOCIO-SEXUAL EXPERIMENTS

There have always been and there no doubt always will be people who have visions of making the world better for human beings to live in. Some of these dreams are seeking utopian solutions to man's problems, ideal social arrangements in which everyone is happy and fulfilled. Such dreams are perhaps necessary and worthwhile, for they may lead ultimately to improving man's lot and giving it more meaning. But the nature of man is so complex and the problems confronting him so great and so transient that almost before he has formulated the problem and begun to develop a solution, the nature of the problem has changed. It seems unlikely, therefore, that a Utopia in the classic sense will ever emerge. Societies, like people, may never attain perfection. But also like people, societies can be in a continual state of *becoming*, of improving, of actualizing their potentialities. It may be that the ideal society is not one in which everyone is magically, perfectly happy all the time, but one in which men are free to struggle with the painful problems of living and dying in a way that maximizes their selfhood—that the utopian society is not one in which there are no problems or dissatisfactions, but one in which problems and dissatisfactions are the challenges of living because man can be free to use his strength and ingenuity to try to solve them.

CONCLUSIONS

We have shown that human sexuality is an extremely complex problem and that it is influenced enormously by cultural values. We have also touched on the problem of love and its relationship to sex; we have discussed homosexuality; and we have discussed the family insofar as that institution has been undergoing some change in the light of new attitudes. Some of these topics will be explored further.

chapter 8
power

POWER IN THE PHYSICAL WORLD

The science of physics deals with energy and matter. Energy exists in a number of forms. When energy is directed in such a way as to have an effect upon matter it is called *power*. The history of power is a very long one in the life of man. For most of his time on this planet, man had to use his own muscles as a source of power, and even with the development of primitive tools, man's power came from his own labor. As time went on, man began to resort to the use of animal power to complement his own. And as his understanding of mechanical principles improved, he began to make very simple machines to aid him in harnessing the forces of nature. By the Middle Ages he had learned to use wind and water to transform mechanical energy into forces that could be utilized for his own benefit. By the beginning of the nineteenth century, he had discovered a brand new source of power—steam.

Three kinds of physical power: (left) human power, (center) animal power, (right) mechanical power.

With the Industrial Revolution there came a new series of discoveries which were to raise man's use of power to a level that he could not possibly have imagined earlier. These discoveries included electricity, atomic fission, and atomic fusion. By bringing these natural forces under his control, man appears to have harnessed the most potent forms of energy in the universe.

Utilization of physical power has made irrevocable changes in man's environment. It has made him capable of Promethean feats; he can move across continents, over the seas, fly through the air and even leave his own planet to go visit neighboring worlds. But the control of physical power is not an unmixed blessing. For although we have developed the technology to use it, we have not always had the wisdom to use it wisely. It is primarily the misuse of power that will concern us in this chapter.

THE PSYCHOLOGY OF POWER

Anyone who has observed children realizes that there is a distinct and probably innate need for children to try to have an influence on their surroundings. This tendency begins at birth and is probably one of the most pervasive forces shaping human behavior. For the desire to have some kind of influence on the world is the essential component of the human drive for power.

Power, therefore, from a psychological point of view is not necessarily a desire to control the lives of other men; although it often takes that form. It is the desire to have an effect, to make a difference in the world; it is a desire to mold a part of the world in one's own unique way. For most living organisms there is no problem, for the effects they have are limited by their inability to use any resources other than their own.

For man, however, this limit does not apply. Since we have developed ways of extending our personal power, it is possible for even the most impotent among us to exert power in a very dangerous way.

The drive for power appears to differ widely from person to person. There appears to be no question that the desire to control or manipulate the world to one's advantage resides in all of us to some degree. And although the "power drive" has often been viewed in negative terms, this view is not always necessary. The desire for a certain amount of power is normal since it serves certain essential purposes; it is only when it is extremely exaggerated as an end in itself that we can speak of the power drive as pathological.

Some people think that the power drive is one of the most important motivating forces in human beings. Bertrand Russell (1938) puts it this way:

> Of the infinite desires of man, the chief are the desires for power and glory. These are not identical, though closely allied. The Prime Minister has more power than glory, the King has more glory than power. As a rule, however, the easiest way to obtain glory is to obtain power; this is especially the case as regards the men who are active in relation to public events. The desire for glory, therefore, prompts, in the main, the same actions as are prompted by the desire for power, and the two motives may, for most practical purposes, be regarded as one.

Alfred Adler (1927) proposed a theory of human motivation in which he included the term "will to power." This concept was later changed slightly and called the "drive for superiority." But in terms of our discussion, Adler meant approximately the same thing by both terms. The will to power meant for Adler the desire of the infant organism to overcome what it perceived as its own powerlessness. The human infant is born into the world in a helpless state. He sees very shortly after birth that he is a helpless creature in a world of giants. The adults around him are capable of enormous and magical feats. They can whisk him from place to place, they can drive automobiles, they can produce food, they can move about at will, they can communicate with language, they can manipulate machines that make strange sounds and perform strange functions. To the bewildered child these are miraculous powers and in comparing himself with his parents and other people in his environment, he comes to perceive himself as completely impotent. He can do none of these things, but soon the desire to be able to do them becomes very important to him. To the child the ability to control the environment is the ability to obtain immediate gratification. And for him, power is the *equivalent* of immediate gratification.

Whether immediate or not, gratification is the name of the game in the drive for power. Desire to have control over the world is related to the desire to gratify one's wishes. From the child's point of view, there is an urgent need to gain leverage or to obtain mastery over the environment. To him, such a state of affairs provides the only circumstances under which he can feel competent in terms of satisfying his needs and desires. Lack of such mastery leads to feelings of incompetence and helplessness, giving rise, in turn, to anxiety and depression.

In terms of power, the organism must find that it has some control over its own life. It must feel that it can shape its destiny in some way. Otherwise it suffers the feeling of alienation so common today in heavily populated industrialized areas of the world. Many of the struggles of the last decade between young and old, black and white, students and administrators have been struggles of the powerless to gain a measure of power in order to have an effect upon their destiny.

EXISTENTIAL POWER

Although we have been discussing power in terms of what it does for the organism and how the organism perceives his need for it, there is another dimension to the power drive. There is in the exertion of power, a satisfaction that comes not from its results *but from the very experience itself.* This feeling is illustrated by such activities as hitting a golf ball or a baseball, shooting at a target and seeing it fall, running a powerful machine, giving an order and seeing it carried out, lifting a heavy weight; in short, almost any activity in which our efforts come to a successful conclusion. This experiential component of power is important in its own right. One might say that it is intrinsically reinforcing. It is probably related in a variety of ways to the concept of self-actualization for, as we shall see later, the organism in developing its true potentiality learns to express power in a creative way.

SOCIAL POWER

One of the most important kinds of influence from the standpoint of the psychologist and sociologist is the influence that one person or one group has on another person or group. The relationships among people, groups, nations, and so on, are all colored by the power relationships that exist among them. The dominance hierarchies that exist in every social organization are largely determined by the extent to which the more dominant individuals can exert pressure on their neighbors. In a group of chimpanzees the dominant member is the one who can instill a certain kind of fear or subservience in the other members and, although in human relationships other kinds of coercive influence are used, the use of fear is certainly not unknown.

Social power has been defined as the ability to control the behavior of other human beings. Such control may be exerted in a number of ways. One way is by what is called *reward power*. A person who is in a position to produce outcomes for another person which are pleasant or beneficial has reward power over that person. By either delivering or withholding his reward he can generally affect the behavior of the other in some desired direction. The boss, the foreman, the parent hold reward power and, generally speaking, the reward they control is important enough to be a great influence on the person receiving it.

An important variable in the phenomenon of social power is the perception of the individuals involved. That is, a person has power over another if that other person believes in its existence. That is why, for example, it often happens that an individual suddenly realizes he no longer needs to follow the instructions of his parents—he has learned there is no longer anything that they can do to him. He may realize, in fact, that for a long time he has been following their instructions out of inertia. They had power over him once, and he continues to act as if they had power over him now. Once he realizes that that is not true anymore, their power disappears.

POWER AND DEPENDENCY

There is an interesting interplay between dependency and power. It is quite clear that a person who has others dependent upon him has power over those people because he can control their outcomes. But what is not quite as obvious is that the dependent person very often holds power over the one upon whom he depends. This situation is often seen when a parent becomes extremely dependent upon his grown child. The child feels an obligation to stay with the parent, to never leave, to take care of the parent, and so on. The parent in this situation is using his dependency to control the other person. Sometimes being dependent is the only way a person can gain any kind of leverage. There are other situations in which dependencies may be mutual, such as in the case of good friends. The friends can exert power over one another in particular circumstances. Both are dependent upon one another at different times and therefore can control each other's outcomes. Such relationships are often referred to as *balanced-power relationships*.

Dependency relationships can also be indirect. In such situations the power of an executive, for example, may be wielded through a number of intermediary steps to be brought to bear upon a subordinate who is never in contact with the executive. Most hierarchial institutions function on this kind of power relationship.

FORMS OF COERCION

There are a number of methods by which human beings can be influenced. The most simple and direct is by physical force, by using certain kinds of physical restraint, or by the infliction of pain in order to compel a person to do one's bidding. Another method is by controlling rewards and punishments, so that one can obtain the behavior that he desires by meting out or holding back those things that the individual considers valuable. Money, love, and sex are things that are often used in such a way.

A third way of influencing another person's behavior is to mold his thinking in a desired direction; for example, if you get a soldier to believe in your cause, you can get him to fight for you.

Power over people is the power sought most often by human beings in modern civilized societies. Many people feel a sense of great strength when they are at the apex of an organization over which they exert complete control. This, of course, is one of the main reasons why people seek to gain control over various kinds of organizations by rising in the hierarchy until they reach "the top." Not only do they generally acquire power over the people in the organization this way, but they also enhance their financial status, which, of course, is another source of power.

One of the things that make power so attractive nowadays, especially in democratic countries, is the fact that a man who is born powerless can sometimes rise to great estates of power. This, of course, was not always true. There was a time when power had to be inherited, as when the king in monarchial times gave his power to his son. In those days a man of humble birth had practically no chance of acquiring the kind of power that we are now discussing. But today even very humble origins do not necessarily preclude the acquisition of power when one is resourceful enough. This does not, by any means, mean that everyone who finds himself powerless in this society can under certain circumstances acquire the means by which he can affect his life. As we shall see shortly, many in our society are born powerless, struggle all their lives, and die powerless.

POLITICAL POWER

Political power has to do with decision making. Those who make decisions concerning the way men will be governed are those in whose hands power resides. The acquisition of power in politics is almost always related to the fact that a large number of people consider the person who makes the decisions to be legitimately empowered. Generally speaking this means that there is no society in which tyranny exists without the consent of at least some part of the constituency. At times this may be only a small elite group, such as the army. At other times it may be almost an entire populace, as in Nazi Germany. But the people who make decisions cannot as a rule hold power by themselves. They must have the support of some of their subjects.

It is not necessarily true, however, that those who hold power in a democracy are supported by a majority of the people. In the first place, many people don't vote. In the second place, a candidate is often elected without a majority of the votes, as, for example, when a third party is involved in an election. But beyond this, since nominating conventions do not necessarily consider the will of the general public in their selection of candidates, the men who run for office and are ultimately elected may not be "the people's choice" at all.

If most of the people in a democracy have very little power in selecting those who will represent them and make decisions concerning their lives, there are groups who are completely powerless in this regard. In the United States there are a number of groups who have almost no political power. They are the very poor and the minorities, which include the blacks,

Two seats of political power: (left) the Acropolis of Athens, (right) Los Angeles City Hall.

Mexican Americans, Indians, Puerto Ricans, etc. Until recently these groups have had very little opportunity to elect people who would consider their interests and work for their welfare. Moreover, the culture of poverty in which some of these people live most of their lives makes it extremely difficult for any of them to acquire the kind of power in tangible form (that is, money) that would enable them to have an influence on the electoral system. The cries of recent years for "black power" and "brown power" are new attempts by the powerless to gain some form of leverage by which they can have some control over their own lives.

The most notable trend in political power in the twentieth century has been the *concentration* of power.

> The history of modern society may be understood as the story of the enlargement and the centralization of the means of power—in economic, in political, and in military institutions. (Mills, 1963)

Political power has moved into fewer and fewer hands, especially in great nations, so that it now resides in the hands of a very few individuals; these individuals make decisions that affect the lives of millions of people.

Political power is seen by some as the ability and opportunity to create history. This can be a very intoxicating thought for some people. The desire to sit at the throttle while history is being created by their moves, decisions, and judgments can be overwhelming. It is easy to imagine how exhilarating and terrifying it must be for one to sit with his hand on the nuclear trigger, which could, in one horrendous moment, bring about the annihilation of the human species. It is strange and somewhat paradoxical that with the little political power that we have, we eventually allow the enormous power of nuclear weapons to lodge in the hands of one man.

There are, of course, other individuals who have a great deal of political power. There are men who can, in fact, frustrate the President of the United States when it is in their interest to do so. These men are generally chairmen of very powerful committees in the Congress who can hold up legislation or push bills out onto the floor in order to get them passed, very often in spite of the desires of the president. Other men who could and do wield tremendous amounts of power are the presidential advisors. (Watergate has shown us just how much power some of these men may try to acquire.) In the case of weak presidents, these men may, in fact, wield more power than the chief executive himself. Such advisors are often in charge of some of the bureaucracies in the federal government, and these kinds of organizations have a type of power of their own. Bureaucratic organizations generally move by their own momentum, and it is very difficult and sometimes impossible to turn them around and change their directions.

President John F. Kennedy remarked on how difficult he found it to institute any change that moved in a direction counter to the prevailing point of view.

PERSONAL POWER

> Whether we look back with historians or forward with scientists or inward with poets, we find power, located in individuals, as a constant, unvarying factor in every phase of organized society. Invariably there are powerholders who somehow attain a position making it probable that their commands will be carried out. The area of that probability may be tiny—the mother giving orders to her children—or large—an Eisenhower commanding the expeditionary forces in World War II—or vast—a dictator like Joseph Stalin giving orders to officials, Communist Party functionaries, and police throughout a continental empire. There are all ranges in between. (Berle, 1967)

All power, according to this view, resides in persons. Institutions may be the means through which they express it, but there is no such thing as power in the abstract, at least according to Berle. Power only exists when it is expressed, and it can only be expressed by an individual. Even a group that wishes to exercise its power must somehow choose a leader so that he can administer or direct the energy that flows from the group itself. Without the leader, the group is a lumbering giant with energy but without power. Berle puts it this way:

> It follows that the abstract definition of power—as though it existed independently of a man—cannot take us far. Power in the abstract does not exist. As abstraction, it is a potential—not a social—fact. It becomes fact only when a man or woman following his inborn instinct takes and uses it. This is why power is invariably individual. (Berle, 1967)

Every individual has limitations upon the expression of his power; these limitations may be internal and/or external. Examples of external limitations are police, laws, and other human beings who have other wishes (especially people higher in the status structure). Internal limitations include such things as moral judgments and concern for the welfare of others. People who do not have *internal* controls can be very dangerous, particularly when they express their personal power in the absence of outer limitations. Certain kinds of delinquents and criminals, for example, will do tremendous damage to others when there is no threat of punishment present, especially if such behavior is in their interest. Sometimes such behavior will be engaged in merely for "kicks."

submission to personal power

Under certain circumstances we are all subject to the power of others. Sometimes we submit willingly; at other times we submit in spite of our wishes. No matter how powerful a human being is, there are times when he must yield to the wishes or judgments of others. Even the president must listen to Secret Service agents when they tell him what is safe and what is unsafe in terms of his behavior in public places. Hitler had a great deal of power, but even he, fortunately for the rest of us, gave way to the whims of his astrologer and decided not to invade Britain at a time when that nation was tottering on the brink of defeat.

For the rest of us, however, following is not so difficult a task. There are many times in our lives when we relinquish our power happily to submit to the jurisdiction of others. We follow the advice of a doctor or lawyer—we follow the directions of a policeman or even a traffic sign—we submit to majority will in an organization—we even allow our children to influence our choice of a vacation site.

authoritarianism

Other kinds of power relations between people are not quite so benign. Adorno and his associates (1950) have described what they call "the authoritarian personality," which they see as a distinguishing characteristic

The police have power over us because they can use sanctions against us when we disobey the law.

of certain kinds of people. The authoritarian person is very much concerned with power and, according to Adorno, he seems to have certain stable attributes. He is acutely aware of authority relationships and emphasizes the importance of power in all interactions. He is exceedingly submissive to those in authority and responds without question to their commands. At the same time he expects and often receives similar reactions from those who are in subordinate positions to him. If he is a parent, he is very likely to impose such attitudes on his children. Adorno lists a number of other attributes of the authoritarian personality which might be of some interest. The authoritarian is generally very rigid and unyielding in his adherence to middle-class values. He often denies sexual motives in himself and has a tendency to see sexuality in others, particularly in minority groups. He tends to be exploitive in his relationships with people who are beneath him in the status structure, at the same time feeling exploited by those above him. His thinking tends to be extremely rigid and categorical and he has a tendency to stereotype other people, particularly minority groups, to whom he often directs a great deal of prejudice. In terms of power, the authoritarian personality is concerned mainly with imposing power on those below him and acquiescing to the power of those above.

The roots of the authoritarian personality are believed to have their source in early childhood. The child is generally subjected to a very severe and moralistic kind of discipline, and he is not allowed to question, or hesitate in obeying, his parent's dictates. Punishment is usually severe and the child learns to fear not only his parents but, after a while, all authority. At the same time it is believed that the child suppresses a great deal of hostility toward the authority figure. Since it is unsafe to express this feeling toward its real source, it is generally displaced onto those who are in no position to retaliate.

The extent to which people will follow the instructions of those they perceive to be legitimately endowed with power has been demonstrated by a number of studies. Milgram (1963) did a study in which he wanted to determine to what extent a person would act in accordance with instructions even though the behavior in question might be against his better judgment. He designed an experiment in which he told his subjects that he was measuring the effects of punishment on learning. What he was really measuring was the reaction of the subject to the instructions of the experimenter. The subject was told that he was to administer a shock to another "subject," who was, in fact, a confederate of the experimenter, every time the "learner" made a mistake. The situation was rigged so that the learner would make a number of mistakes at various intervals. The real subject believed that he was administering shocks to the learner, who was ostensibly in another room. In fact, the learner was not in any way connected to the electrical equipment being used. An important aspect of the experiment was that the subject was required to increase the voltage of the shocks every time he administered one. It was also noted somewhat off handedly that the learner had a bad heart.

As the experiment wore on and the shocks increased in intensity, there were loud cries to be heard coming from the other room. If the subject hesitated, he was instructed by the experimenter to continue with the procedure. At a given point in the experiment, when the voltage reached a rather high intensity, the learner could be heard crying out in pain with the administration of every shock. Then as the intensity was increased further, he began to ask to be released, crying that he was in great pain and that his heart was beginning to bother him. In spite of these entreaties, however, the experimenter instructed the subject to continue with the experiment and, if the subject objected, the experimenter explained that he must go on—that the experiment once begun could not be stopped.

The question for the experimenter was to find out how many subjects would go all the way to the highest voltage available, which in this experiment was 350 volts. More than half the subjects, when confronted by the experimenter and asked to continue, went all the way to the end of the experiment, in spite of the fact that they showed a great deal of reluctance to do so and wanted a number of times to stop. The conclusion drawn from this type of research is not very encouraging. It shows that in yielding to power which they perceive as legitimate, people will inflict great pain and suffering on other people, even though they are quite reluctant to do so.

One can see from this study why it is so easy for leaders of nations to coerce their subjects in many ways. If an experimenter in a laboratory wearing a white coat can influence a person to respond in the ways described above, it is quite obvious that a president or a premier or a king can have tremendous influence on his subjects. The most unfortunate thing about this quality of human nature is that those who love power are aware of this and seize upon it knowing that they can use it to their advantage. The leader who understands this phenomenon can persuade the people to follow his lead—and because of the prestige of his office, most people will do his bidding without questioning the value of the policies or the leader's motives. We have seen very recently how such behavior can lead to dreadful consequences. The readiness of people to follow their leaders into wars in the last three decades has generally resulted in disaster.

POWER AND VIOLENCE

There is no question that violence or the threat of violence is often used to enforce the will of one group upon another or one person upon other people. There are, of course, different kinds of violence. Some kinds are institutionalized—they are part of the society itself. Other kinds are non-institutionalized; they simply occur between people at various times. The expression of power by violence is often seen in pure destructiveness. There are times when people merely have to break things up, destroy them, shatter them, to feel a sense of power. A great deal of the violence during the riots of the 1960s was related to this feeling of expressing one's power through destruction. People often lash out in anger and try to destroy in order to feel a sense of effectiveness, which to some extent helps to dissipate some of their anger.

We have already noted that other forms of violence are portrayed in the media to show certain characters as powerful. The ability to knock another man down with a blow or to kill him with a gun are expressions of power. And we have noted that both the hero and the villain are extremely powerful.

Institutionalized power is of a different sort. The violence of the forces of government is used as a threat to prevent people from breaking certain rules or violating the freedoms or privileges of others. This violence may be held in check a great deal of the time and used merely as a deterrent. However, when the rules are broken or laws violated, the violence of the state may be severe, as in the case of capital punishment, in which the state kills the offender. The violence of the army is similarly held in check at times to be used merely to prevent other nations from acting in ways that are considered to be in violation of the interests of the state. However, when these nations defy the state in question, the violence of the armed forces may be brought into play in an attempt to change their course of action.

When violence is used to enforce power relationships, it is not necessary for the subjects to acquiesce or even to perceive the perpetrator of the violence as legitimate. The use of force generally guarantees that the victim will behave in a desired way regardless of his feelings in the matter especially while he is being watched. This use of power, therefore, has no need to change the opinions of the people subjected to it, for their opinions are of no consequence. The use of violence forces them to behave or, in extreme cases, eliminates them entirely.

The threat of violence is a very real one in the area of power politics. Nations that wish to control certain parts of the world must use their armies as a threat, if not as an actual mediator of violence, in order to gain their ends. The great nations sometimes use their power with a certain degree of restraint. But at other times they become, in the words of Senator Fulbright, "arrogant" and use their power with no concern for the welfare of others. Such naked power becomes dangerous in the hands of insensitive leaders, for they may enforce it with no consideration for the millions of people whom they affect.

Within the state, violence used by those who are not in constituted authority is generally called *crime*. Violence used by the institutionalized forces of the state, on the other hand, is usually called *justice*. This is true even though the two kinds of violence may be quite similar. In international affairs, however, violence used by one nation against another is almost always justified by that nation, although it may be seen by others as unjustified or even criminal. And even though the United Nations may brand an act by one nation as aggression, the nation itself, if it is very powerful, can easily ignore this accusation. Therefore, the problem of what use of force is legitimate in the international sphere is a very difficult one to answer. In fact, many people feel that the reasons usually given to justify war are not the real reasons that wars are fought. An interesting comment was made in this regard by Aldous Huxley (1963):

> There may be arguments about the best way of raising wheat in a cold climate or of re-afforesting a denuded mountain. But such arguments never lead to organized slaughter. Organized slaughter is the result of arguments about such questions as the following: Which is the best nation? The best religion? The best political theory? The best form of government? Why are other people so stupid and wicked? Why can't they see how good and intelligent *we* are? Why do they resist our beneficent efforts to bring them under our control and make them like ourselves?

Huxley is arguing that the real reasons for war are not as humanistic as the ones generally given. The real reasons for war are egotistical. In terms that we have been using in this book, we might say that many times the real reasons for war are for the protection of a national PR image.

The use of power by great nations is for that reason a very dangerous phenomenon. As Senator Fulbright (1966) says:

> Power tends to confuse itself with virtue and a great nation is peculiarly susceptible to the idea that its power is a sign of God's favor, conferring upon it a special responsibility for other nations—to make them richer and happier and wiser, to remake them, that is, in its own shining image. Power confuses itself with virtue and tends also to take itself for omnipotence. Once imbued with the idea of a mission, a great nation easily assumes that it has the means as well as the duty to do God's work.

The temptation of the great nation to exert its influence either by the force of arms or by a threat of such force is sometimes overwhelming. And it is very simple for the leaders of such a nation to find rationalizations for such behavior. When the leaders express these "reasons" the people, generally speaking, tend to go along with this point of view. Senator Fulbright explains this tendency this way:

> The more I puzzle over the great wars of history, the more I am inclined to the view that the causes attributed to them—territory, markets, resources, the defense or perpetuation of great principles—were not the root causes at all but rather explanations or excuses for certain unfathomable drives of human nature. For lack of a clear and precise understanding of exactly what these motives are, I refer to them as the 'arrogance of power'—as a psychological need that nations seem to have in order to prove that they are bigger, better, or stronger than other nations. Implicit in this drive is the assumption, even on the part of normally peaceful nations, that force is the ultimate proof of superiority—that when a nation shows that it has the stronger army, it is also proving that it has better people, better institutions, better principles, and, in general, a better civilization. (Fulbright, 1966)

This is a pretty good illustration of the PR personality working on a national level. We may notice that many of the qualities attributed to nations are very much like the qualities that we have attributed to the heroic figures upon which the PR personality is based. There is no question, therefore, that it is sometimes satisfying for individuals to identify with the great power of the nation, thereby enhancing their feelings of personal importance.

Related to this idea is the one we often hear expressed concerning first-class or second-class nationhood. It is often alleged that it is necessary for the United States to avoid making the kind of errors that Great Britain made which resulted in her becoming a second-rate power within a very short period of time. The implication here, of course, is that a nation must be ranked as the *most powerful* in order to be *worthwhile*. Such an assumption does not consider the question of whether the people in such a nation are better off, worse off, happier, unhappier, and so on. In fact, this kind of statement tends to presuppose that such considerations as happiness and well-being are irrelevant. The desire for national power, therefore, is often seen to supersede the needs or desires of the people.

POWER AND OMNIPOTENCE

Freud and a number of other observers have held that there is a drive in the infant to be all-powerful. And at a certain period in his development, he, in fact, begins to have fantasies about his own omnipotence. Such fantasies grow out of the fact that he believes himself to be responsible for most of the responses of others, particularly his mother and father, and he comes to believe that this power is, or can become, universal. The infantile desire and belief in omnipotence becomes tempered by reality as the individual matures. But there are cases in which for one reason or another this does not happen. In some circumstances, this part of the personality may never, in fact, "grow up." In others, the accumulation of power may be such that an individual realistically sees the possibility of becoming all-powerful (for example, Hitler and Napoleon).

It seems quite likely that the drive for power may in some individuals be insatiable. For such people, each satisfaction simply leads to a desire for the next. And since power itself is generally limitless, the desire to acquire more and more of it is similarly inexhaustible.

One of the unfortunate consequences of this fact is that it is often the very kind of person who has dreams of omnipotence who in fact becomes the recipient of power. For it is this kind of person, with this kind of drive, who is most likely to have the perseverance to overcome the obstacles and endure the difficulties which are required for the accumulation of power.

The fact that the power drive is sometimes insatiable is extremely dangerous in a technological age. For the power that is now available to man, even to the ordinary man, extends his capacity for destructiveness far beyond his natural means. An inkling of this kind of power used in a destructive way can be gleaned from the daily newspaper, which describes shootings and bombings, while in modern war the use of machines, chemicals, napalm, and even nuclear weapons have become the exaggerated expressions of man's unending quest for power. When the power drive is related to omnipotence, it will often find its expression in terms of violence. For it is bound to come up against some resistance sometime, and when this happens the exaggerated use of force will be its only alternative.

POWER AND FREEDOM

There is an interesting relationship between power and freedom. A person is free to the extent that he can do those things which he desires to do. But this means that he must have some power. The person who feels powerless therefore perceives himself to be without freedom. Freedom does not mean merely being left alone. Freedom is related to being able to pursue one's goal. But the pursuit of goals is meaningless when one does not have the ability or resources that are necessary for their fulfillment. This means that freedom and power are sometimes synonymous.

All living organisms are purposive. That is, they have motives and goals. But motives are obstructed in the absence of resources with which to achieve them. And in this sense the man without the ability to attain some satisfaction of his motives is not free. For it makes very little difference whether the fulfillment of one's desires is prevented by others or by one's own impotence. The results are the same. A person is free only to the extent to which he can do those things that are important to him. If, as the existentialists say, a man is free because he makes choices, it would appear that freedom would be meaningless unless the choices made could be implemented. To choose to do something that one is powerless to do is, in a certain sense, not a choice at all.

To speak therefore of freedom to people who are powerless is to speak nonsense. That is why it is so frustrating to poor people and others without resources to be told that they are free to accomplish anything they desire to accomplish. Such a statement strikes them as idiotic. For they realize that they do not have the same freedom (opportunity, influence, authority) as other people. Their freedom, therefore, is not the same freedom as that afforded others. The man in jail is not free because he does not possess the power to go his own way. He may *choose* to go, but he *cannot*. In the same way the poor and the deprived in our society may choose to elevate themselves, but they have no more power than the man in jail, and they are therefore not free.

POWER AND POTENCY

Some psychologists believe that there is a relationship between sexual potency and the idea of power. This is especially true in the male, who perceives potency as an expression and proof of his masculinity. In this view the man who cannot perform adequately in the sexual sphere is considered weak and incompetent. Some psychoanalysts believe that the drive for power is, in fact, the drive for an unlimited reservoir of sexual energy which has been sublimated and subsequently expressed in this way. It may be possible, therefore, that the drive for power may be explained as a symbolic representation of a need for sexual potency.

It is probable that all of us, at some time in our lives, have fantasies of omnipotence of a sexual kind. Such fantasies include the idea of being able to seduce any person of the opposite sex at will. And such fantasies carry with them the ability to control the behavior of those other people completely. The rewards from such power certainly appear to be great. Though such fantasies are believed to exist only in the male, the female, especially in our society, may have similar kinds of visions. For the female, to be irresistible to all men is to be able to make them do her bidding. The bitch-heroine in particular, as we noted earlier, has this quality to a high degree.

Such fantasies, when they exist, are infantile, unrealistic expressions of the desire for eternal gratification. But they are soon repressed. People are not likely to admit that they wish to seduce every member of the opposite sex to whom they are attracted. So on a conscious level, the desire for potency in this extreme form may not be apparent. But its expression may be transformed into a drive for power which seems more in accord with the society in which one lives.

THE MOLDING OF OPINION

We have shown that one can have influence over other people by exerting physical force or by using violence to coerce them to act in a required way. But such gross forms of power are not necessarily the most efficient. A more subtle but perhaps a more lasting way of influencing the behavior of others is to affect their feelings with regard to the matter at hand. The ability to influence the *opinions* of others, therefore, is one of the most pervasive and enduring forms of power available to man.

The earliest form of this power lies, of course, with the family. The parents, by many devices, sometimes without realizing it, shape the opinions and attitudes of their children. They teach them what is "good," what is "bad," what is "correct," what is "incorrect," what kinds of attitudes and behaviors are acceptable and unacceptable, what is "true," what is "beautiful," and even what is "real."

But this is only the beginning. For the rest of society also has a hand in the guidance and direction of opinion. The siblings, the peers, the various institutions in and out of government all have a hand in determining the kinds of thought processes, values, perceptual biases, and so on, that a person will have.

the family

The power wielded by the family over the young is well documented. The family is the major socializing force, particularly in the formative years. Freud pointed out that children tend to introject the values and beliefs of their parents at quite an early age. And we have also seen evidence that children may, at certain periods in their lives, rebel against the values and beliefs of their parents and in many cases adopt views that are completely contrary to them. Nevertheless, the family gives a context to the young which is extremely persuasive in terms of their attitudes and beliefs, and even the direction in which their rebellion will take them, if and when it occurs.

Different kinds of families, of course, have different kinds of effects on the young. The traditional family tended to make the children in its own image. But with changing times, there has been more flexibility in family life and, as a result, more differentiation in its influence. Moreover, different kinds of families in the different areas of our culture have a variety of effects on the socialization of the young. The more traditional kinds of family, for example, tend to leave less room for the assumption of individual roles and result in more stereotyping from generation to generation. In the more modern families, in which creativity and innovation are more acceptable, there has been a tendency for the young to find ways of developing their own attitudes and values which may at times differ somewhat from those of their parents. In this sense it may be said that the family has given up some of its traditional power in the interest of individuality.

peers

Some sociologists believe that the peer group has a greater influence on the attitudes and values of a human being than does the family. Whether true or not, such a belief points to the tremendous effect that the peer group can have upon its members. The particular peer group to which one belongs has a set of rules. All participants are expected for the most part to observe the rules and to abide by them. There are often severe sanctions leveled against those who do not live up to the expectations of the peer group, and as a result such expectations soon tend to become adopted by the individuals themselves. Some peer groups transmit the values of the greater society while others may have values that are completely opposed to it. Generally speaking, with adolescents, when the peer-group values differ from those of the family, there will be a tendency for the peer-group values to win out and for the family traditions to begin to recede.

the communications media

Values of the family and the peer group do not spring into being full blown. They result from and contribute to other influencing organs. In a civilization like ours, there is no question that the communications media have an enormous impact upon the beliefs, values, and attitudes of the people. Newspapers, magazines, films, television all carry many messages, implied or expressed, which inform the individual of what is expected, what is valued, what feelings are appropriate under what conditions, what kind of people he should like and dislike, and so on. Moreover, these sources of information and entertainment are often extremely selective in what they expose to our view. Selectivity is not necessarily a diabolical plot to keep us from being informed about other facets of life in the world. It is perhaps to some extent necessary and automatic to represent only those things that relate to one's particular mode of life while omitting those that relate to any other. Yet in so doing these instruments tend to mold opinion in particular directions. The viewer or reader comes to perceive the world in certain particular ways, to think in certain distinctive channels, and in general to respond to a certain class of stimuli in highly specific ways.

One result of this narrowness is the tendency of people to perceive their own culture as the only "normal" mode of living. Our customs and traditions become the yardstick by which we judge other societies. Our mode of dress, for example, is acceptable, whereas those of other peoples may appear strange or funny. Our religion is the only religion, while everyone else's religion is merely superstition. Our form of government is the best form of government, while every other form is seen as evil or inferior.

The communications media, therefore, not only bring us information and entertain us, they also indoctrinate us, influence us, mold us. This, therefore, places the people who are in control of the media in an exceptionally powerful position. For whether they desire to consciously or not, they control the behavior of millions of people by controlling their attitudes.

organized religion

There is no question that the traditional organized religions of man have always had an enormous influence over the thinking of their subjects. Religion, by its very nature, is usually *prescriptive*. That is, it has a doctrine, or a body of principles, which are expected to be followed, both in thought and in action, by its adherents. This adherence is enforced by very powerful, but often subtle, sanctions. Breaches of acceptable modes of behavior can be severely punished. But it is not only the behavior of the individual in which the church is interested. The church is also interested in the thought processes and beliefs of its subjects. Therefore, to think certain thoughts or to hold certain beliefs which are considered taboo to the particular religion in question can also lead to very severe condemnation. As a consequence, any religious institution exerts enormous control over its "believers."

The effect that religious leaders have upon their subjects is in many ways more powerful than other molders of opinion in a society. For he who would resist the dogma of almost any religious sect is threatened with very drastic punishment. There is usually no room for doubt or individual judgment, for such attitudes constitute heresy. Heretics are punished by excommunication or by damnation, and it is not likely under these circumstances that many people will risk such penalties for the questionable rewards of being free to make up their own minds. Religious institutions also have the sanction of sin for those within their jurisdiction who break the rules or even think forbidden thoughts. Guilt, as we know, arouses a great deal of anxiety and as a result most people will try to avoid any thoughts or experiences that lead to it.

Another form of control in most religions resides in the "rewards of the faithful." For those who abide by the doctrine, various good consequences are promised. Happiness and peace in this world or the next are among the important benefits derived from observing the doctrine. These prospects are, like the more unpleasant ones, difficult to ignore. These are a few of the reasons that religious institutions have such pervasive effects.

political institutions

Many sociologists believe that political dogma is very nearly as persuasive as religious dogma insofar as the effects on opinion are concerned. We are often warned of the dire consequences of voting for the "other party," and there is a remarkable amount of agreement and cohesion among party affiliates with regard to almost any policy. In this connection, many *isms* are often believed to be more like religions than like political beliefs. And they are very often supported in fanatical ways by their adherents.

But even when political doctrine is not so extreme, it is still a very powerful tool for the control of attitudes. Political leaders are clearly aware of this fact and can easily make use of it by appealing to the loyalty of their followers. With such a device and a little rhetoric, they can often influence their constituency to go along with almost anything they advocate. It is interesting to note the circularity in this relationship. For political leaders gain their power through the consent of their constituency, but they gain this consent by virtue of their political leadership.

the educational establishment

Of all the institutions created by any society, it may be those which undertake the formal education of the citizenry that are the most persuasive. For educational systems, like the family and peer groups, are mirrors of the values and attitudes of the larger society. In fact, one of the explicit aims of education is enculturation. And this in the long run may be even more important than its other functions.

Generally speaking, education has two aims. One is, of course, the development of the potential intelligence of its citizenry. And the other is, as we have noted, the socialization of the individual. When most people think of the educational establishment, they think of the first function. However, the second function has a long tradition. In eighteenth-century England, for example, colleges were intended to produce "English gentlemen." And the early colonial colleges in the United States were estab-

The educational establishment exerts power by influencing the values and attitudes of its students.

lished mainly for the purpose of training clergymen for the ministry. The idea that the schools disseminate social and cultural values is not a new one.

The influence of the school over the minds of the young is exerted in a number of ways. One way is by presenting what it perceives as The Truth. For example, for a long time American children were told that the Indians who were discovered in the new land by the early explorers were wild, bloodthirsty savages who were continually attacking the peaceful white settlers who had merely come to colonize the New World. Such a "truth" carried with it the implication that the white men were always "right" and the red men were always "wrong." Aside from the falsity of such absolute beliefs, the damage done to an entire generation of people who misperceived the character of these native Americans is incalculable.

Another means by which the school transmits the values of the larger society is related more to its *methods* than to its *content*. Such indoctrination is not as obvious as some other kinds since it is not taught directly. But the attitudes and values of teachers and administrators, as well as those implied in the choice of curricula itself, become absorbed more or less automatically by the students—until they themselves espouse these values without realizing that they have been "indoctrinated." The educator, without necessarily realizing or intending it, wields great power. For those who mold the opinions of the young hold the key to the direction in which a society will go.

knowledge and power

The power that educators have to influence the thinking of their constituency in ways that are approved by their culture is only one kind of power relationship between educators and students. There is another kind. For education (that is, knowledge) ultimately becomes the student's instrument of power. If it is true that "knowledge is power," then the school is society's agent for its distribution. It is clear, therefore, that the educational process has the effect of imparting power to those it serves. Knowledge, whether scientific, magical, or even imaginary, has always enabled man to have an effect upon his environment.

Most of the forms of power that we have discussed have been related in some way to a body of knowledge. The power of the witch-doctor, no less than the power of the scientist, is dependent upon the things he understands (or believes he understands), and those outcomes over which he has some effect are directly related to this knowledge. In the modern world, of course, power is intimately related to what we know. The power of technology depends upon our understanding of the physical world and our application of its forces. The power of a ruler depends upon his understanding of diplomatic procedures and the like. And the power of the common man depends upon his knowledge of the world in which he lives and the methods available to him to help him obtain the things he needs and do the things he wishes to do. In this sense the educational institutions of a society distribute power to the extent that they impart knowledge.

POWER AND HUMAN EFFICACY

Power and competence are necessary requirements of all living organisms. From what we have seen, it is obvious that every human being needs at least a minimum degree of competence and efficiency to function normally. And groups of all kinds find it necessary to vest power in the hands of certain individuals at certain times in order to perform whatever functions they have assigned themselves. In these instances, power is necessary and useful. But there are other situations in which, as Lord Acton has said, "Power tends to corrupt; absolute power corrupts absolutely."

Power becomes destructive when it is sought as an end in itself and when it is glamorized to such an extent that those who possess it are slavishly admired by those who do not. When power, like status, becomes so much an admired end in itself, the person possessing it tends to be perceived as "larger than life." Such a perception is likely to lead other people to view those with power in an unrealistic way—and to follow them more obediently than they otherwise might. It seems likely, therefore, that it is necessary for a person to bear in mind the implications of this "halo effect"[1] with regard to those who are powerful. In terms of the discussion above, the tendency to perceive one as very powerful may also lead to his being seen as infallible, omnipotent, or magical. Because of our tendency to hero-ize the powerful, we allow them to get away with almost anything. They can lead us into disaster and we will follow. And when they commit unheroic acts (crimes, etc.) many of us try not to believe it. We have invested our PR image in them and cannot bear to have them (us) disparaged. It is as if we have become identical with them through this process of identification, and must now use the same defenses to protect their PR image that we would use for our own. The necessity, therefore, for us to understand the difference between power as a human resource and power as a means of ego enhancement and ego investment is obvious. It is only through a clear understanding of these differences that human beings can reach a high level of efficiency in terms of influencing their own lives.

[1] The tendency to allow certain characteristics of an individual to overshadow our total perception of him in such a way that we lose sight of many of his other attributes.

man, nature, and psychopathology

chapter 9
pathogenic trends in modern life

MAN'S NATURE AND SOCIETY

It is probably true that all societies, to some extent, arise out of a need to solve problems for which man has no instinctive responses. Unlike other animals, man does not have an instinctive set of behaviors that will automatically satisfy his needs. He has therefore found it necessary to form groups and to find innovative ways of dealing with these needs.

In the formation of all societies, certain traditions, beliefs, and attitudes become embedded in the cultural milieu over a period of time. Some of these may arise because they are useful, some because they have aesthetic value, some because they are of ethical necessity, and still others may occur almost by chance. Over the years many of these beliefs and attitudes are modified, or integrated with others, or perhaps lost completely, but the end result is often a complex series of interacting traditions and beliefs which give direction to the life of any given society.

233

From the standpoint of the psychologist, many of these traditions and beliefs can be seen to be antagonistic to man's nature. Since they were arrived at through a long series of innovations usually without a clear understanding of their long-range consequences, many of the attitudes that develop in a society may have detrimental effects on individuals. Although this is probably true of all societies, in our discussion we are interested in those trends in our own culture which, from the psychological point of view, may be said to be *pathogenic*. By pathogenic we mean anything that may be damaging to the psychological integrity of the individual.

The purpose of this chapter, therefore, is to examine those trends in our society that may have this kind of effect, in order to attempt to counteract them. For a clear understanding of such phenomena is essential if we are to avoid being disabled by them. The individual can do a great deal in his own behalf when he becomes aware of the forces that act against his own healthy psychological development.

Some statistics show that more than 60 per cent of the people in the United States suffer from some kind of emotional problem serious enough to require psychotherapeutic attention. Some people believe the percentage is even higher. A number of psychologists and sociologists believe that the society itself is "sick" and that what we are observing in individuals is simply the manifestation of those illnesses which are built into the very structure of the culture itself. The period in which we live has been called "the Age of Anxiety" because many people suffer from neurotic anxiety a good deal of the time. If there is even a little validity in some of these claims, it behooves us to look into those areas of our collective life which may throw some light on these difficulties. Let us therefore consider where some of these problems may lie.

LACK OF CLOSENESS

A great deal of research testifies to the fact that human beings have fundamental needs for contact with their fellows. This need is so important in infancy that if it fails to be met, normal development will be severely impaired. Although the need is crucial in childhood, it is also extremely important throughout life. Moreover, it is a need for actual physical contact or touching, not simply for social interaction.

As noted earlier, Americans except in special circumstances, do not make physical contact with one another very much. In our day-to-day encounters we are, in fact, as a rule very careful to avoid touching one another. And when we do come in contact with strangers in crowded places, for example, where we might accidentally brush up against them, we tend to excuse ourselves, as if we have done something reprehensible.

This in itself would not pose a very great problem if it were not for the fact that some people have almost no opportunity in their lives to touch other human beings. Unlike Europeans, we cannot put our arms around our neighbors or walk down the street with them arm in arm, for such intimacy is frowned on in our society, and as a result a great many people are deprived of the therapeutic value of having physical contact with others.

The physical distance that we maintain between one another has its psychological correlates. Where people in other societies often feel close to one another and have a sense of community, Americans, perhaps because of this lack of physical proximity, often lack this sense of intimacy with others. Many people complain nowadays that they feel alone and lonely even in the midst of large crowds in the centers of busy cities. Such people often report that they have strong desires to touch others in an affectionate way but that they feel strange because of the conventional attitudes related to physical contact. Thus we have the ironic situation of many, many people wandering by one another, wishing to express their affection, and being unable to do so. Such a situation ultimately leads to feelings of rejection by "others" with a subsequent arousal of hostility toward them. Thus we have come full circle. The need for affection has been thwarted and in its place we have isolation, rejection, and hostility.

family ties

A corollary to the closeness problem is the demise of the family unit as it was known in earlier times. Until the 1930s and 1940s there existed

People in other cultures often have more opportunities to cultivate close relationships.

what has been called the "extended family." The extended family not only included the parents and siblings, it also included the cousins, uncles, aunts, and grandparents. This large group was a very important source of comfort for people in the past. This was particularly true in times of stress or bereavement. But it also had its counterpart in happy times when the family would get together for celebrations. There were frictions and antagonisms, of course. But even these lent one the opportunity to bounce his ideas and feelings off others. And it supplied a certain amount of intimate contact with others to whom one felt some relatedness.

To a great extent all of this is now gone. In the first place, many of us now have smaller families. With fewer siblings, there is less opportunity to interact. Sometimes in a family of two children, for example, the age difference may be so great that they appear to be generations apart. So that with the advent of smaller families, there has also been a corresponding decrease in the opportunity for intimacy in one's life.

But the increased mobility of Americans in the last thirty or forty years has had an even greater effect on the fragmentation of the extended family. In the past, people were born and lived their lives within a few miles of their kinfolk. But this is no longer the case. People follow employment from one part of the nation to another and are often separated from their relatives by thousands of miles. Such separation, over a long period of time, results in the estrangement of the two groups to such an extent that when they do meet again years later, they often view one another as strangers. The physical distance that has been placed between them has resulted in a psychological distance of the same magnitude.

Another contribution to the disintegration of traditional family patterns is the increase in the rate of divorce. In years past, when divorce was frowned upon, many couples stayed together regardless of their feelings of unhappiness, and this, of course, created some problems of its own. But although this situation may have had little to recommend it, it did provide a kind of relatedness for the children. For they generally had two parents upon whom they could depend and with whom they could identify. Although this arrangement may have been more difficult for the parents, the new one is often more difficult for the children especially where one parent is permanently separated from them. For very often the children, after having formed strong attachments to particular persons, find themselves torn away from one parent and forced into a new relationship. For some youngsters this situation is repeated several times. Not only are feelings of closeness destroyed by such circumstances, but there may also be a tendency on the part of many to shy away from close relationships since they have already been badly hurt by at least one. For the child often sees divorce as a form of rejection.

There is another factor related to this one, which contributes to the feeling of isolation and loneliness that we have been describing. People who have been brought up in these ways, in which society, in fact, reinforces coolness, aloofness, and so on, often become incapable of developing a sense of relatedness to anyone. When these people become parents, they may find themselves unable to give themselves and their love to their children in a way that is satisfactory to both. The result is that they pass this tendency on to the younger generation. And we have the vicious circle in which alienation breeds further alienation.

One should not necessarily surmise from what has been said above that the older modes of living were necessarily better or healthier than the newer ones. The older modes created their own problems, which were in many ways as serious as the modern ones. But change creates the necessity for adaptation. And the new life styles have come upon us rapidly, creating new problems which we have not yet solved. We shall attempt to deal with these difficulties later.

One last area that might be mentioned with regard to the family is that in which the parents try to express themselves and try to achieve their own successes through their children. Because of the value placed upon success which can be publicly validated, there is a tendency for some parents to use their children as status symbols by driving them toward the success they themselves failed to achieve. The detrimental effect upon the children can be very great in these circumstancs because they become aware, on some level, that the parents are on an ego trip. As a result, they come to see their parents' interest in them as a form of manipulation rather than love. Moreover, the parents come to resent their children to the extent that they cannot perform in the required manner. If their children fail in school or on the ball field or in the social world, the parents may become very hostile or even punitive.

Youngsters have often been subjected to great abuses for simply getting B's instead of A's in school or making a faux pas in the presence of someone "important." This kind of relationship is pathogenic both for the parent and for the child, for the parent alienates himself from his own children and loses the opportunity for whatever closeness might have existed, and the child experiences rejection and disparagement and feels himself driven further away from the intimacy with the parents that he so urgently needs at this time of life. In any case, this situation tends to increase distance and further the loss of contact.

EMOTIONAL INHIBITION

If societies are formed in order to help men procure the necessities of life, what can be said of their efficiency in other areas of human endeavor? Henry (1963) believes that all societies tend to neglect certain human needs. Henry puts it this way,

Throughout history, in jungle and desert and on coral atolls and stone pavements inhabited by men, society has been established primarily for the purpose of guaranteeing food and protection. And from this primitive necessity has emerged the central problem of the human species: the fact that inner needs have scarcely been considered. Man has been so anxiously busy finding ways to feed himself and to protect himself against wild animals, and against the elements, and against other men, that in constructing society he has focused on these problems and has let even sex (not marriage) take care of itself. Within its formal legal institutions, no organized society has stipulated the procedures and guarantees for *emotional* gratification between husband and wife and between parents and children, but all societies stipulate the relationships of protection and support. The very efficiency of human beings in ordering relationships for the satisfaction of these external needs has resulted in the slighting of plans for the satisfaction of complex psychic needs; everywhere man has literally had to force from an otherwise efficient society the gratification of many of his inner needs.

Whether Henry is right about all societies or not is not the point. It is certainly true that many societies have, in fact, provided poorly for certain psychological needs. In our society the expression of emotion is one such area. The expression of emotion is probably the most natural thing for all the higher organisms with the exception of man. And for Americans the expression of emotion is often so confused by contradictory kinds of information that it is an extremely difficult and confusing part of our lives. This difficulty is not lessened very much by the attempts of psychologists to study the emotions, since the emotions are, by their very nature, not easily or clearly evoked in experimental situations. A number of problems related to the emotions can be clarified, however. One question concerns the physiological disturbances that occur in the presence of emotion. Another concerns itself with the expression of the emotion—that is, how the person behaves during an emotional display. And a third is related to the experience of the emotion—this is the subjective side of emotional life— the feeling that the subject experiences in a given emotional state. For the most part we will not be too much concerned with the physiological states of emotion. Our interest will lie with the latter two phenomena.

From childhood on we are told that certain emotions are "good" and others are "bad." That is, we are told we must feel certain emotions and must not feel other emotions. In addition we are often told we must not *express* certain emotions, whether we feel them or not, especially under certain circumstances. And the whole question of feeling and expressing becomes confused. If a child finds himself *experiencing* a certain forbidden emotion, he will try not to express it, but in so doing he will also often repress the *feeling* (that is, the emotion) itself, so that it no longer exists in his conscious mind. We can see, therefore, that experiencing an emotion and expressing it are related but not identical—and that we can sometime *experience* an emotion and *not express* it and we can sometime *repress both the experience and the expression of an emotion.*

It is considered a sign of a cultured individual to be calm, unemotional, self-contained, and cool, and the flagrant expression of emotion is very often considered gross, vulgar, and inelegant. We are therefore taught by our parents, who were taught by their parents before them, that emotional expression is often something that should be inhibited.

Another belief related to emotion is that people who lose their temper, or cry, or laugh raucously, especially in public, are crazy. A picture of the raving maniac is someone who is continually screaming and yelling and generally being too free with his emotions and too open with his feelings. Emotional expression, especially when it is exaggerated, is seen as either uncultured or insane.

the gender of the emotions

It is not yet clear to what extent males and females differ in terms of their emotional life. But it is quite clear that our society has decided that certain emotions are appropriate for one sex and not for the other and vice versa. Little boys are taught, therefore, that they must not cry, that they must not feel fear; moreover, they are ridiculed when they exhibit any of these undesired feelings. The little girl finds herself in a similar situation. She is not allowed to be assertive, to express anger, to raise her voice. She is allowed to feel fear and to cry and to express love under certain specified conditions. In later life men are not supposed to show too much tenderness or too much gentleness, for such feelings may easily be misinterpreted as softness or weakness. Women are required not to be overly sensuous, too flighty, or flamboyant in their emotional expression. Both sexes are expected to have their emotions under a certain amount of control at all times.

problems raised by inhibition of emotion

We have noted earlier that the failure of a person to recognize and experience his own feelings leads to certain kinds of difficulties. These difficulties are related to the *experiencing* of emotions and not to the *expression* of them. When we do not acknowledge our feelings, we distort a part of our being. The difficulties we have which relate to emotion are of this sort. Since we are taught that certain emotions are inappropriate or bad, we tend to repress them. And as we have noted before, repression means that we drive the emotion out of our conscious awareness.

A society can tell you how to *act* but it cannot realistically tell you how you must *feel*. A person's emotions are more or less spontaneous responses to situations that arise in the environment, paired with internal cues relating to the processing of this information. To tell a person that he cannot express certain emotions is one thing, but to tell him that he must not *feel* them is to force him into a difficult conflict.

The fact that society does, in fact, dictate what we can feel (should feel) and the inappropriateness of certain emotional responses leads us to be very confused and/or inhibited about our feelings most of the time. We have on the one hand people who have strange, unexplainable feelings about many things, and on the other, people who complain that they feel almost nothing. Both types of responses are probably related to the fact that real emotions have been repressed, have become unconscious, and therefore are no longer being experiencd in their own right—and have been altered in such a way that they no longer seem to correspond to the external events that aroused them.

emotion and control

Some people argue that it is necessary in a civilized society for people to "control" their emotions. It is sometimes said it is a sign of immaturity for one to simply express the emotion that he feels without restaint. But in making such statements, people often neglect to differentiate between the experiencing and the expression of an emotion. It is true that adults do not always express emotions that they are experiencing for a variety of reasons. But most psychologists believe that the healthy, mature individual is *aware* of his own feelings *regardless of whether he expresses them or not*.

compelling emotion

There is a corollary to the fact that our society frowns on the expression of certain emotions because they are considered inappropriate for one reason or another. And that is the attempt to compel us to experience those emotions that are considered valid or appropriate in certain situations, whether we feel them or not. Not only must we *not* feel hate for our parents, for example, we *must* feel love. And so people often try to experience feelings of love for their parents when in fact those feelings may not be present, at least for the moment. People also report terrible distress because they are not happy at the right time, sad at the right time, sentimental at the right time, and so on. For example, one young man was extremely disturbed because of the fact that he could feel no grief at his father's funeral. Another expressed concern because he felt unhappy when his mother came to stay with him for a short while. Situations like these often arouse feelings of guilt; and to avoid this, the person very often tries to force the appropriate emotion into existence.

Another version of the same kind of conflict occurs when people are engaged in activities in which they feel that they should be having a good time and find that they are not. One young lady was invited to a party by one of her best friends. But while at the party, she became ill. It was later learned that what had upset her was the fact that she thought that she should be having a good time, in order not to hurt her friend's feelings. But she was bored by the guests and found the party quite dull. She felt so guilty and disloyal to the friend who had invited her that she became quite disturbed. A similar situation occurs in cases where people go to a particular place for a vacation and then feel so obligated to enjoy themselves that they literally compel themselves to have a good time. Sometimes they are paying a great deal of money for this particular period of recreation, and they feel that the money will be wasted if they do not get a reasonable return on it in terms of pleasure and enjoyment.

Whether we try to inhibit emotions that are present or force into existence those that are not, the result is falsification of self-perception. And if the society traps us into situations in which we must falsify our ways of perceiving ourselves, it can lead to pathological behavior. A rich, authentic emotional life is an important element in healthy development. Being open to one's own emotional experiences enriches the scope of human experience. A society that prevents this impoverishes the life of its people.

THE PURITAN ETHIC

There are a number of beliefs related to the puritan tradition which, when held too rigidly, are often maladaptive. These beliefs, like others we have mentioned, are contrary to man's nature but generally believed to be universal laws of "good" human behavior. Many of these beliefs come under what has often been called the *work–sin ethic*. This set of beliefs is the underlying philosophy of most Western industrialized countries. It has its roots in the Protestant Reformation, and although it was originally mainly a religious doctrine, it has more recently found its way into secular life because it has had salutary effects upon the economic systems, especially in capitalist societies.

The beginning of the Reformation is generally said to have begun with Martin Luther. But it reached its most influential form, from our point of view, in the writings of John Calvin. Where Luther had taught that salvation lay simply in having faith in the existence of God, Calvin taught that this in itself was no guarantee. It was not man who chose God. It was God who chose man. Calvin believed that God ordained at the beginning of time who would be saved and who would be damned. Those who were "chosen" could not alter their destiny, no matter what they did in their life-time. The same was true of the damned. No amount of supplication, prayer, unselfishness or good works could change what was preordained in the first place. But how did a person know to which group he belonged? Was he one of the saved or one of the damned? Calvin had a very interesting answer to this question. Material success in this life was a sign of God's favor. There-fore, the desire to succeed was enlarged even beyond its ordinary scope. And the drive for success took on new meaning. Beside the ordinary re-wards that material wealth could bring and which are desirable enough in themselves, there was added to this the extra incentive of eternal happi-ness in the next life. One can see that this ethical outlook could be mate-rially helpful to economic systems of the Western societies of the nineteenth and twentieth centuries.

It was a short step from the idea that material success was a sign of divine grace to the designation of work as man's most important function in the eyes of God. As this idea grew, a clear separation appeared between anything that was considered "work" and anything that was associated with pleasure. Work, self-denial, a life of sacrifice became virtue. Pleasure, idleness, activities that were not "productive" or difficult all came to be considered the devil's work. The extension of this kind of thinking finally brought forth the work–sin ethic.

The Puritans brought this philosophy to the New World and, in one form or another, it spread rapidly. And for most of us, although we are not necessarily descendants of the Puritans, their ethic, to some extent, has taken hold. Many of us feel at least mildly guilty when we sit around doing nothing. Some of us worry a good deal even when we are working if that work does not produce something tangible toward which we can point as a product of our efforts. To many people work must be unpleasant to be considered work at all. And there is a clear distinction in our lives between work and play. It is interesting to note that adults in our society seldom use the word "play" in its general sense. Children go out to *play*; and in this sense the word means almost any kind of activity that can be pursued with a little imagination. Adults either go out to work or if the word "play" is used, it is usually meant in a structured content (play golf, play tennis). Children have *fun*. Adults almost never use this word. Fun is contrary to the work–sin ethic.

sin

We have already noted that anything that gives rise to feelings of worthlessness and guilt leads to self-disparagement, which in turn leads to fears and anxieties that are harmful to the organism. The work ethic has this effect because it makes impossible demands upon the conscience of the individual. No matter how much productive work a person does, he can always find more of one kind or another that he feels he should have done. Or he may berate himself for not having done the work he has already completed, faster or better. Every time he finds himself too tired or perhaps even too bored to continue, feelings of guilt or worthlessness are likely to follow. But if idleness or the desire for idleness creates guilt, it is nothing alongside the guilt created by the concept of sin. Sin is defined as the willful transgression of divine law, or violation of the laws of morality or religion. To commit a sin, therefore, is to behave in the most reprehensible manner possible. There are all kinds of sins in the Puritan ethic, but the most important is the one from which we are all believed to suffer—that is Original Sin.

The idea that all men are conceived in sin lies at the foundation of much of Christian theology. According to this doctrine we are all sinners, even before birth. There is no way for us to escape our nature, for our very existence testifies to the sinful deed through which we were conceived. This, of course, is the most extreme expression of this doctrine, and most people today no longer accept it in this form. However, many of us are still influenced by it. And the feeling that we are "bad" is not an easy one to dispel.

Christianity made an attempt to overcome this problem. The Christian God is charitable and forgiving. And He loves us in spite of our sins. All we need do is accept Him, and we are redeemed. This, in some ways, was a noble attempt to undo the damage that the doctrine of sin had done. But from a psychological point of view, it has fallen short. To *forgive* may indeed be divine. *To be forgiven* is to forever be disparaged. This is true because the communication of forgiving is a put-down. It says, "You are bad. You are evil. You are a sinner. But I am loving and charitable, therefore I forgive you." The very act of forgiving stresses the difference between the forgiver and the forgivee. And the temporary relief that is gratuitously received is short-lived.

The act of confession also has as its aim the eradication of guilt. But it does not always have this effect. The person coming to the confessional, carrying with him the feelings of guilt that go with the "sins" he has committed, does not easily forget about them when he is "absolved." The fact that he has had to carry them in his mind for some time and that he has to divulge them to another human being is likely to have lasting effects. Rather than reducing guilt, this procedure, for many, tends to increase it. And the feelings of worthlessness that result are not easily dispelled. A lifetime of weekly visits to the confessional is not likely, therefore, to lead to feelings of self-esteem.

sex

We have already considered the problems of sex and will therefore have no need to devote a great deal of attention to them here. However, in the context of our present discussion, it seems necessary to make certain observations. Any taboo against biological functions is likely to present serious problems to the individual. The taboos against sex, arising out of the Puritan ethic, can clearly be shown to be pathogenic. Once again it should be pointed out that a society can place restrictions on one's behavior but not on one's thought. The puritan tradition not only labeled sexual behavior as bad, it also implied that sexual thoughts belonged in this same category. The results, as we have seen, have been disastrous.

The same might be said of the sex roles that we have been forced to play. Male and female natures do not comfortably fit the roles we have devised for them. Attempts to fit into these roles with the subsequent necessity for denial and repression have created a great deal of confusion and anxiety.

The reason that such traditions are viewed as pathogenic is because they lead to self-deception. A quote from Maslow (1968) may make this clear.

> Freud's greatest discovery is that *the* great cause of much psychological illness is the fear of knowledge of one's self—of one's emotions, impulses, memories, capacities, potentialities, of one's destiny. . . In general this kind of fear is defensive, in the sense that it is a protection of our self-esteem, of our love and respect for ourselves. We tend to be afraid of any knowledge that could cause us to despise ourselves or to make us feel inferior, weak, worthless, evil, shameful. We protect ourselves and our ideal image of ourselves by repression and similar defenses, which are essentially techniques by which we avoid becoming conscious of unpleasant or dangerous truths.

The dangerous truths we wish to avoid in regard to sex and sex roles are those that do not fit the prohibitions of the Puritan ethic. If we feel sexy when we shouldn't or enjoy doing something considered inappropriate for our sex role, we are forced to use the defenses described by Maslow to avoid acknowledging these facts. It is this clash of one's real nature with the traditional views of his society that can often lead to psychological disturbance.

the puritan morality

There is a great deal of controversy about whether the traditional morality is *really* moral in any sense. And young people nowadays are asking a great number of questions regarding the values of our society. But from the psychological point of view, one serious problem related to the whole question of morality is the one concerning conscience.

> The ideas of the Enlightenment taught man that he could trust his own reason as a guide to establishing valid ethical norms and that he could rely on himself, needing neither revelation nor the authority of the church in order to know good and evil. The motto of the Enlightenment, "dare to know," implying "trust your knowledge," became the incentive for the efforts and achievements of modern man. The growing doubt of human autonomy and reason has created a state of moral confusion where man is left without the guidance of either revelation or reason. (Fromm, 1947)

If the Enlightenment told us that we could trust our own reason, we did not heed its advice very well. Men generally sought the word of authority as the simplest means of ordering their own lives. This meant that for most people that which was considered moral and immoral was always what *someone else* said it was. The acceptance of this kind of morality prevented us for a long time from trusting our own reason to tell us what was good or evil.

The introjection of this kind of morality has been ably described by Freud in his concept of the superego. But Freud thought that all morality was thus introjected. And it now appears that he may have been speaking of a special case—of a certain kind of moral judgment—which is common but not universal. In the Freudian superego, the child, because of the attachment to his parents, comes to act in ways that they see as moral long before he can make such judgments for himself. As he grows older, he incorporates these values into his own thinking and they become the core of his conscience. When he acts in ways that contradict this set of beliefs, the guilt that he feels is the result of breaking a code of ethics whose validity he has come to accept. And when he acts "morally," he does so because he feels that he must, not because he feels that he would like to. The superego is a hard taskmaster; and when we disobey it, it does not forget easily.

There is another kind of morality, however, one that is not based so much on guilt. This other kind of morality is not introjected in the same way as the guilt morality is. It is not necessarily based on the value systems of one's parents or of society. It may incorporate a number of the same values, but that would be partly coincidental. This morality is the one of the healthy individual.

Maslow has shown that the healthy person tends to be free of the conventional restraints of his society.

> The point I wish to stress here is the detachment, the independence, the self-governing character of these people, the tendency to look within for the guiding values and the rules to live by. (Maslow, 1968)

Healthy people evidently fulfill the promise of the Enlightenment. They use their own reason and judgment to arrive at their own value system. But the values they hold are not those that have been dictated to them by an authority—whether that authority be the church, parents, peers, or any other person or group of individuals. The values they hold, they hold because they feel them intimately as worthwhile. They are strongly empathetic and they want for others the same things that they want for themselves. When they break their own code of ethics, they do not feel guilty in the same sense as the person who believes in authoritarian morality. But they feel pain—pain related to the fact that they have hurt someone else. That in essence is the basis of their morality, to be considerate of themselves and of others. And if they fail in this they are disappointed and unhappy because they can experience the unhappiness of others. They do not act out of a sense of guilt but out of a sense of concern—or, if you will, love. They act morally not because they are afraid that they will be punished but because it makes them happier to do so.

There is an interesting difference between this kind of morality and the other. In the introjected morality, a person accepts whatever kinds of moral judgments are given him by his parents and other authority figures. He makes no judgments about them for himself. Therefore, when a Napoleon, Hitler, Stalin, takes over, he follows him blindly. He does his bidding whatever that may be. For, by definition, that which the authority decides is moral, is moral. The healthy person reacts in a different way. When the tyrant starts to change the rules, he is immediately sensitive to it. He has a sense of values that are not so easily alterable. He sees the injustice and the immorality and he resists it. It is therefore impossible for the tyrant to get the healthy person to give him his support. Perhaps if we were all healthy, there would be no tyrants.

COMPETITION

Some degree of competitiveness is probably natural and healthy. Individuals striving for mastery very often have to measure themselves against others to have a standard of evaluation. Sometimes the only measure we have for the performance of a certain type of ability or achievement is the performance of other human beings. Such things as intelligence and aptitude are generally measured in this way.

But beyond the use of these kinds of comparisons, competitive behavior, when it becomes excessive, can become pathogenic. In our society, in a number of areas of our life, the competition becomes so keen that it is harmful or destructive to those engaged in it. The forms that this destructiveness takes are varied. They may affect the person engaged in the competition himself, or they may be harmful to others who are not directly engaged in the competition but "innocent bystanders" who become victims as a result of the process itself.

feelings of incompetence

One aspect of competition to which we have already alluded is its contribution to feelings of disparagement (see Chapter 3). In most competitive enterprises, there are a large number of losers and a small number of winners. Where a great deal of value is placed on the idea of winning, the resulting feelings of self-devaluation among those who do not succeed are often great. Moreover, since no one succeeds all the time, everyone in a competitive society has the experience of losing, and feeling disparaged, a good deal of the time. It is an interesting phenomenon in our society that even the most "successful" among us tell their psychiatrists that they very often feel worthless without understanding why. Competition, of course, is not the only reason for disparagement. But it is a very important one.

stress

The unrelenting pressure of competition leads in some people to a chronically high level of tension. Stress and tension in moderate amounts are not believed to be unhealthy and, physiologically speaking, the body is equipped to deal with them efficiently. In fact, it is probably necessary to be stressed occasionally and for short periods of time in order to keep these adaptive mechanisms in tune. And there is evidence to suggest that when stress and tension are absent from a person's life, they will be sought, as if they are a physiological requirement for normal functioning. However when stress becomes chronic—when the tension that exists keeps building from day to day over a long period of time and when the emotional accompaniment reaches a high level of intensity, severe physiological disturbances, beyond the organism's tolerance are likely to follow. The result is very often physical as well as psychological disorganization. The disabilities that result are often called psychosomatic or psychophysiological reactions. These disabilities will be considered more fully later.

The stress reaction is a temporary "alarm reaction" which is a nonspecific adaptive response to severe but temporary stress. Since it is only geared to temporary crisis situations, it it maladaptive when the situation evoking the response is extended over a long period of time. A continual high level of tension is evidently not natural to the human organism. In the primitive state it is likely that man met with crises of short duration to which he reacted quickly and from which he was able to withdraw within a short period of time. This kind of reaction to stress, perhaps because of its adaptability, has survived into the complex industrial world of today. But it was not developed to handle the competitive drive of modern man. As a result, we have no way to deal with the continual stress that modern life places upon many of us.

Since we are not endowed with a mechanism to cope with this kind of "continual crisis," we break down under the strain. The physiological processes that were intended to respond to short, threatening situations now continue to operate long beyond the point where their functioning serves the purpose for which they were intended. And the body, under the onslaught of this long-lasting pressure, finally breaks down. The illnesses that result are clear indications of the pathogenic nature of stressful competition.

ethic of self-gratification

One of the by-products of a competitive way of life is its effect on human relations. We have already mentioned the way in which competition tends to move people away from one another. While it is doing this, it is creating another kind of climate, in which a person learns to gratify his wishes at the expense of others. The competitive game is played in such a way that the one who wins can only do so by defeating his rival in some way. If competition is raised to a virtue, then gratifying one's self, by taking something of value from others, also becomes praiseworthy. The result is an ethic that accepts self-indulgence at the expense of others as one of its prime values.

There is no question that all organisms are interested, to some extent, in the gratification of their own wishes. To this degree they ignore the wishes of other organisms of their own species in order to achieve this end. But most other animals are limited in the kinds of acquisitions they can make or the kinds of possessions they can acquire, and these limitations tend to keep this tendency within bounds. Man, having no such restraints, tends to overstep the kinds of restrictive boundaries that might keep such behavior in check, with the result that some human beings take a great deal of what is valuable in modern life with no consideration for the needs of others. This narcissistic attitude, which dotes on self-gratification and which prevents the maturation of those affected by it, is one of the signs of our times. Psychiatric descriptions of neurosis abound with characterizations such as the following: self-centered, narcissistic, immature, incapable of understanding the needs of others, inability to feel and express love. The ethic we have been describing encourages the development of such characteristics. And the ethic in turn seems to be nourished by some of the competitive aspects of our lives.

failure

Competition has the paradoxical effect of increasing a fear of failure while increasing the incidence of failure. Keen competition leads to winners and losers; as a rule, losers outnumber the winners by a wide margin. The realization of this is likely to increase the fear of many people, especially those who are insecure in the first place. Fear of failure itself, however, acts as a self-fulfilling prophecy, for it creates anxieties that are liable to be counterproductive in almost any endeavor. The result is that failure is likely to be the outcome under a large number of circumstances.

Fear of failure has another result. It often prevents a person from accomplishing that which he is capable of because success would place him in a new, higher echelon of competition where his inadequacies might show. Many people, therefore, often prefer to fail and remain in the existing situation than to expose themselves to this kind of danger.

Some people consider failure and/or losing a form of humiliation. The late Vince Lombardi equated winning with "manhood" and told his players that to lose was to be stripped of their manhood and humiliated before thousands of fans. Failure viewed in such a guise is a frightening thing, indeed. From a psychological point of view, it is one thing to strive for excellence—it is another thing to equate losing with humiliation. Since in every competitive enterprise there is necessarily a loser, it would be more reasonable to make losing what it in fact is—a part of the struggle in life which must be faced by everyone at one time or another.

limitations

A highly competitive society tends to punish the person who has less ability in certain enterprises than others. Most people, in fact, think that this is just as it should be. After all, if a man is not capable of acquiring the things that his society has to offer by his own ability or ingenuity, then he does not deserve them. Such a view, although common in our society, is not universal. After all, why should a person be punished for the fact that he lacks certain abilities? It's not *his* fault. That's the hand he was dealt. No one is incompetent deliberately. If we had the choice, we would all be "good" at all those things that would make us better competitors. It is true, of course, that one often has to work hard in order to develop certain skills, but even so, he must have the necessary potentialities to begin with. We do not, for example, think that a blind person should suffer simply because he does not have the ability to see. But we do tend to have this kind of attitude toward other types of "disability."

A lack of the skills necessary to do well in a competitive situation is, in some ways, like any other disability. However, it is not generally as obvious to another observer. And our society does not act with the same kind of understanding and compassion toward these limitations[1] as it does to others.

As a result, people who are not adept in the competitive sphere get very little sympathy or help from the rest of us. And this is very unfortunate, since many of these people might possibly make valuable contributions to our society if they were given a chance. The society offers many kinds of opportunities for those who are competitive but very few for those who are not.

> It is no problem at all to locate jobs requiring an orientation toward achievement, competition, profit, and mobility, or even toward a higher standard of living. But it is difficult to find one requiring outstanding capacity for love, kindness, quietness, contentment, fun, frankness, simplicity. (Henry, 1963)

Our tendency is to show those who do not compete well that they are not very valuable to our culture. There are very few niches which they can fill, and when they find one, it often carries a low status along with its low wage. Henry (1963) refers to the competitive tendencies as *drives* and the cooperative ones as *values*. He says, "If you are propelled by drives, the culture offers innumerable opportunities for you; but if you are moved mostly by values, you really have to search, and if you do find a job in which you can live by values, the pay and prestige are usually low."

In this way society communicates what it prizes. It tells those who are noncompetitive among us that they are inadequate. And the unspoken implication is that this inadequacy is their own fault and that the rewards that they get are commensurate with their value as human beings. As a result, a great many individuals see those very qualities which make them more human as liabilities and limitations and try to eliminate them insofar as they can. It is quite ironic that those qualities which most thoughtful people agree are the most virtuous (love, kindness, quietness, consideration) are, in the competitive marketplace, the least valuable. Thus we find ourselves in a situation where, very often, virtue has no value, and value, very little virtue.

---

[1]The word "limitations" is used here only in the sense that these kinds of qualities are perceived as such by the society at large. An argument might be made that these are not limitations at all but simply different kinds of orientation toward one's environment. What we consider abilities and/or limitations depends upon our particular culture.

poverty and deprivation

The competitive attitude means that there must be winners and losers; one important result is that there also must be wealth and poverty. The existence of poverty is both a cause and a result of psychological distress. Poverty tends to perpetuate itself because it destroys the individual in ways that very often make it impossible for him to climb out of the trap. The culture of poverty as it now exists in the United States is all the more destructive because it exists side by side with affluence. This comparison makes poverty more difficult to bear and causes the perceptions of the poor to be distorted so that they see much of the rest of the society as hostile. Moreover, the feeling of being less valuable, less important, which usually accompanies the experience of poverty, is disparaging and painful—leading to a whole host of responses from avoidance to aggression.

All of our research points to the fact that psychiatric disorders among the poor are many times what they are among the other socioeconomic groups.

Numerous studies suggest that the form of adult deprivation implied by lower social class position is a significant determinant of severely disordered psychological functioning. (Fried, 1970)

Two contrasting views of life. Imagine the differing psychological effects of the two environments. Some poor people never have the chance to break out of the culture of poverty or to experience an environment like the one on the right.

The stressful conditions of poverty are numerous enough to be disabling in many ways to a large number of people. Although arguments can be advanced which purport to show that the psychopathology of the poor is a *cause* of their poverty rather than an *effect,* they are not very convincing. It may be that some people are poor because they are psychologically disturbed, but it is also quite apparent that some people are psychologically disturbed because they are poor. Knowing what we do about human functioning and the kinds of stress under which people must live in the deprived areas of our society, it is reasonable to believe that poverty gives rise to a great many social ills, of which psychopathology is only one.

We must not make the error of believing that poverty is simply an accident or unfortunate consequence of "the way things are." We often hear the phrase "the poor will always be with us." This is a widespread belief. And it reflects an attitude which says: "This is the way the world is and there is nothing we can do about it." This is an unfortunate attitude. And it probably stems from the idea that in a competitive society there must always be a lower rung, which, for the most part, does without the more valuable commodities that society can produce.

This is not necessarily true. Even in a competitive society, it is possible for the least capable, the most poorly educated, the disabled, the infirm to live in a reasonably comfortable way, without deprivation and poverty, if their society desires it. The fact that between 30 and 40 million Americans do not simply testifies to the fact that we do not desire it enough to make it happen.

Research has shown that in addition to creating the conditions for mental illness, the culture of poverty has other detrimental effects on the human organism. Among these is the impairment of intellectual functioning. It is, of course, well known that poor nutrition in the early years of life can retard or destroy the integration of the central nervous system. What is not as well known is that the deprivation of the sense organs can have an equivalent kind of effect. That is, if the child does not get certain kinds of stimulation in the early years of life, he may develop biochemical deficiencies that will permanently affect his intellectual capacity. It is likely that there are critical periods in the development of the child when sensory stimulation of the different modalities is necessary for their full development. In the deprived environments of the poverty groups these kinds of stimulation either do not occur or, if they do, may not be sufficient. There appears to be a relationship between these kinds of inputs and biochemical processes in the central nervous system which, if not brought into play at the proper time, results in subtle physical defects that may be correlated both with pathology and intellectual deficit.

Poverty, of course, is not a value in our society. Most people would agree it is something that we would like to eradicate. Yet in spite of all of our dreams of the millenium—in spite of our good intentions and sincere efforts—poverty remains in our midst. It remains, not because it is inevitable, but because we do not wish to pay the price to abolish it. It is, at least partly, a symptom of a set of values that places material progress and personal ambition above the value of human welfare.

possessiveness

The idea of owning things is related to the concept of self. Animals, as a rule, do not own very much. Most of the things they need are available in nature and are obtained by their efforts or those of a mate. Nevertheless, within certain limits, animals will be possessive about certain things. They will protect their young, they will protect their "home," and they will protect their territory.

The concept of territoriality requires some attention. It is quite clear that there is a drive for territorial possession among many species of animals. For the most part this drive takes the form of defending an area of space whether it be earth, air, or water against intruders, usually of the same species.

> In most but not all territorial species, defense is directed only against fellow members of the kind. A squirrel does not regard a mouse as a trespasser. (Ardrey, 1966)

To this extent the territorial drive is a competitive one. Ardrey, in fact, belives that territoriality is even more important than sex.

> As a general pattern of behavior, in territorial species the competition between males which we formerly believed was one for the possession of females is in truth for the possession of property.

Whether this is true or not, the fact is that the drive to gain and defend a certain area of space which the individual organism can protect is an important one. But attempts to make inferences from animals to human beings must be done cautiously. We must remember that human beings change and often exaggerate the biological tendencies that exist within them because of their unique ability to innovate. Where the drive to acquire territory and property for an animal is limited so that all animals of the same species have roughly the same kind of territory to defend, this is not true of man. Tendencies such as these in the human species often become infinite. The desire for property and territory in man can become limitless. In human societies, therefore, some people acquire great territorial holdings while others acquire nothing.

Fences are often used to denote lines of demarcation between territories.

Possessiveness in this sense becomes pathological because the desire for infinite holdings in terms of wealth, property or territory, and so on, is obsessional on the one hand, and on the other, for those who have no territory or possession, it is destructive because it frustrates a natural need. Competitive possessiveness, in which the idea is to continue to gain material goods and/or territory at an increasing rate and without limit, is therefore a perversion of the natural territorial drive.

Although territoriality in the animal species is competitive, it also has an element of cooperation about it. The proprietor of the territory stakes out a fair proportion of the available area. For the most part he has little trouble driving off intruders, who, in some sense, appear to realize that they have stumbled into another animal's jurisdiction. They themselves may have a territory elsewhere which they defend in the same manner. Cooperation exists in the fact that all these animals implicitly agree to keep their distance and to allot enough space to each individual or family to assure the survival of the species.

In the human organism this is not the case. The desire to continue to acquire territory and other possessions beyond one's immediate need has eliminated the cooperative aspect of animal territoriality. And the result is that only the competitive aspect remains. This means that some individuals continue to acquire territory, not by driving off intruders, but literally by drving off *proprietors*. This kind of acquisitiveness throws the entire territorial economy off balance. It results in a distribution of the available space that is extremely uneven. The consequences are frustration, conflict, paranoid defenses of the status quo against equally paranoid attacks upon it, constant confrontation and the inevitable stresses and pressures which are their result.

It should be pointed out that not all animals are territorial, for some have life styles which are antithetical toward it:

> There are many species, of course, for which the territorial tie would be a handicap to survival. Grazing animals for the most part must move with the season's grass. Elephant herds acknowledge no territorial bond, but move like fleets of old grey galleons across the measureless African space. The gorilla, too, is a wanderer within a limited range who every night must build a new nest wherever his search for food may take him. (Ardrey, 1966)

Animals (and perhaps men as well) who are nomadic do not have the same territorial need as those who spend their lives in a fixed locale. It might be that as modern man becomes more mobile, the necessity to defend a fixed measure of the environment may be less pressing. Moreover, since there are so many individual differences among human beings in this regard, it seems hazardous to make general assumptions about territoriality being "natural" or "genetic" in the same sense that these statements might apply to animals. Nevertheless, it is undeniable that territoriality exists and is often perverted by man in ways that lead, for some, to exaggerated acquisitiveness, and for others, to a situation in which they have no territory whatsoever to defend. The resulting disequilibrium ultimately becomes destructive to both parties.

vested interest

Just as the territoriality of animals is self-limiting and no single individual acquires large tracts of property at the expense of others, man also occasionally develops his own safeguards in this regard.

> Most, though by no means all, primitive societies are provided with intuitive limits on how much property may be accumulated by one person, and the variety of ways in which primitive society compels people to rid themselves of accumulated property is almost beyond belief. Distributing it to relatives, burning it at funerals, using it to finance ceremonies, making it impossible to collect debts in any systematic way—these and many other devices have been used by primitive culture, in veritable terror of property accumulation, to get rid of it. Rarely does primitive society permit the permanent accumulation of vast quantities of wealth. The fact that our society places no ceiling on wealth while making it accessible to all helps account for the "feverish" quality Tocqueville sensed in American civilization. (Henry, 1963)

By erecting safeguards against the excessive accumulation of property, primitive people avoid the possibility of having a situation in which property can become a subject of serious conflict. This is not to say that the distribution of property is perfectly even—for there is privilege even here. The chief, for example, may have a large tract of land, a larger house, or more wives. But his acquisitions cannot go on infinitely. And so, in primitive societies, it cannot occur that any one person or group of people can have a great deal of property while large numbers of others have none. This, of course, to a great extent, cuts down much of the motivation for the intrasocietal conflicts that are so prevalent in our culture.

These arrangements, which are so common and automatic for animal and primitive human societies, have somehow been lost sight of by Western man. Somewhere along the way we lost whatever traditions we had that determined the limits of what an individual could own. In the early days of American history, when the frontier was so broad that it seemed limitless, the idea of limitless holdings was very exciting and full of promise. (Even then, the property that we took was not ours—for there were people here before us—a fact that we tend to forget.) Although such an attitude may have appeared to be justified in those times, it no longer has the same rationale. Nevertheless, through inertia, it is still retained as one of our most "cherished" goals.

The highly competitive attitudes of modern life, coupled with acquisitiveness (which for all intents and purposes appears infinite), leads to a certain kind of self-indulgence, which is very often destructive, because of its rigidity. People who have accumulated a certain amount of wealth, or have risen to certain positions in the status structure, are loath to allow changes to occur which they feel might threaten the status quo. As a result, a great many bureaucratic structures have grown up around people, professions, careers, and so on, that are designed to protect their vested interest against the encroachment of change. The result is that the more people acquire, the more frantically they defend what they have; at the same time, it becomes more and more difficult for others to accommodate their own needs if, in so doing, these vested interests are jeopardized.

There is no question that many of the conflicts within our society are generated by this set of circumstances. Moreover, the effect on both sets of individuals—those with the vested interests and those without—are paralyzing. Those who wish to defend the status quo become so rigid that they cannot change even when change becomes desirable, and they often become so fearful that they are likely to perceive every event, no matter how innocuous, as potentially threatening. The other group of people, those without large holdings, are likely to view the world in opposite terms. They see themselves with nothing while others are becoming wealthy at their expense. They are likely to constantly be agitating for change, but, for them, change either comes much too slowly or not at all. Their perception of the world may also be hostile since they see it as large, impersonal, immovable, and lacking in compassion.

INDUSTRIALIZATION

The Industrial Revolution was a true boon to mankind, for it presaged the coming of an age in which it would be possible for all human beings to have the necessities of life. But the advent of sophisticated machines meant the growth of large urban centers which would house the operations of the machines and bring together the raw materials from which the new manufactured products could be made. Machines may be efficient, but they are seldom beautiful, graceful, personal, loving, or responsive to the most basic human needs. And it appears that there is a direct relationship between the number of machines (that is, the level of industrialization) and alienation.

Industrialization brings with it a new kind of environment for which man's evolutionary history has not adapted him. Large cities, in general, are not conducive to the kinds of fulfillment that are possible in a rural setting. Of course, cities have other kinds of compensations. Museums, libraries, art galleries, theaters, business and commerce—all kinds of activities go on in cities which could not take place elsewhere. And these broaden man's horizon and make life more interesting. But there is a price to be paid for these advantages. There is the dirt, the pollution, the noise, the ugliness—there is the alienation. Large cities, especially the older ones, can have devastating effects on human beings. One need only visit any major city in the United States and look closely at the faces of the people to observe these effects. There is tragedy and despair in the eyes of many. And there is hostility and desperation, coldness, cruelty, indifference, or apathy almost anywhere one looks. These are not merely subjective impressions. A great deal of clinical evidence testifies to the fact that these observations are accurate. Large urban centers can have powerfully depressing effects upon their inhabitants.

A great deal of clinical research tends to support the contention that there is more mental illness in cities than in rural areas. And it is abundantly clear to anyone who has looked into the matter that the industrialized areas of our world are often destructive and antithetical to the development of healthy personality. There appears to be no question, therefore, that life in large cities—particularly for the poor but often also for the well-to-do—can be pathogenic.

density

The first impression that anyone gets on visiting a large city anywhere in the world is the sense of overcrowding. We have already seen that there is evidently a minimum amount of territory that appears to be required by an individual in order to carry out his life functions. In the city these territorial requirements are often not fulfilled. The large numbers of people crammed into relatively small geographical areas precludes such considerations. As a result there is a widespread feeling of having one's privacy invaded, of being thrust into close physical contact with strangers, of having other people in "one's way," or of simply being overwhelmed by mere numbers. Some experiments have shown that overcrowding often leads to breakdowns in what is considered "normal" social behavior and that conflicts and criminality sometimes result. Although these reactions may not be completely attributable to density, it seems that what is happening in our cities today might reasonably be said to result from such a pattern.

The density is all the more disheartening because paradoxically in our large cities, where people are thrown together in such close physical contact, their psychological distance, as we have noted above, remains very great. So we have the spectacle of people being in very close physical proximity while often experiencing a very profound sense of loneliness. Such conflicting perceptions are often extremely stressful.

alienation

The large industrialized state builds into its fabric certain kinds of insulation which prevent the "man in the street" from reaching the levers of power. This is not necessarily done deliberately—it is more likely simply an outgrowth of the large, bureaucratic, impersonal structure of modern civilization. And, of course, in order to deal with large numbers of individuals, it becomes necessary to lose sight of their separate identities and to treat them in ways that ignore their uniqueness.

Those of us who are caught up in this kind of situation generally begin to resent the kind of impersonality with which we are treated by others. People who have dealings with one another come less and less to look at each other both in the physical and the psychological sense. Numbers and computer codes replace names—plastic cards carry identification marks (that is, identity) with which we transact business. Other human beings do not know us and, worse, appear not to want to know us. In fact, we are known better by computers than by other people and find ourselves responding like computers in turn.

Industrialization and its concomitant, mass production, contribute to alienation in other ways. Workers become further and further removed from the finished products to which they contribute. They see themselves as replaceable cogs in a machine that cares nothing about their existence. If they become ill or disabled or even dissatisfied, they can be immediately replaced and the machine plods on without them. Intelligence, will, creativity—all of these are superfluous. Even worse, they are counterproductive. Every quality that increases humanity and contributes to a feeling of being alive is antagonistic to the system. The worker learns to repress and deny such feelings and attitudes, further deepening his noninvolvement.

The alienation of human beings in highly industrialized society is aggravated in still another way. The massive, indifferent technological system, which appears to be separate from him and unresponsive to his needs, creates feelings of helplessness and apathy which are the hallmarks of this syndrome. A person simply withdraws. He gives up whatever hope he had that life could be meaningful. His senses become deadened and his feelings become shallow. He becomes a passive recipient of all that is presented to him. Like Camus' hero in *The Stranger*, the alienated man feels very little and cares even less. He is not very much concerned about what happens because it makes no difference to him. Life, death, love, hate—these things are irrelevant for him. They are all the same. At best, he is only marginally involved.

The alienated man lives a life that often borders on despair. In the most extreme case he sees himself as useless and expendable. He feels not only that he does not count, that his actions can have no influence on the world, but also that his disappearance would also go unnoticed. He believes that nobody cares and he himself stops caring. He simply goes through the motions of living as if he were under an anesthetic.

The alienated man has almost lost the capacity to feel boredom because boredom is his natural state. Even the few diversions he seeks out have little effect on him. He has hobbies that he pursues "in order to have something to do." But they are joyless. They occupy him but they cannot move him. He has long ago lost the capacity to be really moved or interested in anything.

Three dehumanizing forces of modern life: Industrialization, frustration, depersonalization.

Alienation as we find it in modern society is almost total; it pervades the relationship of man to his work, to things he consumes, to the state, to his fellow man, and to himself. Man has created a world of man-made things as it never existed before. He has constructed a complicated social machine to administer the technical machine he built. Yet this whole creation of his stands over and above him. He does not feel himself as a creator and center, but as the servant of a Golem, which his hands have built. The more powerful and gigantic the forces are which he unleashes, the more powerless he feels himself as a human being. (Fromm, 1955)

The alienated man is, as Fromm has shown, a captive of his own creation. He has unwittingly created a way of life that is devoid of meaning. He comes to perceive everything as being pointless—he goes from one thing to another in a kind of trance. He moves like an automaton from his home to his job, back to his home again through the evening routine to bed—then the whole thing is repeated again and again—the routine is deadening and he withdraws more and more from involvement with it. If one were to ask him why he persisted in his routine, he would have difficulty explaining. He feels that there is no sense to it, but he cannot stop. For him there is no meaning to his life—only a dim feeling that he must go on. And so he does.

powerlessness

One very pervasive feeling of people in modern industrial societies is the sense of powerlessness. The vastness of the country, the tremendous number of human beings, the distance of the average man from the regions where decisions are made—all contribute to the sense of helplessness that people feel regarding their lives. One need not be alienated in the sense that we have noted above to have this overwhelming feeling of impotence. Even people whose lives are otherwise meaningful and enjoyable find themselves completely ineffectual in terms of shaping policy or making changes in the established structure. Each man sees wrongs that must be righted, problems that must be solved, injustices that must be undone, but he feels like a small voice crying out in the wilderness where no one can hear.

Whole groups in our society find themselves, because of their small number, without the resources to have any effect whatsoever on their own lives. Elderly people are discarded by their children, by the society, taxed out of their homes, forced to live on fixed incomes that are continually eroded by inflation, and they are unable to bring any pressure to bear on their government to change these conditions because they do not constitute a large enough segment of the society to have an effect on its political life. Elderly people are not only made to feel useless by being forced to retire while they are still able to do worthwhile work, they are also treated as second-class citizens once they are out of the mainstream by being pre-vented from exerting influence in their own behalf. This form of *involu-tional uselessness* is only one example of the powerlessness that other in-dividuals and groups feel.

The frustration experienced by groups of this sort who are cut off from the mainstream of life sometimes gives rise to violence and lawless-ness as a release for the pent-up feelings. But in the case of the aged, even this outlet is unavailable; the only alternatives available to the elderly are depression, apathy, melancholia, and the like.

materialism

One of the most pervasive values in our society, and one that leads to a great deal of human misery, is the attitude toward *things*. It has often been said that we take better care of our cars than we do of our bodies. And there is, of course, some truth in this statement. We would never, for example, consider putting something into the carburetor of an automobile that would interfere with the flow of air through it. Yet we have no com-punction about doing just such a thing to our lungs with cigarettes. But if we have little concern for the health and welfare of our bodies, we have even less for those of other people.

It seems clear that our society values *things* above *people*, and ma-terial above life. In fact, in a certain sense, it might be said that Americans have come to worship things—and that possessions have become the twen-tieth-century religion.

The desire by most Americans to accumulate goods at an ever-increasing rate is one of the strongest motives in modern life. The need for these objects is sometimes so great that people will deny their natural feel-ings for other human beings to justify this pursuit. Even in a period of affluence, when most people have more of the "good things" of life than they ever had before, they feel cheated and betrayed when their govern-ment asks them to share some of their wealth with those who are less for-tunate. In fact, one hears a great deal of criticism about the poor—accusa-tions that they are lazy, stupid, unwilling to help themselves. Much of this criticism comes from people who would like to consume more than they are able to by the present tax structure. And since much of their taxes goes toward helping poor people, a lot of resentment is generated toward this group.

The need to create a consumer society seems to be a necessity if the economic system is to function. The materialistic attitude is therefore strongly encouraged in order to guarantee this eventuality. But to do this we have to create needs and desires where none existed previously.

> The contrast between primitive culture's assumption of a fixed bundle of wants and our culture's assumption of infinite wants is one of the most striking—and faithful—differences between the two cultural types. It contributes to stability in one and restlessness in the other. (Henry, 1963)

This assumption of infinite wants is the basis on which the production of material things is carried out. And it is the job of the advertising industry to create these wants in order to guarantee continued consumption. With the introduction of new products there is a concomitant campaign to create, in the minds of the people, the feeling that these new products are necessary to their happiness and/or survival. This ensures a perpetual demand for products in a spiraling curve that continues toward infinity.

With such needs and/or wants, the average person finds himself always in a state of relative deprivation, in terms of the things he would like to own. And there is a tendency on the part of many, as they struggle to satisfy these desires, to lose more and more of their humanity along the way. For other people become obstacles or status rivals rather than human beings.

For many Americans the struggle for *things* becomes so totally absorbing that they lose their interest and sensitivity for other kinds of pursuits. And they dedicate a lifetime to the accumulation of products that become substitutes for their own personal growth. For by equating what they possess with themselves, they see themselves as growing only in terms of these possessions. Their interests become centered upon accumulating more of such things, to the neglect of cultivating changes within themselves.

The accumulation of possessions and the enhancement of status are just other forms by which the PR personality manifests itself. But the desire to enhance one's self-image by the use of such techniques, as we have already noted, is fraught with difficulty. Attempts to improve one's feelings of self-worth by "decorating" the individual with fancy ornamentation from the outside is usually futile. Changes in self-perception of the kind generally sought have to come about by somewhat different means if they are to be stable and convincing to the individual himself.

PARENTAL ROLE

There is a great deal of research to show that parental neglect or disparagement have very damaging effects on the development of chlidren. And in a certain sense most of the pathogenic trends we have been discussing are transmitted to the children by their parents or their parents' representatives (schools, churches, governmental institutions). Moreover, the cultural attitudes toward children in any society usually determine the relationship that exists on a one-to-one basis between parents and children. However, when we look at the attitudes toward children in our society and then look at the ways in which children are treated by their parents, we find some puzzling discrepancies.

A great many people in our culture claim that their parents either did not love them or, if they did, were so deficient in the ability to express it that for the children it came to the same thing. Why this should be true in a society in which children are highly valued and esteemed is somewhat puzzling. But a few explanations present themselves.

instincts and human behavior

Most animals make good parents. It is extremely rare to find cases of parental neglect or rejection in the animal kingdom. This, of course, is true in nature and does not necessarily hold for animals in captivity or those that have been domesticated. In their natural surroundings most animals have well-developed procedures for caring for their young. These procedures generally ensure the healthy psychological development of the next generation. But since man lacks these predetermined modes of behavior—since almost everything that man does is influenced by learning, there is a wide variety of ways in which different human parents interact with their children, and some of these differences are related to traditional societal beliefs.

A great many youngsters in today's "pampered generation" come into psychotherapy and counseling with the same complaint. They may phrase it differently or even try to disguise it somewhat, but what they are almost always saying is this: "My parents never let me feel that I was loved." This complaint, which is widespread, must be related in some way to some of the issues with which we have been concerned in this chapter. Let us see how.

emotion

If we feel ashamed of our emotions or if we repress them because we consider them bad—then we are also unlikely to be able to express love. In fact, many parents are ashamed of openly demonstrating feelings of love, or they are simply unable to do so because for them such expressions are anxiety-provoking—and, as a result, they have no way of communicating what love they might feel. In fact, as a result of repression, they may feel very little love. Our traditional attitudes toward emotion may therefore make it difficult or impossible for many parents to communicate love to their children. The kinds of problems that can thus arise can be very serious indeed.

puritanism

The puritanical attitude has its effect on parenting because of its negativism and authoritarianism. Its negativism lies in the fact that the Puritan ethic demands so many inhibitions that the parent who accepts it must almost always be saying "no" to whatever his child desires to do. Moreover, the parent has to invoke the adjectives *good* and *bad* to describe almost every behavior. And it turns out that almost anything that a young child is likely to want to do will be labeled *bad*. Moreover, he will usually be told that *he* is bad for wanting to do it or if he gets away with it when his parent is unaware of the fact, he will feel guilt for having engaged in the forbidden activity. In any case a serious negative feeling about the self is the logical consequence of such activities.

The authoritarian aspect of puritanical attitudes destroys the parent–child relationship because it promotes *passive acquiescence*. The child is taught that he must accept the values expressed by the parents, that he must never question these values, and that when he does not obey them, he must be punished or otherwise atone for these transgressions. The loving relationship so necessary in the parent-child bond is undermined by these interactions. For the parent who is more or less forced to say, "You do it because I say so!" is destroying any respect for the individual in his relationship with the child. Children are aware of this and they rightly resent this kind of treatment.

competitiveness

It may be that one of the most important contributions to a subtle form of parental neglect in American society is related to our competitive nature. The "rat race" in which many people find themselves is so engrossing and exhausting that many parents who would otherwise be reasonably warm and loving simply have no time for their children. A great many middle-class children complain to their counselors in school that their parents come home tired, drained, angry, and simply cannot or will not relate to them in this state. Moreover, the types of activities in which they have been engaged throughout the day leave very little room for the kind of sentiment that is a necessary ingredient in parental love. It is not an easy matter for them to simply "turn it on" after spending a day in this other, very different, state of mind.

If middle-class children have these problems, they are even more acute for the youngsters of lower socioeconomic families. Here very often there is only one parent. That parent often has to work as well as keep a house and family together. The neglect that can occur in such situations has been well documented and needs no further comment here.

industrialization

Industrialization and its accompanying syndrome, alienation, are obviously not conducive to good parenting. People who have given up on life are not likely to be loving parents. People whose feelings are so shallow that they can experience no emotion will not find it easy to express love to their children. Moreover, since a person's frame of mind is determined to a great extent by his surroundings, the people who are forced to live in the dirt, the noise, the garbage, the ugliness will often find "loving and caring" to be luxuries that they cannot afford.

materialism

And finally the attitude that values things above people, objects above life, money above joy, tends to create a population in which deep human relationships are difficult or impossible. People who hold these values, whether parents or not, will not exhibit the kinds of attitudes that psychologists believe are essential to the healthy development of the young. These people, it is true, will often shower a great many material things on their children—but material things are not love and their children sense this. These attitudes merely perpetuate the problem either by creating a new generation with the same attitudes, or by giving rise to a generation of young people who because they have always felt unloved come to view themselves in negative terms. Both attitudes are destructive because they are antitherapeutic—in one way or another they do not contribute to the psychological well-being of the individuals in whom they reside.

We have concerned ourselves in this chapter with the pathogenic forces believed to contribute, in our society, to psychological distress. Some of these beliefs and values are not, of course, exclusive to American life. Some appear elsewhere, and there are different pathogenic forces at work in other human societies. But it is hoped that an understanding of these beliefs and attitudes will lead us to a better understanding of the prevalent pathological syndromes and, as a result, to certain modes of behavior that may be instrumental in counteracting them.

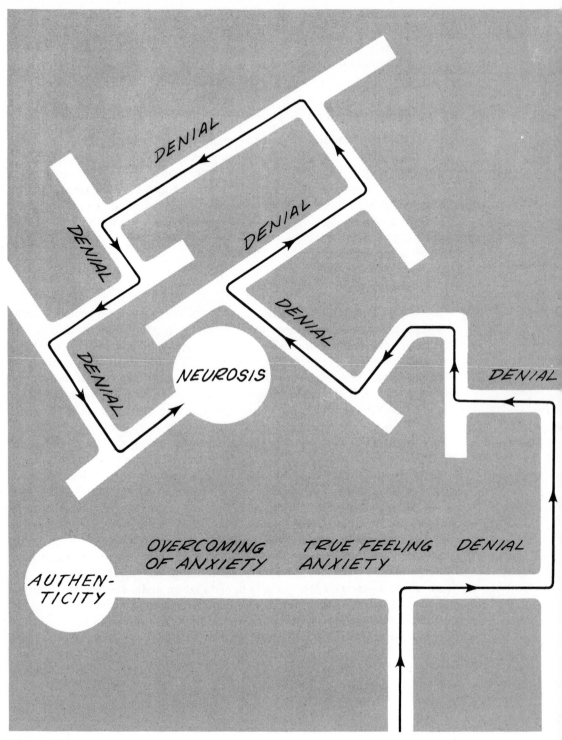

Neurotic Maze.

chapter 10
strategies of defense:
the self in conflict

THEORETICAL FORMULATION

Insanity has always held tremendous fascination for people. What is it, we wonder, that can cause a human being to lose control of his rational faculties, to "take leave of his senses" and become "mad"—a man without purpose, reason, without the ability to function in the present, to plan for the future, to anticipate the consequences of any of his acts? Insanity is both frightening and fascinating—frightening because we don't know what to expect from creatures so afflicted and fascinating because we know that with just a little impetus any one of us might easily be pushed over the edge, into the dark, terrifying region of the deranged. The *neurotic maze* on the opposite page shows how each attempt to avoid anxiety by using defense mechanisms leads further and further away from authenticity—finally leading to neurotic kinds of solutions.

267

the continuum

It is not a simple matter to define psychopathology. Almost any definition is subject to a certain amount of criticism and controversy. But it is generally agreed that what we call "abnormal" is not a discrete entity separated from normal behavior—it lies rather at one end of a continuum of behaviors that shade gradually into one another. At one end of the spectrum we have an idealized state which we might call "perfect health." At the other end is a state that might be called "total derangement." Neither of these extremes actually exists. There is probably no one who is totally psychotic any more than there is anyone who is perfectly sane. However, we use the two parameters as boundaries for the kinds of behaviors that do exist.

One of the most important questions from our point of view is, How does it happen that an individual, in the course of his lifetime, sometimes moves from the healthy end of the spectrum toward the pathological end? Knowing that, what forces can be brought to bear to reverse that process— to change the direction of his movement so that he begins to travel back toward the side of the continuum associated with psychological well-being? Such a reversal of momentum may not always be possible without outside help. Nevertheless, some understanding of the kinds of events that contribute to pathological states can be very helpful toward ameliorating them. Moreover, such knowledge contributes greatly to improving our dealings with other people, especially those who may be suffering from such "afflictions."

the nature of pathology

As we have noted, there have been a great many approaches to the problem of defining pathological behavior, and no particular one is universally accepted. But from our point of view, in terms of what we have been considering in this book, we may define pathology as *estrangement from the self*. And we can assume that the degree of pathology is directly proportional to the degree of this estrangement. Given such a definition, we can now examine the kinds of circumstances that contribute to movement along the continuum that leads, in one direction, to self-knowledge, self-acceptance, and psychological health, and, in the other direction, to self-deception, self-negation, and finally to a loss of contact between the self and reality.

THE DEFENSE MECHANISMS

One of the most remarkable insights of Freud's genius was the discovery of the mechanisms of defense, by which human beings can alter their perceptions or transform their feelings in order to meet certain adjustive demands or to face certain kinds of stressful situations. In a sense we can say that the defense mechanisms are strategies that the individual initiates to decrease a portion of his awareness with regard to the self. All defensive maneuvers, although some are occasionally useful within reasonable limits, are, in the final analysis, finely calibrated movements away from authenticity.

denial

We have already met the defense mechanism of *denial*, in earlier chapters. Denial is one of the simplest and most common of the defense mechanisms and in fact may be present in some form in most of the others. It is, simply stated, a method of avoidance. It is a means by which the mind simply does not see that which is present by ignoring it or "forgetting about it." On an unconscious level, when there are unpleasant thoughts or events that we would rather not acknowledge, we simply "make believe they are not there." In a sense we figuratively turn away from the unpleasant thoughts, sights, or feelings which may beset us. If a situation is dangerous or traumatic or disparaging to the self, we simply turn our attention elsewhere. We selectively perceive those situations which make us comfortable and fail to perceive those which cause us anxiety or pain.

An interesting example of the use of denial is the case of a young girl who was abandoned by her lover. The girl, unable to face the fact that her lover had changed his mind, became convinced that he had contracted some serious disease which had affected his mind. She kept calling him and telling him to go for help in spite of the fact that he continually explained to her that he no longer wanted to have anything to do with her. His continual rejections, however, had no effect on her. She simply continued to shake them off as aberrations of his "illness."

One can see in such an example a clear attempt to protect the PR image in at least two ways. In the first place, the young lady simply denies the rejection that is so obvious to everyone else. In the second place, she can persist in pursuing him, without feeling humiliated, by ascribing all of his evasiveness to his illness. Although one might say that the defense mechanism has in this case served a purpose, one might well question the cost. As long as the girl persists in perceiving that which is untrue for her—the fact she no longer has a lover—it will prevent her from making any realistic attempts to deal with the situation.

rationalization

The defense mechanism of *rationalization* is one that is so common and so much a part of our everyday life that we often fail to realize how much we use it. There are almost an infinite number of situations which are disappointing, embarrassing, anxiety-provoking, or simply just very unpleasant. But the technique of rationalization can often help us avoid the impact of these problems by the simple device of creating logical and justifiable reasons for their existence. If, for example, a person under hypnosis is given a posthypnotic suggestion that within one minute after awakening he will get up and open the window, he will usually follow the suggestion. That is, after being awakened, within a minute or so, he will often get up and open the window. But when asked why he did so, he will often say that he simply felt too warm. Now since the hypnotist's suggestion contained nothing about the room's temperature, the explanation that the subject has given is most likely an attempt to make sense out of a behavior whose real reasons he does not understand. And since it would be embarrassing to admit that he opened the window without knowing why, he rationalizes—he creates a reason that seems plausible.

It is usually a very simple matter for us to think up reasons to justify doing things that we should not do or to allow us to avoid doing some of the things that we feel we should. For example, we may spend a great deal of money on a car that we know that we cannot really afford, and then convince ourselves that it really didn't cost us so much because it has a higher resale value than the less expensive models.

Although this a very mild form of rationalization, it can also often take some very bizarre forms. The heroin pusher who rationalizes his behavior by saying, "I'm only giving people what they want" or "If I didn't do it, someone else would" may be trying to assuage severe guilt feelings.

Although rationalization and other defense mechanisms are commonly used by normal individuals, at least to a mild degree, it must be noted that such behaviors are tendencies along the continuum away from authenticity. This is not serious when the movement is slight and the distortions of perceptions, minimal. But even rationalization can become a serious problem when greatly exaggerated. Simply creating false reasons to justify our behavior is one thing. But the firm belief in events or facts that are untrue when stubbornly maintained in defiance of contrary evidence is delusional. Rationalization, when carried to its limit, can bring about such a state.

projection

The defense mechanism of *projection* is one of the most remarkable of all the defensive maneuvers. Projection is often intimately tied up with guilt, and it reflects an individual's need to free himself from this guilt by ascribing it to an outside source. Projection serves a double purpose. It allows a person to transfer his own unacceptable wishes, desires, fears (that is, unheroic traits) to others—and it also allows him to see others as the cause of his own weaknesses, shortcomings, misdeeds, and so on, when he *does* acknowledge their existence. Projection, in other words, gets us off the hook. It is the perfect strategy for blaming the external world for those traits that we cannot possibly accept in ourselves. We have noted earlier that there is a certain amount of paranoia in the perceptions of certain extreme groups. Projection is the *sine qua non* of paranoid thinking. There are many kinds of examples of this technique. The girl who allows herself to be seduced by a young man to whom she is very much attracted, says, "I couldn't help myself. He swept me off my feet." An impartial observer, however, would notice that she had engaged in a great deal of "leading on" by giving many nonverbal cues about her availability. On a conscious level, however, she does not realize this. And if she could see a film playing back her own behavior doing the flirtation, she might be very much surprised by her seductive behavior. Another example might be a young man with unacceptable homosexual tendencies, who sees homosexuality in other men almost everywhere he looks. He may in fact believe that these men have homosexual designs on him, when in fact it is he who is doing all the designing.

Projection need not always take such extreme forms. In some cases it is merely the tendency to see in others qualities of personality that exist in ourselves. These characteristics appear to us to be so automatic that we simply expect to see them in everyone else. Thus if we are generally honest, we tend to believe that others are likewise generally honest. If we are selfish, we may believe that others are selfish. If we are unhappy, then perhaps everyone is unhappy. It might be argued that these examples are not defense mechanisms at all. For they may not be used to *defend* ourselves against a particular threat. They may simply be ways of perceiving the world based on our own implicit assumptions that other people are very much like ourselves. Nevertheless the element of projection exists even in these situations. For we are seeing the qualities that we ourselves possess, in others. This, of course, is a natural tendency in all of us. Within certain normal limits, we tend to perceive the world in terms of our own psychological functioning. Projection, therefore, is a ubiquitous form of human behavior.

fantasy

One of the methods by which human beings make life tolerable, even under the most difficult of conditions, is through the use of *fantasy*. We are all, at times, wont to imagine things that are not true but that we would like to *come true*. It is a simple matter for any of us to sit down and imagine a world that would be ideal, or an event that could bring us great pleasure. Flights of fancy of this sort are means by which all of us can escape the pain or anxiety that reality sometimes inspires. But in other situations our fantasizing works against us—as when we allow ourselves to believe in the flattery of the con man or the exaggerated claims of the salesman or we believe that the person we love actually possesses all the superhuman qualities that we would like him to have. These kinds of fantasies generally lead to disillusionment because they cannot stand up against the harsh, persistent facts of reality.

Most fantasy is a result of feelings of frustration that arise out of the fact that many of our basic needs do not receive immediate gratification. The postponement or even the total prevention of certain gratifications can lead to a great deal of discomfort. In these situations a person may fantasize the acquisition of the desired goal in order to render that discomfort somewhat less disturbing. In our reveries there are no unfulfilled wishes. Even the past failures that we have suffered can be wiped out in a moment of fanciful reliving.

We have already noted that one prevailing fantasy that we all seem to embrace is the hero or heroine playing various roles and exhibiting various attributes. In James Thurber's *Secret Life of Walter Mitty* the main character continually fantasizes himself in heroic roles. He sees himself as rich, powerful, as a great surgeon, an athlete who wins the game in the final minutes, or a courageous soldier who wins the day through his daring and resourcefulness. In almost all his exploits, Walter Mitty receives the applause and admiration of all who come in contact with him. This kind of fantasizing seems to be related to PR striving.

Other kinds of fantasies come to us ready-made and we do not have to make use of our own imaginations for them. Movies, television, books, plays all give us the opportunity to escape the everyday real world and move into "more pleasant surroundings." Fantasy when used this way is sometime called *escapism*. This use of fantasy is generally helpful in aiding people who have boring lives. And it also helps those who may have failed to realize their dreams in real life to make greater efforts when the next opportunity presents itself. But like other defensive maneuvers, if this becomes extremely exaggerated, and an individual loses his clear-cut recognition of the difference between fantasy and reality, serious consequences may result.

repression

One of the most remarkable insights that Freud gave us is the one concerning *repression*. Until Freud's time it was generally not understood that an individual could simply "forget" thoughts or events that he found dangerous or painful and on a conscious level be completely unaware of their existence. This phenomenon is probably one of the most important discoveries in the history of psychology. Repression often acts to spare us from memories whose recollection would be so painful that they would be almost unbearable.

A young man was driving his car with his mother and sister as passengers when he was involved in a serious accident in which he crashed into the rear end of another vehicle. The man was immediately thrown clear, but his mother and sister were pinned in the wreckage. The gas tank of the vehicle he struck burst into flame, and within moments his own car was engulfed. The young man was seen by witnesses running around the car trying to free his mother and sister, whose screams could be heard as the flames closed around them. He became hysterical—he tried to reach his mother and sister but was driven back by the tremendous heat. The smell of burning flesh was overwhelming. The young man continued to circle the car screaming in anguish as he watched his mother and sister die in the flames.

A few days later this individual was unable to recall the incident. He knew that his mother and sister were dead, but he could not recall the events which were testified to by witnesses. The injuries that he himself had were very slight, and there was no evidence of concussion, thereby ruling out the possibility of memory loss caused by a head injury. In a follow-up study six months later, the man was still unable to recall any part of the incident.

This is an extremely dramatic example of the defense mechanism of repression at work. The memory of such a tragic episode was simply too painful for this person to bear. He may also have felt a certain amount of guilt, since it was he who was driving when the accident took place. But even without guilt, the traumatic effect of such an experience is simply so great that repression comes to our rescue and drives the memory of the event from consciousness.

Another example of the use of repression in forgetting traumatic past episodes is the case of a man who had been involved in an accident some years before in which a child had been killed. Since the man had been shown to be at fault, he considered himself responsible for the death of the child. As a result, the entire episode was blocked from his conscious memory. Even several years later he was unable to recall any part of the incident. This is a clear case of repressing unacceptable memories, for it is obviously unlikely that anyone who participated in such an event could simply have it "slip his mind." The only way one could forget such an incident would be to actively drive it out of his awareness. And this is precisely what repression does.

Besides making unacceptable memories unconscious, repression also acts to simply prevent our experiencing some events in the first place. When we are unable to accept our own "bad" emotions—when we are afraid of our sexual feelings, homosexual tendencies, anger, hostility, even love, we can simply avoid experiencing them on a conscious level by repressing them and remaining unaware of their existence.

Such repression is not always complete, and in many cases, some residue of the repressed feeling or experience may call it to our attention, if only occasionally. We may have vague feelings of discomfort or guilt without being able to attribute them to a particular cause. Sometimes some of our repressed desires may become manifest in our dreams, our fantasies, or in various kinds of behavior which we cannot easily explain.

It is important to make a distinction between *repression* and *suppression*. In the latter case we are dealing with a conscious process. We suppress something simply by deciding to avoid thinking about it. We consciously choose to turn our attention away from it—to think of something else or to turn our focus in another direction—thereby putting the event out of our minds, at least temporarily. But with repression there is usually no conscious choice. The mechanism appears to work automatically. It is as if the unconscious mind makes a choice to push an event or feeling out of awareness *just before* the conscious mind can take cognizance of it. And we say, therefore, that the whole process takes places on an unconscious level. We repress but we are unaware that we repress—and at the same time we are unaware of *what* we have repressed.

The most severe form of repression is *amnesia.* Sometimes, under intolerable conditions, people repress an entire segment of their life. The repressed portion is so large that we use the term "amnesia" rather than simply calling the phenomenon repression. In amnesia a person may forget his name, his occupation, the fact that he is married, that he has children; he may forget his occupation, the town in which he lives; his whole past may be a blank. Yet interestingly enough he remembers many of the normal processes of life, such as reading, writing, mathematical operations, and most of the rest of his functioning appears unaffected by his problem. We shall consider the specific dynamics of amnesia later when we deal with psychopathology.

Repression, like denial, which it resembles closely, appears to be prominent in most of the defense mechanisms. It is probably the most efficient maneuver we use in our strategies to avoid self-understanding. Those parts of *ourselves* that we find unacceptable or intolerable (and the term *ourselves* is really equivalent to *all* of *our experience*) are simply truncated or separated from those portions of our minds which are engaged in conscious processes—so they become alien and estranged from the self. It is by this method that we prevent our own perception of our unheroic qualities, our misdeeds, our unacceptable wishes, our unbearable hurts, and therefore great portions of our being. In all the conspiracies and strategies by which we attempt to avoid knowing who we are, the defense mechanism of repression is in some way implicated.

reaction formation

One of the most resourceful ways in which we can hide our own dangerous desires is to take a position diametrically opposed to the desire itself. If I have a need of which I am ashamed, a simple way to convince myself and others that no such need exists in me is to campaign against it loudly and vociferously so that everyone becomes a witness to my position. If I speak long enough and passionately enough against a particular desire, it is not likely that most people will discover that I harbor that desire myself. Of course, under some conditions, reaction formation becomes apparent to others because of this very tendency toward exaggeration. Shakespeare expresses it well when he has one of his players say, "My lord, methinks the lady doth protest too much." His meaning is quite clear. She says "no" so much and with such passion that an observer is led to believe that what she really means is "yes."

Reaction formation is used therefore whenever a person, in attempting to hide his real feelings, becomes an advocate of the opposite point of view. This is sometimes a very effective kind of defensive maneuver because we ordinarily believe, when we hear someone defend a particular position with a great deal of conviction, that he means what he says. And because such a belief is widely held, reaction formation usually does its job extremely well. Like the other defense mechanisms, it convinces the person using it just as effectively as it convinces the individuals toward whom it is directed.

The adoption of a point of view opposite to the one a person really holds can be very effective in erecting obstacles that can then serve to prevent the feared behavior from manifesting itself. This reinforces the defense mechanism itself, since it reduces the anxiety which arises as a result of fear that the forbidden activity may make its presence known.

Sometimes reaction formation can be recognized in others because of the fanaticism and intolerance which often accompany it. Very often the issue may not seem very important to others, but to the person involved, it often takes the form of a holy crusade. Some of the most fanatical reformers in man's history were probably acting under the influence of this defense mechanism, and without realizing it were struggling to hide their own repressed impulses with regard to a particular (for them) unacceptable behavior.

Reaction formation has a dual purpose for the fanatical reformer; it provides him with two kinds of satisfaction. As an example, let us take the pornography fighter. For most of us, the fact that many people are interested in or excited by displays of nudity, sexuality, or even written descriptions of such things does not seem terribly disturbing. However, for some people, these practices cause a great deal of discomfort. Some of the people who appear to be most adamantly opposed to the existence of pornography are, in fact, aroused and titillated by pornographic material. But since their idea of "decency" cannot allow such feelings to reach conscious awareness, they are forced to deny them and, by repression, render them unconscious.

But such a maneuver does not always do its job completely. The unconscious feelings continually threaten to break through the defenses and force themselves into awareness. To avoid this, the second part of the defense mechanism comes into play. On a conscious level, the person adopts the opposite point of view. He becomes an advocate of thoughts and actions that are one hundred and eighty degrees away from his real feelings. In short, he becomes a crusader for the abolition of pornography.

Thus the crusader obtains two satisfactions. He presents an image to others and himself of great virtue and high moral purpose, while providing himself with the opportunity to go see all the pornographic movies, books, plays, and so on, in order to pass on their "suitability" for viewing by the rest of the general public. Thus this self-proclaimed guardian of our moral behavior affords himself the opportunity to be titillated by those things which arouse him, while he appears to be on a crusade to "protect" society.

Reaction formation, therefore, is one of the more insidious of the defense mechanisms in that it prevents us from knowing who we are by trying to convince us that we are in fact something quite different. By our insistence that our feelings are opposite to what they really are, we take a stand that requires a great deal of bolstering. Once committed to such a position, we are continually on guard lest our true nature should reveal itself. As a result, reaction formation is perhaps more of an obstacle to self-knowledge than some of the other maneuvers. For once one has taken a position that is diametrically opposed to his own feelings and attitudes, he has a long way to go to come back to that position. The fanatical crusader, for example, is not likely to admit that he is really stimulated and excited by the very elements against which he rails. Reaction formation, therefore, tends to be somewhat more resistant to change than are such defense mechanisms as rationalization, for example.

undoing (atonement)

We have all had occasions on which we did something, or said something, or even thought something, which we later wished we had not. And we have all had the experience of wanting to have a moment back again in which we could undo something that we had done. In situations such as these, we often resort to the defense mechanism called *atonement*.

Certain kinds of transgressions tend to produce guilt. And guilt is a very uncomfortable feeling. There is, as a result, a great need to reduce the guilt by whatever means are available. In the Puritan ethic, one way of reducing guilt is to "pay for one's crime." Having done something wrong, we feel guilty until we have made some form of restitution. By the act of apologizing, or performing a task that is considered proper penance, the slate is wiped clean. The guilt disappears and the person starts anew.

The defense mechanism of atonement, therefore, comes into play when a person feels guilty about having thought or done or said something that is seen as a vice in his particular value system. By submitting to punishment or paying a penance, this guilt can be irradicated. Sometimes the mere admission of the crime itself is enough to do the job. And often, by so doing, we hope to avoid serious punishment later. It is bad enough to do the forbidden deed, but failing to admit it is another transgression. The whole purpose of confession, therefore, grows out of the feeling that if we acknowledge our sins, we can be forgiven for them.

The Judeo-Christian belief that all wrongdoing must be punished is probably one of the most important factors leading to the adoption of this defense mechanism. Many people feel guilty about what they have been doing all week and feel that their attendance at church on Sunday is important in mitigating these feelings. Moreover, they see atonement as protection against a more serious punishment at a later time, and therefore it serves as a safeguard against this frightening eventuality.

The main danger involved in the use of this particular defense mechanism is that it might lead to drastic self-punitive measures which are so overwhelming that they influence the entire life style of an individual. The person who constantly feels guilty, unworthy, sinful, and so on, may have to spend most of his time alternating between disparaging himself for his shortcomings and going through rituals to atone for them. Usually this is not a perfectly efficient device and, as a result, a certain amount of residual anxiety is left. The acts of confession, penance, apology, retribution—the experience of punishment, of humiliation, of begging forgiveness—all have a dual effect. They reduce the feelings of guilt and anxiety in the present, but their very nature produces other feelings of worthlessness, shame, and humiliation. For the fact that one has to be punished—to confess—to make retribution—these very acts carry with them the feelings that they are designed to eliminate.

It may therefore be reasonable to assume that atonement is not the most efficient of the defense mechanisms. This may account for the fact that many people who go to confession week after week, still, although they have been assured to the contrary, report feelings of guilt and anxiety as an almost chronic accompaniment to their lives. It should be noted at this point that atonement is not alone in its lack of efficiency. All the defense mechanisms share this quality to some extent. It is likely, however, that atonement is more inefficient in this area than are some of the others.

compensation

The defense mechanism of *compensation* is related to a number of the themes in this book. We have noted earlier that people who suffer from feelings of inferiority or feelings of self-devaluation will generally be driven to find ways to overcome them—to make up for the pain that such feelings evoke. In so doing they often use the defense mechanism of compensation.

In some ways the PR image is really a complex and exaggerated form of compensation. For it is used to cover up feelings of inadequacy or inferiority and to make up for these feelings by presenting an image of competence and efficiency. In this particular case, the compensatory mechanism is fabricated—that is, it is imaginary and it is superimposed over the feelings of inferiority in an attempt to blot them out. As noted earlier, when the PR image is sold successfully to the self, this mechanism does its job, at least on a conscious level.

Other forms of compensation are more realistic attempts to overcome inadequacies by really developing competencies or skills in other areas. By this device people very often become so proficient in the area of their compensatory behavior that they gain fame, success, and notoriety from the endeavor. Theodore Roosevelt is perhaps an example. As a boy, he was very frail and sickly. But through great determination and concentrated effort, he became a physically robust man of action later in life. Helen Keller overcame both blindness and deafness to become one of the world's most inspiring and influential women.

Some forms of compensation are not as benign as those mentioned above. The child who feels insecure and inadequate may become the egotistical or narcissistic "center of attraction." And the boy who feels fearful about his adequacy with other boys may become a bully with smaller children. In some extreme forms of compensation, people may commit crimes or start fires simply because they feel that they are "invisible" unless they do something to attract attention. One somewhat extreme form of this mechanism is illustrated by the case of the child who believed that he wasn't "good" at anything. But there was one thing that he could do so well that it always obtained for him the attention he desired. And that one thing was to be "bad." Since he only received recognition when he was doing something wrong, and since some form of recognition is often essential for a person to feel that he exists for others, the boy became very good at being very bad. It is likely that we reinforce criminality and delinquency in many youngsters in just such a way.

The competitiveness of our society makes compensatory mechanisms extremely important in daily life. The need to excel at something becomes so essential in a situation where one is always being compared with others in a rank order or hierarchy of value that individuals must always struggle to hide their "defects" and to build up other abilities to extreme degrees in order to feel worthwhile. It might be that his particular defensive maneuver is not as important in societies in which competition is not so strongly stressed.

emotional insulation

In *emotional insulation* the individual attempts to reduce his affective involvement in a given situation by separating (that is, insulating) his feelings from his cognitive reactions to a situation. This device is useful because, in many cases, it protects us from being badly hurt or disappointed by circumstances beyond our control.

Sometimes when we look forward to an important event, we find ourselves holding back our anticipation in order to prevent great disappointment in case something should go wrong. If we like someone but are unsure of his or her affection, we may hold down our own emotion to avoid being hurt by a possible rejection. We will often intellectualize about the situation rather than commit ourselves emotionally to it until we have been assured that there is not too much danger of being disappointed. Such behavior prevents us from experiencing pain, but it also tends to blunt our emotions. If we engage in such behavior continuously, our emotional life is likely to become very shallow and extremely dull.

In extreme cases, where people have been in unhappy circumstances for a long time, insulation frequently makes its appearance, giving rise to a kind of apathy or resignation in which a person appears to have lost hope for any kind of happiness in his life. What he has lost, of course, is not hope, but commitment. He has repressed the hope because he has come to believe that there is no hope. As a result, he insulates himself from the disappointments that are sure to occur wherever he turns.

Another form of insulation occurs in the case in which a person is afraid of ego involvement in a particular situation. If a young man wants to ask a girl for a date and he is afraid that she might refuse, which for him would be a disparaging experience, he can reduce his ego involvement by not asking her at all, or by lessening his emotional commitment to her, thus implying that her opinion is of no consequence with regard to his attractiveness, masculinity, sex appeal, and the like.

We can also use insulation to separate emotional experience from thought processes by using *intellectualization*. We may use a word like justice and have intellectual discussions about what justice is or is not, while in fact we are masking the feeling that for some people there exists no such thing as justice. For some people there is misery, inequality, poverty, illness, and unending despair. But to know this would either make us feel guilt for the little that we have done, or cause us great discomfort as we empathize with the victims. But by the technique of intellectualization, we can avoid all these feelings by concentrating on the cognitive rather than the affective component of the situation.

Intellectualization is also used very often in psychotherapy. The patient, unwilling to delve into the areas of his life which are painful, threatening, anxiety-arousing, and so on, talks, in cognitive terms, about the situation—*about* the emotions—but without allowing himself to *experience* those emotions. By such a technique he hopes to fool the therapist and himself into believing that he is really dealing with his problem. In effect, however, he is avoiding the problem; a good therapist will quickly detect this behavior as a defensive maneuver aimed at avoiding pain. It is sometimes the case that certain parts of the therapeutic process are painful, so the patient may try to avoid them. However, when he attempts this, he is merely stalling. As we shall see later, getting in touch with one's feelings is the sine qua non of most therapies; and avoiding them is the sine qua non of most neurotic behavior. Intellectualization, therefore, like other defense mechanisms, very often serves to prevent self-knowledge.

THE DEFENSE MECHANISMS AND SELF-KNOWLEDGE

We have discussed the defense mechanisms in some detail because understanding them is essential to a knowledge of how an individual distorts his perception of himself. It is true that many of the defense mechanisms, especially in mild form, are adaptive—in that they provide an individual with a means of reducing anxiety or eliminating pain which might otherwise make his life more difficult. Of course, within normal limits, we all use these defensive maneuvers for these purposes. But even while these techniques are enabling us to function, they are distorting our perception of ourselves and our world. When they become greatly exaggerated, the distortion becomes so serious that it impairs rather than enhances our ability to adapt to our world.

But the use of defense mechanisms has another outcome which is of interest to us since it concerns the processes involved in identity formation.

For if a person is to know who he is—if he is to be authentic—if he is to feel a harmony wthin himself and a sense of peace about himself, he must come to see that defensive maneuvers are obstacles to attaining his goals. The authentic person is generally free of these techniques. He takes the risk of allowing himself to experience his feelings even though some of these feelings may be painful. But he prefers that kind of pain to the pain of not knowing who he is.

On the other hand, the defensive person—especially the extremely defensive person—is taking steps along the continuum away from a state of health and authenticity toward psychopathology. One of the consequences of extreme forms of defensiveness is a distorted perception of reality which must be maintained at all costs. The individual finds himself functioning within very narrow limits. He perceives anything beyond these limits as dangerous and threatening. Such a state carries a great deal of tension and anxiety with it and will generally lead to even more defensive behavior.

In line with what we have been saying in this book, it seems reasonable that we can define psychopathology in terms of a lack of self-knowledge. We can say, therefore, that there is a correlation between a lack of self-knowledge and psychological distress. Or, stated differently, the more an individual knows himself, the healthier he is. The search for identity, therefore, is the search for psychological well-being.

In Chapter Eleven we shall examine the more serious consequences of inauthenticity. We shall see that the behaviors that we variously call "neurotic" and "psychotic" can often be seen as extremely elaborate attempts at the prevention of self-knowledge by the individual.

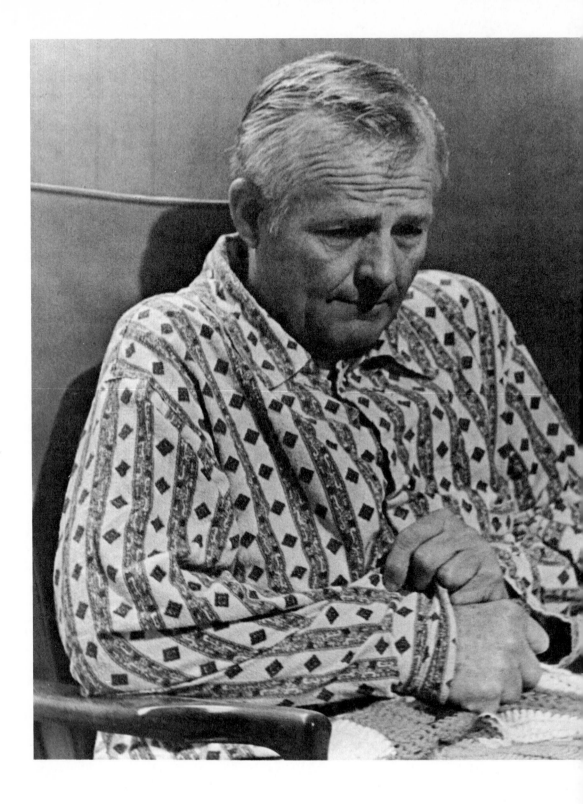

chapter 11
psychopathology: alienation from the self

There are a number of ways to look at the phenomenon of psychological distress, and each way has theoretical explanations that attempt to present a rationale for the various syndromes. For a long time psychiatrists and clinical psychologists used a medical model—a model in which psychological disability was viewed as an illness, and the intervention of a therapist was viewed as an attempt to "cure" the patient. This was a natural outcome of the fact that psychiatry had grown out of medicine and that most of the people who were practicing psychotherapy were physicians. Although Freud himself felt that it was unnecessary for psychoanalysts to be physicians, for a long period of time most of them were.

But there were a number of problems with the medical model. For example, psychological distress is not usually associated with the kinds of things that physical illnesses (for example, infection, organ dysfunction) are associated with. Moreover, since psychotherapy is not, generally speaking, a *medical* cure, the health–sickness dichotomy does not seem appropriate. A more serious difficulty with this kind of conceptual framework is the fact that there is no clear line between those people who are termed "normal" and those who are termed "abnormal." And most psychotherapists have come to believe that the difference between these two types of individuals is merely one of degree. In other words it has become apparent that those people who are suffering from psychological distress are doing so not because they are different from anyone else, but because certain events have occurred in their lives that were so painful and stressful that their only recourse was to seek refuge in the dark caverns of disordered thought.

If such disorders do not fit neatly into the medical model inherited from the biological sciences, how are we to understand them? In their severe forms the syndromes that psychiatrists and psychologists describe seem very mysterious and bizarre. And at first sight they seem explainable only in terms of some strange affliction. But there have been a number of objections to this kind of approach in recent years, especially by such writers as Szasz (1970). He contends that the whole idea of "mental illness" is merely a myth—that some people are different from their fellows, and this difference gives rise to a certain amount of anxiety in "normal" people, who explain away the deviant behavior as "illness." Szasz objects to this labeling, contending that what we generally call mental illness is nothing more than certain problems encountered in living.

There are other difficulties with the models of psychopathology we have inherited. Because there is a great range of "abnormal" behavior, there has been an attempt to classify a number of separate syndromes so that psychiatrists from one part of the country to another, in various institutions and in private practice, might all have a similar idea of what they were dealing with by using a few uniform terms. This gave rise to the classification of the neuroses and the psychoses, the organic and functional disabilities, the character disorders, and some miscellaneous classifications.

Although all of this was an attempt to clarify and simplify the many kinds of reactions so that they could be dealt with in specific ways, the result was a conglomeration of categories and designations that were largely fictional. And although textbooks of abnormal psychology classify these syndromes and give their specifications, in truth there are very few "textbook cases." The symptoms of any one syndrome can be seen in almost any other. In fact, one sometimes has the feeling that what he is dealing with is really one large problem with a number of different variations, some mild and some severe. Karl Menninger (Menninger et al., 1963) has made the suggestion that these variations can be viewed simply as a series of steps or orders of dysfunction. By this he means that mild defensive behavior, for example, would be in the first order of dysfunction while what has been called schizophrenia would be found in a higher order of dysfunction.

Such an idea has a lot to recommend it. For, viewed this way, all human functioning from the highest level of health to the most disturbed level of maladaption can be viewed as a continuum along which every one of us can be found to move.

Textbooks of psychiatry and clinical psychology list a number of syndromes that describe a certain group of behaviors generally considered to be pathological. These syndromes are named and classified and presented as if each one is a distinct entity that can clearly be delineated by a competent diagnostician. However, a number of research studies have shown that what looks like manic-depressive psychosis to one clinician, for example, may be diagnosed as paranoia or schizophrenia or even as compulsive neurosis by another. The reliability between different practitioners in terms of recognizing and labeling psychiatric entities has proved to be quite low.

It might be that the reason for this is that those entities which we have wished to describe as separate and distinct do not exist. Some therapists (Rogers, for example) have suggested that the whole idea of diagnosis is largely irrelevant. In the final analysis it may be that all psychological disability is really a series of variations on a single theme. That theme might be termed *self-alienation.*

If we define the self as the sum total of all the perceptions, feelings, and memories, that are at least potentially retrievable, then we can say that pathology results from any process that diminishes our experience of these. This is not very different from the Gestalt view that pathology is a diminution of the *contact* that occurs at the organism/environment boundary. (Perls et al., 1951). The Gestalt notion of *contact* is almost identical to the concept of *perception* as used here. If the Self is the sum total of all perceptual processes, then any diminution of these processes attenuates one's total experience. Defensive behavior with its use of repression and denial is believed to be one of the most pernicious sources of this reduction of self-awareness.

From the standpoint of what we have been saying in this book it seems reasonable that we can look at most psychopathology as movement along a continuum from self-knowledge on one end to self-deception on the other. Our reasons for deceiving ourselves are many. But it seems apparent that alienation from the self is instrumental in all the "syndromes" with which we shall now deal.

THE NEUROSES

We have already seen that when stress, anxiety, painful memories, and so on, become too much for the individual to bear, he usually resorts to defensive measures to spare himself from the discomfort of such experiences.

But we have also remarked about the fact that these techniques do not always do their jobs completely. As a result, a certain amount of anxiety is often left over. When this occurs we are usually forced to adopt more sophisticated measures and thus we begin building defense mechanisms upon already established defense mechanisms until we have a rather complex structure which has removed us even further from our selves than we were before.

Usually such an elaborate system of defenses becomes cyclical. That is, anxiety causes the adoption of defense mechanisms which give rise to higher levels of anxiety, which in turn gives rise to further, more elaborate defense mechanisms, which in turn gives rise to more anxiety. The final result is a cyclical condition which seems to feed on itself. The neurotic is generally immature—he tends to perceive certain common life situations as terribly threatening—he is usually beset by severe anxiety—and as a result he resorts to neurotic defensive maneuvers in order to cope with these feelings. The final picture includes the appearance of vicious circles which prevent him from extricating himself from the situation and result in a number of secondary symptoms or psychosomatic afflictions that are even more disabling.

It should be noted that this description of the *neurotic individual* can be applied to all of us at some time or another. We all occasionally fall into situations in which these kinds of symptoms occur. But for most of us, these situations are temporary and the symptoms mild. The reader, therefore, should not be concerned if, in the following descriptions of neuroses, he recognizes some tendencies which he himself has. This does not make him neurotic. It simply proves that he is human.

anxiety reaction

The most pervasive experience of a person suffering from the neurosis is the feeling of *anxiety*. Anxiety has often been defined as *psychic pain*. In an *anxiety attack*, the anxiety is usually quite severe, although it appears to have no particular source. The person is terribly afraid, panicky, filled with dread, but he is at a loss to explain why. The anxiety seems to be "free floating." It is almost as if it exists outside the individual and he is immersed in it. The person undergoing an anxiety attack seems to have a premonition of impending doom. But he has no explanation for this feeling and no idea what the dreadful event is that so terrifies him.

This reaction is one of the most common of all neurotic patterns. It is said to be involved in about 30 to 40 per cent of all neurotic disorders. However, such a statement may be misleading since anxiety is present in large amounts in most neurotic reactions. As a result it may be somewhat artificial to separate this reaction from the others. The main purpose for giving it a separate status is that it may be the *only* symptom in this particular situation, and the anxiety itself may be quite disabling.

The person who suffers from an anxiety reaction is incapacitated in a number of ways. In the first place he or she may become the victim of an attack at almost any time, without any warning. This fact in itself is terribly frightening and tends to limit the kinds of behaviors in which a person can engage. For he becomes wary of moving too far away from familiar environs, fearing that an attack in a strange place may be even more difficult to deal with than it is at home.

The fact that an anxiety attack appears "out of nowhere" and without any kind of warning increases its intensity. For if a person is aware of the reason for his fears (a difficult examination, athletic contest, job interview) he also realizes that when the critical moment has passed, the anxiety will decrease. But without this knowledge, and with the apprehension that this mysterious fear may continue indefinitely, an even greater fear is superimposed on the first. As a result, the anxiety reaction begins to snowball, taking on enormous proportions. Along with these psychological symptoms, there are a number of physiological changes that are both accompaniments of, and instigators of, further anxiety. These changes may include increased heartbeat, with rates sometimes as high as 180 to 200 beats per minute, as well as increased blood pressure, difficulty in breathing or extremely fast respiration, sweating, nausea, dizziness, and so on. Needless to say, all these physiological responses to the original anxiety give rise to a higher level of fear and trepidation which further incapacitates the individual.

If the individual could only know that these symptoms seldom last very long, the attack itself would not be so severe. But because there is no object in the environment to which he can point as a source of his fear, he feels powerless to end it. And he becomes afraid that it will never end. This, of course, feeds the fear and raises it to a higher intensity, just as do all the other symptoms. In fact, it seems as if everything conspires to make the anxiety attack more severe and disabling than it would otherwise have to be. And fear being one of the most painful experiences that a person can undergo, the anxiety attack is a very difficult one for the individual to deal with.

The person who suffers from anxiety reflects the tension he experiences in strange postural movements, muscular spasms, digestive discomforts, and difficulty in sleeping. He tends to be "on edge" a great deal of the time even when he is not in the grip of an "attack." He may develop aches and pains which are vague and not easily identifiable. And he is likely to be generally unhappy and excessively vigilant as well as extremely sensitive to the behavior of others.

Most psychologists and psychiatrists agree that the anxiety that is found in all the neuroses generally comes from the repression of an event, feeling, attitude, or desire. In other words, anxiety, generally speaking, is the result of some form of self-alienation—some separation of a portion of a person's being from the self in such a way that this area of the personality is prevented from becoming conscious.

Very often the cause of anxiety is related to the threatened breakthrough of dangerous desires which are being kept out of awareness by rather strong repressive measures. Feelings of hostility or sexuality that are unacceptable to the individual may have been repressed or disguised by means of projection or reaction formation—but very often in such situations the defense mechanism has not done its job well enough and the person experiences a strange uneasiness, as if the undesirable feeling or tendency is about to become conscious. The individual is afraid that if he acknowledges the real feelings against which he has been protecting himself, he will be (a) forced to act upon them, thereby doing something "horrible," or (b) perceive himself as "worthless," "useless," "evil." Much of this "thinking" takes place on an unconscious level and, as a result, the individual is able to insulate himself from its content. However, he is not able to insulate himself from its emotional concomitants—fear, panic, premonitions of impending doom.

Typically people who suffer from these kinds of difficulties are unable to deal with feelings of hostility and tend to repress them, presenting a mask of compliance, affability, and passivity. As a result, they develop even stronger feelings of hostility because they perceive the world as restraining them from expressing their true nature. This hostility in turn is repressed, and a vicious circle is established. This helps to make the reaction self-perpetuating. The person experiences a constant threat that his defenses are going to give way and that the hostility will come out in overt behavior.

Very often these people have the feeling that they are going to do violence to a particular person or group of people and they are afraid that they will not be able to restrain themselves. *Because of the fact that they offer resistance to their feelings, the feelings themselves become exaggerated and seem even more dangerous than they really are.*

A young woman had terrible anxiety attacks whenever she had to drive her mother into town from the farm on which they lived. The attacks grew even more severe when they passed the reservoir on the way. The girl was unable to explain her fears and did not at first realize that they were related to the mother, on the one hand, and the body of water, on the other. The situation seemed all the more mysterious because she drove that route almost every day without any anxiety. It was only on the occasions when her mother was in the car with her that she experienced any discomfort. She also had a vague fear that she might turn on her mother and do her some harm.

As time wore on, this young lady's anxiety generalized to a number of other situations and she finally sought psychiatric help. In therapy she learned that there had been a great deal of hostility between her and her mother which she had almost entirely repressed. Her mother had driven off a number of suitors "for her daughter's own good"—and she had made a number of other decisions affecting the young girl's life without considering her wishes or asking for her consent. The girl was very resentful but unable to experience these feelings, since it had always been impressed upon her that everything her mother did was for her own welfare. As time went on, fewer and fewer young men were available and the girl started to believe that she had lost the best opportunities. This further intensified her anger toward her mother because she perceived her mother as responsible. The hostility thus aroused gave rise to some fantasies in which the young girl saw herself drowning her mother. These were quickly repressed and were not remembered again until they were brought out in therapy some years later. However, when driving by the reservoir, the feelings threatened to break through into consciousness and caused a panic and a consequent anxiety reaction.

Sometimes anxiety attacks are brought on by a change in a person's status which he perceives as a threat. A promotion, for example, may bring with it a greater degree of responsibility—and a person who feels insecure or inadequate may see this responsibility as dangerous. Because he feels inadequate, he believes that he cannot do the job or handle the new situation competently; as a result, he becomes highly anxious when he is confronted with the possibility of failure. As we have noted earlier, failure is not in the repertoire of the hero and many people are loath to admit that there may be areas in which they are incompetent.

A young man came into psychotherapy complaining that he became terribly anxious every morning just before leaving for work. He also noted that this reaction occurred on weekdays but not on weekends. When the therapist inquired how long the feelings had been occurring, the young man reported that they started several weeks ago. The therapist noticed that the attacks coincided with a recent promotion. The promotion carried with it a great deal of responsibility and required certain abilities which this individual thought he lacked. It turned out that his anxiety was a warning which prevented him from going to work—to avoid the failure he unconsciously believed was inevitable.

Threats to the self-image have already been shown to be very serious kinds of challenges to psychological stability. For the insecure person generally holds his PR image together with a great deal of defensiveness. Any kind of pressure that makes him feel that these defenses will not be able to maintain themselves leads to an unconscious feeling that the PR image is about to crumble and that the underlying inadequacy will be exposed. The anxiety that the person in this situation experiences is simply the conscious component of this entire dynamic—that is, he has separated himself (insulation) from the object of his fears and experiences only the fear itself.

Some anxiety attacks are related to guilt and fear of punishment. We have noted that most of us, because of our upbringing, believe that if we have done anything wrong, we must pay for it with a form of punishment which is in some way commensurate with the "crime." Thus when we have purposely or even accidentally done something we consider to be wrong, we may find ourselves feeling extremely uncomfortable because of the guilt we feel or because we expect to be punished in some way. Such feelings, when repressed, can cause a great deal of anxiety to appear on the surface, but the person as a rule will not be able to explain what his anxiety is related to.

In a certain sense a person who suffers from a great deal of anxiety, although we have been emphasizing his weaknesses, also has very many strengths. He has the courage to maintain himself in the face of a great deal of psychic pain and he does so over a long period of time. Moreover, he does not resort to the more exaggerated defense mechanisms which could lead to even more serious kinds of disability, such as psychosis. In a certain sense, he struggles to maintain himself in the state in which he exists because even though it is very painful, it is preferable to losing touch with reality entirely. This is one escape that may be open to him but one which he decides not to pursue. It is these resources of courage and tenacity with which the psychotherapist tries to work in helping this kind of individual overcome his difficulties.

aesthenic reaction (neuraesthenia)

In an age in which we have so many diversions, entertainments, hobbies, and creative pursuits, it may appear incongruous that one of the most common complaints that people have is that they are bored, depressed, and almost always tired. This reaction constitutes a great deal more than simple fatigue related to overwork or lack of rest. It is a quite serious and rather widespread phenomenon in our society. It has perhaps been common in all ages, but it has special significance for us for it is related intimately with the feelings of alienation and emptiness which we have already described.

The symptoms of this reaction can be quite variable. Generally speaking, the individual reports that he has a lack of interest, desire, energy, strength. He appears to be tired all the time and yet finds that he cannot sleep deeply and restfully and does not feel refreshed when he awakens. Even the smallest efforts seem for him to require a tremendous amount of energy.

Curiously enough the kinds of people who often suffer from this kind of reaction are those who in other ages would have "had it made." That is, these are generally people who are reasonably well off, in their middle years, who have all of the labor-saving devices and conveniences that modern technology can provide, who have steady incomes, healthy families, and what would appear to be reasonable prospects for the future. Yet in spite of all these things—perhaps because of them—these people feel alienated, alone, tired, depressed, and they see their lives as empty and meaningless, sterile, dull, worthless, and in many cases even tragic.

In addition to these kinds of feelings, the person who is suffering from an aesthenic reaction reports certain kinds of somatic symptoms such as minor headaches, dizziness, vague feelings of irritation or weakness, vague aches and pains that they cannot clearly delineate, and other such complaints, which seem almost to change daily. This kind of individual may also be somewhat hypochondriacal and show a great deal of concern for his physical condition. In extreme cases he may become quite morbid in his thinking, to the extent that he may believe that he has a terminal illness, that he has ingested poison which is slowly killing him, or that if he does not use the latest drug or diet, he will suffer grievous consequences.

This particular syndrome seems to be most common among middle-class, middle-aged, overweight American housewives. These women often feel discouraged and frustrated in terms of fulfilling their own potentialities, for many of them have been forced into the housewife role by the socialization process, and they may feel either unfulfilled or incompetent in it. Moreover, such women often seek escape in such pastimes as watching television soap opera and reading romantic novels or fan magazines, or they try to gain vicarious satisfaction through back-fence gossip. But these activities only heighten their feelings of frustration, and, by comparison, show them how empty and dull their own lives really are.

In the past it was believed that aesthenic reactions could be attributed to a disease of the nerve cells. Attempts were made to find the physiological processes that were responsible for the problem. But as time went on it became apparent that this syndrome was strictly psychological. Modern explanations therefore, no longer resort to finding physical determinants.

The modern view of the aesthenic reaction sees it as a defensive maneuver designed to avoid acknowledging a painful real-life situation. In most cases the person who suffers from the reaction is one who has had to endure a great deal of frustration, disappointment, and hopelessness. Moreover, along with these experiences, there is usually an accompanying lack of dedication to anything that is interesting, important, or meaningful to the individual. It is as if a certain element is lacking from his life—an element so fundamental that he hardly thinks about it, yet one so important that it can hardly be ignored—the element of excitement.

There is literally nothing in these people's lives that is exciting. One reason is, of course, that they are not interested in anything in particular. But another reason lies in the fact that they have walled themselves off, because of their neurotic pattern of defenses, from anything that entails any risk. And excitement is generally related in some way to risk. As a result these people feel cheated and thwarted by a world that seems completely uninteresting and meaningless to them.

The aesthenic may also feel tired and sickly a great deal because the work of maintaining the kind of defenses he usually has is fatiguing. The continuous maintaining of defensive measures requires a great deal of energy, and the person so engaged must expend this energy or run the risk of losing control of his elaborately constructed fortification, which would then leave him exposed and barren before a hostile world. The expenditure of such energy for so long a time is exhausting.

Aesthenic reactions, like all forms of extremely defensive behavior, very often have secondary gains which are important to the individual and which therefore perpetuate their existence. A person who is tired and sickly all the time cannot be expected to do very much or to work very hard. Moreover, he often gets a good deal of sympathy from the rest of his family, who may see him as a very courageous person fighting against very great odds. But, generally speaking, such relationships will not last indefinitely. Other people finally give up on an individual who is continually negative, continually complaining, continually unable to hold up his end of the family obligations. So in the final analysis, this reaction, which may have served an individual well for a long time, may outlive its usefulness. When this happens the person may be forced to use other defensive measures or perhaps, with some help, find more realistic and worthwhile solutions to his problems.

Research shows that the aesthenic individual is usually immature, lacking in self-confidence, and generally dependent upon others for the solutions of serious life problems. He generally feels inadequate in terms of dealing with stressful situations and as a result is likely to give up without trying rather than to make the effort and be humiliated by failure.

The person suffering from an aesthenic reaction seldom has insight into his problem and believes that his symptoms are physical. For this reason he is not likely to make strenuous efforts to change his perception of himself in order to alleviate them. As a result, he may not seek help. And if he does, he may seek the wrong kind of help. If he goes to a physician who does not correctly diagnose the problem, he may be treated for years for a variety of illnesses which are, in fact, imaginary. Unlike the anxious person, the aesthenic individual may never seek psychiatric help. Since he believes his ailments to be purely physical, and, in fact, secretly hopes to find real physical causes to justify his behavior, the idea of going to a psychiatrist or psychologist offends him. Moreover, since very often the level of his anxiety is not as high as that of some other kinds of individuals, he does not feel a strong need to seek immediate help in order to reduce it. This is unfortunate, for it appears, at least at the present, that drugs (either tranquilizers or energizers) are not too effective in treating this type of reaction. Generally speaking, psychotherapy is the best approach in dealing with this problem. (We shall consider psychotherapeutic procedures later.)

It may be that in this generation we are seeing a new kind of aesthenic reaction. For something like this syndrome very often afflicts the young. Whereas in the past this kind of behavior was seen mostly in middle-aged and older people, we now see something that looks very much like this reaction among people in their late teens and early twenties.

One interesting aspect of this particular problem is that it may be related to affluence. It now sometimes appears among students, young working people, or other people under thirty who are generally reasonably well off but appear to have no direction in their lives. And it may be that this lack of direction or goal is one of the underlying contributors to this problem. For just as in the case of the middle-class housewife who has attained most of the things that she once thought would make her happy, young people today are also often in possession of many of the commodities which the society produces, but still feel unsatisfied.

It seems certain that for an individual to be psychologically healthy, he must have certain kinds of goals toward which he is striving, and which appear, with a reasonable degree of probability, to be achievable. Such goals give life meaning and make the anticipation of the future worthwhile and exciting. When such goals are absent, there tends to be a feeling of floundering—of disorientation—of being adrift without power or sense of direction. With such perceptions, we tend to see the future as empty, without challenge—or even foreboding.

It seems that there are two ways in which a person can get into such a situation. One is by having no particular goals in the first place, and the second is by having certain goals, reaching them, and then realizing that they are not what one expected them to be. It is likely that this latter situation is the case for many of the people who suffer from aesthenic reactions in an affluent society. They saw affluence—suburban living, labor-saving devices, status, comfort—as very attractive goals when they were not in possession of them. But having attained them, many people came to realize that they were not enough.

While striving for the goals, they could not of course realize that their attainment would be meaningless or empty. As a result, during this time their life had some meaning. But with the realization that the acquisition of these things did not bring them the happiness they expected, there came a feeling that they had wasted their lives. They had worked and sacrificed and gone without, only to arrive at a point at which they discovered that the things they had thought they wanted had not really been worth the struggle.

For the middle-aged generation this realization came slowly and was perhaps partly repressed. As a result, what they felt was a vague kind of uneasiness or depression or tiredness or apathy, without clearly realizing why. But for the younger generation the same kind of realization occurred earlier. Having been brought up in an affluent world, they could clearly see what perhaps their parents could not see—that the goals toward which the parents had worked did not really contribute to making life more meaningful. To live with affluence is to take it for granted and to know its real value. It is worthwhile in supplying man's more basic needs, but it does not enrich his life in other ways. Aesthenic reactions in the young appear often to be related to this fact.

There are other reasons for depression and apathy among the young. One obvious one is, of course, the fact that there are hands that are always poised close to the nuclear trigger. Such a fact makes day-to-day living difficult and future planning almost meaningless. And the thought that everything we do, everything we produce, everything we think, may be obliterated in one blinding flash is a sobering one. Such facts cannot help but contribute to this depressive kind of reaction.

Another contributor to aesthenic reactions among the young is the overwhelming feeling of loneliness that many of them have. Many move away from their families at the earliest opportunity. They either live alone or, for a while, with one friend or another. But they feel rootless.

Rootlessness and loneliness are widespread among young people today because of the trend away from the extended family of the past, the speed and ease of transportation, and the depersonalization of modern life. Even on college campuses, where one might think that there was a certain amount of camaraderie, students complain that they feel alone. Those who work are similarly alienated. The loneliness and meaninglessness of their lives are often reflected in aesthenic types of reactions or even more serious behaviors.

conversion reaction (hysteria)

A *conversion reaction* is one in which an individual defends himself from a difficult or intolerable situation by becoming ill. Although the illness appears to be real in many particulars, a physician cannot usually find any underlying physiological or organic pathology. Conversion reaction has been one of the most fascinating psychological reactions in man's repertoire because it clearly shows the extraordinary effect which the mind can have over the functioning of the body. For in this reaction the individual may experience some very severe somatic symptoms, even though, in a physiological sense, his body in functioning perfectly.

The word *hysteria* comes to us from ancient Greece. Hippocrates, the great Greek physician, and others of his time believed that this particular reaction was confined to women. Moreover, these practitioners had a rather naive picture of human physiology and anatomy. They believed that organs were not fixed in a particular place and might move, at various times, throughout the body. Hysterical reactions were therefore believed to be related to the wandering of the uterus (hysteria coming from the Greek word for uterus) throughout the body in frustration because of an unfulfilled desire for children. In its wandering it was believed that the uterus might become lodged in various parts of the body, thereby causing symptoms in that area. The fact that the uterus was implicated in the disease, however, shows that even in these earlier times, hysteria was in some way linked with sexuality. And Hippocrates thought, in fact, that one of the best solutions to the problem lay in marriage.

Freud, of course, was quite intrigued by this particular kind of problem and, in fact, may have been first attracted to psychiatry by it. For it was mostly through studies of hysteria that he discovered the concepts of repression, the unconscious mind, and the importance of sexuality. Freud used the term *conversion hysteria* to indicate that the individual was repressing some particular thought and *converting* those thoughts into physical symptoms. Those thoughts, for Freud, were almost invariably sexual in nature. And so he saw the conversion reaction as an attempt to repress sexual thoughts. The subsequent disability served the purpose of hiding from the individual his own forbidden sexual feelings.

Although the dynamics underlying the Freudian view of conversion reaction are still believed to be valid, most theorists nowadays would agree that sex is not the only problem that can account for it. Any unacceptable impulse or feeling might be repressed and, if the situation seems to warrant it, give rise to physical symptoms that might afford the opportunity for the individual to escape some difficult or undesirable situation.

Some of the most common kinds of conversion reaction have occurred in combat situations. Very often a person in a terrifying situation may wish to run away but be unable to face his "cowardice." In repressing his fear, he drives out of consciousness his desire to run. But on an unconscious level, the fear and desire to escape still exist. As a result he may become blind (hysterical blindness) and consequently, through no fault of his own, he has to be removed from the combat situation. An examination of such an individual shows nothing wrong with his eyes or nervous system. And he is completely unaware on a conscious level of what has occurred.

Once in the rear area, his vision may return quite quickly, especially with psychiatric help.

Hysterical reactions may take other forms, such as *anesthesia*, or loss of sensitivity; *hypesthesia*, or partial loss of sensitivity; *hyperesthesia*, or excessive sensitivity; *analgesis*, or loss of pain sensitivity; *paresthesia*, or exceptional sensations such as tingling. There may also be such things as *tunnel vision*, in which only a partial blindness occurs; *deafness; paralysis*, in which the use of a limb or limbs is lost; *tremors*, or muscular shaking; and even serious *spasms* or epilepticlike seizures are occasionally seen.

> The ability of hysterics to simulate actual disease symptoms is almost unbelievable. In a pseudo attack of acute appendicitis, not only may the patient evidence pain in the lower abdominal region and other typical symptoms of acute appendicitis, but his temperature may also shoot up far above normal. Even cases of psychogenic malaria and tuberculosis have been cited in the psychiatric literature, in which patients showed all the usual symptoms—coughing, loss of weight, recurrent fever, and night sweats—without actual organic disease. (Coleman, 1964)

The fact that conversion reactions can imitate almost any known disease sometimes complicates the issue from a diagnostic point of view. The individual himself is almost always convinced that his illness is, in fact, a real physical one. As a result, he can be of very little help in terms of clarifying the situation. Moreover, it must not be imagined that the person is merely malingering. Competent people can usually tell the difference between conversion reaction and deliberate attempts at deception. It is, of course possible for mistakes to be made—and occasionally people have been treated for "diseases" or even had surgery performed upon them, when, in fact, their real problems were largely hysterical.

There is no question that the hysterical person is severely limited in self-knowledge. He has had to deny certain feelings and to "create an illness in order to escape these particular perceptions." He has generally been successful in reducing the anxiety that he would feel if he were to acknowledge these feelings. But this comfort has been purchased at a very high cost to himself. For he has to make an invalid of himself, to deny large portions of his emotional life, in order to gain this very precarious semblance of adjustment.

Like many of the other reactions that are categorized as neurotic, the hysterical reaction is very often a face-saving device. The person, unable to admit a failing, retreats behind the veil of illness—and thus relieves himself of the responsibility for the particular "shortcoming." The not-too-good gymnast who becomes lame before every competition—the mediocre singer, who becomes hoarse before every important audition—the night flyer who loses his night vision but is quite normal during the day—these are all people who are desperately trying to protect their PR image against what they perceive as dangerous possibilities of exposure.

One serious complication with regard to conversion reaction is that most of the individuals who become involved in this kind of behavior are highly suggestible. As a result they are very easily influenced by the mere mention of symptoms of any kind. A physician may unthinkingly ask them if they ever have certain kinds of reactions and, although they may not have up to that point, they might begin to manifest them from then on. Well-meaning friends may also contribute to the situation by discussing various kinds of illnesses. Moreover, nowadays the media are saturated with medical "information," which gives the prospective hysteric an almost endless supply of syndromes from which to choose.

It should be noted that most so-called neurotic individuals are highly suggestible and, as a result, most of the reactions that we have been describing are easily influenced by outside events. The hysterical person, of course, since he is desperately looking for a mode of escape in the form of an illness, is extremely sensitive to information from external sources and is therefore easily influenced by them.

dissociative reactions

The remarkable power and versatility of the defense mechanism of repression is aptly demonstrated by *dissociative reactions.* These responses utilize rather extreme forms of defensiveness in such a way that very often one part of the person is completely unaware of some other prominent part of his own personality. Such behaviors as amnesia, fugue, multiple personality, and somnambulism are included in this group.

Each of these types of behavior seems to use repression and insulation in very exaggerated forms. Amnesia is the inability to recall certain episodes or events in one's past life. Although amnesia can occur as a result of organic changes in the brain, we are not here concerned with that form of the reaction. As noted earlier, in psychogenic amnesia the person typically loses his memory for specific events while retaining his normal capabilities in other areas. For example, although he may forget his name, where he lives, even whether or not he is married, he will often retain his ability to read and write, to do certain kinds of work, to drive, ride a bicycle, play tennis, golf, and so on. In amnesia, the forgetting appears to be selective. And that which is forgotten is very often that which is most threatening to the integrity of the individual.

Amnesia is sometimes accompanied by fugue or flight. In this particular manifestation, the individual simply blanks out for a period of time and leaves the scene, to turn up days, weeks, or even years later in a new locale, with no memory of his past life. The fact that the amnesiac's memory does come back or can be brought out by hypnosis shows that the memories have been repressed rather than forgotten.

Amnesia and fugue appear to have the same kind of dynamics as conversion reactions. The major difference is that instead of getting sick to avoid a difficult or intolerable life situation, the person simply forgets (represses) the pertinent information. Instead of getting sick, the amnesiac simply loses contact with the situation, as if it no longer exists. Indeed, for him it no longer does have any reality.

In this reaction the individual literally cuts himself off from some part of his personality. Those areas of his psychological life that are unacceptable are simply driven out of consciousness and insulated or dissociated from the rest of the person's life. On a conscious level he no longer has any contact with the disagreeable parts of the self, but on an unconscious level these parts continue to affect him. As a result, he may sometimes suffer from other kinds of neurotic symptoms. But these are generally mild enough for him to function adequately.

The person suffering from amnesia, therefore, may very often present a picture of a fairly well adjusted individual in his new setting. After a short adjustment, he will tend to keep away from people who may be curious about his past life, in an effort to avoid thinking about it himself. He will therefore usually lead a rather restricted kind of existence, for this is the only way he feels safe from discovery. Of course, most of this kind of motivation orginates on an unconscious level, and the individual himself is generally unaware of the reasons for his behavior. But he finds himself shunning people who ask questions about the distant past and selecting as friends only those individuals who do not seem interested in talking about "the old days."

In multiple personality we have an even more exaggerated form of the defense mechanism of insulation. Although this syndrome has gotten a great deal of publicity in the media, in clinical practice the incidence is quite rare. But because of the dramatic possibilities inherent in the idea of a person having more than one distinctive personality, movies, novels, and television have all had some interest in depicting these kinds of reactions—often, unfortunately, without too much real concern for scientific accuracy.

In multiple personality an individual usually manifests two or more distinct systems of behavior, each with its own separate emotional and attitudinal aspect, each presenting what appears to be quite different kinds of individuals with almost completely different life styles. The personalities are so discrete to the individual that he often calls them by different names. In some cases one or more of the personalities may be completely unaware of the existence of the others. Where this happens, a person may switch from one personality to the other, sometimes rather quickly and suddenly, and be unable to remember or account for the activities of the other personality. There may, therefore, be great periods of time for which the individual is amnesiac.

Very often in cases of multiple personality, the individual has two kinds of needs and desires which he cannot reconcile. Perhaps he has been brought up rather strictly and has a very strict code of ethics, on the one hand, while, on the other, he has strong sexual desires or affiliative needs which cannot be satisfied in his ordinary mode of life. In order to satisfy these needs, the individual very often separates himself from them and allows this segment of his personality to gain dominance for a certain period of time—during which he goes about fulfilling those desires that are forbidden to the more rigid personality.

In some cases of multiple personality, the individuals are so different from one another that they have different vocabularies, grammatical sophistication, and even IQ. Lipton (1943) sites a case in which a young lady with two distinct personalities was given separate intelligence tests for each. Her IQ on one was 128. But on the other, a more immature personality, her IQ was 43. Her other intellectual capacities, such as use of vocabulary and grammar, also showed very great differences.

There are other differences reported in Lipton's study. The two personalities had very different life styles. For example, one dressed very gaudily, wore a great deal of makeup, and colored her fingernails. The other dressed very conservatively, never wore makeup, and seemed loathe to draw attention to herself. One of the personalities was a chain smoker and often expressed a great need for cigarettes, while the other one did not smoke at all. One was promiscuous sexually, while the other one felt all kinds of guilt in terms of sexual behavior.

This case of dual personality shows very clearly how one part of an individual can be completely insulated from another part, with which it is incompatible. In this case, as in many others, it appears that one part of the personality cannot accept certain kinds of wishes, desires, and needs and, as a result, it separates itself from those particular segments of the self. In this way it affords the repressed part of the personality a certain amount of freedom to engage in its desired activities, while the other part of the individual is protected from knowing about it.

In the famous case of Eve White and Eve Black (Thigpen and Cleckley, 1954) the dynamics appear to be similar. In both cases there is a sedate, naive, sexually inhibited personality who longs for sexual freedom and expression but who, because of a puritanical upbringing, has generally repressed these feelings, so that on a conscious level they do not exist. But these feelings, which strive for expression, are strong enough to manifest themselves in the behavior of another personality, which is unknown to the dignified, conservative personality that is the dominant one in the individual's life. The resulting dissociated personality becomes the only means of expressing both personalities for this person.

Somnambulism is another kind of dissociative reaction, in which it is believed that the ideas that are repressed from waking life become manifest during sleep. In a typical case the individual usually goes to sleep and sometime during the night arises and carries out a particular act which may be as complex as driving several hundred miles to a specific location. He usually returns to bed without awakening and finishes his night's sleep. In the morning he cannot recall any of the events of the previous night. During the sleepwalking the person's eyes are generally open and he is able to respond to commands or avoid obstacles, but occasionally he may injure himself because of the fact that his attention is very narrowly focused. One sleepwalker, for example, was struck by a car while crossing a street.

Although it is commonly believed that it is dangerous to awaken a sleepwalker, this has not been borne out in practice. Usually when awakened a sleepwalker will be puzzled, surprised, and perplexed to find himself out of bed and engaged in whatever it is that he is doing, but he is not likely to be violent. Somnambulism, like the other so-called neurotic reactions, does not exist in a vacuum. It is also often accompanied by other symptoms, and somnambulists often find their way to a psychiatrist because of anxiety, psychosomatic symptoms, conversion reaction, and so on. In many cases they may not even be aware of their somnambulism until the fact is brought out in therapy.

It is believed that somnambulism is the attempt of an individual to escape a difficult situation or to reduce anxiety through motor activity. Since this activity is probably inhibited during waking hours, it has its only opportunity for expression during sleep.

Some investigators believe that during adolescence somnambulism is related to sexual conflicts and dependence–independence concerns. In adults the picture seems to be somewhat different. Somnambulism is often believed to come on during times of severe stress, either after a severe traumatic experience or at a time when one is expected. The imminent death of a parent, for example, may be one such event.

The somnambulist very often tries to carry out during sleep certain activities that have been forbidden and repressed during the day. For example, one patient got up every night and walked over to a picture of his brother, with whom he had had a serious argument months before. He kissed the picture and returned to bed. In psychotherapy it was found that the young man had lost contact with his brother, who had moved to another city, and he had repressed the desire to find him and reinstate their former relationship.

phobic reaction

A *phobia* is an irrational persistent fear that exists in the presence of certain stimuli which for other individuals are not threatening. The subjective experience of the phobia may be very similar to what an individual feels in an anxiety attack. The major difference is that in an anxiety attack there is no perceptible object in the environment which the person fears.

In a phobia the individual can usually point to a specific object or objects or situation which, he feels, elicits his fear. The interesting thing about this kind of reaction is that the person himself realizes that the object which is so frightening to him is not really one that should be feared. It makes no sense to the victim whatsoever to be afraid of what is obviously a nonthreatening object or situation. Yet he finds himself unable to shake the fear, and the more he tries to use logic to argue himself out of it, the worse the fear becomes.

Occasionally the phobia may be referred to a real object of concern such as fire, illness, and certain kinds of animals. But once again the fear that the individual experiences is far out of proportion to the real threat involved with these particular objects, and he realizes that. The person suffering from a phobia very often shows a number of other kinds of symptoms. He may have headaches, back pains, upset stomach, dizziness, and so on. Besides these psychosomatic complaints, he may have psychological ones, such as feelings of inferiority, fear of serious organic disease, fear that he is losing his mind. These accompanying symptoms simply demonstrate the fact that reactions such as this are generally part of an overall picture of the personality which is related to feelings of inadequacy and self-alienation.

There are a number of interesting explanations for the existence of phobias. One is that phobias, like anxiety attacks, are defenses against dangerous impulses which are threatening to break through to consciousness. One woman, for example, exhibited fears of all sharp objects because of a repressed desire to stab her husband. Of course all she experienced was the fear, not the reason for it. One young man found himself terribly afraid in the company of children. It turned out that he had repressed desires to molest them sexually, and in their presence he became frightened that these impulses would break through his defenses.

Another explanation for the existence of phobias is that they represent anxiety that has been displaced onto another object or person. For example, a person who may be afraid that he might be fired from his job because of incompetency may develop a phobia for driving—since he must drive every morning in order to get to work. The same person, however, may have no fear whatsoever when he takes the family for a ride on the weekend.

Intense guilt feelings that are repressed may also lead to phobic reactions. One young lady was terrified of keys. In therapy, it was found that she felt exceedingly guilty about her sexual desires and that, for her, the key represented the penis because of its ability to be inserted so easily into a lock. Without her realizing it, whenever she saw a key, she was reminded of her own sexual feelings. But what she experienced on a conscious level was merely the fear that had been displaced from sex to the symbolic representation, the key.

A third explanation for the existence of phobic reactions is conditioning. There appears to be no question that conditioning plays a part in almost all forms of maladaptive behavior. This is one reason why the changing of this kind of behavior presents such a difficult problem. When two stimuli are presented simultaneously, they soon become associated, so that the presentation of one elicits the expectation of the other. When one of these stimuli is fear, it will tend to occur whenever the other stimulus appears.

Thus a mother may condition her child to be afraid of insects simply by responding with a great deal of fear in the presence of one. This is especially true if the behavior continues for any period of time. In the same way a parent may condition a child to be afraid of the dark, by frightening him in regard to it—or to a storm, airplanes, and so on—simply by exhibiting great fear in the presence of these particular stimuli. Very often there is generalization of the fear so that similar objects come to have the same kind of effect as the original one. And one may, for example, find himself afraid of all animals when his original fear was only related to dogs.

obsessive-compulsive reaction

In obsessive-compulsive reactions, an individual is compelled to behave in certain ways even though he realizes that his behavior is irrational. An *obsession* is a thought which a person cannot get out of his mind. A *compulsion* is a behavior in which he must engage. Obsessive-compulsive behavior is extremely incapacitating, since it is very likely to interfere with a person's daily life.

All of us have experienced thoughts which have some degree of obsessional urgency, such as a melody that we cannot forget—the imagined smell of a perfume that will not leave our nostrils, a commercial jingle that goes through our mind at night, keeping us awake for hours, or even the thoughts of an impending trip, date, new assignment. All of these are normal manifestations of mildly obsessive tendencies.

On the compulsive side, we all walk down the street stepping on cracks, or avoiding cracks, or counting fence posts, or touching every other fence post, or counting our steps from one end of a block to another. Such behaviors are generally normal and almost all of us engage in them from time to time.

One reason for these kinds of behaviors is that they are intended to ward off disaster. We often feel that if we do not do certain things, something dreadful might happen. If the thing we have to do is as simple as not stepping on the cracks in the pavement, that seems a cheap enough price to pay to ward off the impending event. Pretty soon we forget why we started such a ritual and just continue the behavior itself. Most of us do not believe that knocking on wood will prevent catastrophe, yet most of us will indulge this little compulsion because it is simple to do, and because, even though we do not believe in it, somewhere deep in our superstitious nature we feel that it might be true.

In more neurotic form, obsessive fears may be the kind in which people fear that they are going to kill someone, shout an obscenity in public, disrobe in public, rape somebody, and so on. Obsessive ideas are almost never carried out in action. But for the individual, this fact is of little comfort. The feeling that he has makes him certain that he is about to act upon his terrible desires.

In compulsive reactions the patient feels that he must perform certain ritualistic kinds of acts even though he realizes that what he is doing makes absolutely no sense.

A young man was unable to eat unless he sterilized all the implements he was about to use. The situation was extremely difficult for him because he could hardly go anywhere except to his own home to have his meals. Before every meal he would put his dishes and silverware into a pot and boil them for at least a half hour, then put them on a table and cover them completely with napkins and not allow anyone to touch them until mealtime. He would refuse all invitations to go out to dinner, to visit other people's homes, and even to go on vacations where he might have to eat food with implements that had not been sterilized.

Obsessive-compulsive reactions may often be substitutive thoughts and behaviors designed to mask more threatening ones. Some people, for example, must continually keep busy doing something. And they find themselves unable to relax even for a few moments because as soon as they do, they start to have thoughts or feelings which make them feel guilty, worthless, or evil. For these people, activities represent escape from uncomfortable feelings that would overwhelm them if they allowed them to have free rein. As a result, such people are continually in search of work to keep themselves busy. They find it very difficult to relax. And they often feel guilty if they are engaged in an activity that is not "accomplishing something."

In some cases obsessive-compulsive reactions represent reaction formations. For these kinds of people the compulsive reaction may represent the opposite of a feeling or thought which they secretly harbor. A person may try to mask his hostility by continually taking up humanitarian causes. He may react against his feelings of sexual inadequacy by trying to seduce every woman he meets. He may try compulsively to atone for guilt by performing ritualistic tasks over and over again.

This form of compulsion is very well depicted in Shakespeare's *Macbeth*. In a famous scene, having persuaded her husband to kill the King, Lady Macbeth is seen washing her hands over and over again in an attempt to clean the "blood" from them. The blood, of course, is a symbolic representation of guilt. In an attempt to wash the blood away, she is symbolically trying to remove the guilt she feels so strongly for her part in the deed. But since the act of washing does not really rid her of the guilt, she must continue to do it over and over again almost endlessly. In our society the almost compulsive emphasis on cleanliness may be related to our early indoctrination about sex—which often links it with dirt.

Many obsessive-compulsive reactions are related to an attempt to order the world in the face of insecurity and unpredictability. The less tolerance an individual has for surprise, the greater attempt he will make to order his environment in such a way that he can always keep contingency within manageable bounds. Very often people develop rigid patterns of behavior which seem to assure them that nothing surprising will occur to upset their pattern. It has also been noted that in some cases of brain damage people develop rather rigid compulsive ways of behaving, to deal with situations for which they have a very narrow capacity to respond. And when situations arise that require responses beyond their restricted capabilities, a great deal of discomfort and anxiety result.

People who suffer from obsessive-compulsive reactions are usually similar to those who suffer from other neurotic-type behaviors. They are generally rigid, methodical, submissive, suggestible, and they tend to suffer from feelings of inadequacy, guilt, and fear of punishment. They also tend to perceive the world as a threatening place and must be continually on their guard.

THE NEUROSES IN RETROSPECT

We have examined the pattern of so-called neurotic behavior to show that what we call pathological is simply an extension of defensive responding, and that both kinds of patterns have one common denominator. The common denominator is self-alienation. Defensive behavior and its extreme exaggeration, neurotic behavior, are both methods of dealing with the self (and included in this concept is the perception of the world, which is also, for our purposes, a part of the self) in such a way as to deny some part of it access to consciousness. The resulting symptoms are the consequences of such strategies. It might be said that to some extent we cannot alienate a part of ourselves without paying for it by a disruption in our way of life. The neuroses are the forms our payment takes.

In Chapter 12 we shall see that, for some people, even the neurotic responses are not adequate to maintain them, and when these strategies fail they have to fall back on more severe pathological kinds of responses in order to cope with their world. The results are even more distorted ways of perceiving and behaving and almost complete withdrawal from reality.

chapter 12
psychopathology: the fragmented self

THE FUNCTIONAL PSYCHOSES

In the classification of "abnormal" behavior, the psychotic reactions are the most severe. Although it must be emphasized that there is no clear line between neurotic and psychotic kinds of behavior, there are certain criteria that are often used to describe the difference. Let us further reemphasize the fact that although these reactions are described as "abnormal," all of us at one time or another engage in some or all of these kinds of behaviors, at least temporarily. To express it another way, we are all neurotic and psychotic at times. The difference between most of us and these more extreme reactions is one of degree and duration. In these latter situations the reactions are both exaggerated and persistent. Moreover, they are so disruptive of the individual's life that he usually cannot function effectively at all. Nevertheless, in reading about these reactions, it should be kept in mind that from time to time we may recognize some of these symptoms in ourselves. This is not necessarily a cause for alarm. Thoughts such as "I'm afraid I'm going crazy" can only give us added problems to worry about.

The major differences between the neurotic and the psychotic kinds of reactions are related to the person's perception of reality. In both situations, as we have already noted, there is a certain amount of distortion in terms of self-perception and perception of the external world. In the psychotic reactions, these distortions are so great that we tend to talk of an individual as having "lost touch with reality." That is, he appears to behave in ways or to respond to stimuli which, to another observer, do not exist. Under these circumstances we can reasonably say that an individual has gravely distorted his world.

In our discussion we shall be mainly concerned with the functional rather than the organic disorders. The psychotic reactions, resulting from brain injury and/or insult, will not concern us here. We shall focus on those reactions which come about through psychological rather than physical factors. These are the *functional* psychotic reactions.

delusions and hallucinations

The most outstanding characteristics of psychotic reactions are the existence of *delusions* and *hallucinations*. Delusions are false beliefs. In psychotic reactions individuals very often have many beliefs which cannot be corroborated by investigation. Nevertheless, the individual tends to defend these beliefs with great vigor even though it is perfectly clear that holding these beliefs is in itself highly disadvantageous to him in terms of social functioning.

Delusions may take many forms, and psychotic individuals are ingenious in creating and embellishing new ones from time to time. But there are a number of types of delusional systems, which are quite common. Two very prominent kinds are *delusions of persecution* and *delusions of grandeur*.

In a certain sense these two kinds of beliefs are related. In delusions of persecution, the person typically believes there are powerful forces dedicated to his destruction. These may be other people, animals, mystical figures, forces of nature. Their main characteristic is that all these things desire to destroy, thwart, injure, or otherwise interfere with the life of the individual. Delusions of grandeur help explain why the delusions of persecution occur. The psychotic individual very often believes that he is extremely important, powerful, influential, heroic, and remarkable and that because of this great importance, there are people who are dedicated to preventing the expression of his great power. The psychotic, therefore, sees his persecution in terms of his *importance*. An unimportant person would invoke the wrath of no one. But an extremely important person attracts powerful enemies.

Related to these delusions are the *delusions of reference* and of *influence*. In the former case the individual believes that people are talking about him, making fun of him, referring to him, portraying his life in television and movies, and so on. In the delusions of influence, the individual believes that "enemies" are putting thoughts into his head, wiring him up with electrical devices, causing him to behave in ways contrary to his own wishes, or "pouring filth" into his mind. Again one can note that in these processes there is an underlying delusion of grandeur and/or persecution.

Other kinds of delusions relate to hypochondriacal reactions, in which a person believes he has terrible diseases or that his body is rotting away or being eaten away by strange microorganisms. Another set of delusions are related to nihilistic thinking, in which the person believes that nothing exists or that he died some time ago and that only his spirit exists or that the world is simply a world of shadows, without substance.

Hallucinations are false perceptions. A person suffering from hallucinations believes that he is having certain sensory experiences, which he relates to the external world but which, when examined by others, seem to have no appropriate source. The most common hallucinations are auditory. People typically hear voices emanating from God, friends, enemies, or sources that they cannot identify. Other kinds of hallucinations are visual, olfactory, tactual, or even gustatory. A person may see visions, angels, demons, animals—he may smell gas, taste poison, feel bugs crawling on him or underneath his skin.

It appears reasonable that the elaboration of defense mechanisms such as projection and reaction formation are instrumental in the development of hallucinations and delusions. There is also, of course, a certain amount of fantasizing in terms of wish fulfillment related to these severe distortions of perception.

In psychotic reactions we have a very substantial movement along the continuum in the direction away from self-knowledge and self-understanding. The person has moved so far from the acceptance of the self that he has completely altered the meaning of the stimuli which are acting upon him.

This is true of both the internal and the external stimuli, but in the final analysis, it makes no difference. In the final analysis all stimuli are really internal stimuli, in the sense that they must be processed by the organism in order to make sense to him and to find a place in his perceptual scheme.

The alterations that take place between the time that energy impinges upon a receptor and a perception occurs are phenomenal. These changes are related to the needs, desires, fears, and biases of the individual—and by the time these impulses are processed, they have little or no resemblance to the original stimulus, even in healthy people. In psychotic people the degree of alteration becomes so great that there is very little correspondence between the original stimulus and the final perception. Moreover, since many of these stimuli arise from the inside of the organism, the distortions mean that the person is not properly processing the communications from his own body. Since all impulses, even those originating from outside stimuli, become inner processes immediately after impingement, all these processes can be said to truly be parts of the self. In this sense the psychotic individual can be said to be almost completely alienated from the self because of the radical alterations in meaning which he has given these inner processes.

It should be noted that the classification of specific psychotic reactions, like that of the neuroses, is largely a convenience. There is a great deal of overlap in the symptomatic and subjective experiences of people with "differing" psychotic classifications. Some people, in fact, believe that the classifications are largely a fiction. It may be that it is a better idea simply to think of all psychotic reactions as extreme forms of self-alienation.

manic-depressive reactions

Many of us in our own lives notice changes of mood that seem to correspond to certain rhythms or cycles of bodily functioning. For most of us these alterations in mood are generally mild and cause us little concern. In the manic-depressive reaction, the alteration of mood can be extremely exaggerated. Some people experience periods of elation, excitement, stimulation, agitation, during which they engage in an enormous outpouring of energy. At the other end of the emotional scale, a person may feel extremely depressed, unhappy, hopeless, worthless, and so on. In some individuals these reactions alternate; and the person is manic for a period of time, and then the mood changes to one of despair and depression. In other patients either the manic or the depressive phase is prominent throughout most of the reaction.

In the manic phase the person generally feels extremely optimistic, excited, agitated. He may be boisterous, excessively energetic, even violent toward anyone who appears to be interfering with his activities. He is often making grandiose plans and appears to be engaged in all kinds of exciting activities. Delusions of grandeur are common in this state and the individual very often believes that he has discovered a great new truth, invented a miraculous device, or found a solution to one of the world's most pressing problems.

In the depressed state the person may experience a profound state of sadness or hopelessness as well as an overwhelming feeling of loneliness.

To him the whole world appears tragic and joyless. Moreover, it appears to be doomed to remain that way. For the depressed person there appears to be no hope. In this state many of his thoughts are self-accusatory. He may accuse himself of indulging in all sorts of forbidden behaviors. He may also have delusions that his body is being destroyed by a number of strange, incurable diseases. In the depressed state, suicidal thoughts are common and, given the opportunity, suicidal attempts may occur.

The manic phase of the disorder seems to be a manifestation of the defense mechanism of reaction formation. The person desperately tries to overcome his feelings of failure, worthlessness, incompetence, and so on, by adopting the opposite point of view—that he is a great and important person engaged in exciting and relevant ventures that will have enormous consequences, usually for all mankind. These kinds of thought processes are usually successful, at least temporarily, in overriding the underlying feelings which he desires to conceal. Moreover, this attitude provides him with a great deal of activity which keeps him busy so that he does not have time to allow his *real* underlying thoughts to surface.

Some patients stay in the manic phase indefinitely. Others stay in the depressive condition for an indefinite period of time but in some patients there is a kind of seesawing between the two states, and in these cases the mood swings may be very severe, so that the change from extreme excitability to one of deep depression can be very pronounced.

The depressed phase often comes about as a result of a state of exhaustion which has followed the tremendous exertion of the manic behavior. With the exhaustion comes the feeling of failure and the admission that the projects that were so important and so exciting a little while ago have all come to naught—and with this realization the feeling of hopelessness becomes complete. Thus the cycle of manic-depressive behavior can be seen as one state running its course and giving rise to the other, and, in turn, being replaced by the former phase once again.

Many explanations have been offered for the existence of manic-depressive reactions but, whatever their nature, they all seem to include one thing. The person involved has had very severe feelings of inadequacy or worthlessness, and these feelings have been repressed and overreacted to in a particular way. Either the person trys to fight the feelings by the manic expressions and delusions, or he gives up and in despair falls into the depressed state in which he often comes to see himself as a victim of his own evil deeds.

In either case this is an example of highly exaggerated defensive behavior, which represents a desperate attempt to cope with difficulties that are overwhelming for this particular individual. Because of its severe nature and because of the exaggeration and elaboration of defensive strategies, this kind of reaction exists at the far end of the continuum.

paranoia

Many of us have had the experience of walking down the street and passing a group of people engaged in conversation who, just as we pass by, break out in laughter. Most of us, at such a moment, would probably wonder if the laughter were directed at us. We might even have the feeling that there was something wrong with our dress, or the way we walk, to evoke such a response. Most of us would shrug off the suspicion and continue on our way. Such a reaction is normal for most of us and limited in its effect.

But for some people these reactions become so important, and so intense, that they cannot easily dismiss them. When such reactions become elaborated to the extent that a person believes he is being watched, persecuted, attacked, then we say that the person is suffering from *paranoia*.

Paranoia very often appears in individuals who seem to be reasonable and logical in most of their behavior. Except for one area of their personality, they are generally competent and functional in their everyday lives. Moreover, the delusional system which they have is itself quite logical and systematic; as a result, these people may get a job, function within a family unit, even be important members of the community without other people being aware of their problem. In paranoia the person typically suffers from delusions of persecution and/or grandeur. We have already shown that there is often a relationship between these two kinds of delusional systems. For the paranoid person, however, and very often for others who are acquainted with him, there is enough logic embedded in the delusional system to be almost convincing until one follows these delusions to their ultimate limit.

The paranoid person tends to exaggerate or overinterpret real events so as to perceive them as threatening, dangerous, evil, and so on. Two people whispering, for example, are interpreted as talking about *him*. Someone who looks angry is angry at *him*. This overinterpretation of real facts sometimes makes it difficult for an outsider to know whether some of the things the paranoid person reports are true. This is especially likely in the case where the delusions themselves are well systematized and logical-sounding. Some paranoics can convince outsiders that some of the things they believe are true.

Paranoics often come from severely authoritarian family backgrounds. As children they are often loners. They are generally suspicious and aloof and seldom have the kinds of friendships that characterize normal children. In these individuals, like other neurotics and psychotics that we have described, there is often a need for a facade of superiority which is meant to overcome severe feelings of inadequacy and inferiority. This kind of attitude tends to destroy most of the social relationships which they try to form, but they are likely to see this as the fault of others, so that the pattern of projection may begin quite early.

In later life paranoics tend to show the pattern of arrogant, demanding, rigid behavior which often marks the extremist or fanatic. And like these individuals, paranoics often lack a sense of humor. They are often likely to see everything in black and white and are unable to conceive of any shades of gray in between. They often have unrealistically high aspirations which, when the psychosis is full blown, may account for the delusions of grandeur which they have about themselves. After a long period of frustration, they finally imagine that they have achieved the impossible goals which they had set for themselves.

In a sense the paranoic represents the PR image driven to the most extreme position. Strong feelings of inferiority are masked behind a rigid mask of superiority and self-importance. But even with this, these patients show a great need for praise, approval, and recognition. They become terribly upset when these kinds of responses are not forthcoming. Criticism or rejection can completely destroy them. They show extreme hypersensitivity to anything that can be interpreted as disparagement. It is as if their PR image is all they have and any threat to it is seen as a potential disaster.

schizophrenia

The most common, the most misunderstood, and the most disturbing of the psychotic reactions is the group of behaviors which come under the heading of *schizophrenia*. There is a certain amount of misunderstanding about this particular entity because of the popularization in the media of certain kinds of reactions that are often wrongly labeled schizophrenia. For example, the phenomenon of multiple personality is a neurotic, not a psychotic, reaction. But the popular press often refers to this particular syndrome as split personality. This leads to a certain amount of confusion because of the fact that *schizo* is the German equivalent of *split*. Schizophrenia is not, properly speaking, either split personality or multiple personality. It is probably more accurate to describe it as *fragmented* personality. The split in schizophrenia is not the splitting off of one part of the personality from the other—it is more like the splitting of the personality into a large number of fragments which seem to be out of phase with one another. One might say the personality is disintegrated.

Schizophrenia typically involves a number of kinds of behavior. In the first place, like all the psychotic reactions, the schizophrenic has lost touch with reality. He sometimes appears to be completely uninterested in the people and things around him. The schizophrenic also seems to be concerned largely with an inner world of fantasy rather than with real events or people. He suffers from delusions and hallucinations, particularly delusions of influence and persecution, and he tends to hear voices, which may be talking to or about him.

The emotional life of the schizophrenic individual is often quite shallow or blunted. It seems to any normal observer to be distorted. The emotional responses seem to be inappropriate to the situation in which the person finds himself, and it is difficult to predict the kind of emotional response that a schizophrenic patient will give under any circumstances. Very often the individual's behavior is bizarre, peculiar, or even childish. His posture, his gait, and other kinds of reactions seem awkward or peculiar and many of his acts are antisocial.

The schizophrenic's thought processes appear to be irrational, disorganized, and erratic. He is unable to follow any train of thought for any length of time and there appears to be no logical sequence to the flow of his ideas. His thoughts flit from one thing to another, often in rapid succession, almost as if his brain is being subjected to a large number of short circuits.

Schizophrenia is the most common of the psychotic reactions. It may come on suddenly or the onset may be prolonged. In the latter situation, the early signs of schizophrenia may be overlooked. The prognosis is not as good for the cases of prolonged onset as for those in which the onset is sudden. It may be that long-standing needs for defensiveness, which become more and more exaggerated as time goes on, are more difficult to alter by psychotherapeutic methods.

Schizophrenia has been classified into a number of types. These include hebephrenic, catatonic, paranoid, and one or two other classifications. These types differ somewhat in certain symptomatic reactions, but it is believed that the underlying core has certain common elements. The behavior of the hebephrenic is often characterized by inappropriate, childish reactions. It occurs most often in young people who act in silly, childlike ways. They may sit alone and giggle or talk in childish fashion to nobody in particular. They appear to be engrossed in an inner world of fantasy, and their emotional responses are blunted and inappropriate.

Most of the behavior in the hebephrenic reaction appears to be a kind of childish withdrawal from the world in the face of overwhelming difficulty. It is as if the individual has completely given up resisting the unbearable forces of his environment, and in this renunciation he has turned the entire situation into a bizarre joke. He laughs, he clowns, he fantasizes, he withdraws, and in all of this he is symbolically "throwing up his hands" in terms of any realistic solutions to his problem.

Catatonic schizophrenia very often develops much more slowly than the hebephrenic type, but in catatonia the withdrawal from reality is expressed in more overt physical behavior. The catatonic individual often alternates between stupor and agitation. The stupor is marked by a lack of activity which can become so extreme that the person gets into one position and holds that position for long periods of time, sometimes up to many hours, without moving. These positions are often extremely uncomfortable, and an ordinary person trying to maintain one for fifteen or twenty minutes would suffer a good deal of distress. But the catatonic, apparently unaware of these feelings, remains immobile and inaccessible for long periods of time. Sometimes these positions are held for several days and the hands and feet may become swollen and blue because of the circulation failure that results.

The patient in a catatonic stupor is often very resistant to the attempts of others to change his position. He also is often very negativistic, mute, inattentive to bodily needs, and in general appears to be in another world. Surprisingly enough, however, although the individual may appear to be completely oblivious to events around him, later he is often able to relate those events in great detail. The catatonic is aware of what is going on; he simply choses to withdraw from it.

During the catatonic stupor, he often has hallucinations and delusions. He may hear voices informing him of plots against his life, or he may believe that he is in such a precarious position that any movement on his part could lead to disaster. Some people believe that the catatonic state is a state of extreme emergency in which the individual is so uncertain of what to do, and in such a great panic, that the fear of making a wrong move becomes overwhelming. And he simply cannot move at all. Some of the strange postures in the catatonic reaction are symbolic. They often represent, for the patient, very important ideas or events, and the individual feels compelled to hold these postures because of the importance of these events in his delusional system. Thus a certain posture may signify that God is approaching. Such an event is of such great importance that it is unlikely that an individual will allow anyone to change his position or to interrupt his fantasy until the "event" has occurred.

paranoid schizophrenia

This type of reaction is by far the most common of all the schizophrenic types. And one might say, when we have reached this particular kind of disturbance, that we have come to the far end of the continuum. For this is the most disturbed and the most disturbing psychotic reaction. The syndrome seems to be a case of schizophrenia with a superimposed set of paranoid delusions which, however, in this case, are not as logical and systematized as they are in true paranoia.

The clinical picture in paranoid schizophrenia is one of a severely disturbed individual who shows the bizarre thought and fragmented personality of the schizophrenic along with delusions of persecution and grandeur and a great deal of projection which tries strenuously to locate the individual's problems in the external world. The person usually suffers from a series of illogical and absurd delusions in which he is suspicious of almost everyone at one time or another or believes that strange machines are operating on him, sometimes from great distances, destroying his body and his mind or injecting filth, terrible thoughts, or other kinds of threatening ideation into his mind. The individual may believe he is being watched, attacked, poisoned, injected with disease. He may also believe that he is one of the most important people on earth, which, of course, explains his persecution, and this delusion may include real people such as great figures in history (Napoleon, Lincoln, Caesar).

The person also often hears singing or the voices of his enemies talking about him or of God or angels advising him.

The paranoid schizophrenic's behavior can be so erratic and so volatile that it may be dangerous to himself or to others. He may attack "his enemies" or, in response to a "command," he may injure himself. The intellectual functioning of the paranoid schizophrenic is often so badly impaired that he may not understand what does or does not have survival value and, as a result, especially during an acute attack, he may engage in a great deal of irresponsible behavior.

Since most of these reactions are acute, they tend to clear up after a short period of time, especially with appropriate treatment. However, where schizophrenia is chronic, that is, where it is of long duration and gradual onset, it is often very difficult to remedy completely.

There are a number of theorists who believe that repressed homosexuality is sometimes an important factor in the etiology of paranoid schizophrenia. Studies have shown that paranoid schizophrenics have more homosexual episodes in childhood, more concern with homosexuality during psychotherapy, and more indications of latent homosexual tendencies than control groups. Some research tends to show that this may not be as true of female paranoid schizophrenics as it is of males.

etiology of schizophrenia

It is believed by many that there is a constitutional predisposition which is a necessary but not sufficient condition to bring about schizophrenia. That is, it may be that there is a susceptibility factor which determines that some people will become schizophrenic under a great deal of environmental stress while others will perhaps respond in some other way. These studies are by no means conclusive, but if it turns out that this is the case, then we are here dealing with a functional psychosis superimposed upon an organic condition which is its prerequisite. Some researchers have pointed to the fact that in childhood schizophrenia there is atypical and retarded development from the earliest stages of infancy. In these cases there appears to be lack of integration of various functional systems such as the autonomic nervous system, and the respiratory system, and it is upon the integration of such systems that normal behavior depends. Of course, these irregularities themselves may lead to stress between such children and their parents and/or siblings or peers, and in that way give rise to an extremely difficult life situation which may itself precipitate psychotic reactions.

Many studies have been made of the mothers of schizophrenic patients. These mothers are typically seen as rejecting, cold, domineering, possessively overprotecting, and unable to identify with the feelings of others. The mother of the schizophrenic very often keeps the child so dependent upon her that he never has the opportunity to develop mature competences. Very often, also, the parents of schizophrenics are rigidly moralistic, especially with regard to sexual behavior, so that almost any sexual experience, especially in childhood, may provoke fear and horror. In many cases the mothers of male schizophrenics are extremely and subtly seductive, tending to complicate his sexual problems even further.

In schizophrenia, as in most of the other severe emotional disturbances, there appears to be a failure on the part of the individual to integrate a meaningful and consistent sense of identity.

> In general, the mother–son relationship in schizophrenia appears to foster an immature, anxious youth who lacks a clear-cut sense of his own identity as a person, is handicapped by a distorted view of himself and his world, and suffers from pervasive underlying feelings of inadequacy and helplessness. (Coleman, 1964)

The lack of a consistent feeling of the continuity of the self is probably the most shattering experience that an individual can undergo. In its extreme form, which we choose to label schizophrenia, the individual's experience of the self and his world seems to be so fragmented that from one moment to the next, the self appears to have almost no continuity.

A number of researchers have chosen to view emotional disturbance in terms of expectations or predictions. Phillips (1956) and Kelly (1955) have developed theories that relate pathological behavior to failures of prediction. The general theory of these two writers involves the idea that we make certain bets about the outcomes of all our behaviors, and in the healthy person most of our bets or expectations are confirmed by experience. But the unhealthy person tends to make a large number of bets concerning himself and the world that are contradicted. This means, in effect, that this individual is a poor observer of reality because he has not learned what he can accurately expect from his past observations. In the case of the psychotic person, his predictions or expectations are so unrealistic and so unlikely to be confirmed that almost every one is contradicted by the real world. These disconfirmations cause him to withdraw into a world of his own making, to avoid further confrontation with the painful realities of life. This withdrawal into the fantasy world constitutes his psychosis. If we can imagine an individual who is making one prediction after another, each of which is being contradicted by his experience, until he has absolutely no capability of knowing what to expect from moment to moment—we can get a feeling of what psychotic behavior really means. The psychotic does not know what to expect, how to react, what steps to take to alleviate his fears, and as a result the world is so disordered and chaotic from his point of view that he is forced to create his *own* world, in which at least some of his predictions or expectations can be confirmed.

In terms of self-alienation, the psychotic separates himself from the part of the self that is in contact with reality (that is, the real self), so that the separation has become complete. Schizophrenia, therefore, is the most radical division of the self from its own being that human beings are capable of.

Like other emotionally disturbed individuals, the schizophrenic is an outer- rather than an inner-directed person. He takes his cues from others, is overly concerned with their approval, and begins to feel that he himself has no control over his own behavior. In this context it is no surprise that as the feeling of control passes from the self to others, the individual comes to believe that all of his own thoughts and actions emanate from the external world.

DRUG PATHOLOGY

Addiction to various kinds of drugs has become a major concern in our society in recent years. Although the concern may be recent, the problem has been with us for a very long time. Addiction to chemical substances such as alcohol, morphine, and heroin, are problems of long standing. But the reason for the recent furor is that now the drugs have reached a large segment of the young people of our nation.

It is no secret that we live in a drug-oriented culture. And it is also no secret that many people from middle-class backgrounds indulge to excess in the use of a number of substances, some of which are legally prescribed by physicians. But the modern problem of drug addiction is related to the problem of "the street." For it is here that many young people, in an attempt to experiment with new kinds of "kicks," may become "hooked" on some very dangerous substances.

Let us at the outset distinguish between two broad classifications of substances in order to clarify a rather confused situation. For a long time many people classified all of the substances that could be procured on the street as addictive drugs. In so doing, they included a number of substances which, in fact, are not physiologically addictive at all. However, the confusion that resulted from this kind of classification led young people to disbelieve almost anything that the adult generation said concerning the action or ingredients of these substances. The unfortunate result was that a large number of young people were not able to discriminate between those substances that could do serious physiological damage and those that could not. And because of their distrust of the older generation, many of them rebelliously tried everything that became available on the street. The result for some was disastrous.

In one group, let us classify the *psychedelic* substances. These substances have the ability to alter the state of consciousness of the user to a very great degree (mind expanding and consciousness altering) on a temporary basis, but they do not have physiologically addictive properties. We will speak of these substances shortly. The other kinds of drugs to which we have referred are those which produce physiological changes in the body, which then require further administrations of the drug, usually in an increased dosage, for indefinite periods of time. Most of these drugs have serious physical side effects as well. Included in this group of substances are the amphetamines and the barbiturates.

the amphetamines

The amphetamines are the most common stimulants used by the medical profession to produce temporary feelings of well-being in people who are depressed. These are the "pep pills" or "uppers," and they have been taken by a large number of people under all kinds of circumstances. In this group of substances are Benzedrine, Dexedrine, and methamphetamine (Methedrine). The latter substance is often called "speed," especially when it is taken hypodermically.

The amphetamines will rouse a tired person, excite a depressed person, elate an apathetic person, excite a bored person. These effects seem desirable and, to most people, achievable at low cost to themselves. That is, it seems to most individuals that it is easier to change one's mood by the injection or ingestion of a drug than it is by changing one's life or, even worse, changing one's self. This makes the use of amphetamines extremely attractive to many people. For most of them do not see the long-range consequences of using such substances.

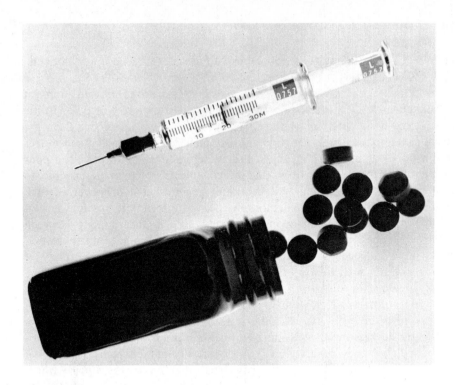

the barbiturates

Whereas the amphetamines are stimulants, or "uppers," the barbiturates are depressants, or "downers." These substances have a sedative, hypnotic effect and are used most often to relieve tension and anxiety or to produce sleep. The barbiturates are particularly dangerous for two reasons. In the first place, overdoses of these substances cause coma and death. In the second place, there is a tendency for individuals who use them continuously to develop a tolerance to them, which then results in their finding it necessary to increase the dose to get its benefits. The continuous use and the accompanying increased dosage lead to physiological dependence. When such a pattern has been established, withdrawal of the drug leads to very serious physical illness, which may include convulsions, delirium, and temporary psychotic behavior. Excessive doses of the barbiturates lead to loss of emotional control and impairment of judgment, both of which can lead to serious criminal behavior and/or accidents that may involve not only the user but other individuals as well.

Both the amphetamines and the barbiturates become serious problems when an individual who is dependent upon them needs such large doses that he has to obtain a great deal of money to support his habit. (This is even more true of the opiates, as we shall see shortly.) Because large doses of these drugs are generally expensive, individuals often turn to crime as the only means to get the money to pay for them. Although the crimes of addicts have usually been petty, they seem to be increasing in seriousness as well as in violence. The more desperate an individual becomes, the less he is concerned about the behavior he indulges in to obtain the money to keep his supply of drugs coming.

It should also be noted that the amphetamines and barbiturates are abused by the "straight," middle-class, middle-aged citizen, who gets the drugs legally by prescription from his physician but becomes so dependent upon them over a period of time that he is almost unable to function without them. This form of drug abuse is serious because it is often unrecognized by the individual himself and also because young people, seeing their parents "hooked," are not likely to listen to their admonitions to stay away from drugs.

Another group of substances, which are not related chemically to the barbiturates but have somewhat similar effects, are the sedative and tranquilizing drugs introduced in the early 1950s. These drugs include Miltown, Equanil, Doriden, Valmid, Placidyl, and Librium. Excessive use of these agents over a long period of time in large doses may lead to physical dependence. Once again these drugs are used generally by people who get them legally through their physician, but they can also be obtained illegally on the street.

the narcotics

Under federal law the term "narcotic" includes the opiates and cocaine, and in some cases marijuana has also been classed with this group. However, recent research has shown that marijuana belongs with another class of substances. The term "narcotic" refers to certain substances that induce sleep, dull the senses, or relieve pain. But in the United States the term "narcotics" is a legal one that refers to the opiates and cocaine.

the opiates

The opiates refer to those substances that include opium, morphine, and their derivatives and compounds. The most important derivative of morphine is the drug *heroin*. This is one of the most dangerous of all the drugs and one of the most often abused. Generally speaking, heroin is a depressant. It relieves anxiety and tension and often creates a euphoria which some people have described as the most powerful experience of their lives. The sensation is so overwhelming that it has been compared by many to a "central nervous system orgasm." Repeated use of the drug leads to tolerance and physiological dependence. The withdrawal from heroin can be pure hell.

Permanent organic damage does not occur from doses to which an individual is tolerant. Overdoses, however, can lead to respiratory failure, coma, and death. Moreover, the individual addicted to drugs very often injected under the skin or intravenously ("mainlining"). In the latter two paired.

Heroin, like morphine, can be introduced into the body in a number of ways. It can be smoked, "snorted" (inhaled in powder form), eaten, or injected under the skin or intravenously ("mainlining"). In the latter two cases, hypodermic needles are used, and there is a great danger that heroin users will contract a variety of serious infectious diseases from dirty needles. One of the most common of these diseases is hepatitis, which damages the liver.

cocaine

Cocaine has been listed under federal law as a narcotic, but its action is opposite to that of the opiates. Cocaine is a powerful stimulant that does not create physiological dependence or tolerance. Cocaine may be introduced into the body, like the opiates, by sniffing, swallowing, or injecting. Like these other drugs, it gives rise to a euphoric state lasting from four to six hours. During this period, the user often experiences serene, blissful feelings of peace and contentment.

Although cocaine has had its booms in popularity from time to time, it has not generally presented the kind of problems that accompany heroin addiction. But some people have recently become alarmed, because young people, knowing the pitfalls inherent in using heroin, have been turning more and more to other substances, cocaine being chief among them.

Although, as we have noted, there is no physiological addiction to cocaine, there very often is developed a psychological dependence, especially for people who need escape. This dependence can be very great and many people find it very difficult to give it up.

the psychedelics

There are a group of substances which are variously called *hallucinogens* or *psychedelics* which are somewhat different from the substances we have been speaking of. These substances include LSD, mescaline, psilocybin, DMT, and marijuana. Among these psilocybin, mescaline, and marijuana come from natural plants. The other substances are generally synthesized. Some of these substances have been used for generations in connection with religious ceremonies in various parts of the world. For example, mescaline, which comes from the peyote cactus, and psilocybin, which comes from a mushroom in Central and South America, have both been used by the Indians of these regions in connection with their religious rituals as far back as there are records.

The actions of these substances appear to be similar, although there are great differences in potency. One effect is a tremendous enhancement of visual experience. A number of writers have observed that the "high" one obtains from the psychedelics differs in important ways from that of the other drugs we have been considering. Some serious researchers, among them Aldous Huxley, Gerald Heard, Alan Watts, and Sidney Cohen, have reported that the major effect of these substances comes from what they consider a "new perception of the universe." Thse drugs somehow have the capability of reordering our mental set in such a way that the old categories break down and we begin to think in completely new ways.

> All this evidence leads to the conclusion that these drugs, so different in chemical composition, operate through a common mechanism and bring into action a capacity present in the human psyche but not ordinarily used. This capacity can be defined as the power to transcend temporal limitations, verbal definitions, the limitations of name and form. Somehow these chemicals release the awareness from certain fetters that ordinarily bind it. The doors of perception are cleansed. The taste of the infinite is obtained. The isolated awareness, imprisoned in the illusion of its ego-sense, is suddenly liberated from its fetters. Ecstasy is the result, for ecstasy means nothing more or less than standing outside of one's self. A man dies at one level and is reborn at another. (deRopp, 1968)

There has been a lot of controversy concerning the psychedelic drugs, and some of the research is somewhat contradictory. But it appears that certain conclusions are beginning to emerge. In the first place, none of these substances are physiologically addicting. Tolerance does not develop and dosages do not have to be increased. Moreover, a person who has used any of these substances, for any length of time, can usually stop without withdrawal effects. Psychological dependence is rare, although it can develop in certain instances. The feeling of well-being that arises in connection with the use of these particular substances seems to be a result of the thought processes themselves, not a euphoric response to physiological changes. The ecstatic experiences, when they are reported, appear to be related to a new vision of the self and the world, and when such a vision is not forthcoming, the experience may not be at all pleasing. There appears to be some danger, especially with the use of the stronger substances, that a number of people can have extremely disturbing experiences—or even what appear to be psychotic breaks. In very rare cases, the psychotic reactions do not clear up even after the effects of the drug have worn off.

One controversy surrounding LSD has been related to the possible effects of the substance upon chromosomes. Some researchers have suggested that LSD may cause chromosomal damage, but other investigators, in follow-up studies, have failed to find any such effects in moderate dosage levels. Additional research will have to be completed to resolve this issue.

In addition to the existence of "bad trips" and possible chromosomal damage, there is another serious side effect of the use of LSD. Approximately one in twenty users of the drug experience "flashbacks" of their psychedelic trip. Flashbacks are spontaneous recurrences of the hallucinatory images which occur after the effects of the drug have worn off. These recurrences may continue for weeks or even months, and they are generally frightening in their nature. Flashbacks can be very disturbing to some individuals and can precipitate anxiety reactions or, in extreme cases, psychotic behavior.

The mildest psychedelic is marijuana, especially as it is usually found in the United States. It has not been shown to have any harmful physical effects, at least in short-time use. Research is in progress to see if it has long-term deleterious effects, but so far there is no clear-cut evidence that it does. The effects of marijuana, like all the other psychedelic substances, depends to a great extent upon the user's state of mind, his purpose in using the drug, the setting in which the drug is used, and the potency of the particular substance. In comparing marijuana to alcohol, many people have pointed out that whereas both appear to reduce inhibitions, marijuana, unlike alcohol, does not seem to give rise to aggressive kinds of behavior and, in fact, often seems to have the opposite effect.

why drugs?

Why do people resort to the use of substances that alter their thought processes, disturb their emotional states, distort their perceptions, create physiological dependence, impair their judgment, or cause them to commit crimes? There may be many reasons—many answers to this kind of question. But the simplest answer is that for one reason or another the individual who uses drugs wishes to change the state of awareness in which he finds himself. In other words, he does not like the way he feels at the moment and desires to change it. One way to do this quickly, is through the use of substances that can rapidly affect the state of mind.

In a certain sense, we might consider any kind of motivation a desire to change one's state of consciousness in one way or another. If we want water, or food, or sex, it is because we believe that these things will change the way we feel, presumably for the better. Those who use drugs use them for the same purpose. Unfortunately, sometimes they ignore the other consequences of drugs (the *long-range* effects may be to change the state of consciousness for the worse). In other words, we buy a *temporary* state of well-being, often at the cost of very great personal distress.

In some cases the desire to alter one's state of consciousness relates to a need to *remove* one's self from the state in which he is at the moment. The present situation is one that is so undesirable that the individual seeks to escape it in the quickest and easiest way. As one drug user put it: "The world is a terrible place and if for a few minutes I find a way to escape the pain and experience a little bit of happiness, why should I not do it? Sure it's a crutch. But when reality is as awful as it is, a crutch may be the only way to avoid the pain."

For those who see the world in this way, it is understandable that they might desire an easy form of escape. The rehabilitation of such people involves an entire reorganization of their ways of perceiving themselves and their world so that they come to see it as worthwhile, exciting, beautiful, as well as painful, sad, ugly. With a realistic, balanced view of the world, the use of drugs for escape becomes less necessary.

There is another state of consciousness which people sometimes strive to reach through the use of chemical substances. In this case they are not trying so much to escape the present situation as they are seeking to explore a new and mysterious realm of consciousness. This use of drugs is often an attempt not to "cop out" but to "tune in" to a new kind of awareness. This is the kind of experience that is so sought after by individuals who have in the past used the psychedelic substances for this purpose.

These people are not, generally speaking, maladjusted individuals seeking to escape from an oppressive present. They are, on the contrary, usually individuals who are happy and successful in their personal and professional lives, but who are convinced that there are other realms of consciousness which are of great value to the human spirit but which are seldom explored. Although the use of psychedelic drugs may not be the best method of achieving such states of awareness, for some of these people it has been one method that they have utilized in this pursuit. It appears, however, that we are on the threshold of discovering other methods which will be more suitable and less dangerous.

The entire question of the use of these substances in the body, whether addictive or nonaddictive, psychedelic or narcotic, especially in the young, seems to be related to a prevalent feeling that the state of the world is so desperate that it hardly matters what one does to one's body. This is an unfortunate attitude. Young people have to realize that the real world does not go away while one is under the influence of these substances, which temporarily take us out of the area of our immediate problems. When we come down, the world is still there. In fact, it may be a little worse because the problems that we have been running away from have not been solved. If there are any answers to the problems that beset mankind, they will surely require clear heads, perseverance, and a sense of direction. Such commitment also alters consciousness, although in a somewhat different way.

It is important to note once again that the use of drugs is widespread in our society and is not limited to the young. Many middle-aged and older people, who begin the use of tranquilizers and/or energizers under the care of a physician, become "silent abusers" of these substances over a period of time. And since these people use the drugs in their own home and are seldom brought to public notice, it is literally impossible to obtain dependable statistics about the phenomenon. However, it is generally agreed that this kind of abuse is widespread.

One final problem must be considered before we leave the subject of drugs. Because of the widespread use of many substances intended to alter an individual's state of awareness, there are often certain combinations of substances that can be extremely dangerous. Drugs obtained on the street are of unknown quality and may often be combined with very toxic substances in order to give them more "kick." It is axiomatic, therefore, that drugs obtained in this way may not be what they are claimed to be—and they may, at times, be laced with certain substances which can cause death. (For example, some drugs are mixed with strychnine, which is a deadly poison.) Another serious problem related to drug use is the fact that many people who use drugs drink alcohol at the same time. Even the mildest kinds of tranquilizers and energizers can be deadly when combined with alcohol. And it is difficult to predict when an individual will have a very serious reaction to this combination. Many people mix alcohol and drugs occasionally. And every once in a while, one of them dies. No one is certain why. The fact that a person has mixed these substances before and has not had a serious reaction does not guarantee that he will not have one, even a fatal one, in the future. The best advice, therefore, is never to mix drinking with any of the pharmaceutical substances.

We have examined the various conditions which are generally classified as pathological. We have tried to show that, to a great extent, all these conditions are related to some form of alienation from the self. In later chapters we will discuss what procedures are available to us to try to change the direction of movement along the continuum away from pathology and toward health. Some of these procedures are called *psychotherapy*. Some of them are simply called *authentic living*. In what follows we will be changing our orientation from the psychology of despair to the psychology of joy.

IV

the psychology of joy

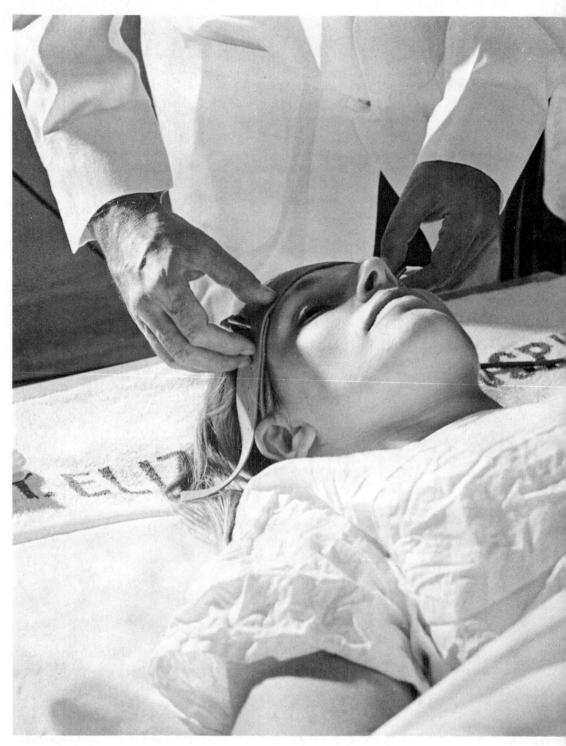

Electro shock therapy.

chapter 13
psychotherapy

STRATEGIES FOR MOVING TOWARD AUTHENTICITY

Psychotherapy has often been thought of as a means of helping individuals who are emotionally disturbed to overcome their difficulties so that they can function adequately in their environment. Although this is one way to look at psychotherapy, it is not the only one. For psychotherapy should be more than that. It should not only help solve the problems of disturbed individuals, it should also be of value to "normal" people in enabling them to find more fruitful and valuable experiences with which to give meaning to their lives.

There are a number of therapies that are biological in nature—that is, they are involved in some way in changing the biochemical functioning of the nervous system, through drugs, electroshock, implantation of electrodes, or whatever. Some of these methods are in experimental stages and are not widely used; some, like chemotherapy and electroshock therapy are in common use. However, for the purposes of this book we will not deal with any of these. What we are interested in in this book is what the individual can come to understand about himself that will better enable him to fully function and fully experience the richness of his life. In that sense we are defining psychotherapy as the search for joy.

Every form of psychotherapy is an attempt to reverse the direction of the pathology in which the individual finds himself. This means that the methods and techniques of any psychotherapeutic procedure will be directly dependent upon the theory of human behavior to which that therapy subscribes. If, for example, as some people have sometimes believed, the insane are possessed by demons, then exorcism is the proper methodology with which to deal with that problem. If, on the other hand, pathology is related to alienation from the self—which, of course, is the underlying assumption of this book—then the solution to the problem lies in methods and procedures which bring the individual back into harmonic relationships with his essential being. Most of the modern psychotherapies, although they may not always explicitly express it in so many words, are essentially trying to do just this.

In general, all psychotherapy aims at helping the individual move in the direction of maturity, self-actualization, competence, and happiness. There are seven general ways in which the therapeutic procedures which we will examine try to do this:

1. There is an attempt to increase the insight and understanding of the individual with regard to his own specific problems, with the aim that understanding will lead to more realistic solutions.
2. There is an emphasis on the clear, undistorted perception of the individual's identity.
3. There is an attempt to attack underlying conflicts which may be working at cross purposes in terms of integrating the personality.
4. There is a great emphasis on changing the undesirable conditioned responses which tend to disable or cripple growth and openness.
5. There is a desire to improve the interpersonal competencies and interactions in order to create viable relationships with other human beings.
6. There is a concentrated attack upon the inaccurate or irrational assumptions or traditional beliefs about one's self and the world.
7. There is the attempt to open or enlarge the individual's awareness and appreciation in order to enrich in each individual the capacity for joy.

These are not simple aims. And they are not easily attained. It may be accurately said that no single form of therapy attains these goals consistently, and some would say that all of them are never attained. Nevertheless, these are the aims of psychotherapy, and any progress toward these goals is certainly a valuable contribution to an individual's life. Let us therefore examine the methods that are available to us in the hope that such knowledge will lead to a better understanding of our own individual situations.

OLDER VIEWS

Throughout man's history there have been attempts by one individual to "help" another, to relieve his fears, to reduce his anxieties, to alleviate his sadness, and to return him to a state of normal functioning. These procedures took the form related to the particular theory about emotional illness that was in vogue at the time.

For a long time in man's history it was believed that an emotionally disturbed person was possessed. Through some means, a demon had gained access to the soul of the individual and was now in possession of his body. This meant that the demon had to be exorcised. And very often the unfortunate individual had to undergo a series of torturous "treatments" in the hope that the demon would be made to suffer so much that he would leave the body. However, for the individual who had to submit to these drastic measures the treatment was probably far worse than the disease—moreover, it is unlikely that it did anything but make the person's condition worse.

There have also been times in history when it was believed that those people who acted in strange ways were "bad" people. For them, therefore, the appropriate treatment was punishment. In some sense we still believe that this is true—and we still treat many emotionally disturbed people as criminals.

There have been times in the history of man when kindness rather than brutality became the *modus operandi* of those who attempted to give aid to these unfortunate people. Although kindness and consideration are important elements of the psychotherapeutic process, by themselves they are no more than merely palliative measures that have only temporary effects.

Another form of psychotherapy which has been used through the ages comes under the general heading of *meditation*. These methods have been used for thousands of years, mostly in Oriental countries. We will have more to say about these methods presently.

psychoanalysis

The term *psychoanalysis* has generally been used incorrectly in the media and elsewhere, giving the impression that all psychotherapy is, in fact, psychoanalysis. That is not the case. It is important, at the outset, for us to realize that psychoanalysis is only one of a large number of psychotherapeutic procedures and techniques presently being used all over the world. It is not true, for example, that everyone who goes to a psychotherapist is being "analyzed." The word "analysis," usually meaning psychoanalysis, is thrown about so carelessly by individuals who are really talking about psychotherapy that it has become almost synonymous with the latter term. But psychoanalysis is a specific technique based on a particular theory of the origin and treatment of emotional disturbances. The other psychotherapeutic procedures, of which there are many more than most people realize, are also based on their own theoretical formulation about the nature of health and illness—and so we must look at psychoanalysis as merely one of many kinds of procedures that come under the heading of psychotherapy.

Psychoanalysis is based on Freud's theory of the structure of the psyche. Freud saw the mind as divided into three parts: *id, ego*, and *super-ego*. The id was the storehouse of all of man's instinctive drives. And of course, for Freud, man's instinctive drives were mainly sexual and aggressive. In other words, for Freud, man's essential being was animalistic. All the energy of the psyche was contained in the id.

The id was aware only of its desires—but it had no realistic means of satisfying them. For this purpose there developed the *reality principle* of the mind: the ego. The ego was the director of the energy of the id. It could perceive the environment accurately and act upon these perceptions. Unlike the id, the ego would recognize the difference, for example, between real food and the fantasy of food. It could therefore act in the former case and restrain itself in the latter.

But with the id, the source of all instinctive energy, and the ego, the reality principle and executor of the mind, there was still no moral principle to prevent man from acting upon his destructive instincts and behaving in ways that would be unacceptable to society. This task fell to the superego.

The superego, in Freud's system, is man's conscience. It consists of the introjected values of an individual's parents and the rest of society. These values generally act in opposition to the forces of the id and, as a result, suppress behavior that would otherwise be immoral, unlawful, evil, and otherwise socially unacceptable. This is the task to the superego—it is the superego that represses, and drives into the unconscious, those impulses which society has deemed undesirable.

In psychoanalytic theory, repression is the major factor in the etiology of human disorders. For although repressed, the libidinal energy (that is, the energy from the id) is not lost. It exists somewhere. And it brings to bear a pressure on the system which leads to its inevitable expression. However, since the normal form of this expression has been blocked, it will be expressed in some altered form. Very often this new form is symptomatic—it is experienced as anxiety, depression, as a phobia, as a compulsive reaction, and so on. In some cases, according to psychoanalytic theory, repressed energy finds its way out in socially acceptable forms. In this case it makes use of the defense mechanism of sublimation and may be expressed as artistic creativity, in nurturant behavior (nursing), or in some other acceptable activity which might be of value to society. But this would be the exceptional case. Most repression, from the Freudian point of view, results in more serious consequences. And when the repression is massive, especially with regard to childhood memories that have been traumatic, the result is usually symptomatic.

Psychoanalytic therapy consists of uncovering these repressed memories, motives, desires, and so on, and bringing them to light in the present so that the patient can gain insight into their nature. The uncovering of a long forgotten event, which is believed to have triggered the neurotic reaction in the first place, is often a signal to the psychoanalytical therapist that he has reached the very core of the neurosis. The remainder of the therapy consists of helping the patient to integrate this new understanding into his adult personality so that instead of repressing it, he acknowledges it as part of his experience. This acknowledgment and integration is believed to be the "cure" of the neurotic disorder. The psychoanalytic approach to the treatment of psychosis is essentially the same. In the latter case, however, it usually takes somewhat longer to uncover the important repressed material, since presumably in psychoses they are more deeply repressed.

Psychoanalysis uses a number of techniques which are considered essential to its success. Among these are *free association, dream interpretation*, and *analysis of transference*. If the patient's problems all lie in the unconscious, then it is necessary to find ways of penetrating this realm to uncover those hidden elements which are their cause. One of these techniques is free association.

In free association the patient is asked to lie down and relax as much as possible and to allow his thoughts to flow freely without trying to steer them in a particular direction. He allows one thought to lead to another, even though the sequence of associations may seem completely illogical. Freud believed that although the thoughts in free association may appear to be random, in reality they make sense in terms of the patient's unconscious processes. It is the job of the therapist to discover this sense in these seemingly random processes by interpreting their hidden meanings. These interpretations are subsequently used by the patient in order to help him gain insight into his difficulties. The interpretations given are generally in accord with the psychoanalytic theory of psychosexual development. Thus the psychoanalyst is always on the lookout for evidence of oedipal striving, castration fears, sexual conflicts, and so on.

The second technique is dream interpretation. Freud felt that when an individual is asleep, his superego is relaxed. This means that there is an opportunity for repressed materials to surface, in a somewhat less restrained way, in dreams. But although our inhibitions are somewhat relaxed, they are not completely eliminated, and even dreams contain a certain amount of repression, so that a great deal of the material representing unconscious motives is presented in symbolic form. It becomes the task of the therapist, therefore, to interpret this symbolic material in order to determine its real meaning for the patient.

Freud considered dream interpretation so important to his therapy that he made it a central part of his procedure. He referred to dreams as the "royal road to the unconscious."

Once again the interpretation placed upon the dream by psychoanalytic theorists is conceived in light of their theory. Some people have objected to this, claiming that the psychoanalyst is likely to force his own interpretation, based on a rigid theoretical outlook, upon the patient. Whether this is true or not, it is generally agreed that dreams do contain various kinds of meaning for the dreamer, but there is less agreement on who should do the interpreting and how they should be interpreted.

The third technique is the analysis of transference. The idea of transference is closely related to the concept of stimulus generalization in learning theory. Both ideas relate to the fact that we tend to perceive similar objects in similar ways. In terms of reacting to people, we have all had the experience of meeting someone who looked like someone we knew at an earlier time, and we often reacted to that person in ways which were consistent with our reactions toward that other person. In psychotherapy it often occurs that the patient comes to view the therapist in the same way he once viewed significant people in his life. He might come to see the therapist as his father, his mother, a sibling, a friend. He may come to experience love, fear, aggressive tendencies, and so on, toward the therapist, whom he now views as this other individual.

In psychoanalytic therapy, the therapist keeps looking for signs of the transference because he uses it as a tool to reeducate the patient. If, for example, the patient is perceiving the therapist as his father—and if his father was rejecting—then the patient can now experience "his father" in a new way. He can now have the experience of having a "good" father, and presumably he can now work through the feelings that he has repressed with regard to his father, as well as the feelings of self-devaluation and humiliation that he experienced in his presence. In general, the feeling of acceptance that now replaces the old feeling of rejection leads to a new resolution of the ancient conflicts that have plagued the individual.

In practice the patient's response to the therapist is often ambivalent.

He may, at the same time, love the therapist and hate him or distrust him —he may see him as a symbol of authority and react in whatever ways have been customary for him. And in some cases it may be that what passes for the transference is a real feeling of love and affection and/or sexual attraction which can easily develop between two people engaged in such intimate disclosure. In fact, as we shall see, in some other forms of therapy a feeling of mutual trust and affection is seen as necessary for the therapeutic process.

What we have been presenting here is generally the classic psychoanalytic approach to psychotherapy. These approaches have been modified in recent years by people who have succeeded Freud in the psychoanalytic tradition. Traditional psychoanalytic therapy is time-consuming and expensive. Moreover, there has been a great deal of criticism about its results or lack thereof. Many of the neo-Freudian analysts, therefore, have altered their procedures to some extent.

For the most part, the new therapists spend less time on the historical past and the childhood experiences that may have begun the maladaptive pattern. Instead, they concentrate on the current situation and try to determine the elements that maintain the symptoms in the present. For although a traumatic event in the past may have *begun* a neurotic reaction pattern, it is often something quite different that *maintains* its existence in the present.

Although there have been changes in modern psychoanalytic procedures, there is still a great deal of criticism regarding the time it takes and its therapeutic efficacy. We shall now consider some of the newer therapeutic procedures which have arisen in more recent years.

CLIENT-CENTERED THERAPY

There have been many objections to traditional psychoanalytic therapy, a good number of these coming from psychoanalytically trained people themselves. Among these objections were the facts, already mentioned, that psychoanalysis was lengthy, expensive, and often unreliable in terms of its results. Moreover, the emphasis upon the interpretation of the therapist was seen by some as completely authoritarian. The entire course of therapy was dependent upon the theory and attitude of the therapist, and the patient was forced to more or less accept the interpretations that were given him as "the truth."

One of the most vocal critics of this authoritarian attitude in psychoanalysis was Carl Rogers. Rogers' theory of man differs radically from the theory that comes to us through Darwin, Freud, and most traditional Western religious views. The latter view mainly contends that man is innately destructive or evil and that his socialization consists of teaching him to live in the world by *controlling* these tendencies. Rogers, along with Maslow and others, sees man from an almost opposite point of view. For Rogers, man is innately creative, trusting, and loving. The problems that he has, therefore—the pathology which is seen all around us—result from society's suppression of these innate tendencies. Given the opportunity, man will fulfill these potentialities. But the restraints of society, the pressures toward conformity, the belief that many of our natural feelings and functions are bad, all tend to prevent us from expressing these inborn, natural qualities. The result is that we become confused, frustrated, hostile, depressed.

But the tendency to realize, to discover our real nature, never leaves us. It always remains within us, waiting for the moment when it will become free to express itself. That moment comes during therapy. But it does not come about through anyone else's guidance. The solution comes about through the vision of an inner wisdom which exists in everyone. This inner wisdom, given a chance to be free, discovers its own solution.

Client-centered psychotherapy, therefore, attempts to be non-directive. In this form of therapy, or counseling as Rogers prefers to call it, the client (rather than the therapist) steers the course of therapy himself. The counselor tries to be a mirror which shows the client where he is, in an emotional sense, at any given time. Under these conditions the client becomes capable of seeing his own problems in a new way for the first time. This enables him to create his own solution—to find his own way to fulfill the potentialities which he, and *only* he, has.

The main technique used in client-centered therapy is called *reflection*. The counselor attempts to reflect back to the client the feelings which underlie the words he speaks. Since it is believed that most people who seek therapeutic help are alienated from their own feelings, it bcomes necessary for the counselor to put them back into contact with these feelings. Rogers believes that once an individual knows how he feels—what emotional responses he is making to a particular set of stimuli, appropriate solutions to his problems will begin to present themselves to him. He will then be able to make enlightened choices among the alternatives that are available and thereby alter the pathogenic process.

If, for example, the client says, "I just had a fight with my wife," the counselor might respond, "You are angry at your wife." In such an exchange, the counselor is reflecting the feeling which underlies the statement that merely reports an incident but which is devoid of any emotion. Such a response might seem quite obvious and almost unnecessary to the uninitiated. However, it is extremely important since many people are entirely unaware of the emotions that underlie their behavior. And it is often this lack of awareness that gives rise to their difficulties. The bringing to awareness of this heretofore repressed emotional life is, in Rogers's view, absolutely necessary for the insightful discoveries which lead to a resolution of the individual's problems.

The techniques of client-centered therapy have undergone some refinements in recent years. And although the underlying concepts are still the same, Rogers has come to see that the most important factor in a therapeutic relationship is an authentic dialogue between individuals. These may be client and counselor or they may be members of an encounter group. But the essential ingredient is honesty presented in an atmosphere of acceptance and support. If a person sees other people willing to explore and share embarrassing or painful feelings, then he, too, may be encouraged to so respond. Rogers's theory is very much concerned with the self.

The self consists of the totality of experiences and perceptions attributable to the "I" or "me." A very important part of this self-system is the affective or emotional component. To disregard or deny any of one's emotions is to deny that part of the self. But many people, in order to protect a self-concept which they have been socialized to accept, do in fact exclude certain emotional experiences from their consciousness. This leads to a state of incongruence in which a person's perceptions of himself are falsified with regard to his feelings.

We have already noted how such denial leads to emotional difficulties. The Rogerian technique attempts to undo this pattern, to bring the denied feelings back into the spotlight of awareness so that the individual literally comes to reaccept those parts of the self that he has been afraid to face. The result is a congruent individual who can learn to take control of his own life, who can experience the richness of living in a new way, without the disabling and neurotic defenses that were necessary before.

It is interesting to note that, for Rogers, one of the most important measures of psychotherapeutic effectiveness is increased self-esteem. Much research has shown that clients who come for psychotherapy usually have a very poor self-concept. However, after a number of weeks of client-centered therapy, most measures show a greatly improved self-image. Moreover, as the self-image continues to improve, other neurotic tendencies tend to disappear.

One of the most important considerations of client-centered therapy is the resolution of the feeling of dependency that the client tends to develop in almost all psychotherapies. Rogers believes that client-centered therapy, as opposed to some of the other directive therapies, is less apt to give rise to powerful feelings of dependency in the client, since he is not allowed to rely on the counselor—that is, he does not come to depend upon the counselor but must use his own resources in dealing with his difficulties. By such a strategy, Rogers hopes to gradually condition the client to become a mature, independent human being. In contrast, other psychotherapies usually have an authoritarian type of structure. This means that the therapist is the one who knows all the "right" answers. And the client or patient relies on the therapist to give him these answers. The result is that even after he is "well," he may still feel unable to depend upon himself when new problems arise.

Although theoretically plausible, it turns out that even in client-centered therapy, dependency is one of the major problems with which the counselor must deal. For the type of people who generally come for psychotherapy are people who perceive themselves as dependent, and who, in fact, obtain many secondary gains from dependent behavior—as a result, they often cling to their dependency with great tenacity. And even client-centered therapy has a good deal of difficulty trying to alter this relationship.

What has been described above is the original formulation of Rogers's theories. With the passage of years the theory has undergone a process of maturation, and it now exists within a framework that might be called *the humanistic movement in psychology*. We shall consider the approaches of these therapies next.

HUMANISTIC–EXISTENTIAL THERAPY

American psychology and psychiatry have been dominated for the past half-century by psychoanalysis and behaviorism. Although both of these views give valuable insights into human behavior, many students of the human condition think they do not go far enough. For one thing they concern themselves mostly with past events and unconscious motivations—and for another they concern themselves with segmented, isolated responses which do not take into account the complexity of interaction throughout the entire organism.

As a result of the shortcomings of these two major forces in psychology, a "third force" has appeared on the scene in recent years, whose scope and impact appear to be so great that it has begun to influence the other two schools of thought in some radical ways. The concept of humanism is related to the *nature of man* as distinct from all other organisms. It concerns itself with what it means to be human, but directs its attention to the needs, motives, aspirations; to all the hopes, dreams, fears, which are exclusive to the species: man.

The cerebral cortex differentiates man from all other organisms. To be human, therefore, is to be something apart—to conceive of the world in a completely different manner from the animals from which we evolved. It also is to perceive the self in a way that is impossible for other organisms.

Existentialism joins humanism in the new psychology because the existentialists also deal with the human condition. The existentialists attack such questions as loneliness, alienation, death, love, and the dilemmas of mortality and vulnerability. These problems cannot be attacked from the old frames of reference. For the behaviorist, they hardly exist; for the psychoanalyst, they are largely irrelevant. Yet for the existential humanist, they are crucial. These are the problems with which man must deal. These are the critical predicaments that exist only on the human level.

The therapies related to the humanistic–existential conception of man are concerned with making the problems of human existence clear to the individual so that he can face them and deal with them through his own efforts. These therapies are generally concerned with the search for self-understanding through the utilization of the ongoing process of awareness. They are concerned with the here and now rather than the past and with the inner needs of the organism rather than environmental influences. They do not discount the importance of the past or the environment, but they see both of these as having an influence on the present state of awareness and, consequently, on the present state of pathology.

The existentialists, particularly, see man as having a high degree of freedom. In a sense it is his freedom which creates his difficulties—and it is his freedom which can remedy them. Existentialists believe that man must come to know that his choices are meaningful. He must learn that the kind of person that he becomes is directly related to the choices he makes. That he, in fact, *chooses himself*. Even if he decides to conform completely to the will of others—even if he gives up choosing, even that is a choice. He must therefore become aware of his freedom, so that he can start to make his choices in an intelligent fashion.

Existential psychotherapy, perhaps more than any other, concerns itself with human *values*. One of the most important and fundamental values from the existential point of view is individual authenticity. The individual must look inside himself, find out who he is, allow himself to *be*, to *become*, and by following his true nature, find *meaning* in his life. Frankl (1963) believes that there is an existential neurosis which results from the fact that most individuals have no sense of purpose, no worthwhile goal (that is, meaning) in their lives. The task of the therapist, therefore, is to get the person in touch with his authentic self by concentrating on the existential process—the process of being and becoming, so that the individual comes to know his authentic self and uses this knowledge to find his own significant way of being-in-the-world.

The existential therapist is not concerned merely with adjustment, with mere coping behavior. He seeks more than this. To merely be capable of balancing one's self among the antagonistic forces of instinct, on the one hand, and society, on the other, is not enough. The existentialist is interested in growth. He seeks a *process* rather than a state of equilibrium.

And the process arises from within the individual rather than from the external pressures of the environment.

In existential therapy there are no standardized techniques, no stereotyped procedures in which the therapist can engage to obtain the desired results. The therapist himself proceeds existentially. That is, he experiences the patient and himself as two human beings in an encounter, and proceeds *along with the patient* to explore the state of being in which they both find themselves. The intimate relationship that results gives the patient the opportunity to experience himself in a new and meaningful way. And this results in a new perceptual organization of the self, its values and its meaningful relation to the rest of the world.

gestalt therapy

A recent approach to psychotherapy which falls within the area of humanistic–existential thought is *gestalt therapy*. Gestalt psychology is concerned with the organization of perception. It considers the perceptual field of the organism to have a powerful, wholistic effect upon the individual. The individual is in a continuous state of interaction with the environment, but the gestalt psychologist sees no separation between organism and environment.

Human beings tend to "block out" certain aspects of their perceptions, for a variety of reasons; as a result, there are portions of the personality that are incongruent with the rest of the individual. Blocked-out areas prohibit "contact" (which, for the gestaltist, is synonomous with growth), creating problems and difficulties in living. The task of the gestalt therapist is to increase self-awareness in the here and now, to unblock those portions of the personality that are inhibited from making contact. Unresolved traumas or conflicts are areas of blockage or "unfinished business" which the therapist must help the patient resolve so that he broadens the front of his awareness at the point of contact which is the organism/environment interface.

The language of gestalt therapy is somewhat difficult. But it can be translated into the language of other psychotherapies. What it seeks is simply a more open and defenseless approach to self-perception and therefore to perception of the world. It believes that to accomplish this the individual must deal with the present rather than the past and put himself into the conflicting situations which he has generally avoided. Gestalt therapy relies a great deal on fantasy and role playing, especially where the individual can take the part of an adversary or even an inanimate object.

One of the jobs of gestalt therapy is to make the implicit feelings explicit in the psychotherapeutic situation, thus heightening the individual's awareness of who he is at any given moment. The therapist looks for clues in the individual's behavior which may betray the facade he is trying to present. The therapist confronts the patient with his inconsistencies. He challenges him to see his "phoniness." And he invites him to try to be congruent with his real feelings.

In the safety of the psychotherapeutic situation the individual is offered the opportunity to experience feelings, attitudes, and traumatic memories, and to realize that the world does not come to an end when such things occur. As a result it is hoped that he will allow himself to integrate these perceptions into his life where they genuinely belong, so that he can live as a whole rather than a fragmented individual.

RATIONAL–EMOTIVE PSYCHOTHERAPY

In Chapter 3 we spoke briefly of rational psychotherapy as a tool in dealing with feelings of disparagement. But that, of course, is not its only use. Rational psychotherapy attempts to deal with all kinds of emotional problems by attacking the assumptions upon which those problems are based. Albert Ellis maintains that during our life, especially in the early years, we learn a number of self-defeating propositions which we incorporate into our thought processes. These statements or sentences which we continually reiterate to ourselves generally lead to unrealistic expectations concerning ourselves and the world. When these expectations are contradicted by reality, we suffer from frustration, repression, defensiveness, and so on.

For example, let us examine the assumption, widely held in our society, that sex is evil. People who accept this assumption suffer from feelings of guilt and disparagement whenever they become conscious of their own sexuality. Guilt and disparagement, as we have seen, lead to psychopathology. Since these underlying assumptions are generally tacitly accepted without any critical assessment, the job of the rational psychotherapist is to attack these assumptions, to give the individual an opportunity to reexamine these beliefs and, seeing their irrationality, to reject them.

The tool that the rational psychotherapist gives us is a very important one. The ability to look at our own assumptions is essential in many areas. The philosopher, for example, wrestles with this question a great deal of the time. But that of course is his professional responsibility. In other walks of life, assumptions are no less important. Our beliefs about psychological health, for example, determine what we designate as pathological. One psychotherapist, for example, might believe that a woman is ill because she rejects her role as a wife and mother. Another might believe that she is, in fact, trying to actualize herself by finding other, more fulfilling modes of expression. The assumption about a "normal" woman's role would obviously differ in both cases.

The great value of rational psychotherapy is that much of the time, with a certain amount of practice, most of us can apply it to ourselves. We can learn to look at all of our beliefs with a degree of skepticism, to accept none of them without investigation, and to reject those that we find irrational or self-defeating. In fact, an intelligent person should always be engaged in this process. All our assumptions need reexamination from time to time. Nothing fights rigidity and fixedness like the ability to occasionally reexamine our beliefs and alter them when the circumstances call for it. In a world in which the rate of change is accelerating daily, such flexibility is practically a necessity.

ENCOUNTER THERAPY

It is not a simple matter to characterize the new procedures that come under the general heading of *encounter therapy*, because encounter occurs in a large variety of contexts, and also because this particular philosophy of therapy draws from many of the procedures already mentioned. Moreover, encounter groups have been described and dramatized in the media, and in many cases their depiction has given an erroneous conception of their procedures and intent.

Let us first endeavor to define the term *encounter*. The idea of encounter is distinguished from other human interactions in a number of ways. We have already noted that in most civilized societies, the interactions between human beings are superficial. This may be necessary to provide for the smooth functioning of the society. For a variety of reasons, it is practical, in the day-to-day business in which most people engage, to keep these interactions short and shallow.

But although such behavior is practical in the business world, it tends to overflow into the social life of many of the citizens of our society. We have already noted that such isolation leads to feelings of alienation. But the tendency to be superficial in our dealings with one another results in a tendency to be superficial with ourselves. If we have become unable to experience and express our feelings with other human beings, it is usually a result of our own defensiveness and repression—and we have already seen how such tendencies are destructive and antagonistic to authentic being.

Encounter tends to overcome this situation. In the safety of the therapeutic relationship, whether it be individual or group, each person is encouraged to encounter the other. That is, he is invited to reach deeply into himself, to discover those feelings which lie hidden below the surface niceties of everyday conversation, and to express them—*to feel* those areas of his being that he has hitherto been afraid to explore. Encounter means the *real* meeting between two or more individuals. It means the shedding of the

Encounter is the genuine meeting between human beings.

masks—the discarding of the PR personality and the authentic communication of the self to another individual.

One of the outstanding characteristics of encounter therapy is that there is a great deal of flexibility in terms of goals, procedures, and outcomes. If psychological health is a process that is unique to each individual, then it is impossible to predict beforehand what kind of behavior is desirable from a given person. Most encounter therapists subscribe to this view of psychological health, and therefore they remain open on the subject of what kinds of changes should occur in the course of therapy. Moreover, the methods used may vary from one therapist to another, or from one group to another, for any procedure may be considered worthwhile if it produces the phenomenon of encounter.

The main emphasis in all the encounter philosophies is mutual self-disclosure. That is, two or more people meet in a situation in which they discard their masks and reveal themselves to each other with as much candor as they can muster. Self-disclosure, as we have noted earlier, is closely related to self-discovery. And it is through this process that the individual comes to perceive himself more accurately, more acceptingly, and in this sense, becomes better able to know who he is.

The goals of most modern psychotherapies are increased self-knowledge, self-esteem, and growth. In addition, it is necessary to be able to form *genuine* relationships with others. The process of encountering, of self-disclosure, and of acceptance of the non-heroic self are the elements emphasized in this particular form of psychotherapy.

343

BEHAVIOR THERAPY

One of the major contributions of American psychology to the understanding of human behavior comes out of the area of learning theory which has been based largely on the behavioristic model. Behavior theory holds that the activity of any organism is dependent upon reinforcements (either rewards or punishment).

The behavioristic tradition begins with the classical conditioning experiments of Pavlov and continues into the modern era with the operant theories of B. F. Skinner. Essentially what the behavioral theorists maintain is that an organism develops a habitual way of responding to given stimuli because these stimuli are continually reinforced, but that very often these responses prove to be maladaptive. Another way of saying this is that emotional disorder is a "bad habit." On this, no doubt, most other schools of psychotherapy would agree.

If psychopathology is merely a habitual way of responding, and if the principles of learning are understood, then it should be theoretically possible to apply these principles of learning to recondition the maladaptive responses. If we can learn what it is that reinforces the undesirable behavior we can try to remove that reinforcement or substitute in its place reinforcement for a more desirable response, and thereby break the old pattern (the bad habit). In other words, the aim of the behavior therapist is to substitute a new, healthy response for the unhealthy one.

There is no question that an understanding of the influences of conditioning is necessary to anyone undertaking to change the behavior of any organism. We all know how tenacious and persistent conditioned behavior can be. And there seems to be little doubt that conditioning of one kind or another is implicated in a great deal of psychopathology. In fact, if we believe that maladaptive behavior is learned, then we must acknowledge the role of conditioning in its etiology.

Although the behavior theorists do not concern themselves with inner conflicts or phenomenological processes, their procedures are extremely important in terms of altering the processes that give rise to subjective symptoms of discontent. For it makes no difference what model we use, an individual who is in distress is expressing a subjective fact. If, for example, he has a phobia, he has a phenomenological experience. If his phobia is a result of conditioning, which, in all likelihood it is, it is because he has learned to *perceive* some aspect of the world as threatening. Therapy, if it works, will have an effect on this perceptual tendency. And the resulting behavior will be changed.

Where the behavior therapist differs from the more traditional theorists is in his use of reinforcement. He structures the situation in such a way that the maladaptive responses are no longer reinforced and, as a result, begin to disappear. Or he simply reinforces new behavior, which is then substituted for the old. Two major procedures used by behavior therapists are systematic desensitization and operant reinforcement.

systematic desensitization

Jacobson (1938) and others have shown that complete muscular relaxation and anxiety are incompatible states. That is, it is impossible to relax all the muscles of the body and at the same time to experience anxiety. The understanding of this principle has given the behavior therapist a great tool in the elimination of certain kinds of anxiety. Wolpe (1969) has developed a procedure that makes good use of this information. By having the individual contract and then relax all the muscles under his voluntary control, it is possible to facilitate a state of almost complete relaxation. Once in this state it is possible for the therapist to introduce anxiety-arousing stimuli in a mild form. Since the autonomic accompaniments of anxiety cannot occur in a state of complete relaxation, the patient confronts the fear-arousing stimulus without experiencing fear. Now, gradually, the fear-arousing stimulus is increased in its intensity. Soon the individual finds himself in a situation in which formerly he would have experienced great anxiety, but now he is able to confront the stimulus without fear. A number of repetitions of this procedure generally lead to the disappearance of the fear reaction.

Let us illustrate this technique with an example. Let us assume that a person is suffering from an irrational fear of dogs. Wolpe would get the individual to relax completely and then bring a dog into the room, keeping it in a cage a good distance from the patient. Then, over a period of days or weeks, he would bring the dog closer to the patient, still keeping it in the cage. As time went on the patient would perhaps be encouraged to pet the animal through the bars of the cage. Finally, the dog would be let out and the patient would pet him and play with him until his anxiety disappeared entirely. All of this would occur while the patient was in a state of complete relaxation, so that the experience of anxiety would be absent. It is believed that by such a method the feeling of comfort in the presence of this one dog would generalize so that the patient would become comfortable in the presence of other dogs as well.

Systematic desensitization has been valuable in dealing with phobias, impotence, frigidity, neurotic anxieties, and a variety of generalized fears. It has been criticized on the grounds that it attacks only a few symptoms in an otherwise faulty personality, but there is no question that it gives us aid in dealing with conditioned or habitual tendencies which are difficult to remove by other methods.

the use of positive reinforcement

Operant conditioning is based on the idea that all behavior has consequences in the environment, and that these consequences inform the organism about whether to continue or discontinue that specific behavior. The feedback that we obtain from the environment has either pleasant or unpleasant effects upon us. If the effects are pleasant, it is likely that the activities will be further engaged in. If they are unpleasant, then the likelihood is that we will discontinue that behavior. Feedback that is satisfactory or pleasant to the organism is called *positive reinforcement*. As used in psychotherapy, positive reinforcement attempts to bring out those behaviors which are desirable (that is, nonpathological) and to allow undesirable behaviors to disappear.

A great deal of work has been done to show that people will begin to alter their behavior if they are positively reinforced for doing so. Moreover, operant theorists believe that, in a number of subtle ways, mental health workers may inadvertently reinforce "unhealthy" responses. For example, a patient may be ignored on the ward when he is engaged in no particular behavior which draws him to the attention of the nurse or doctor. But if he suddenly begins to scream or to disrobe or to attack another patient he suddenly becomes the center of attention. This, in many cases, can be more rewarding than simply being ignored. As a result, it is believed by those who adhere to the operant model of behavior that, in this particular situation, the individual's deviant behavior is being reinforced.

The use of positive reinforcement, therefore, can be structured in such a way that desirable behaviors can be maximized while the patient is in the structured situation. In a number of institutions, even psychotic patients have shown improvement when rewarded for such things as making their beds, working cooperatively with others, and arriving at the lunch room on time. The reinforcers in this situation are often tokens that can later be exchanged for desirable objects or activities. Such programs have met with a good deal of success, often with very difficult patients (schizophrenics, autistic children).

One beneficial result of the use of positive reinforcement is that it has made some patients amenable to psychotherapy who otherwise were unapproachable. This is true of other forms of behavior therapy as well. An individual who is paralyzed by fear may have difficulty relating to a psychotherapist, or to a group, and in that sense may be very difficult to deal with. In addition, psychotic patients are often so involved in their own fantasy world that they do not often respond to the efforts of others to help them deal with their problems. The techniques of behavior therapy have, at times, been very helpful in making these individuals accessible to the procedures of psychotherapy in general. It should be noted that all psychotherapies are only partially successful and that therefore any form of treatment which is helpful to the individual, regardless of its theoretical formulation, is worthwhile if it can help to reduce the misery that most psychopathology produces.

PSYCHOTHERAPY IN PERSPECTIVE

Traditionally, psychotherapy has been used to help individuals who were having difficulty or experiencing severe distress in the enterprise of living. The whole concept of therapy is devoted to the idea that someone becomes disabled, needs help, and is provided with that help in one form or another. But more and more this orientation is changing. And a new way of looking at therapy is emerging. It is being seen not as a way of "curing" people who are ill, but as a way of providing the conditions for growth for all human beings whether they are emotionally disabled or not.

The proliferation of encounter groups and growth centers throughout the United States testifies to the need for psychotherapeutic encounters for a large number of people. This means that people who have no overt symptoms of neurosis or psychosis nevertheless feel the need to enrich their lives, to investigate their potentialities, to deepen their interpersonal relationships, to find new ways to give their lives meaning. These are goals that go beyond merely adapting or adjusting. These goals transcend mere coping behavior and seek to establish new horizons toward which human beings can aspire.

Moreover, the new psychotherapeutic philosophies are at least as interested in prevention as they are in cure. It is believed by most counselors and therapists today that an understanding of both the personal and social causes of psychopathology and a society dedicated to the elimination and/or neutralization of these causes could produce a society in which people are growth-oriented, free of most forms of psychopathology and generally able to experience joy in living. Psychotherapy, therefore, is becoming more interested in such problems as creativity, exploration, artistic appreciation, love, and pleasure. In concerning itself with these kinds of problems, psychotherapy and the science of psychology are exploring new life styles in order to assess their contributions to the quality of human life. In the following chapters we shall concern ourself with these kinds of problems as we consider psychology's further exploration of the psychology of joy.

chapter 14
health as growth

For many years psychology has concentrated on the problem of psycho-pathology and its management. But during this time there has been growing a new vision concerning the nature of man. And this new vision has been concerned not with pathology but with health.

As we have seen, the Freudian view perceived man as a kind of sophisticated or civilized ape. His animal instincts held him prisoner, and the best he could hope for was to make some accommodation between these instincts and the restraints of civilization.

But a number of psychologists began to find this model too limited. They believed that there was more to life than simply adjusting to the demands of society. In fact, they had noted that there were individuals who did not seem to fit the Freudian model. And it occurred to them that perhaps these exceptional individuals might differ radically from Freud's idea of the "adjusted individual."

SELF-ACTUALIZATION

One of the pioneers in the study of the psychology of health was Abraham Maslow. Maslow believed that man's nature was not instinct-oriented but growth-oriented. For Maslow the human organism has innate needs to develop its potentialities as a continuous part of living. But in order to recognize these needs, certain requirements must be met. The reason that there are so few self-actualized human beings is that these requirements are very seldom fulfilled, especially in civilized societies. When these basic requirements are not met, they halt the process of growth and literally "hang up" the individual at a low level of development. The result is that a series of coping strategies designed to alleviate the stress and frustration are thus generated.

the hierarchy of needs

Maslow has developed a sequence of needs which, he feels, must be fulfilled in order for self-actualization to occur. These needs exist in a hierarchy in the sense that some are more powerful and more prepotent than others. Maslow has demonstrated that when the basic needs in the hierarchy remain unmet, the higher needs do not even appear.

The needs have the following position in the hierarchy:

1. Physiological needs
2. Safety needs
3. Love and belonginess
4. Esteem needs
5. Self-actualization needs
6. Cognitive needs
7. Aesthetic needs

Maslow differentiated between the first four needs and the last three. The first four are deficiency needs, designated *D-needs*. These arise through some lack or inadequacy, some differential between what the organism needs to function adequately and the supply of that commodity. The last three needs, on the other hand, arise not out of deprivation but out of abundancy. These are what Maslow termed the being needs, or the *B-needs*. These needs arise only when the D-needs have been so well satisfied that they no longer present a serious problem. It is for this reason that Maslow believes that most people in our society never reach the state of satisfying their B-needs adequately.

Let us examine these needs in turn and see what each involves. The physiological needs, the lowest needs in the hierarchy, are the ones that appear to be most basic to the survival of the organism: the need for food, water, air, sex (to a certain extent). These needs all arise in physiological processes and are linked in some way, with the exception perhaps of sex, to the survival of the organism. The deprivation of most of these needs leads to increased striving, on the part of the organism, to fulfill them. And, of course, their continued deprivation leads to death. But from Maslow's point of view, the important consideration is the subjective state of the organism when one of these basic needs is unmet.

The starving man, for example, is totally absorbed in his hunger and the search for food. Hunger encompasses his entire existence. He can be concerned with no other enterprise until this need is fulfilled. The experience of hunger in this situation becomes a wholistic organismic concern. The person is totally involved in satisfying this one need.

It is only when a lower need becomes reasonably well provided for that the next higher needs can emerge. The man who is starving cannot concern himself with his safety. In fact, he may risk his life—he may do what would otherwise appear to be very foolish in order to obtain food. But once he is well fed, he becomes concerned for his safety. This need includes stability, security, freedom from fear, freedom from chaos, the need for structure, order, law, and dependency. Such needs, to a greater or lesser degree, are present in all children. And they seem to appear as soon as the physiological needs are met. In infancy they are usually gratified by the same person (the mother), who supplies the physiological necessities as well. But when these needs, for one reason or another, are not gratified, the organism may become completely dominated by them. Once again, the individual will be able to think of almost nothing else, until they are satisfied. For the deprivation of these particular needs gives rise to fear. And constant fear is an all-consuming experience.

Speaking of these needs Maslow says

> They may serve as the almost exclusive organizers of behavior, recruiting all the capacities of the organism in their service, and we then may fairly describe the whole organism as a safety-seeking mechanism. (Maslow, 1970)

The need for safety is to some extent related to the need for predictability. An individual cannot feel comfortable in a world that continually surprises him. There is therefore some degree to which an orderly and predictable world is necessary to the satisfaction of these safety needs. This phenomenon helps explain the fact that people are afraid of novelty and change, especially if they have been brought up in such a way that the novel or unknown was described as dangerous. The most extreme form of an exaggerated safety need is the obsessive-compulsive neurotic, who must create artificial order in his world in order not to be "surprised" by an unfamiliar situation.

The love and belongingness needs emerge when the first two needs, lower in the hierarchy, have been satisfied. In Maslow's hierarchy, love and belongingness appear after the gratification of the physiological and safety needs. But it may well be that the love and belongingness needs, in fact, are even more basic and necessary than the other two groups. For we have found that survival does not depend on the satisfaction of the physiological needs alone. Studies of infants in orphanages, who are well fed and kept clean but given no love in terms of physical touching and fondling, show that these infants very often stop taking nourishment and sometimes even die, simply because of the lack of love. These children often allow themselves to waste away, even though the physiological and safety needs are ostensibly well provided for. So it might be that these needs are at least as basic as the other two. We shall deal with this problem later.

In Maslow's hierarchy, the love and belongingness needs, especially in later life, become prepotent when the lower needs have been neutralized —that is, rendered nonexistent by their prompt and adequate gratification.

The need for affiliation, for love and belongingness, often finds expression in our society in the forming of various kinds of coalitions of individuals who come together, ostensibly to promote a common cause, but also because this is one of their few opportunities to feel that they have common bonds with others. Moreover, the appearance of communal life styles, the popularity of T-groups, of encounter groups, of the whole human potential movement, testify to the fact that belongingness is a very powerful and often neglected need in our society.

We have noted earlier that the hero in our society is often depicted as a loner, a man without ties. This encourages people to wear the mask of the loner while inside their need for community remains unfulfilled. There results a kind of a taboo on closeness and affiliation in our overt behavior, while unconsciously the longing continues to cause us great distress.

The esteem needs are probably the most important and most difficult needs in the hierarchy to understand. This is so because *self-esteem* is based on a number of factors. In the beginning, self-esteem comes from the esteem of others. A person comes to value himself in great degree through the responses of his parents, siblings, and peers. At this stage also it often depends upon certain competencies, abilities, and mastery. Positive evaluations in all these areas lead to feelings of confidence in one's worth. But because the basis for this kind of esteem comes from the reactions of others, the danger exists that an individual will sabotage his own existence (that is, use the PR image) and thus lose touch with who he is. So there comes a point in his life when he must choose authenticity over the approval of others and still maintain self-esteem.

This means that the healthy individual finally comes to accept his *real* self with whatever deficiencies, fallibilities, liabilities, that might exist and still maintains a feeling of self-worth.

It might be that the esteem needs become important in a society in which affluence predominates. For in such a society, the lower needs are often provided for. This would permit the emergence of the esteem needs, making them extremely salient for the individuals in such a culture. It appears likely that this is the area in our society in which many people find themselves stalled. In other words, they get this far in the hierarchy, and because of frustration of the esteem needs can go no further.

When the esteem needs are satisfied, a new need arises.

> The need for self-actualization is described this way. Even if all these needs are satisfied, we may still often (if not always) expect that a new discontent and restlessness will soon develop, unless the individual is doing what *he*, individually, is fitted for. A musician must make music, an artist must paint, a poet must write, if he is to be ultimately at peace with himself. What a man *can* be, he *must* be. He must be true to his own nature. (Maslow, 1970)

The idea of self-actualization is not a new one. It has been used in the past by such writers as Jung and Kurt Goldstein. But in the present connotation, it is related to an individual's uniqueness. Self-actualization is not the same thing for each human being. It is specific to the individual nature of each person. It is a need to become what is in one potentially to become. The specific form that self-actualization takes cannot be determined by someone other than the person involved. Other people may help and even influence one's choice, but the final outcome is always a consequence of some inner prompting which is highly personal and individualistic.

It must be noted that self-actualization is not necessarily related to vocation or career choice. A person may actualize himself by being an excellent parent, for example. From Maslow's standpoint, self-actualization is not primarily concerned with *results* of a particular kind of activity—it is concerned with the experience of the activity itself—not the composition but the *composing*—not the work of art, but the creative process by which it is produced—not the taste of the food, but the creativity in the cooking of it. This is not to say that the product has no importance. What Maslow is emphasizing is the fact that the self-actualized person is fulfilling his potentialities *in the act itself*. A byproduct of this creative act is a unique outcome. He may admire the result of this process. But the enjoyment of the process itself is also extremely important. *The ability to enjoy the experience of being*, therefore, is one of the essential capabilities of the healthy individual.

The cognitive needs emerge most fully in the self-actualized person. There seems to be no question that such needs are different from the ones lower in the hierarchy. For the need to know is not based on a physiological deficiency but seems to be an essential part of the human personality, which emerges when the deficiency needs have been abundantly satisfied. It is probable that this particular need is present at birth and never completely disappears. The clear evidence of curiosity in small children and also animals attests to this particular quality in many living organisms. The fact that it appears to be more prevalent in self-actualized persons is explained by Maslow by the fact that the gratification of the other needs has allowed it to flourish. In this sense this need, as well as the other B-needs, are based on abundance rather than deprivation.

Men have always been attracted to the mysterious, the challenging, the chaotic, and have shown a great desire to unravel, to solve, to explain, to understand such phenomena. In a certain sense one might even say that this is the function of man as man. For the evolution of the human cortex, transcends mere survival needs. The higher processes, which are unique to man, in a sense create their own needs by their very presence. And Maslow's studies indicate that such processes are more apparent in healthy individuals.

Self-actualized people are generally less bored with themselves and with life, and it is very likely that this is a result of the continued expression of curiosity, learning, philosophizing, experimenting, and so on. Such activities involve a great range of interests which almost guarantee relief from boredom. One of the most important arguments of the feminist movement concerns these cognitive needs, which are often neglected in intelligent women. The woman who is curious, intelligent, and innovative but who is playing the conventional role of housewife often becomes depressed, apathetic, and bored, and shows all the other symptoms of neurasthenic reactions. However, when such women begin to immerse themselves in the areas of their interests, and once again begin to take an active part in satisfying their cognitive needs, these symptoms usually vanish. There appears to be no question that, especially in self-actualized people, the deprivation of the cognitive needs can lead to serious difficulties.

The aesthetic needs are the last of the B-needs in Maslow's hierarchy. There is not a great deal known about these needs, but certain facts seem to be clear. Beauty, however defined, is apparently necessary to healthful functioning. Even if we use only a subjective definition of beauty, it appears to be clear that an individual responds to that which he considers beautiful in a positive and happy way and that he reacts to ugliness in an opposite manner. Moreover, the need for beauty may be more important than we have hitherto realized. There is some evidence that some people become ill when they are forced to exist in ugly surroundings and improve dramatically when given the opportunity to experience beauty in some form. The use of music and poetry in psychotherapy is a recognition of the need for beauty, providing aesthetic experiences to patients who may be suffering from their absence.

The aesthetic needs also seem to include the need to create beauty as well as to appreciate it. From the very beginning of man's existence on this planet, he has been fascinated by the exploration of new forms in design, in music, in storytelling. The production of beauty appears to be a uniquely human phenomenon. And the development of sophisticated forms of art is certainly one of the most important developments of human culture.

Creativity is one of the hallmarks of self-actualized individuals. Maslow notes that it is one of the important indicators of psychological well-being. It is often artistic, but it need not be so. For example, the self-actualized individual is innovative in such areas as problem solving and novel cognitive processes and in such things as cooking, and in developing a life style. The main thing about the self-actualized person is that he is always seeking new ways to do what the rest of us might do in stereotypical fashion.

Creativity is one of the hallmarks of self-actualization. Most children are naturally creative.

THE CHARACTERISTICS OF PSYCHOLOGICAL HEALTH

Psychologically healthy people differ from the rest of us in a variety of ways. It is informative to observe these differences, for it gives us an indication of where we fall short and also some insight into our own actualizing tendencies.

more efficient perception of reality

The self-actualized individual has less need for defensiveness and therefore less need to distort reality. He is more likely to perceive the world as it is (that is, with more realistic expectations), and as a result he is less likely to be disappointed, frustrated, surprised. This is not to say that he does not sometimes experience all these emotions. He does. But he experiences them in relation to real events and not in relation to his own inaccurate perceptions.

Healthy people are less likely to engage in "wishful thinking" because they do not allow their own desires, anxieties, and fears to affect what they see or what they predict. They predict things on probability rather than on the basis of what they would *like* to see happen.

The neurotic person and certainly the psychotic person perceive the world inaccurately because of their needs to distort, to defend, to repress. The neurotic's use of defense mechanisms to protect himself against threat, anxiety, and pain results in an alteration of his world which is less real, less authentic, and more prone to error and fantasy.

The healthy person is also more comfortable with the world as it is and more accepting of the nature of things. When he perceives things that are unjust, dangerous, unhealthy, he can take realistic steps to change them, so he is more effective as well as more accepting in the real world.

acceptance of self and others

Another important area in which self-actualizing people differ from others is in their nonjudgmental acceptance of themselves. Maslow says that they seem to have a lack of overriding guilt and crippling shame and also to be free of the anxieties that usually accompany these feelings.

> They can accept their own human nature in the stoic style, with all its shortcomings, with all its discrepancies from the ideal image without feeling real concern. (Maslow, 1970)

Such feelings of comfort and acceptance with the self are extremely important in terms of laying down a tone that underlies a person's whole existence. The difference between happiness and unhappiness is related to this tone.

The healthy individual does not strive to live up to an ideal, perfect PR image. He sees himself as human and therefore as unheroic in the naive sense. He acknowledges his "shortcomings," his "deficiencies," his "inconsistencies." In short, he acknowledges his imperfections without being disparaged by them. Being accepting of his frailties, he can also be accepting of those of others. And the healthy person demands neither more nor less of others—he is willing to acknowledge human nature in all human beings, both in others and in himself.

One very important area in which self-actualizing people are accepting is on the animal level. They accept their animal nature without shame, without guilt, with a kind of gusto or *joie de vivre*. They are lusty in their love of food, sex, excitement. They tend not to feel shame or disgust with the functions of the body on an animal level. Thus they are less likely to respond negatively to these basic organismic needs.

spontaneity

Healthy people tend to respond to the world without guile or premeditation. This is not to say that they do not plan or take precautions for safety and health. It means that they respond to the world without concerning themselves with whether their response will be acceptable, approved by others, or in some way have an effect on their self-image. In this sense they allow themselves the luxury of spontaneous responses to beauty, sex, love, hate, sadness—the whole range of emotional life which has often been truncated in other people.

It must not be assumed that the healthy person simply acts impulsively. He responds spontaneously, in the sense that he knows his feelings immediately in relation to a given situation. But he may not always act upon them, for he also knows that the actions may not always be appropriate. He is therefore able to allow himself to experience the world without inhibitions, while he may or may not act upon this inner experience, depending upon the situation.

Maslow points out that the healthy individual usually experiences the world in unconventional terms. But this does not necessarily mean that he behaves in an unconventional manner. When he is among conventional people, he generally observes the conventions, which to him may be silly or unnecessary. But he recognizes the needs of other people, and tends to act in accordance with them when possible. However this conventional attitude can easily be quickly discarded when he is in the company of people who, like himself, do not require it. Then his unconventional, unpredictable ways of responding to the world become apparent.

One aspect of this tendency toward spontaneity is the retention of a childlike quality of perception. These people have retained the ability to see things with a kind of freshness and newness which most of us lose as we grow older. This quality gives them the opportunity to continually see the world from a fresh point of view. Like children, they can extract the novel and the beautiful out of things which, for the rest of us, become mundane and trivial.

There is a profound difference in the orientation of the self-actualized individual, in terms of his ordinary motivation. The healthy person is existentially in contact with his being, to a greater extent than even so-called "normal" individuals. His ability to experience naturally and spontaneously enables him to exist in the here-and-now in a much more expanded fashion. Moreover, he is less encumbered by a superimposed PR image which, for others, obscures or clouds the existential moment, producing a kind of watered-down state of being. Because of a lack of what we might call PR-striving, the emphasis in healthy people is on the satisfaction of the abundancy needs. Having met the needs for belonging and esteem, these people can now concentrate on creative and growth needs. This means that they are describable in different terms from most people. They are free to explore their own natures, to be open to constant redefinition of themselves and to enjoy this exploratory process in their own unique way.

the need for solitude

Most of us feel very sorry for people who are alone. We believe, with a certain amount of justification, that anyone who is alone is lonely. This, of course, is true for a large number of people. It is particularly true for those people who have not had the love and belongingness needs adequately satisfied.

But in the healthy individual, these D-needs have been satisfied. As a result, there is a need for another level of encounter—with the self. To be solitary, to be alone, is not necessarily to be lonely. For the healthy individual, *to be with himself* is to be in good company. As one individual put it, "When I'm alone, I'm with my best friend." For many of us, other people are a welcome distraction, for they prevent us from experiencing ourselves and our anxieties, but the healthy person has little need for such distractions. He generally feels very comfortable with himself.

autonomy—authenticity

Maslow's healthy subjects showed a high degree of self-generated behavior. By this we mean that these individuals were less influenced by societal demands and by the other pressures which are brought to bear on all of us from time to time. This is perhaps one of the most important qualities of the self-actualized person. It is the complete antithesis of what has often been considered "normal." The healthy individual is a unique person. He is dependent upon his own development and his own perception of his potentialities rather than on the conventions and customs that are so powerful in influencing most people.

It is in this sense that self-actualized people are authentic.

> A person is authentic in that degree to which his being in the world is unqualifiedly in accord with the givenness of his own nature and of the world. (Bugental, 1965)

Self-actualized people are authentic because they are true to their own nature and at the same time involved in a realistic relationship with the world. Autonomy and authenticity go together because the individual who is true to his own nature, who behaves in accordance with his own inner prompting (even in defiance of the rest of society), is both autonomous (self-initiating) and authentic (true to himself). In this area Maslow's view is very much in agreement with the existentialists, who see authenticity as a state of *being*, without interference.

From Maslow's point of view, the authentic individual, having satisfied all the deficiency needs, and having become independent of the approval of others, is now free to make his own choices without fear of criticism. This is not to say that he will never receive criticism. It is merely to point out that criticism does not have the disparaging effect upon him that it does on other people. In fact, the healthy individual must be relatively free of the fear of disparagement in order to go his own way. It is the self-actualized individual who is "doing his own thing."

A very important quality of the self-actualized person which is corollary to what we have been discussing is their ability to disregard praise much in the same way that they disregard blame. The healthy person's head is not turned by fame, awards, honors, popularity, or prestige. These things are merely the other side of the disparagement coin. They are mostly embellishments for the PR image and, as such, not important to the healthy individual. To one who already has a strong feeling of self-esteem, the plaudits or complaints of others have little consequence. If this were not so, the praise of others would act as reinforcement for certain kinds of behavior, leading to their increase, with a resulting loss of autonomy for the individual. To remain authentic, the healthy person resists the temptation to be seduced by these outer determinants and remains true to his inner promptings.

One interesting sidelight of this particular quality of self-actualized people is the fact that they are very similar regardless of the society from which they come. Since they are not culture-bound, their personalities tend to transcend cultural stereotypes, and they are more like one another than their backgrounds would expect one to believe. Thus in a certain sense the self-actualized person is a universal person.

One of the most important qualities of the mature individual is the quality of *independence*. That quality, of course, is intimately related to the ideas of authenticity and autonomy. Perhaps independence can best be described in contrast with its polar opposite, dependency. The dependent person is in great need of others in many areas of his life. He requires the confirmation of other people's judgments in relation to his own. He does not choose his own mode of life, for he is insecure about his identity. His love relationships are often dependent relationships—that is, he "loves" only those people who can support him, and he feels helpless and impotent without their support.

Deficiency-motivated people are in need of other people in order to help them fill most of their needs. Maslow points out that this is true because love, safety, respect, prestige, belongingness all require human beings for their fulfillment. Even the need to have someone else dependent upon one is itself a dependency need. For the person who needs others in order to function adequately, no matter what the reason, is dependent upon these others and generally feels incomplete without them. There are, therefore, a large number of human relationships in which one person needs to be dependent, while the other needs someone to be dependent upon him. Such relationships are sometimes called *symbiotic*. The very nature of symbiotic relationships in human affairs demands that each individual in the relationship be dependent upon the other. We shall see shortly that many marriages that appear from the outside to be stable acquire their stability through neurotic, symbiotic dependencies.

The independent individual does not *need* other people in this way. This is not to say that he will not have deep and lasting relationships with others. For he will. But his relationships will not be deficiency-motivated. Moreover, most of his other behaviors will be similarly free of D-needs. This means he will feel competent to make his own choices, to run his own life, to be his own person. Independence means the lack of need to rely upon the support of others in the creation of one's style of life. In some ways the healthy individual is *hampered* by other people since the requirements of conventional social activities are often inhibiting to him.

Psychological independence is often related to financial or economic independence. It is rather difficult for someone who must depend upon others for the basic requirements of life to be able to make all his own choices in regard to the life he lives. There can be a beginning tendency in this direction but, generally speaking, the people who pay the bills will often try to influence those in their care. This makes the acquisition of independence difficult, especially for adolescents in our society. For financial independence does not usually occur until a later stage in life. But the process of becoming independent, especially in the psychological sense, can begin at this time.

Whether we use the word authenticity, autonomy, or independence, the self-actualized individual is a person who has developed the ability to steer his own course through life. He does not allow others to take hold of the tiller. In the process of setting his course and guiding his movements, he is his own helmsman.

the peak experience

Peak experiences or mystical experiences are difficult phenomena to describe. This is especially true because they are so infrequent for most of us. And yet such experiences are probably universal. From the standpoint of psychological health, the interest lies not in the fact that self-actualized people have peak experiences but in the fact that they seem to have more of them than the rest of the population.

There is a certain amount of misunderstanding regarding this particular experience. It is often related to some kind of supernatural or occult phenomenon. And though it has been described in those terms for thousands of years, such an association is not necessary. That the mystical ex-

Music can sometimes be the vehicle for the peak experience.

perience can be a *religious* experience seems undeniable. On the other hand, the same state of awareness has been described in nonreligious terms as well.

The peak experience is a very powerful state of involvement in which the individual becomes fused in some sense with an event. It may, for example, be a hearing of a piece of music that the person has heard many times before. But in this particular instance the person is in a particularly receptive mood, and the experience has an impact upon him which is so overwhelming that he is transported beyond the usual boundaries of "normal" experience. Peak experiences and mystical experiences are truly self-transcendent states in that an important element in their existence is the fact that the self-as-object disappears. Usually this process is accompanied by great joy, wonder, awe, a change in the perception of time and space, and the feeling that something profoundly important and beautiful has occurred.

It may be that all of us, at times, have a few such experiences. But in Western society, with the emphasis upon practicality, such experiences are played down in importance. We might in fact even be ashamed to admit their existence, since they often carry with them tremendous emotional impact. And it is likely that most of us do not cultivate experiences of this sort, with the result that they easily become extinguished.

Self-actualized people, however, tend to value these experiences very highly and to cultivate their intensification. Some people attempt to produce these experiences through the use of psychedelic substances. And many experimenters have claimed that these substances do, in fact, expedite this process. Others have argued that the mystical experience is an important human potentiality which must not be tampered with. And its only real value occurs when it is produced naturally (without chemicals).

The acute peak experience appears to be an intensification of any experience in which the self, especially the PR personality, disappears from view. It is as if the PR image is always superimposed upon our perceptions of the world, cutting down, diminishing, attenuating our capacity to incorporate the world of our perceptions within ourselves. But when an experience becomes so intense that our self-image is simply erased by it, then the peak experience has the opportunity to occur. These experiences can be extremely joyous, but they can also be fearful. This may be especially true for the individual who has a great need of maintaining the ego boundaries which he uses defensively for protection. Stripped of such defenses, such a person may feel helpless. Even so, if the fear is not *too* great, the experience can be valuable. The child going down the big hill in the roller coaster is both fearful and thrilled. The fear is usually great enough to overcome concern with his self-image, and the thrill of excitement that ensues may be partly a result of this. It is certainly clear that in a roller coaster ride, a person must "give up control" and allow the experience to overwhelm him. In that sense, perhaps, a roller coaster ride may be said to be a mild kind of peak experience. We shall speak more of this phenomenon in Chapter 15.

interpersonal relations

Healthy people have deeper and more profound relationships than do other adults. Their friendships are deep and lasting, although they may be few. Such friendships occur more on an encounter level than on a surface level. By this we mean that healthy people have friendships that transcend mask wearing, so that one individual is in contact with the genuine part of the other. To put it another way, the two friends are authentic with one another.

Because the friendships of healthy people are intense and deep, they are generally long-lasting. They may often be retained through long years of separation, to be renewed again if and when the opportunity presents itself.

There is a certain kind of exclusivity but not snobbishness in the deep relationships of healthy people. There may be only a few people with whom they relate in this way. Nevertheless, as we have seen, they are generally accepting and friendly, but in a less intimate sense, with a large number of people. Thus these people are generally kind and accepting to almost everyone. This should not be thought of as a social mask. It may, on the surface, appear like one. But this is a superficial resemblance. Their kindness is genuine. They are not nice to others because they wish to be accepted or approved by them. They are that way because they genuinely feel affectionate to others. Maslow points out that they are especially fond of children, and in a sense they feel a strong attraction to the child in everyone.

Self-actualized people are generally likable and for that reason often attract a number of friends. However, the fact that other people like them can sometime become a burden to them. They usually have things to do, for which they need time. And the demands made by others often impinge on this need. They may therefore sometimes appear to be more brusque than they intend with some people. And they may even seem somewhat cruel in cutting off unwanted relationships.

faith in the integrity of the organism

Self-actualizing people have a good deal of faith in nature, in general, and in the cues that they receive from their bodies, in particular. Because of the fact that they are unafraid to experience themselves as they are, healthy people are intimately in touch with the messages that their bodies send. And because they tend to trust and respond to these cues, they are in harmony with their physical organism.

This trust leads to a heightened sense of experience of the body, so that even very ordinary activities can become extremely meaningful for them. Thus they can enjoy many bodily activities, such as walking, dancing, eating, sex, with a kind of gusto that is often lacking in others.

Trust in bodily processes is probably an important element in the prevention of psychosomatic illnesses. It is believed by some psychologists that people who resist, whether on a conscious or unconscious level, the normal bodily processes may be doing themselves some injury. Recent experiments with the conscious control of autonomic processes demonstrate the real ability of psychological processes to influence even the most automatic physiological activity. It is likely, therefore, that attitudes which are contrary to the natural organismic needs result in interference with these natural functions, producing psychosomatic reactions.

self-actualization and imperfection

An examination of some of the qualities that are observed in healthy people might give one the impression that they have no faults. This, of course, would be ridiculous. Maslow does not take a Pollyannaish attitude toward the nature of man. He believes it is good, but he does not claim that it is perfect.

Self-actualizing people are no more perfect than anyone else. They have their faults and limitations, but the difference is that they can accept them as part of being human. The self-actualized person is not the traditional hero. He is not true blue, completely courageous, handsome, infallible. Such a character, as we have seen earlier, is a caricature. He is a result of the individual's own wish for perfection and his projection of that perfection onto some heroic figure. Maslow points up this difference between the heroic figures of fiction and self-actualized people.

> It is my belief that most of the novelists who have attempted to portray good (healthy) people did this sort of thing, making them into stuffed shirts or marionettes or unreal projections of unreal ideals, rather than into the robust, hardy, lusty individuals they really are. (Maslow, 1970)

Maslow goes on to show that his subjects show many of the nonheroic characteristics of ordinary people, at least at times. They can be silly, selfish, wasteful, prideful, even ruthless on occasion. Sometimes even their kindness can lead them into difficult situations, which they later regret. For example, they may feel sorry for someone, allow themselves to be involved for that reason, and later regret the relationship and perhaps cut it off somewhat ruthlessly when they finally have been annoyed by it too much.

Essentially what this means is that there are no perfect human beings and that psychological health does not necessarily mean the absence of *any* shortcoming. It simply means that these shortcomings are minimal, often temporary, and for the most part, do not dominate the personality to any major degree.

We have devoted this chapter to Maslow's discussion of the healthy individual in order to lay the groundwork for the discussion of the psychology of joy. Joy and happiness are reasonable goals toward which any individual might strive. Indeed, most individuals if asked would contend that these are in fact their goals. But happiness is elusive. And most people fail to find it.

Yet happiness is almost synonomous with the idea of health. Health is an essential prior condition for a happy life. And happiness, therefore, is more abundant in the lives of self-actualized people than it is in those of others.

Happiness is not as much dependent upon a series of fortunate events as it is upon the state of being which already pre-exists these events. Moreover, it is not a goal that lies at the end of a great struggle. It is really a by-product of a life style that is meaningful and fulfilling. Instead of being an end product toward which one must work, it is a feeling that runs parallel to the experience of living because it includes all the richness and variety and excitement that life can offer to the growth-oriented person.

In a very real sense, happiness appears to be related to self (PR personality)—transcendence. It is related to the ability to experience fully without the interference of a superimposed ego. This is the highest level of development of human consciousness. In Chapter 15 we shall consider some of the implications of such states of awareness.

chapter 15
joy

Joy has been defined as a feeling of happiness which arises out of a sense of well-being. It is obvious that all of us are capable of experiencing joy, but for many of us this experience may be very rare. According to what we have said in Chapter 14 it is probable that self-actualized people experience joy more regularly than the rest of the population.

It seems that one reason for the lack of joy in the lives of many is that they have forgotten how to achieve it. Children have no difficulty experiencing joy—that is, given the necessary requirements of health and well-being. But adults, having gone through a long process of enculturation and learning, have forgotten how to enjoy their lives.

Joy depends upon a number of other feelings. These include pleasure, fun, and happiness. And the most exquisite experience of joy, sometimes called ecstasy, has a further requirement—self-transcendence. Since the real experience of any of these feelings requires a certain degree of transcendence, it will be profitable to explore this phenomenon before discussing the others.

THE METAPHYSICS OF THE SELF

Self-transcendence is easy for children and animals because they have not yet developed an image of themselves, by which they judge most of their activities. They can literally be *beside themselves* with almost any emotion because they are not yet aware of their awareness. For an adult this process becomes progressively more difficult as the demands of culture and conformity perseverate. But the difficulty may be as much in our philosophical attitudes, as in our conventional modes of behavior.

some philosophical considerations

The world has traditionally been viewed in two ways. One way is to see the physical universe as a series or collection of physical objects in space. These objects are generally considered to be separate from one another, as entities in themselves, or to interact with one another at various times.

The other view of the world is not concerned with objects, but with mind, being, process, and so on. Although philosophers can defend both positions with reasonable degrees of validity, it is this latter view, more or less foreign to Western man's thinking, that we would now like to explore. The two major areas which most importantly influence this view of the world in the twentieth century are the Oriental philosophies and existentialism.

THE CONTRIBUTION OF ORIENTAL PHILOSOPHIES

It is not a simple matter for Westerners to grasp the underlying meanings of Eastern thought. It is not that these ideas are so difficult or esoteric, it is more likely that their simplicity eludes us. We don't understand their basic tenets because we don't accept their basic assumptions. The most important of these assumptions is that the world is not composed of "things." That is, the world of material objects existing in space, which has been the cornerstone of Western science until the beginning of this century, is for the Eastern philosopher an illusion. There are a number of reasons for the persistence of this illusion. One reason is linguistic and the other is sensory. These two are not independent of one another, for although one's mode of perceiving gives rise to the development of language, the effects of language on perception, being less obvious, are probably more far-reaching.

A subject-object language tends to rigidify the organization of the perceptual field in a way that can falsify reality.[1] And the tendency to label that which we can see while we ignore (that is, not include within the context of the label) that which we cannot see but which we know is there creates for us a universe of objects which appear to be separate and generally unrelated. Moreover, our language as well as our perceptions tends to freeze time so that we do not see the dynamic flux of persons and things changing and interacting through different intervals. We see them instead as fragmented, isolated entities limited to *this* moment and *this* space as if this were all they were. That is, we perceive objects (and people *as* objects) encapsulated by their outer boundaries as if there was no interaction between them and their environment. And although we know that this is not true, we largely ignore this fact. We act as if the *separateness* rather than the *relatedness* were real.

A more accurate perception would be possible if we could perceive the *relations* between things as clearly as we now see the things themselves. If, for example, it suddenly became possible for us to see how an organism utilizes various parts of the environment, changing it and being changed by it, how different our conception of man would be. If we could see the large volume of air moving in and out of a man's body and if we could note through time how some parts of the "external" world are ingested, changed, and used to become part of the organism itself, our definitions of "organism" and "environment" would change radically.

Moreover, if we could increase our level of magnification and see electrons and protons, what then would define the boundaries of those objects which we now see as separate? And if we could see electromagnetic waves and gravitation, what object in the universe could we say existed without some relation to every other? The objections to the usual modes of description are made not only by the mystic (Watts, 1961) but also by the modern physicist (Barnett, 1957), who sees in the principle of indeterminacy and the theory of relativity testimony that relatedness is a fundamental law of nature. One cannot make an observation on the "ultimates"

[1] If a language tends to emphasize nouns (and pronouns), it influences the perception of the environment in terms of "things." If it emphasizes verbs, it influences perception in terms of processes. In most Western tongues, the dominant linguistic pattern places a subject and object into a relationship with a verb. Something is always doing something to something or someone. Things don't happen—they happen *to* something. As a result, we feel that the world can only be described in terms of objects in space.

We must not mistake our description of the universe for the universe itself. The world can also be described in terms of mind, being, or process. In fact modern relativistic physics and Eastern mystical philosophies come much closer to one another in their description of the universe than most of us realize.

of existence without affecting them. In a certain sense, then, we are making an observation on *ourselves* or an *effect of ourselves*, which is the same thing. This is no different from the Eastern philosopher's statement that he and the universe are inseparable. Carrying this point a bit further, we might say with Teilhard de Chardin (1959):

> Considered in its physical, concrete reality, the stuff of the universe cannot divide itself but, as a kind of gigantic "atom," it forms in its totality . . . the only real indivisible.

The implication of these facts for modern man are profound. For if it is true that there is a oneness that we can experience with the world and one another, then anything that destroys that experience destroys the harmony between what we normally call the individual and what we term the environment. To the extent that we falsify our relation to others and the world, we place impediments in the path of the free-flowing relationship between ourselves and the rest of existence. In another sense, what is being said is that our customary modes of perceiving ourselves are, to a great extent, fictions. Our social, role-playing ways of responding to and perceiving the environment prevent our recognizing the relatedness that exists between us. The contribution of the Eastern philosophies is that they see through these social games and it is in this that they help us understand our nature.

The ways of liberation of the East and the enlightened forms of psychotherapy in the West both seek to distinguish between the definition of what man is according to a cultural system and what he is in fact. Liberation comes when a person realizes that he is not what society tells him he *should* be or *must* be, but that he *is*. When this realization occurs he is, in Watt's terms, both universal and unique.

> He is universal by virtue of the inseparability of his organism from the cosmos. He is unique in that he is just *this* organism and not any stereotype of role, class or identity assumed for the convenience of social communication.

Another contribution of the philosophies of the East is the recognition that the use of labels tends to dim awareness. As Aldous Huxley has pointed out:

> All men of great religious insight are agreed in regarding the theologian's preoccupation with words as being almost as dangerous to the individual's chance of liberation as are the preoccupations of the crusader and the inquisitor with violent action. (Huxley, 1960)

Words are dangerous in two ways. First, they may and are often completely misunderstood. But even more important, they are sometimes mistaken for the thing they stand for. Moreover, labels are used to categorize experience, thus dulling its impact in the here and now. The recognition and classification of an event or an object places the experience in a pigeonhole in which a past experience is superimposed on the present one (recognition) and the ongoing event is partially or totally ignored. The use of the label is generally instrumental in this process of "adapting out."

The designation of the "I" as a label of a separate self tends to encourage the fiction that one is autonomous and distinct from that which we call the external world. Vedanta, Taoism, and Buddhism all deny the existence of this ego entity which persuades itself that it is the experiencer rather than the experience.

THE CONTRIBUTION OF EXISTENTIALISM

The marriage of existentialism and psychology is not a recent one. Tillich (1959) has pointed to the development of psychoanalysis (in its broadest possible connotation) and existentialism as mutually interwoven systems. He sees depth psychology and existentialism as growing from common roots. They have, he says, "been connected with each other from the very beginning; they have mutually influenced each other in the most radical and profound ways." And certainly we must agree that Kierkegaard's insistence on the subjective experience has focused the attention of psychology on that dimension more forcibly. Moreover, the concern of the existentialist with such questions as meaninglessness and loneliness has opened the way for psychotherapy to wrestle with these problems overtly instead of ignoring them or relegating them to theoretical categories.

In an age when the old explanations no longer seem valid, when the threat of nonbeing has become more imminent, when the ideas of salvation and eternal life are no longer convincing concepts, existentialism has been willing to confront such issues. And it has recognized the anxiety that these problems engender. It faces the existence of chance and contingency in human life and accepts the necessity of risk as a requirement for authenticity.

But the most important contribution made by existentialism toward the understanding of man is its emphasis on the subjective process. The existentialists claim that all our knowledge about the world is phenomenological. It comes to us through our private experience. Even our philosophical speculations about the existence of objects and space and time come about because of our private perceptions of such things. And if the existence of such a world is based upon so faulty a process as human perception, then its reality can be brought into question. That is exactly what many philosophers do.

If objects in space with their attributes are illusory, then this is also true of persons and *their* attributes. And the *real* person is not a physical thing at all; *he is a phenomenological process.*

METAPHYSICS OF PLEASURE

This short excursion into philosophy has been presented to demonstrate that transcending the self is really transcending nothing. For self-transcendence merely means to forget the ego, the PR image, the self-as-object, and to allow the experience to involve fully the phenomenological self, the self that is identical with the world. Any one of these descriptive statements explains the experience of being beside-one's-self. And it is only during such an experience that one can be said to discover joy.

Pleasurable experiences exist on this same level. The organism experiences pleasure through a phenomenological process. The experience of pleasure is most satisfying when the individual is not concerned (or, better still, completely unaware) of his objective existence. When this occurs, pleasure completely floods the awareness of the individual, obliterating everything else.

This is the true experience of pleasure. As children we all automatically knew and responded to pleasurable feelings. But as adults we have been socialized away from true pleasure. And in its place there exists a kind of ersatz pleasure which is largely unsatisfactory. The capacity for joy is based at least partly on the capacity for pleasure. And if this capacity is lacking, then happiness is likely to be lacking as well.

> Pleasure is a bodily experience. It is a response in the brain of some sensory input which produces for the organism a sense of well-being. Without pleasure, there is no fun and no happiness. Underlying any experience of true fun or happiness is a bodily sensation of pleasure. (Lowen, 1970)

The feeling of pleasure is related to physiological processes which occur in response to particular sensations and which stimulate certain portions of the brain. The subjective experience of pleasure, of course, is one of the most powerful in terms of motivation. Freud, in fact, believed that the pleasure principle was the guiding force in most human behavior.

There is no question about the fact that pleasure determines our actions to a very great extent. But adult human beings cannot always succumb to their need for pleasure. We learn to restrain this desire under certain circumstances and to delay many gratifications until appropriate conditions arise. Ordinarily such demands on the organism are reasonable, but because of certain cultural traditions and values, many adults have almost lost the capacity for true pleasure once they have left childhood behind.

One of the reasons for this inability to experience pleasure lies, as we have already noted, in the metaphysics of our self-perception. One who is too concerned with his objective image, with the way he appears to others, with a desire to appear "cool," must limit his pleasurable experiences by this preoccupation. Moreover, the cultural idea that adults should be blasé, unruffled, unemotional, inhibits an individual from allowing his body to respond physiologically to the cues that would otherwise produce pleasure.

We have all seen children shriek with delight, unashamedly expressing their pleasure in a particular activity. And perhaps most of us can remember incidents in our childhood when we so behaved. It is unfortunate that we do not allow ourselves this luxury more often as we grow older.

Biologically, pleasure is a survival mechanism. Most of the things that bring pleasure are good and healthy for the organism. Most of the things that bring pain, on the other hand, have negative value in terms of survival. This means that we should, biologically speaking, pay attention to those cues and respond to them appropriately. This means that we should look at pleasure in a positive rather than in a negative way.

Not only is pleasure a cue to what is good for the body, it is also a result of health itself. A person in good health feels pleasure in the very act of being alive. To move, to breathe deeply, to see color and form, to hear sound and music—all of these things are joyous to the healthy person. So pleasure is an important feeling that both contributes to and results from the health of the organism.

pleasure and play

There is a widespread feeling among Americans that play is a serious business. Thus individuals play games in which they are so concerned with the result or the outcome that they cannot really take pleasure in the playing. Many people play cards this way and are miserably unhappy when they lose. And, even if they win, the pleasure they receive is not related to the playing of the game but to the winning.

Another example of this type of indulgence can sometimes be seen in the weekend golfer. Usually he is a person who wants to get away from his work and relax and have some "fun" out on the course. But he is often so concerned about playing well or beating his old mark or defeating his opponent that he has a miserable time. If such an individual becomes upset every time he makes a poor shot, there will be very little pleasure in his day. This is particularly true because golf is a difficult game to master and most people who play it only occasionally do not do well consistently.

If one examines the opportunities for adults to have pleasure in their day-to-day life, he will find very few. Pleasure and fun are things that appear to be set apart, to be engaged in separately, and to be absent from the everyday affairs of men. Life, for most adults, is serious. Fun and pleasure belong to another part of their lives, the part called recreation.

We noted earlier that many of the activities in which people engage that are supposed to be pleasurable really do not fulfill this requirement. For many people recreation is simply a period of time devoted to something other than their "important business" but which provides them very little pleasure. In many cases, people move from one kind of boredom to another, because they have forgotten how to have fun.

Pleasure or fun are spontaneous, partly biological, reactions to sensory stimulation. We cannot control pleasure. That is, we cannot have pleasure on purpose—by an act of will. We can indulge in an activity that we know will be pleasurable, but we cannot force an activity to be enjoyable simply because we believe that it must. Nor can we make something enjoyable because we have paid a high price for it. If it is not enjoyable, none of our persuasion will be successful in making it so.

pleasure and homeostasis

The theory of homeostasis maintains that every organism seeks a state of balance in which all its basic needs are satisfied. According to this theory, needs develop that throw the organism into a state of temporary imbalance, and such states as hunger and thirst are merely conscious manifestations of the need to bring the organism back into equilibrium. Pleasure, in this view, is merely a subsidiary conscious state, the satisfaction of which restores the balance of the organism. Satisfaction, therefore, becomes a state of quiescence.

This theory is opposed to another theory of motivation, which sees pleasure in a quite different light. A quiescent state, according to this thinking, is not a satisfactory state, but one in which new kinds of needs arise. This idea is in accord with Maslow's hierarchy, in which B-needs arise when the D-needs are satisfied.

A state of perfect balance, especially in regard to the basic needs, often gives rise to a need for *excitation*. Quiescence, for many organisms, is simply boredom. And excitation becomes necessary for the experience of pleasure. People deliberately increase their tension and their excitation in order to better enjoy certain kinds of activities. Some people, for example, cannot play a competitive game unless they bet on the game—thus heightening the stakes which can be won and lost, adding to the intensity of the feelings thus aroused. The person who is always seeking challenging situations, such as competitive sports or dangerous ones, like shooting the rapids or climbing mountains, does so because such endeavors increase the excitation, which then enhances the pleasure of the particular activity.

Children are clearly aware of this, and one can see in their behavior many attempts to increase the excitation by doing "dangerous" things. The enjoyment of a roller coaster ride is mainly generated by the fear, which increases the excitation and makes the experience frighteningly pleasurable.

This point of view differs sharply from the homeostatic theory of motivation in that homeostasis is concerned mainly with survival, while the excitation theory is concerned mainly with joy. As Maslow has shown, once the survival needs are met, these new B-needs become prominent. And when they are not dealt with, very often the result is mere boredom. This may be one of the reasons why boredom has become one of the most pressing problems with which affluent Americans must deal.

Affluence and the development of a highly structured civilization have taken a great deal of risk out of everyday living. In addition, they have also eliminated, to a large degree, the unexpected. People more or less know what will happen from day to day, and they are not subject to very many surprises. This means that they can go through the motions of living with a very low level of excitation. Although such living may be perfectly functional in a survival sense, it is absolutely antagonistic to happiness. Happiness requires pleasure. And pleasure requires some novelty and some excitation.

> Pleasure and survival are not identical. Life does not aim at a static equilibrium, for that is death. Life includes the phenomena of growth and creativity. That is why novelty is such an essential ingredient of pleasure. (Lowen, 1970)

If the experience of novelty can be perceived as a process of assimilation or learning, then we can see that pleasure and growth are very intimately related. Many people have testified that the assimilation of new knowledge or the discovery of new ways to deal with people and the world are pleasurable. All these activities increase the excitation of an otherwise homeostatically balanced system.

What we have been saying is that the healthy person is "turned on" by life. He is excited and stimulated by the ongoing processes of which he is a part. He takes pleasure in the healthy functioning of his body. And he

The ability to have fun is an important element of healthy living.

enjoys the discoveries and innovations of his intellect. Pleasure underlies many of the activities in which he engages. Instead of being indifferent, depressed, apathetic, alienated, in a quiescent state, he is activated, inspired, enthusiastic, even exhilarated by most of his experiences.

THE PSYCHOLOGY OF FUN

The ability to have fun is the ability to engage in pleasurable activities in such a way that one gives one's self over entirely to the experience. This means that the individual does not *try* to have fun or to force something to be pleasurable which is not. It means that he chooses activities that are pleasurable for him and allows himself to be "carried away" by the activity in such a way that it fully engages his consciousness.

A child romping in the surf might be used as the prototype of fun. He delights in the movements of his body and the feeling of the water that splashes around him. He shrieks with excitement as the bigger waves crash close by. The smile that literally covers his face testifies to the sheer delight he experiences. He is not distracted by any consideration of past or future or by concern about whether his behavior is appropriate or dignified or productive. At this moment we can truly say that he has transcended any self-concept he might have. He is literally beside himself with joy.

This behavior is so easy for a child that we simply take it for granted. In a way, we are sometimes condescending toward a child who behaves this way. "After all, he's just a kid. He doesn't know any better." But it may be the adults who have lost the ability to experience this kind of joy to whom we should be condescending.

One of the reasons that it is difficult for adults to experience pleasure, fun, and joy is that they have been taught that time should not be wasted—that time is a commodity and that it should be spent only in ways that have valuable consequences in a *practical* sense. Children may play and have fun. But adults have to be productive. To spend time doing something "silly" simply because it is enjoyable does not fit in with the Puritan ethic. To romp in the surf and giggle and scream—these are activities that we expect from children, because children are by nature impractical and unproductive. The task of socialization, of course, is to enculturate them as they become adults so that they can learn to live their lives seriously and to stop being so infantile that they enjoy it. This makes adulthood a very grim business indeed.

the ethics of pleasure

For centuries man has been warned against living "merely for the flesh." He has been admonished against excessive indulgence in sensuality. This attitude has become a cornerstone for many traditional points of view. Thus we have come to look upon pleasure as bad, wasteful, or even sinful. It might be that the confusion about pleasure arises from the fact that different kinds of feelings are described as pleasurable. For example, a person who suffers from anxiety feels a sense of relief (pleasure) when that anxiety is reduced. Although this feeling may be called pleasure, it is not the kind of pleasure we have been describing. The relaxation of inhibitions through the use of alcohol and other drugs is also described as pleasurable. Again this differs from the biological state with which we are dealing.

A life based on the pursuit of these kinds of activities could reasonably be said to be wasteful. And a life devoted only to sensual pleasure might be criticized on the grounds that it lacked richness. But this is different from condemning the behavior as sinful. For the concept of sin, as we have already seen, can be extremely destructive to the individual. An understanding of man's nature demands that we include pleasure as an essential and important part of his life. In that sense, a reasonable pursuit of pleasure, which does not adversely affect the welfare of others, is a moral undertaking.

ECSTASY

Ecstasy is defined as an overwhelming state of rapture—a feeling of pleasure which has reached its outer parameters. It is the experience of joy at its highest intensity.

The feeling of ecstasy occurs in a number of situations. But it is most common in what Maslow has called peak experience. Sexual orgasm has often been described as one such peak experience. Childbirth has also been so characterized. But perhaps the most intense and most long-lasting ecstatic experience is the state sometimes called cosmic consciousness (Bucke, 1972).

For thousands of years the literatures of all peoples have described a state of consciousness which is one of the most profound, most compelling, and most meaningful of all states of human awareness. This state has been called cosmic consciousness, oceanic experience, mystical experience, religious union, state of grace, and so on. As Aldous Huxley has pointed out, it has been a perennial philosophy throughout man's history (Huxley, 1945).

Although we discussed the mystical experience briefly in Chapter 14, we are concerned in this chapter with its relationship to joy in the life of the individual. The overwhelming feeling that accompanies the recognition of oneness with all being is inexplicable on rational grounds. The experience itself is nonrational and the feeling it elicits is similarly mysterious. It might be said that the perception of the self-as-world is so exquisite that ecstasy is the natural reaction to it. Perhaps one might speculate that the universe is ecstatic, and to discover one's identity with it is to experience that ecstasy.

Although, as noted in the previous chapter, this experience has often had a religious connotation, it is not a necessary one. Whether religious or not, the experience has such an effect upon the individual that it often changes his life. And it almost always contributes to a feeling of optimism about man and his relation to the world which colors the life of the person from that time on. It is no wonder, therefore, that people seek to create this experience from time to time, by whatever means.

One thread that seems to run through all the literature describing this state is that it gives rise to a new form of understanding and knowledge which cannot be achieved through sensory or intellectual means. The new knowledge is direct, immediate, without the intervention of the senses or higher thought processes. In that sense it is revelatory. It is often described as knowledge, directly apprehended, which reveals a oneness and unity of all being.

A significant part of this experience appears to be dissolution of what is sometimes called the ego boundary. Perceptions become extremely intense, but the separation of the viewer and the viewed breaks down. The individual has the experience of being a part of the perception itself. He does not *see* objects; he becomes the objects themselves. Or, put differently, the objects of his perception are somehow a part of him, emanating not from out *there*, but from within. The boundaries between the self and the external world have vanished. In their place is a kind of total existence in which the concept of "boundaries" is meaningless. In the religious interpretation of the mystical experience, the ecstatic vision occurs when an individual suddenly realizes that he, God, and the universe are really all the same thing. The recognition that God and man are one is said to be the most profound and important realization of which man is capable. However, he does not learn this truth simply by being told about it by another human being. It is only through his own personal experience that one can come to know who he really is, in this sense.

HAPPINESS

Happiness is the name of the game. What we have been discussing throughout this book, has been related in one way or another to human happiness. And by now it should be apparent that some of the requirements of a happy life are related to many of the things with which we have been dealing.

But happiness is not a simple term to define. And many books which have been written on the subject of happiness make assumptions about its nature that this discussion would hold to be invalid. For example, books that teach people how to be popular, to be influential, to become wealthy, to develop *charm*, all purport to bring the reader happiness. But from what we have already said in the previous chapters, it must be apparent that happiness is not related to any of these, except perhaps in a peripheral way. In fact, it has already been shown that living one's life in such a way as to gain the approval of others, accumulate great material wealth, acquire power—such quests often have the opposite effects and bring about a great deal of unhappiness because they are often inauthentic modes of living.

If these commonly accepted paths to happiness are unfulfilling, what alternatives are available for modern man? For a life to be happy, it seems that there are a number of requirements that must be met. And these requirements exist on different levels.

In the first place, happiness requires a certain underlying tone or harmony which serves as a kind of constant *motif*. This means that there is a feeling of comfort and optimism which pervades the individual's existence most of the time. It is interrupted occasionally by tragedy and pain. But it is a resident part of the personality and, as such, it is almost always present.

This feeling of harmony and optimism cannot be voluntarily imposed. It comes about as a result of satisfaction with the self—it is a part of the comfort that one feels in being true to his real nature. It is self-satisfied but not smug. It is the experience of one who allows himself to be, and does so without anxiety.

Such an underlying tone gives a kind of coloring to a person's experience that allows him to look forward to the future with a feeling of engaged curiosity. He is interested in life, and he is bold in his approach to it. He allows himself the experience of pleasure on many levels. He enjoys creating, and his own life is one of his creations.

happiness on different levels

The underlying tone of harmony with one's self creates a foundation but is not in itself a guarantee of happiness. It is a necessary, but not a sufficient, requirement. One may have very good feelings about himself and be comfortable about all his needs and desires but be in a situation which is so difficult or painful that he could not truly describe his life as happy. To be happy, therefore, one must experience joy and pleasure on various levels.

Human beings are both physical and intellectual creatures. True happiness, therefore, would seem to require that one experience pleasure on *both* these levels. It may be that those who describe their lives as unhappy are neglecting one or another of these levels.

On the physical level, we have already pointed out the kinds of pleasure and/or fun which tend to increase one's satisfactions with his life. It would appear that there are a variety of activities that contribute to feelings of well-being on this level. *Playing* becomes exceedingly important in this context. Some people neglect to cultivate an interest in play, for reasons that have already been considered. This is unfortunate. Play and the anticipation of play are important aspects of a happy life. Too many people work all year for a two-week vacation in which they "play" and then have to give up the idea of enjoying themselves again for another year.

The cultivation of interest in sports, games, in physical activities that bring pleasure, are important aspects of enjoyment on this level. As children we often have a large number of such activities that are of interest to us, but as we grow older we tend to eliminate some or most of them and thus have very few to rely on as adults.

This pattern is particularly true of women who have been socialized, at an early age, to give up the more physical forms of play and to resort to more quiet types of activities. Modern women have been rejecting this passive role more and more, but they still have a great deal to accomplish in this area. A man can usually look forward to a round of golf or a ballgame or a fishing trip, but women have had many fewer options along these lines.

On the physical level it is important to notice that the human body has a biological rhythm which dictates, to a certain extent, when we should work and when we should play. In many ways our bodies tell us what it requires in terms of this rhythmic pattern. Because civilized man lives with schedules that are not in tune with these biological rhythms, he cannot always observe them. However, if he can intersperse periods of play among the periods of work within his day, he can go far in making his life more agreeable. If all work and no play make Jack a dull boy, he must find a way to introduce some periods of enjoyment into his schedule.

One thing that must be noted in relation to physical pleasure is that physical pleasure carried to an extreme often becomes pain. All play and no work can also have adverse effects. And a life of continual pleasure is both impossible and self-destructive. A no-work ethic is just as self-defeating as a no-play ethic. The idea that one can go through life without ever doing unpleasant things is naive. One may live off the land as Thoreau did at Walden. But that required a certain amount of work, which he was will-

Traditional sex roles have often been stifling. It may be necessary to disregard them in order to make life more enjoyable.

ing to do. And if one wears clothes, those clothes must be woven by someone and sewn by someone and shipped by someone. Those people must be paid in one form or another, and it usually requires some kind of work in order to do that. Some young people neglect this aspect of their lives in the pursuit of a pleasure ethic, then find that their cars break down, or they are dispossessed, or they have to go without food for several days. Such experiences do not as a rule lead to happiness. In other words, the exaggeration of either style of life, the overindulgence of pleasure on the one hand or the excessive industriousness of the work ethic on the other, is not likely to lead to a happy life.

One last thing need be said about happiness on the physical level. It must not be assumed that total gratification of the physical needs leads necessarily to happiness. In fact, it appears that the opposite may be true. The physical needs are the D-needs (or deficiency needs) in Maslow's hierarchy. They must receive *reasonable* gratification so that they do not become obsessive in the life of the organism. But this does not necessarily mean that they must be always satisfied, on demand, without delay. Such need satisfaction may lead to a state that Maslow has called "gratification produced pathology" (Maslow, 1970).

The psychological effects of affluence have not been studied for very long. But some data are starting to accumulate. The constant and immediate gratification of basic needs can lead to boredom, apathy, indifference, selfishness, self-centeredness, and a host of other self-defeating reactions. This is particularly true when such needs are gratified immediately upon their inception. For the pleasure of need gratification depends, to a great extent, upon the strength of the need and the *time* that it has been felt. In fact, with some needs (hunger, sex, etc.) we deliberately try to heighten the needs by prolonging gratification in order to increase the pleasure.

And it seems that a certain amount of frustration and tension must be tolerated by the healthy individual if his life is to have any richness. It is likely, therefore, that happiness, on a physical level, is achieved only by a balance between need on the one hand and gratification on the other.

the intellectual level

Happiness on the intellectual level has been very seriously neglected in our society. Even psychotherapy fails to help people deal with this important area. We have seen earlier that our society tends to be anti-intellectual to a great extent. This may be one reason for this neglect. But another reason is probably related to the fact that most Americans do not realize that there is great excitement to be experienced in the intellectual realm. We must remember that the traditional view of the intellectual is that of a stodgy, dull, generally unhappy person who is an intellectual only because he could not "make it" on some other level.

Not only is this not true, but it is a dangerous assumption. The greatest forms of happiness are achievable on the intellectual and/or spiritual level of man's existence. Moreover, this is the one area which need never be relinquished. For the intellect, with the right kind of care, can serve us well into old age. People who live an active mental life usually remain alert and appreciative well into their nineties.

Intellectual and spiritual delights do not, as a rule, come about spontaneously. They usually require a certain amount of training or taste acquisition. No one is born with a love of classical music any more than one is born with a taste for fine wine. The development of intellectual interests requires a period of acquaintanceship. Unfortunately, too many Americans are not willing to invest some time in gaining this acquaintanceship. Or if they begin to pursue their interests, they may be dissuaded by their parents or their peers. If a young boy likes classical music, he may be made fun of. If a young girl likes nuclear physics, she may likewise be ridiculed. Although these attitudes are changing, the vast majority of Americans still support the stereotypes.

Americans have lost the art of reading great books. Poetry has almost become a lost art in our culture. Yet the joys that one receives through these kinds of pursuits are incalculable.

The pursuit of a special intellectual discipline is another source of happiness. The excitement with which one reads of new findings in a particular field in which he has interests is tremendously absorbing. Most people do not realize that the "stodgy scientist in the white smock" is greatly excited by the discoveries he makes. Even a layman's interest in any particular discipline can bring one many happy hours. To a person with even a minimal amount of curiosity, the explorations of the moon and the nearby planets has to be a thrilling episode in his life.

The neglect of the intellectual capacities for enjoyment leads to long periods of boredom or apathy, especially when physical activity is limited by circumstances. One can often see this situation in children, when on a rainy day they have "nothing to do." This is understandable in childhood, but it is unnecessary in adults. If adults have cultivated their intellectual interests as fully as possible, they will not feel bored when they run out of physical pursuits.

Interest in ideas is a powerful contributor to happiness, because ideas are always with us. There is no limit to the amount of reflection we can do, even while engaged in physical activities of various sorts. Thought processes occupy the major part of our existence, and it is therefore important for these thought processes to bring us enjoyment. The person who is intellectually excited about life, therefore, is never very far from rewarding experiences. As a result, his entire life is enhanced.

The most difficult area for most people to deal with in relation to happiness is the area of work. Although work may be a physical undertaking, its contribution in terms of happiness is a psychological one. In that sense we can consider it an intellectual pursuit.

Most of us will spend the greater portion of our waking hours in the pursuit of a particular occupation. The question of what kind of work we will do is therefore a crucial one in the terms of happiness. A person who works day after day, year after year, at a job that he hates is not likely to be a happy person. To look forward day after day to the same dull routine must have negative consequences for the individual. The choice of an occupation, therefore, is one of the most important a person will make.

A person must give very careful consideration to the skills that he has, the things that he likes to do, the kinds of opportunities that are available at the time, in making a decision about his life's work. But even then it is possible to make mistakes. Sometimes our expectations about a particular kind of work differ markedly from the work itself. As a result, we sometimes find ourselves engaged in a kind of work that we dislike intensely.

But we should keep in mind that it is never too late to change. Many people have changed their occupations in their fifties and even their sixties, with the result that they spend many happy years doing something they enjoy rather than remaining in a situation that was creating unhappiness for them.

When a person's work is rewarding and exciting it has a powerful effect on his outlook on life. Each day presents a new and interesting challenge. He looks forward to going to work and, when it is over, he looks forward to relaxing from it. His rest refreshes him for a new start the following morning.

In contrast, the man who hates his work sees every day as a long, agonizing period of travail. Getting up in the morning, the prospects to which he can look forward all day fill him with despair. When he finally comes home from such a day, his anger and hostility are often expressed against his family. Life is one long, meaningless, repetitive routine. It is difficult for a person who is locked into such a situation to be truly happy, even if he has the other requirements we have been discussing. Young people, therefore, must take great care in choosing their work realistically. Since each one of us is unique, it is a decision that each individual must make for himself. To do something because one's parents desire it or because one's wife or husband demands it can be a tragic mistake. This kind of decision is, of course, easier for an individual who has developed some degree of authenticity.

happiness as growth

Happiness is related, to some degree, to the ability to change. The ability to incorporate novelty into one's life appears to be one of the most important human attributes. The human organism craves both novelty and familiarity. But if the need for familiarity becomes too great, many people simply give up the search for the novel. The result is stultification.

The person who is afraid of change is condemned to boredom. The healthy organism seeks to incorporate new experiences into his life space. But to do so requires a certain amount of risk. Change, variety, novelty, all seem dangerous, especially to the neurotic person who compulsively holds on to the familiar, the stereotyped, the comfortable.

The ability to grow is also the ability to look for new horizons. It is the capacity to anticipate new and exciting experiences. People are happy when they anticipate interesting outcomes. Sometimes, in fact, the anticipation is more enjoyable than the event itself. And sometimes the expected event never materializes. Nevertheless, the anticipation itself has been joyful.

The experience of growth and learning is almost always a joyful affair. The accumulation of wisdom, the acquisition of a new skill, the inception of a new idea, are all experiences that enrich life. Those who do not allow themselves these experiences are needlessly limiting their opportunities for a happy life.

loving relationships

The need for loving relationships, for healthy development of the individual, has already been discussed. But in regard to happiness, deep personal relationships are very important requirements. It is not likely that people who are alone in the world, who have no one with whom they share close personal relationships, can consider their lives complete. The need for another individual or individuals with whom one can share his deepest feelings does not seem to end in childhood—but continues throughout life. This need is often supposed to be filled by marriage. But traditional marriage very often fails to accomplish this task. Close personal relationships are possible with members of the same sex or with members of the opposite sex whether this be a marital arrangement or not. These relationships may be between members of the same family. Parents and children, brothers and sisters, cousins, uncles, or complete strangers—all are potentially capable of filling this need for us. The main requirement is that the relationship be a real (authentic) one.

anticipation

A happy life is marked by the fact that one is often contemplating the occurrence of pleasurable events. Anticipation itself is an extremely important component of happiness. The expectation of happy events is one of the most pleasant of pastimes. It gives an underlying tone to the person's experience which is truly beneficial.

But this must not be construed as a Pollyannaish way of looking at the world. Nor must one simply try to cultivate a positive attitude about everything. The optimism of which we are speaking must be based on reality. That is, a person must plan to include within his life space events and activities which are pleasurable to him. These events must be realistically possible. Even so, he may not accomplish all of them. But if they are really not possible, then he is indulging in an escapist world of fantasy, which will make the real world much less palatable when he finally has to come face to face with it.

The anticipation of enjoyable events is a positive force in one's life. A person, for example, may have a long-range goal, such as becoming an artist, lawyer, fireman, or policeman, or he may have a number of short-range goals, such as going on vacation, to a concert, working on a hobby. Or he may have a combination of long-range and short-range goals, the outcomes of which all promise to be pleasant, so that the anticipation of these outcomes is also pleasant. If he is lucky he will accomplish many of these. This should be satisfactory. If he is unlucky, he may accomplish none of them. In that case it is likely that the goals are unrealistic in some way and that they should be revised. In any case, the ability to establish a number of long-range and short-range goals that have some reasonable possibility of being realized, can have an important influence on an individual's happiness.

the phenomenology of happiness

Finally, it is the basic assumption of this book that happiness, joy, pleasure, and so on, are all phenomenological experiences. They are in no way related to the PR image, roles, the approval of others, or any of the other strategies that most people use to acquire happiness. Happiness is an experiential event. It has very little to do with the way we are perceived by others.

The attempt to achieve happiness by trying to change our PR image to gain the approval of others almost always fails. There may be a few minor satisfactions, of a temporary nature, on the way. But these are usually based on the need to reduce anxiety about the way other people respond to us, and although the reduction of anxiety is pleasurable to a degree, it is also insatiable. The anxiety returns almost immediately after it has been reduced, and the same process must be repeated.

We have all been surprised, at one time or another, to hear of brilliant, successful people who have taken their own lives at what seemed the height of their careers. These people, often adulated by millions of fans, did not find happiness through their success. And very often, the probable reason was that they were concentrating on the PR personality rather than the real self. The PR personality cannot be happy. It cannot be anything. It cannot *be* anything because it cannot *experience*. To dedicate one's life to decorating his image in the hope that this will bring happiness is futile. Happiness is a trip into the phenomenological self. The ego trip is a dead end.

chapter 16
love

We spoke earlier about love and the in-love syndrome which is so much a part of our folklore. In this chapter we wish to discuss love in more general terms. We want to consider what love is, especially for healthy people, and also what it is not. We shall see that a great many emotions that are labeled love are not really love at all.

THE LOVE OF THINGS

There is a certain amount of confusion concerning the meaning of love, because we use the same word to describe our feelings toward both persons and objects. When I say I love football or candy or green grass, I am not concerned with the well-being of these objects of my affection. If I say I love candy, I usually mean that I would like to possess it and devour it. It never occurs to me to ask myself how the candy feels about this. This is reasonable because I feel that candy has no feeling. Nor has football. And although green grass may have feeling of a sort, at the moment I am not concerned with that. If I love green grass, I mean I love to look at it.

The condition or response of these objects of my love is relatively unimportant to my loving them. Except for the candy, they are not even changed by my loving them.

To love *things*, therefore, is to love objects which I want to possess or consume—but which I do not consider to have any awareness of my love. To say it another way, objects have no *being*.

With objects, I can be completely narcissistic in my love. I can satisfy myself when and where I desire, with no concern that I will be taking advantage of them, exploiting them, inconveniencing them, or in any other way having an effect upon them that would be negative. I can therefore concern myself only with my *own* satisfactions and I can indulge myself almost without limit. All of us occasionally do just that with things we love, and occasionally we suffer the consequences afterward.

The quality of the feeling which we have for objects differs somewhat from what we feel for people. We desire to use the objects of our love or to obtain them when they are absent, or to go see or hear them when they are available. Objects serve their functions when they are used—an apple is meant to be eaten; a symphony is meant to be listened to; beautiful scenery is meant to be looked at; and perfume is meant to be smelled.

THE LOVE OF PERSONS

When we come to the meaning of the word "love" in relation to other living organisms, especially human beings, we run into a great deal of confusion. This is because there are a great number of meanings to the word "love," and their range is so vast that one can never really know which connotation is intended when the word is used.

When I say I love you, it may mean many things. It may mean that I *need* you; it may mean that I want you to *need me*; it may mean that I want your *approval*; it may mean that I want to *control* you; it may mean that I need to be *dependent* upon you—to have you *dependent* upon me; it may mean that I want you *sexually*; it may mean that I admire some of your *qualities* and wish that I had them myself; it may mean that I want to *use* you, and get gratification from you; it may mean that you have such prestige, that I want to acquire some of it by having a close relationship with you; and finally, it may mean that I love who you are, and want to help you to continue to *become*.

We need not go into the nuances of all these meanings of the word "love" in order to realize that many of them are not genuine. That there are a great variety of emotional attachments that are labeled love, and that are not love, is only too obvious. Our concern here will be to try to establish what kind of love is real, so that we can recognize it in our own lives, if and when it occurs. In order to do that, we have to consider briefly some of the things it is likely to be mistaken for.

love of people as objects

In noting the character of love of things, we noted that it was mainly exploitive. It was concerned only with the gratification of the lover and was indifferent to the fate of the loved object. In many cases love of persons proceeds in the same way. Some people "love" other people as if they are things. They seek gratification from them, or they use and exploit them, but they do not consider the feelings of the loved one at all. To love someone as if they do not have a separate consciousness is not to love *them*, but to gratify one's self *through* them.

There are many relationships in which this kind of exploitive love exists. It exists among parents for their children, among husbands and wives, or among friends.

Generally this kind of relationship exists because the lover has serious deficiency needs that must be met. Such needs take preference over other important psychological functions so that they influence all of the person's love relationships in this way. When love concerns the gratification of the lover only, it is usually because the deficiency-motivated individual can only perceive the other person as an object. He is literally "too wrapped up in himself" to understand the needs and desires of another.

love as need

It may be that the most primitive form of love (that is, the love of the infant for his mother) begins as need. Harlow (1966) has shown the need response of infants for their mothers, especially when frightened or otherwise upset, as one of the rudiments in the development of love. It is clear that the early development of the feelings of love grow out of this state of need. Most likely these needs are related to the need for safety in Maslow's hierarchy. But we have also seen that infants have other requirements (for example, the need for contact) that are also served by this form of love.

However, this kind of love is completely one-sided. The infant *receives*, but for the most part he is too immature to realize that the organism supplying his needs also has feelings.

It is possible that some people never develop beyond this particular stage. They act toward others in the same way Harlow's monkeys act toward their real or surrogate mothers. These kinds of people never *give* love, they can only take it.

the need to be a lovee

Another form of this same kind of dependent, deficiency-motivated love comes from the universal need *to be loved*. Certainly all human beings and probably most of the higher animals as well need to receive love, especially at an early age, in order to develop normally. As Maslow has shown, when this need is frustrated, it can become one of the most pressing in an individual's life. And as we have noted before, in our society, where the physiological and safety needs are reasonably well met, more people seem to be deprived in the area of the love and esteem needs. People who are suffering from inadequacies in this area tend to remain dependent upon the love and affection of others well into adulthood.

As a result these people tend to be lovees. When they are talking about love they are invariably talking about *receiving* rather than *giving*. When they say they are in love, they generally wish to convey the impression that someone loves *them*. Such people may "fall in love" time after time. Or they may claim to love many people at the same time. But what they are usually communicating by these statements is that they are worthwhile because they are loved.

A variation of this syndrome is exemplified by the person who manipulates others in order to gain their love. This individual very often uses, with great effectiveness, his or her sexual and other personality attributes to attract others. He or she will accumulate a large number of admirers and very often will claim to love a number of them. But this, again, is a person who, in a real sense, cannot love others. He is too much involved in receiving love and, as he has not developed the capability of giving it, what he labels "love" is merely his need to be a lovee. In this connection, Stein (1972) makes the distinction between *passive* and *active* love. Passive love is the need to *be loved* by others. Active love is the ability to *give* love. A period of passive love is necessary for the development of the ability to give active love. Without this period of passive love, active love may not develop.

There are many lovees in our society and the reasons for them may differ widely. Some people need love and approval because they have been rejected at an earlier state; some because their parents were incapable of giving love, either to the children or to each other; and some because the parents simply spoiled or smothered them, always giving them *things* but not a feeling of worth. In this latter situation, the feeling is conveyed to the child that he is incapable of doing anything for himself. Parents who smother children may not intend to communicate this. But the way they act—the attitude that says, "Let me do this, you can't"—gives the child a clear picture of his own inadequacies.

LOVE AS AFFIRMATION

We have been discussing different kinds of love, a number of which have been deficient in one way or another. If these many things that pass for love are, in fact not love, what kind of emotional feeling will we accept as authentic in terms of loving? Love is the affirmation of the life and growth of another person or persons. It is love for, and understanding of, the *being* of the other. To love someone, therefore, means to share, to the degree that it is possible, in his phenomenological life. And it is the desire to make that life a happy one. It is to desire for the *other*, joy, pleasure, beauty, and all of the other things that make life worthwhile.

An interesting insight into the nature of this kind of love can be gained from an examination of the love of children for their pets. The devotion that children often show to their animals, whether real or imaginary, has in it a quality that is very close to B-love as described by Maslow. The child, like the savage, tends to attribute awareness to most of the objects in his environment. And he is keenly concerned about the state of awareness of those he loves. He imagines that he shares their feelings intimately. And he believes that he knows when they are happy or sad.

The child is concerned for the happiness of his dogs and cats, and he suffers when they suffer and experiences joy when they are happy. In this sense he is a true lover. He is willing to make sacrifices for the objects of his love. And he is often quite unselfish in doing so.

He is much less concerned with what he can *get* than what he can give. And his happiness is derived largely from the happiness of the other rather than from his own gratification. The child's love for his pet is seldom involved with his ego. (In contrast, many adults keep pets which have prestige value via pedigree or some other special attribute, and use them for their own recognition.) As we shall see when we consider the love of healthy people, the love that children have for their pets turns out to be quite genuine.

THE ABILITY TO LOVE

It seems apparent that some individuals have been so crippled and so hurt by their life experiences that they no longer have the ability to love other human beings. And it may be that many in our society are at least partially impaired in this area. The question that therefore must be asked, is: to what extent is the ability to love cultivated, and in what ways can it be disrupted?

Psychologists generally agree that the ability to love is dependent upon loving relationships in life. We are not born with the ability to love. But we are born with the potentiality. In order for this potentiality to be realized, it is necessary for a child to be loved and cared for in his first few years of life. The absence of love during this critical period may result in a permanent inability to love.

As we have already seen, love in childhood is both a physical and a psychological process. The infant must be physically loved. He must be held, cuddled, hugged, kissed, and otherwise played with physically. His body must be engaged with the bodies of others. Whether we wish to include these behaviors within the concept of sexuality or not is irrelevant. Freud believed they were. Others have argued that they are not. The point is that the physical contact with other human beings and soft cuddly objects is one that is sought after by all children. Neglect of these kinds of contact can lead to serious problems later.

Out of these initial experiences, the psychological component of love evolves. From physically encountering others, the *idea* of affection for others begins. Love then begins to grow into a psychological entity in a person's life.

The love that the infant receives from his parents, siblings, relatives and others becomes the foundation of his own early self-evaluation. Reflecting upon the affection he has received from others, he comes to see himself as good, valuable, and worthwhile. He comes to like himself. And this is one of the most important steps in the ability to form deep attachments with others.

separateness
and encounter

Every individual perceives himself as separate and alone. His loneliness leads him to find ways of relating to others in order to overcome his separateness. Love is, to some extent, the attempt of the individual to overcome his loneliness by encountering others.

> The experience of separateness arouses anxiety; it is, indeed, the source of all anxiety. Being separate means being cut off, without any capacity to use my human powers. Hence to be separate means to be helpless, un-

able to grasp the world—things and people—actively; it means that the world can invade me without my ability to react. (Fromm, 1956)

The way man overcomes the anxiety aroused by his separateness is to love and, by loving, recombine himself with other human beings. But if he has not developed the ability to love in childhood, he will have great difficulty overcoming his loneliness. He may, in fact, become compulsively gregarious, in a vain attempt to overcome the separateness that plagues him. He may try desperately to receive the love of others. Or he may try to force himself to love others. But if he has not developed the ability to do so, most of these strategies will be unsatisfactory.

Fromm points out that in order to escape their separateness, many people give in to the pressures to conform. By being *like* other people, we believe that we are *with* them. This feeling is reinforced by their acceptance. We feel less alone when other people respond in approving ways.

If I am like everyone else, if I have no feelings or thoughts which make me different, if I conform in custom, dress, ideas, to the pattern of the group, then I am saved; saved from the frightening experience of aloneness. (1956)

But conformity is a counterfeit form of love. Both the giving and the receiving are inauthentic. We give love conformingly because we are afraid that we will be abandoned if we do not. We receive conforming love with an understanding that it is a false form of flattery—we are being complimented for what we are not.

LOVE IN SELF-ACTUALIZED PEOPLE

Maslow describes the love of healthy people as different qualitatively from that of others. It is unanxious, freely given, with complete abandonment. Its most important quality is the dropping of defenses. Love in the self-actualized person is the state of defenselessness. The person leaves himself deliberately vulnerable. Vulnerability is a part of the openness that one expresses to another. It is therefore a necessary concomitant to love. The feeling the person has is that he can "be himself." But this also means allowing his own faults and weaknesses (unheroic qualities) to be visible to the other. The idea of maintaining distance in order to be more mysterious, captivating, glamorous is anathema to real love. In fact, the whole essence of healthy love is to *reveal* rather than to *conceal* who one is to the other.

There is therefore a great deal of dropping of *careful* behavior, in favor of spontaneity, freedom, and openness. In a certain sense the person who loves in this way is unwilling to have love on any other terms. For to be free to be one's self in a love relationship, without deviousness, without manipulation, without games, is a luxury that such a person does not want to relinquish.

This openness must generally occur in a climate that is free from threat. This means that we can show who we are to the other person without fearing their rejection. For we cannot love those who threaten us. There is, therefore, a certain amount of safety involved in a real love relationship. The person can allow himself to be vulnerable because he knows that his lover will not take advantage of this state. Openness, in a two-way love relationship, becomes a natural, comfortable way of behaving, devoid of threat.

care

Mature love is marked by the concern of one individual for the welfare of the other. The emotional component of this concern is a deep sense of caring. The person who loves another is deeply concerned with his outcomes. He has an emotional investment in the happiness of the other. He *feels* the other's joy. He also feels his pain.

A person who loves another becomes a part of the person's growth. This kind of love is most clearly represented by the good parent. The good mother or father experiences his child's joys and sorrows as if they were his own. And his efforts are bent toward contributing to the growth and happiness of the child.

Love also means respecting the being of the other. The individual who truly loves, loves not a projection that he himself has created but the authentic other person. He respects the other person as different from himself, and different from what he wishes him to be. And he respects the changing, ongoing process of becoming which has its center in the other. He not only loves who he is, but he also loves (that is, respects) the person he is continually becoming.

responsibility

If I love you, I am, in some way, responsible to you. If I love you, I have communicated to you that you can depend upon me in certain kinds of circumstances. If I love you, I will not abandon you in times of need, in times of crisis, in times of danger. My love is testimony of my responsibility to you. In many instances, I will be willing to sacrifice for you. In some cases, I may be willing to sacrifice my own life.

Responsibility also means that if you put your trust in me, I will not fail. I will be available when you need me, and I will be conscious of the times you are depending upon me. This does not mean that I will try to control you or to force you to live your life in a certain way. It simply means that when you want to reach out to me, I will be there.

One of the most essential factors in the respect for others concerns their uniqueness and individuality. Love in this sense becomes the recognition and affirmation of the uniqueness of the other. It is not the loss of the self or the subservience of one's self to another, but the recognition of the many individual qualities that make up the particular individual and the acceptance of their existence. The lover even respects those qualities of the other with which he is not always in accord.

THE PHENOMENOLOGY OF LOVE

Love is one of the richest, most exciting experiences we can have. When it is strong it fills our whole being with a sense of joy and excitement. It colors all our perceptions so that they seem more beautiful, more meaningful, more alive.

Love is therapeutic. It is a kind of sunshine for the soul. It lights up one's life. It fills one with wonder and awe. As Maslow points out, this kind of joy in love is unrelated to possession.

> We can enjoy a painting without wanting to own it, a rosebush without wanting to pluck from it, a pretty baby without wanting to kidnap it, a bird without wanting to cage it, and also can one person admire and enjoy another in a nondoing or nongetting way. (Maslow, 1970)

Love is an accompaniment to happiness. When one is able to love in the ways we have described not only other people but also, in a certain sense, the world, he is likely to be happy a great deal of the time.

Love in healthy people is an end experience. It is not a means to an end. It is not a step toward a higher state of emotion. It is one of the most powerful experiences we have. In a certain sense, one might say that love is the end of all our striving. We love because that is the essence of our nature. Love is pleasure, joy, ecstasy, and the act of loving is the act of *being* in one of its most intense forms. It is a special state which is at least potentially available to all. But the love that we have described here is not as common as one might suspect. And it certainly is not identical with all those feelings described earlier which are generally designated by the same term.

LOVE IN WESTERN SOCIETY

The ability to love is based upon a feeling of real self-esteem. Unless we can love ourselves in an open, accepting way, we can love no one else. This being true, it becomes quite apparent that what passes for love in Western society is seldom love at all.

Fromm's argument about the disintegration of love in modern Western society (see p. 194) must be taken seriously. People who do not like themselves do not like others. And we have shown that the structure of Western society is such that many people never learn to like themselves adequately.

As a result, many people practice various kinds of pseudo love—narcissistic substitutes for love in the form of ethnic or nationalistic pride—but the experience of loving is empty and is largely absent in these forms of expression. Sometimes love is part of the role we play in an effort to convince ourselves that we are really capable of love. Most of the time, of course, our performance is unconvincing.

One reason for the disintegration of love in the Western industrialized world is that we have come to perceive other human beings as objects and in our own minds have denied their ability to feel. This makes it easy for us to suspend our feelings of commitment toward them in order to manipulate them for our own gain. If we loved them we could not use them, exploit them, bomb them, force useless products on them. If we loved them and desired their happiness, if we wanted their growth, if we allowed ourselves to experience their being, we would be forced to change the way we deal with them politically, economically, and otherwise.

Fromm describes another form of pseudo love which grows out of the inability to love the self.

> If the person has not reached the level where he has a sense of identity, of I-ness, rooted in the productive unfolding of his own powers, he tends to 'idolize' the loved person. He is alienated from his own powers and projects them into the loved person, who is worshiped as the *summum bonum*, the bearer of all love, all light, all bliss. In this process he deprives himself of all sense of strength, loses himself in the loved one instead of finding himself. (Fromm, 1956)

The many forms of hero worship that are so common and that lead to the kind of hero emulation that we described in the early chapters of this book are the result of this kind of crippling of the real ability to love.

LOVE AND THE RISK OF LOSING

One important aspect of loving is that it is not always reciprocal. We may love someone who does not return our love, or we may love someone whom we lose through some other contingency. Such an event very often causes great pain. As a result, many people become fearful of committing themselves.

This is particularly true of an individual who has lost the person he loved, particularly in childhood. The feeling that committing one's self is dangerous can easily be acquired as the result of such an experience.

Nevertheless, the love that one gives to other people must run this risk. For if we love someone we must be willing to face the despair of losing them, the pain of being separated from them, the occasional doubt about their love for us, and all of the other feelings that accompany this great emotion. But if we are afraid of these, then we will guard ourselves against love. And if we do that, we will miss the most powerful experience of living.

UNIVERSAL LOVE

The ability to love in a mature way implies another kind of love, a love that is perhaps the most important of all of man's potentialities. This is what we call *universal love*.

This love, which has also been called brotherly love, love of God, love of mankind, or even love of the universe, is unique to man. Only man can contemplate a universe far beyond his own perception and respond to that universe with love. This is the love that all the religious leaders, all the philosophers, all the sages of all times have advocated.

This kind of love involves the care, respect, and understanding of any other human being with whom one interacts. But it also means more than this. It also means a love of the world itself—it also means an affirmation of life. It literally entails a love for all that exists.

This capacity is not reached by everyone. It is a highly developed capability growing out of self-actualization. It was quite apparent among the people that Maslow studied. And it seems to require a kind of maturity and self-confidence that is rare.

If one has clearly developed a capacity to love, in the terms that we have already described, then it is easy for him to extend that love to all mankind. There is the ability to feel united with all men, to share their pain, happiness, and sorrow, and to desire their well-being. Universal love is based on the feeling that all men are really brothers. It is the clear perception that other people's pain is just as real as our own.

Universal love is also a kind of feeling of oneness with the inanimate world as well. The man who contemplates the stars and enjoys their beauty is, at that moment, engaged in universal love.

Although this is one of the most beautiful and perhaps the most valuable forms of love, it cannot be legislated. One of the great mistakes of the great religions has been to command people to love their fellow man. Such a commandment is doomed to failure if the individual has not developed to the point where he is capable of such love. And, in many situations, such a commandment merely leads to guilt or disparagement because people cannot experience what they have been told they must.

Universal love is often inspired by the beauty of nature. This scene in Yosemite Valley has thrilled thousands of visitors.

Universal love may one day be the salvation of mankind. When all men experience this emotion, there will be an end to manipulation, exploitation, destruction, and all other such maneuvers for personal gain. But that time is not yet here. It is not likely to come about until people are given the opportunity to take the preliminary steps necessary in developing such a capacity. Those steps are the same ones that are essential to self-understanding.

The person who is desperately seeking happiness cannot be concerned with the love of others. The person who is already happy, however, can hardly be diverted by anything else. To be happy is, in a sense, to love the world. And to be happy is to desire happiness for others as well.

The true religious experience, described in the literature of all ages and all times, always contains reverence. Schweitzer's *Reverence for Life* is a perfect example of this. Love of God, love of man, love of the world, all of these are expressions of universal love.

Whether this state is attainable for all human beings is not known. It may be that it is not. There is no guarantee that all human beings are born with this potentiality. However, it is the view of such writers as Maslow and Rogers that this is indeed a true human capacity. It should be noted that this is also the view of most of the great religions, no matter where they have appeared and in what epoch of history. In this sense, modern psychology and ancient religion are not far apart.

That man can seek out and find the beauty that exists in living is a fundamental assumption of the humanistic trend in modern psychology. And the culmination of the development of higher states of consciousness, of more mature functioning, of self-actualization, are all wedded to the idea of man's perfectability in this particular sphere. The ultimate good, therefore, the final outcome for the self-actualized individual, is this ability to love universally. And the ideal outcome of all education would be to create a race of human beings all of whom have reached this stage of development.

UNIVERSAL LOVE AND ETHICS

The attempts to develop new life styles in order to find new and better ways for people to relate to one another have provoked a great deal of thought about the ethics of our own society. Many people have been dissatisfied with the styles of life that they have been forced to adopt; as a result, they have struck out on their own in an attempt to reorganize the world so that universal love could be one of the fundamental principles of their lives. The "hippie" movement of the 1960s, with all its shortcomings, began with just this thought in mind. Having seen their society and found it unsatisfactory, these people tried to create a new society in which the principle of universal love was the basic commandment. When one thinks of it, this is not very different from what Jesus did, what Moses did, what Mohammed did, or what Confucius did. That they met with ridicule and derision is not surprising. They were attacking a life style that was very strongly entrenched. Or at least that is how their contemporaries perceived their actions.

The underlying ethic of the movement of the *flower children* or *young seekers*, as they have been called, was universal love. This was perhaps too simplistic an approach, but it had the essential idea: "people have to reach out toward one another before they can develop a culture in which it is safe for all of them to live together."

Whether the life style that the young people were trying to develop was workable or not is debatable. Cultures of this sort have existed and do exist on this planet quite successfully. In fact, small subcultures in which love and cooperation are primary virtues exist in our own twentieth-century industrialized society. The real point is that the ideal of universal brotherhood was generally rejected by the greater society. There may be a number of reasons for this. People who have been conditioned to a certain way of life are not likely to change quickly, especially when the new life style appears strange or contradicts some of their most basic compulsions (neatness, short hair, inhibited sexuality). The essential point is that universal brotherhood cannot be imposed on people from the outside. It is one of the by-products of psychological health and, as such, it only comes about through the successful struggle for authenticity. This idea is not new. What is new is that we now have a somewhat better model of psychological health than we had before. In a certain sense this new understanding has turned the entire question of ethics completely around.

the morality of happiness

One of the problems that beset all discussions of ethical behavior is the question of defining *what is good*. There have been many definitions and many arguments throughout the history of ethical philosophy, but they will not concern us here. For we can begin simply by defining *happiness* as a basic good.

It is clear that all organisms seek and desire happiness, while seeking to overcome and eliminate its opposite. From this point of view we can say that the organism experiences happiness as a basic value for itself.

We have already defined happiness as the state of fulfilling one's own potentialities, the actualization of one's own capacities, and the ability to love productively not only other individuals but also the created world. It follows, therefore, that self-actualization becomes an essential ingredient in any discussion of ethics or morality.

There is really nothing new in this idea. Spinoza, Dewey, and Aristotle all felt that man must understand his nature, fulfill his potentialities, in order to live an ethical life. For Aristotle, *virtue* was synonomous with *activity*—which meant using one's faculties to their highest potentialities. Happiness was a result of the use of these faculties, while unhappiness was equivalent to their disuse. For Spinoza, virtue had a similar definition.

> To act absolutely in conformity with virtue is, in us, nothing but acting, living and preserving our being (these three things have the same meaning) as *reason* directs, from the ground of seeking our own *profit*. (Spinoza, 1927)

The idea that preserving one's being and developing it to its full potential is a moral act is clearly seen in another quote from Spinoza in which he says that good is anything that "we are certain is a means by which we may approach nearer and nearer to the model of human nature He set before us"—while evil is "everything which we are certain hinders us from reaching that model" (Spinoza, 1927). In more modern terminology, Spinoza is saying that man's ethical duty is to become self-actualized. John Dewey, the twentieth-century American philosopher, held a similar view.

Notice that these ethical systems do not have a series of rules dictating the way that men should live. Any system of rules that is rigidly presented is an authoritarian form of ethical thinking. And most humanists reject this form of thinking. For a rigid system of behaviors cannot make allowances for the many subtle variations that reality imposes upon us. We have seen all too often how rigid adherence to codified laws has led to tyranny, cruelty, and other forms of oppression.

Although the philosophers of the past have asked man to know his own nature and to act upon it, often there was disagreement about what man's nature really was. And although this disagreement still exists, there *is* developing a body of scientific evidence which, perhaps for the first time, is giving us an accurate appraisal of what man really is. So the philosophical insights of the past, coupled with the scientific discoveries of the present, may give us a more empirical foundation upon which to base our ethical system of thought. In a sense, though, we no longer need the philosophical support of the past, because modern psychology points the way to a new kind of ethic.

If we accept happiness as the fundamental good, then it follows that

that which leads to happiness also leads to a virtuous life. We have already shown that self-actualization leads to a happy life. Moreover, we have shown that an understanding of one's real nature—a life that is lived authentically, a life in which a person knows how he feels and responds reasonably to those feelings—is a life in which one can fulfill his potentialities. A person who lives such a life is capable of authentic committed love, and this love can generalize from one or a few persons to the whole world.

It follows that a person with such a system of values, does not have to be taught a codified set of rules which he introjects or superimposes upon his personality. Such a person has no need of a watch-dog conscience. In other words, the Freudian superego becomes superfluous to him.

Such a person is virtuous (remembering that happiness is virtue) in that he desires happiness for others as well as himself. His love, care, concern, and respect for mankind dictates that he desire happiness as a universal outcome. His empathy makes it impossible for him to be happy at the expense of others. He cannot therefore exploit, destroy, or cause suffering to others for personal gain. He need not be taught the golden rule because it is a part of his own nature.

The virtuous (healthy) person may resist unjust laws when he perceives that they are causing unhappiness for others. The authoritarian moralist will never do this. For the latter, laws are to be obeyed, never questioned. The authoritarian moralist obeys laws because he fears punishment. The self-actualized moralist obeys an inner feeling of love for mankind because he is unhappy when he does not. Fear of punishment has nothing to do with *true* morality. True morality is an act of universal love.

VALUES IN EDUCATION AND PSYCHOTHERAPY

There has been a great deal of controversy regarding the place of values in any kind of educational system. And psychotherapy and other enculturating influences can be viewed as forms of education, in the broadest sense of the word. The beauty of the ethic we have been discussing is that it wipes out the need for educators, parents, psychotherapists, ministers, or anyone else to inculcate a set of values. To tell a person who is suffering from paranoia to love his neighbor is as ludicrous as asking a fish to live on land. To tell a starving man who sees riches all around him that he must not steal is to be completely unaware of the power of D-needs to control the behavior of an organism, especially in severe deprivation. Without an adequate understanding of the nature of man, an ethical system is a series of rules that will continually be violated by the majority of people.

The problem of ethics, in terms of a set of rules of behavior, disappears the moment one acknowledges the nature of self-actualization. It becomes unnecessary to inculcate individuals with a set of "values" which are in fact usually a set of biases related to specific cultures. The only requirement becomes the need to help the individual *find out who he is* in education, psychotherapy, or any other endeavor and then allow him to develop the ethic that is the natural result of this experience. If we want universal brotherhood we cannot teach it or preach it. We must allow human beings to once again, as they did in the beginning, perceive themselves as a part of the universe, and love that.

chapter 17
the continuum:
a fantasy in one act

We are often told that the past is dead and we can do nothing to affect it. This is true to a great extent But in a sense, *all* of the past is not dead. What we are doing today will become the past tomorrow. In that sense, we can have an effect on the past that is yet to be.

Someone has said, "Today is the first day of the rest of your life." Today is the day that we can begin to change. If we change now and make our life worthwhile from this moment on, then one day we will look back and say that life was worth living. If we do not, and if we let the days slip away one by one without doing anything to increase our happiness in valid ways, we may look back when it is nearly over and feel the despair of knowing that it was all wasted. A character in a film, illustrating the alienation of modern life, says it well when he sums up his life: "When I die, and they put me into the ground, they'll write on my headstone, 'this was a waste of time.'" Unfortunately, many people look back at their lives in this way. The only way to prevent this is to know what we're about. And

407

that means we must seize the present so that the past that grows out of it will not be "a waste of time."

Let us therefore look at one man who took the opportunity to look back. And let his experience serve as a lesson. At this moment, it is not too late.

the continuum a fantasy in one act

cast of characters

FRED HARRISON (*A businessman*)

STRANGER (*An angel*)

NAPOLEON (*Emperor of France*)

MARIE ANTOINETTE (*French aristocrat*)

JUNKIE (*A drug addict*)

AUNT MARGARET (*Fred Harrison's maiden aunt*)

BILL PHILLIPS (*Old colleague of Harrison's*)

HENRY DAVID THOREAU (*The Sage of Concord*)

OLD MAN (*A man with a province*)

As the curtain rises, the stage is in darkness. The lights come up at center stage, revealing a dark misty place. There is a strong greenish tint, giving the place an eerie glow. This glow gradually brightens, revealing an empty stage with mists swirling mysteriously about. Both ends of the stage, near the wings, are in darkness, and all entrances and exits are made to materialize out of this darkness. FRED HARRISON *wanders on, looking about him with great curiosity. He is a middle-aged man, well dressed and stockily built.*

FRED: What place is this? Is anyone here? (*cupping his hands to his mouth*) Hello-o-o.

(*Enter* STRANGER *out of the darkness. The man has grayish temples, a serious but friendly face, and a quiet manner. He appears out of the mists so suddenly that* FRED *is taken by surprise. He steps backward in an involuntary start.*)

STRANGER: Fred Harrison?

FRED: Who are you? What am I doing here?

STRANGER: What's the last thing you remember?

FRED: Well, I was talking to my wife. . . .

STRANGER: Arguing!

FRED: Well, all right, arguing. Say how do you know? You one of those goddam psychic freaks?

STRANGER: Not exactly. But go on. Try to remember.

FRED (*still looking at him suspiciously*): Well, we were arguing. You know the usual thing. She wanted to go to the ballet. She doesn't even like the damn thing. She just goes to show off the fancy new dress she got from Dior. She thinks she looks so gorgeous in it. To me, she looks like something left over from Halloween! A real spook! That dress cost me plenty, too. Imagine, a thousand bucks for a dress and she comes out looking like the leading lady on Horror Theater! Well, anyway, I didn't want to go to the ballet. I had business to take care of. It was very important. I'm an executive in the automotive industry, you know. And you've got to be on your toes. Got to keep one jump ahead of the next guy, know what I mean?

STRANGER: Yes. So you argued pretty vehemently and got pretty upset.

FRED: That's right. Say, what are you, a private eye or something? If it's about that weekend in San Francisco, that girl's a lot of baloney. I can name four other guys. . . .

STRANGER: No. No. It's not about San Francisco. Go on.

FRED (*again looking at him suspiciously*): Say, you aren't an interior decorator or dress designer or anything like that are you?

STRANGER: No, nothing like that.

FRED (*resigned but not convinced*): Well, I was getting pretty upset and yelling quite a bit even though the doctor had told me not to. And then I began getting this pain in my chest. . . . (*suddenly becomes frightened, gasps and looks around quickly*) Say, where the hell am I? And the pain. Where's the pain? (*feeling his chest*)

STRANGER: There's no pain here. Anyway not that kind.

FRED (*A look of realization comes over him. He is both frightened and fascinated*): Then I'm . . . dead . . . This is it . . . but how, I mean . . . (*Looks around again*) Is this what it's like? (*suddenly becomes happy*) Say, there's no fire.

STRANGER: Did you expect one?

FRED: Well, I haven't exactly been an angel. Uh, no offense. . . . What I mean is, I figured if I went anywhere, it would be, you know . . . Say, is this . . . Heaven?

STRANGER (*smiling a little wryly*): You people all have such a naive idea of Heaven. It isn't a *place*. It's a *state*. Haven't you ever heard the expression, "The Kingdom of Heaven is within you?"

FRED (*apologetically*): Yes, I guess so. I'm afraid I haven't been very religious. I meant to go to church more often but you know, you get busy. . . . (*brightening a little*) I was there last Easter though. (*now becoming chagrined*) Of course, I had to go. Nutso had a new hat. But I really meant to go more often.

STRANGER (*interrupting with a wave of his hand*): All that's not important. The point is that if the Kingdom of Heaven is within you, so is the Kingdom of Hell. This is merely the Continuum, what you call Limbo. But what it becomes is up to you.

FRED: You mean everyone comes here?

STRANGER: More or less, yes. It would be more correct to say that here is where everyone *is* and life is a temporary interruption.

FRED (*dejected*): Then my wife'll be here, too. You call that Heaven?

STRANGER: You made your bed on earth, you'll have to sleep in it here.

FRED (*pleading*): But please, not with her!

STRANGER: You can't undo what you've done. Neither there nor here. The laws of nature are the same everywhere in the universe. And what's been done doesn't vanish magically because you'd like it to. Oh, I know you people think you can live the most horrible kind of life and then repent at the last minute. And you think that makes everything perfectly all right. But if you've done someone harm, how can your apology undo the damage retroactively? No, my friend. You can't get out of it that easily.

FRED: Then how does one get to Heaven?

STRANGER: I guess that depends on what you think Heaven is.

FRED (*uncertainly*): Well, I guess Heaven is a place where your wishes come true.

(*The dark area near the wings at stage right grows light, revealing a large, ornate desk with a name plate facing the audience. The letters spell out the name* FRED HARRISON. *As* FRED *sees it, he walks toward it smiling.*)

FRED: Well, this is more like it. I guess I'm to be an executive here, too. For awhile there, I thought my talents were going to be ignored. (*Walks around behind the desk and sits down, leaning back in the swivel chair.* STRANGER *walks to the front of the desk.*) Well, I suppose I'm to be doing some administrative work. What are my duties?

STRANGER: You have none.

FRED: What, no duties? You must be joking. Why the desk if there are no duties?

STRANGER: Do you remember your most fervent wish in the other life?

FRED: Well, there were so many, it's pretty hard to remember. . . . Oh, I know, you mean when I wanted a desk of my own with my own nameplate on it.

STRANGER: Well, now you have it.

FRED: But who are my subordinates?

STRANGER: Oh, there are no subordinates.

FRED (*exasperated*): But how am I expected to get anything done without a staff?

STRANGER: Who said anything about getting things done? You said that Heaven was getting your wishes fulfilled. You wished for a symbol of prestige, a desk. Well, you've got it. But if Heaven is the fulfillment of wishes for *you*, then it's the same for everyone else. And since no one wishes to be a subordinate, there are none available. But why should you care? You've got your wish and you can enjoy it till eternity. (*turns to go*)

FRED (*jumps up from the chair and runs around to the front of the desk*): Wait a minute! Just sitting behind a desk. That's no life . . . I mean death! I've got to do something important!

STRANGER: I see. So getting a wish to come true isn't enough. It only leads to more wishes. And sooner or later your wishes will clash with someone else's. Whose would you have us grant then? No, Fred Harrison. That's not the road to Heaven.

FRED (*walks dejectedly toward center stage with* STRANGER *as desk fades into darkness*): I don't know. I guess I just don't understand this Heaven business.

STRANGER: That's the first sensible thing you've said.

FRED: But how am I going to learn?

STRANGER: It isn't going to be easy to explain. But perhaps if you speak to others here, it will help you to understand.

FRED: You mean I can see anyone I like? I can meet all the great figures of history, uh, that is, the dead ones.

STRANGER: We don't particularly like the word "dead" here. We prefer to say those who've come back. Yes, you can see them all. Just say the word and they will materialize for you.

FRED: I'd like to see Napoleon. I've always admired him. He was such a great leader.

(NAPOLEON *materializes out of the darkness at stage left. He is dressed as we remember him. He looks about quickly then sees* FRED *and* STRANGER).

NAPOLEON (*disgustedly*): Oh no, not again. Not another newcomer fawning over me. A spirit can't get any rest at all. It's positively indecent the way they gawk at you. (*studies* FRED) This one looks like a real idiot.

FRED (*to* STRANGER): He's not very polite for a great man.

STRANGER: There's no such thing as politeness here. You see, there are no words, just thoughts that become audible. So when anyone thinks anything, it's the same as saying it aloud. Your social niceties are just a pose to try to hide your real feelings. But we know what everyone is thinking, so you see, that kind of politeness serves no purpose here.

FRED: Well, may I talk to the Emperor? I mean, may I think at him?

STRANGER: Think away.

FRED (*bowing*): Your Highness. I'm thrilled to meet you. You've always been my idol. In fact, I consider you the greatest man in history.

NAPOLEON (*annoyed*): Just as I thought. Another adulator and probably for the wrong reasons. In fact, all adulation is a form of conceit since adulation is the sire of emulation. And so since you love yourself rather than me, it is most certainly for the wrong reasons. But why, may I ask, do you claim to admire me?

FRED: Why you were such a great soldier. . . .

NAPOLEON (*leaps at* FRED, *covering his mouth with his hand and looks about surrepititiously*): Quiet, you fool! (*now almost whispering as he releases him*) They don't like soldiers too well around here. Making murder honorable doesn't make it less murderous. Besides, soldiers are always responsible for population explosions here. It gives them a lot of extra work.

FRED: Well, a great leader, then. You almost became ruler of the world.

NAPOLEON: You mean ruler of the *earth*. I wasted a lifetime trying to become the biggest man on a dust particle in space. And you, you idiot, you think that's greatness.

FRED (*a bit bewildered*): What do you call it?

NAPOLEON: I call it insanity, that's what. How would you like to face millions of people every day who suffered and died because of you? Do you think it's pleasant? That's all I hear nowadays. They never let me forget it. And why should they? They're absolutely right.

FRED: If you think that, why did you do it?

NAPOLEON (*shouting*): Because of an underactive pituitary! Can't your moronic brain understand that if I'd been two inches taller, the entire history of Europe would have been different? (*starts whispering*) If only those kids I used to play with hadn't kept calling me a little shrimp.

FRED: But everything you did. All the work you put into it. All the people who were affected. Doesn't any of it mean anything now?

NAPOLEON: After you're here awhile, if you have any brains at all, you learn a few things. (*looks him over disdainfully*). In your case I'd better explain it. You see, when you're out there in that other world, you think of yourself as single, as individual. Everything you do is for the benefit of this one isolated personality. But when you come here, a part of you dissolves into the common pool. What others feel you feel too, because you are a part of them. And the things I did for this individual self destroyed a lot of other selves. So I feel it now.

FRED: While you did them, weren't they wonderful? Didn't they bring you great satisfaction?

NAPOLEON: A little, to the part of me that was singular. But the other part, the part that knew what I was doing to others, no. After all, I'm not a fool. I knew the suffering I caused. I saw men bleeding in the snow. I saw them torn apart by cannon and shell. I saw their women and children starve. I knew all this was by my instigation. But something I couldn't control kept driving me. Even when I wanted to resist it, I couldn't. And now I have to face it every day. Or what's worse, I have to be leered at by fools who think all of that was greatness. (*He turns and walks away dejectedly, vanishing into the mist.*)

FRED: Well, he's a big disappointment.

STRANGER: Did you think there were emperors and conquerors here? You'll find a different set of values in this sphere. Who else would you like to meet?

FRED: How about Marie Antoinette? She was quite a piece of French pastry. Uh, but I don't want to see anyone without a head. (*thoughtfully*) A beautiful body without a head. That might not be too bad at that.

(MARIE ANTOINETTE *appears out of the mist. She is quite dishevelled. She is holding a mirror and trying to comb her hair which is in a rather wild state.*)

MARIE: I must regain my beauty. I'll look good again, you'll see.

FRED: What happened! Why are you so ugly?

MARIE: Oh, it's the beauticians. They won't work here. (*laughing*) You should see Pompadour. Her hair is straight as string. (*more seriously*) Oh, it's awful here. You can't get anyone to do anything. The peasants are terribly independent. And besides, they're still mad at me. (*thoughtfully*) I guess I should never have done that line about the cake. Ah well, it wouldn't make any difference. You see, money's no good here. And you're not even allowed to exploit the peasants. In fact, an aristocrat is considered the same as the dirtiest street rabble. Without money there's no way to tell the difference. Imagine, my family spent generations accumulating fortunes and now we all end up peasants. . . . But I'll show them. After I regain my beauty they'll all want me. I *will* be beautiful again. And they'll all vie for my favors. But I won't be easy to get. Not for a while, anyway. (*gayly*) Oh there'll be parties and balls and things will be like they used to be.

(*She grabs* FRED *and starts dancing around the stage.* FRED *protests all the while. He stumbles around with her, but he is obviously uncomfortable and somewhat bewildered.*)

FRED: Oh please, I'm afraid I can't dance. (*laughing uncomfortably*) I think I'll have to sit this one out.

MARIE (*finally giving up on him and whining*): Oh what a place! You can't have any fun at all.

FRED (*surprised*): Why you're just a child. A little girl wearing grownup clothes. If you can't have your own way, you cry.

MARIE (*pouting*): Well, I can't help it. I've always gotten what I wanted. Oh, if we could only have parties and dances again.

FRED: Would that help? Were you happy at the great court balls?

MARIE: Well, to tell the truth, they became pretty boring. Always the same routine. Always the same people saying the same tiresome things.

STRANGER: But you still kept going.

MARIE: What could I do? A body needs some diversion.

FRED: But was it worth the trouble?

MARIE: Of course not. It never is. But it passes the time and then once in a while there's a new *amour* and it diverts one for a while.

FRED: But I don't understand. If all these things are so dull, why do you look forward to them so much?

MARIE (with a shrug): What else is there? Besides in my position one must keep up appearances. (*continues combing hair and looks into mirror as she exits*)

FRED: What an empty life. Imagine going from one boredom to another.

STRANGER: Yes, but that's the most prevalent form of wretchedness here. You see, Hell, like everything else in the universe, is relative. If you are unhappy, a milder form of misery looks good to you. And that's really what most people settle for. They try to escape one hell and run straight to another.

(*Enter bearded man dressed in beatnik style. He is looking around impatiently and snapping his fingers in time to some mysterious rhythm known only to himself. He dances about wildly for a moment and then he sees* FRED *and* STRANGER)

JUNKIE: Hey man, where do you get some kicks around here? Got to have kicks. Kicks are the whole bit. What do you say, man? (*slaps the* STRANGER *on the back with great fervor*)

STRANGER (*smiles slightly, seems unaffected by the slap*): What kind of kicks do you mean?

JUNKIE: Man, you know. Weed, H., all that jazz. Gotta have kicks.

STRANGER: I say you're wrong. I say there is joy instead of escape, reality instead of delusion, consciousness instead of unconsciousness.

JUNKIE (*looks aghast at* STRANGER *and speaks with great disgust*): Oh no! This place is the squarest! You mean you don't dig kicks?

STRANGER: Not that kind. Even you don't. Not really. They finally became so commonplace that they weren't enough for you. Narcotics became too mild. You needed bigger thrills. Do you know how you died?

JUNKIE (*proudly*): Sure, I got juiced up and tried to beat a train to a crossing at a hundred miles an hour. Man, playing chicken with a train. That's a real gas.

STRANGER: But you lost.

JUNKIE (*indignantly*): It was a tie!

STRANGER: But that wasn't your bet. You gambled your life for a thrill and you lost. Now don't try to weasel. Being alive wasn't enough for you. It finally became bearable only by flaunting death. But now that last thrill is gone. In the end, escape always leads to extinction.

JUNKIE (*angrily*): I knew it. Squaresville! (*exits*)

FRED: Well, he certainly won't like it here.

STRANGER: He didn't like it on earth either. He merely ran away from it. If a soldier runs from death, you call him a coward. But if a man runs from life, you hardly notice. That's where you go wrong. It takes courage to face life, too.

FRED (*suddenly brightening*): I've got it. My maiden aunt Margaret. She was very religious. She went to church almost every day of her life and gave large donations to all the worthy charities.

(MARGARET *materializes out of the mists. Spinsterish and prissy but not old, she still has a trace of late middle-age about her. She is dressed conservatively but not dowdyish*)

MARGARET: Freddie! You here already? (*admonishingly*) I told you to go on polyunsaturates years ago.

FRED: Hello, Aunt Margaret. How are you?

MARGARET: How am I? Awful, that's how. What did you expect?

FRED: But you led such a good life. I thought. . . .

MARGARET: (*interrupting*): Good! You call that stupid life good?

FRED: But you were one of the most religious people I ever knew. Surely you must have your reward here.

MARGARET: Ah, that's just what I thought. I did all those good things, all those stupid unpleasant things, just so I could go to Heaven. Every act, every prayer was a petition to God on my behalf. But what I was really trying to do was bribe Him with my piety. Imagine, I tried to impress God with contributions, self-sacrifice, and chastity. Chastity! What a blunder. I had no fun there and I have no fun here.

FRED: But don't good acts count for anything?

MARGARET: Good acts, yes. But what's good about acting a part? What's good about spending a life being a model of virtue when you know you don't mean it? And I didn't even confine my precious goodness to myself. No fanatic does. I made sure everyone close to me would forego the pleasures I did. I told myself I was saving them from sin. But I was really jealous of anyone who might do the things I couldn't do. No, Freddie. I wasn't good. I was performing like a trained seal. I was trying to buy a ticket to Paradise. Freddie, I'll tell you something I've learned since I've been here. Something I wish I'd known long ago. A good act is one that brings happiness to someone even if that someone is yourself. That's the thing I didn't understand. I hated the things I did. But I did them because I thought I could deceive God. So you see, my whole life was a pose, everything. What you thought was so noble and good. Just a pose. I flaunted my virtue before everyone and secretly enjoyed fooling them. Even you, Freddie. But there are no secrets here.

FRED: Then you haven't found Heaven either.

MARGARET (*sadly*): You can't buy your way into Heaven. Not with money or phony sacrifices or anything else.

FRED: Then what do you do here?

MARGARET: What can I do? You live a lifetime a certain way. You can't change just like that. The patterns are set. So now I go through eternity with my phony pose. But here everyone sees through it. They know I'm a fraud and, worst of all, so do I. (*exits into the darkness*)

(*Enter* BILL PHILLIPS. *He is in his sixties. His expression is sad as he approaches* FRED *and* STRANGER.)

FRED (*frightened*): What's Bill Phillips doing here? I don't want to see him. Get him out of here.

STRANGER: Maybe he wants to see you. These things work both ways, you know.

BILL (*smiling wryly*): So you're finally here. I've been waiting for you.

FRED (*obviously disturbed*): Me? Why me? I would think I was the last person you'd ever want to see.

BILL (*laughing bitterly*): Oh, yes, we weren't exactly good friends, were we? It was you who started that rumor about me, wasn't it? I always suspected you. I had seniority, but you couldn't wait.

FRED: What do you want now? I can't do anything about it now.

BILL: (*sinisterly*): I should have killed you then. (*takes step toward* FRED)

FRED (*backs away, cowering*): Don't you touch me! Stay away from me!

BILL (*laughing*): I can't hurt you physically anymore, look. (*swings violently at* FRED *but his hands stop short of making contact.* FRED *nevertheless cowers toward* STRANGER *and whimpers.*) You see, there's nothing physical left of you to hurt. (*laughs*)

FRED (*recovering slightly and straightening himself out*): Then what do you want? Why don't you leave me alone?

BILL: I'm just going to be around to remind you that you killed me.

FRED: Killed you? That's a lie. You killed yourself. (*turns to* STRANGER) I thought there were no lies here.

STRANGER: There aren't. What he says is true.

(FRED *opens his mouth to protest but* BILL *interrupts*)

BILL: That vice presidency meant everything to me. It was my life. I would have had it too if it hadn't been for your whispering campaign. I was a drunk, you said. A hopeless alcoholic who couldn't be depended upon. And they believed you. Somehow, they fell for it. So you got the job. *You* got *my* job, *my* life. And I stuck a forty-five in my mouth and pulled the trigger. But who do you think put that gun in my hand? Do you think you have to handle the weapon to commit murder? You killed me before I ever picked up that gun. You took my life from me. Isn't that murder? (*almost breaking down*) I was your brother and you killed me.

(*There are a few seconds of silence*)

BILL: So I'll be around to remind you. I'm going now but I won't let you get lonely. Just look around and the man you killed will be there. (*goes off into darkness*)

FRED: Well, that does it. Now I suppose I'll be punished.

STRANGER: When you are going to get it into your head that this is not a kindergarten where someone slaps you over the knuckles if you break the rules? No one has to punish you. You've already done that yourself by being what you are. And you'll continue to do it as long as you remain that way.

FRED: What about Bill Phillips? He was no saint either. He was more ambitious and power hungry than anyone. Why he was as bad as me.

STRANGER: Yes, and he suffers for it. But it's a funny thing about ambition. The man who fails to get what he's after is a little better off. If he has nothing else, he has the dream, the challenge. But the one who succeeds and then realizes that what he's been striving for is really empty—he's the one who really knows despair.

FRED: Isn't anyone happy here?

STRANGER: Of course, millions and millions.

FRED: Show me one.

(THOREAU *enters smiling*)

STRANGER: Meet Henry David Thoreau.

FRED: Oh yes, Mr. Thoreau. I remember reading about you in high school.

THOREAU (*smiling*): It must have been compulsory.

FRED: But it was interesting all the same. Let's see. You went to live in the woods and wrote a book about it, right? (THOREAU *nods*) Have you found peace here?

THOREAU: I've always known peace. Life is good if one looks for goodness. I loved the world instead of myself. That was my whole secret, and it's the only one that will save us. I walked through the woods and saw its beauty. I watched the sweep of summer embrace the countryside while the townsfolk sulked about worrying whether their clothes had gone out of fashion. As if beauty could change with the whim of every insensitive fop. But I noticed that nature brought the same styles back every year and had no concern that they might be outdated. And so while they worried I knew joy. They are still worried, and I still see the beauty of the forest. Man cannot find peace if he loses touch with nature.

FRED: But we haven't lost contact with it. We have our national parks and recreation areas. . . .

THOREAU: Nonsense! You call that nature? You drive through the woods in your luxurious automobiles. Next thing you'll be telling me that you get close to nature when you sniff your pine-scented bathroom spray. I'm talking about living with it as I did.

FRED: And what about your neighbors? Didn't they concern you. Weren't you ashamed to be considered odd?

THOREAU: If I had thought about it at all, I should have thought that *they* would feel ashamed being so much alike.

FRED: Is it so important to be different?

THOREAU: Only if being the same means to be thoughtless. It usually does.

FRED: But living in the woods is hard. Were you happy without conveniences?

THOREAU: Comfort isn't living. A cabbage is comfortable but it's never seen a sunset. I walked through storms soaked and shivering, but I saw lightning split the sky and heard the rain drumming in the forest.

FRED: And what about friends? Didn't you need the comfort of others?

THOREAU: I would rather listen to the chirping of the crickets through the night than the gossip which passes for conversation in the town. Man's time is not to be squandered in meaningless babble. There are a million mysteries waiting to be unraveled, a million places within the mind waiting to be explored. If a man would like to find Heaven, let him look for it where it might be. He will not find it in the mouths of scandal mongers or the comfort of his bed. If he would find Heaven, let him first fill his mind with wonder. (*turns and exits into darkness*)

STRANGER: You see he's happy here.

FRED: Yes, but he's a genius. Are you saying that only wise men can find Heaven?

STRANGER: Not at all. Look.

(*A little old man appears. He is sculpting a large clay form near the wings at stage left as the lights come up. He is whistling cheerfully as he works. The figure on which he works is as large as the man himself but is of no discernible shape. When he sees FRED and STRANGER approach, he stops working and smiles broadly. He is a robust but gentle-looking man, with pleasant eyes and a warm smile*)

OLD MAN: Hello, my friends. How good of you to pay me a visit.

FRED: What are you making, old man?

OLD MAN: Oh, it's nothing very important. It's my province.

FRED: (*puzzled*): A province? What's it for?

OLD MAN: (*surprised*): Why for me, of course.

FRED: But what will it be when you finish it?

OLD MAN: Oh, I'll never finish it.

FRED: Never finish it? You mean you'll go on doing it forever?

OLD MAN (*to* STRANGER): He must be new here.

STRANGER: Yes, he is. And I'm afraid he's never had a province of his own.

OLD MAN: No province of his own, oh my. Everyone should have a province of his own. Even I know that.

FRED: But what *is* a province? If it's so important I'll buy one, oh, that's no good, I'll borrow one.

OLD MAN: Oh, he *is* new, isn't he? Imagine using someone else's province. That's like trying to use someone else's brain.

FRED: Well, is someone going to tell me what a province is?

STRANGER: Tell him, old man. He has a right to know.

OLD MAN (*to* FRED): Well, you see, a province is not something a man *has*. It's something he *does*. It's an activity that he loves and that he is more or less equipped to do. It's a part of the world that he loves just for itself.

FRED: But what practical purpose does it serve?

OLD MAN: None, that's just the point. It's done not for comfort or ease or any of the usual reasons. It's done because it's where you belong. It's what you can *become*. It's your province. Look at this thing I'm doing. (*points to sculpture*) It's not a great work of art. The world would never acclaim it. And it's of no use or value to anyone but myself. But I love it. That is, I love *doing* it. And a man must have something he loves to do.

FRED: But what's the use of doing something that's of no use to anyone?

OLD MAN: It's of use if it makes someone happy. So it's of use to me. I'm someone. It isn't a matter of numbers. Anything that's good for one person is good for the world.

STRANGER: That's right. And anything that's bad for one person is bad for it.

OLD MAN: Look at it this way. A man must look forward to something, something he feels is worthwhile. It might be to climb a mountain or discover a new comet. But it must be something he finds joy in. That's his province. If he has that, he has everything, and without it he's lost. But there's one little hitch. This thing, this joy, must come from outside of his ego. What I mean is, this thing he loves—it must be something that helps him fulfill himself. Oh, yes. Everyone must have a province.

STRANGER: Well, goodbye, old man.

(OLD MAN *waves as they walk away toward center stage. The lights go down and he disappears*)

STRANGER: You see what he means, don't you?

FRED (*still puzzled*): I still don't get it. I wanted to make something of myself and I did. I had position and respect. I was an important man in the community. Maybe that's my province. Is it so wrong?

STRANGER: But were you doing it because you loved it or because you were looking forward to the admiration of others?

FRED: Well, what's wrong with the admiration of others? I thought love was the highest virtue here.

STRANGER: Love, yes. But don't mistake vanity for love. You want to be looked up to by those beneath you. You want them to see you as a man who has something they would like to have. You want their envy. That's not love. It's ego. Besides, the virtue you're thinking of is *loving*, not the desire for adulation. What we've all been trying to tell you is that Heaven is not based on dreams of conquest or false devotion or on the envy of your neighbors. The Heaven you dream of is a fiction from childhood and the phrase that traps you is the one that says, "And they lived happily ever after." Do you know why the story always ends with that line? Because the rest is indescribable. The truth is that the eternal bliss of your dreams would really be intolerable. No one could endure the infinite pleasures of his fancy. In such a Heaven, one would soon find himself pleading for pain. No, my friend. What man wants is joy. Not eternal titillation. What we've been trying to say is that Heaven is really a simple thing, and it's always *now*.

FRED (*finally realizing*): Then what you mean is that dying doesn't change anything. That Heaven and Hell are as much a part of life as they are of death. That we can have them even on earth.

STRANGER: Yes, that's it exactly.

FRED: Well, I'll be damned.

STRANGER: Yes, I'm afraid you will. (*takes his arm and leads him off*)

CURTAIN

epilogue

The courage to grow is intimately related to the realization that our time in this realm is finite. When we are very young, we feel that we will live forever. And when we are very old, we believe that it is too late to change. But in those many years that lie between these two extremes, there are thousands of opportunities to make a decision about altering the course of our lives. With the knowledge that time will run out if we fail to act, we can muster the courage to do so. Let us therefore resolve that that moment is at hand. The process of becoming begins at the moment we make the decision to allow it to unfold. Let that moment be now.

THE BEGINNING

references

ADLER, A. *The practice and theory of individual psychology*. New York: Harcourt, 1927.

ADORNO, T. W.; FRENKEL-BRUNSWIK, E.; LEVINSON, D. J.; and SANFORD, R. N. *Authoritarian personality*. New York: Harper & Row, 1950.

ALLPORT, G. W., and POSTMAN, L. *The psychology of rumor*. New York: Holt, 1947.

ANGELL, N. *Story of money*. Garden City, N.Y.: Garden City Publishing Co., 1929.

ARDRY, R. *Territorial Imperative*. New York: Atheneum, 1966.

ASHLEY, W. R.; HARPER, R. S.; and RUNYON, D. L. The perceived size of coins in normal and hypnotically induced economic states. *Amer. J. of Psychol.*, 1951, *34*, 564–572.

AUERBACK, A. "Swinging." The sexual exchange of marriage partners, in R. R. BELL, ed., *Sexual Behavior*, 1971, 1 (2), 72–76.

BARNETT, L. *The universe and Dr. Einstein* (2nd ed.). New York: Harper & Bros., 1957.

422

BEALS, R. L., and HOJDER, H. *Introduction to anthropology* (3rd ed.). New York: Macmillan, 1965.

BEECHER, W., and BEECHER, M. *Beyond success and failure.* New York: Julian Press, 1966.

BERLE, A. A. *Power.* New York: Harcourt Brace and World, 1967.

BERNE, E. *Games people play.* New York: Grove Press, 1964.

BEXTON, W. H.; HERON, W.; and SCOTT, T. H. Effects of decreased variation in the sensory environment. *Canadian J. of Psychol.*, 1954, *8*, 70–76.

BRANDON, N. *Psychology of self-esteem.* Los Angeles: Nash, 1969.

BREASTED, J. *The dawn of conscience.* New York: Scribner's, 1933.

BUBER, M. *I and thou.* Edinburgh: T. & T. Clark, 1937.

BUCKE, R. M. *Cosmic consciousness.* New York: Olympia, 1972.

BUGENTAL, J. F. T. *The search for authenticity.* New York: Holt, Rinehart and Winston, 1965.

CAMPBELL, J. *Hero with a thousand faces.* New York: Pantheon, 1949.

CAMUS, A. *The stranger.* Trans. by STUART GILBERT. New York: Knopf, 1946.

————. *Myth of Sisyphus and other essays.* New York: Random House (paperback).

CARLSON, C. E. *Behavioral concepts and nursing intervention.* Philadelphia: Lippincott, 1970.

CARRIGHAR, S. *Wild heritage.* Boston: Houghton Mifflin, 1965.

CHILMAN, C. W. If I had another chance at fatherhood. *Today's Health* (April) 1969.

CLOWARD, R. A., and OHLIN, L. E. *Delinquency and opportunity, a theory of delinquent gangs.* New York: The Free Press, 1960.

COLEMAN, J. C. *Abnormal psychology and modern life.* (3rd ed.). Glenview, Ill.: Scott Foresman, 1964.

COOLEY, C. H. *Human nature and the social order.* New York: Scribner's, 1902.

COWLES, J. T. Food tokens as incentives for learning by chimpanzees. *Comp. Psychol. Mongr.*, 1937, *14*, 71–136.

DE ROPP, R. S. *The master game: Pathways to higher consciousness beyond the drug experience.* New York: Delacorte, 1968.

ELLIS, A. Rational psychotherapy. *J. of Gen. Psychol.*, 1958, *59*, 35–49.

————. *Reason and emotion in psychotherapy.* New York: Lyle Stuart, 1962.

FRANKL, V. E. *Man's search for meaning: An introduction to logotherapy.* Boston: Beacon Press, 1963.

FREUD, S. Totem and taboo (1913), in *Complete psychological works of Sigmund Freud* (Vol. XIII). London: Hogarth, 1962.

————. Civilization and its discontents (1930), in *Complete psychological works of Sigmund Freud* (Vol. XXI). London: Hogarth, 1962.

FRIED, M. Social problems and psychopathology, in HENRY WECHSLER, H., SOLOMON, L., and KRAMER, B. M. (eds.), *Social psychology and mental health.* New York: Holt, Rinehart and Winston, 1970.

FROMM, E. *The art of loving.* New York: Harper & Row, 1956.

————. *Man for himself.* New York: Holt, Rinehart and Winston, 1947.

FROMM, E. *The sane society*. New York: Holt, Rinehart and Winston, 1955.

FULBRIGHT, J. W. *The arrogance of power*. New York: Random House, 1966.

GALLOWAY, D. D. *The absurd hero in American fiction*. Austin, Tex.: University of Texas Press, 1966.

GOFFMAN, E. *Stigma*. Englewood Cliffs, N.J.: Prentice-Hall, 1963.

GOLDENSON, R. M. *Encyclopedia of human behavior: Psychology, psychiatry and mental health* (Vol. I). Garden City, N.Y.: Doubleday, 1970.

GREENE, T. A. *Modern man in search of manhood*. New York: Associated Press, 1967.

GURKO, L. *Heroes, highbrows and the popular mind*. Indianapolis: Bobbs-Merrill, 1953.

HALL, E. T. *Silent language*. New York: Doubleday, 1959.

HARLOW, H. F., and HARLOW, M. K. Primary affectional patterns in primates. *Amer. J. of Orthopsychiatry*, 1960, *30*, 676–684.

_____. Learning to love. *Scient. Amer.*, 1966, *54*, 244–272.

HENRY, J. *Culture against man*. New York: Random House, 1963.

HOFSTADTER, R. *The paranoid style in American politics and other essays*. New York: Knopf, 1965.

HOLLENDER, M. H. Prostitution, the body, and human relatedness. *Int. J. Psychoanal.*, 1961, *42*, 404–413.

HOROWITZ, M. J. Spatial behavior and psychopathology. *J. of Nervous and Mental Disorders*, 1968, *146* (1).

HUXLEY, A. L., *After many a summer dies the swan*. New York: Harper, 1940.

_____. *The perennial philosophy*. New York: Harper, 1945.

_____. *On Art and Artists*. PHILIPSON, M. (ed.) New York: Harper, 1960.

_____. The politics of ecology. *Santa Barbara center for the study of democratic institutions*, 1963, p. 6.

ISHERWOOD, C. (ed.) *Vedanta for the western world*. New York: Viking Press, 1945.

JACOBSON, E. *Progressive relaxation*. Chicago: University of Chicago Press, 1938.

JAMES, W. *Psychology* (Vols. I and II). New York: Henry Holt & Co. 1890.

JOURARD, S. M. *Personal adjustment*. An approach through the study of the healthy personality. (2nd ed.). New York: Macmillan, 1963.

KANTER, R. M. Communes. *Psychology Today*, 1970, *4* (2).

KELLY, G. *The psychology of personal constructs* (two volumes). New York: W. W. Norton, 1955.

KEYNES, J. M. *Essays in persuasion*. New York: Harcourt, 1932.

KINSEY, A. C., POMEROY, W. B., and MARTIN, C. E. *Sexual behavior in the human female*. Philadelphia: Saunders, 1953.

_____. *Sexual behavior in the human male*. Philadelphia: Saunders, 1948.

KINZEL, A. F. *Time* (June 6), 1970.

KNIGHT, J. A., *For the love of money*. Philadelphia: Lippincott, 1968.

LAMBERT, W. W., SOLOMON, R. L., and WATSON, P. D. Reinforcement and extinction as factors in size estimations. *J. of Exper. Psychol.*, 1949, *39*, 637–641.

LEGMAN, G. *Love and death: A study in censorship*. New York: Breaking Point Publications, 1949.

LIPTON, L. *The erotic revolution: An affirmative view of the new morality*. Los Angeles: Sherbourne Press, 1965.

LIPTON, S. Dissociated personality: a case report. *Psychiat Quart.*, 1943, *17*, 35–56.

LOBSENZ, N. M. *Is anybody happy?* New York: Doubleday, 1962.

LORD RAGLAND. *The hero*. London: Watts & Co., 1936.

LOWEN, A. *Pleasure*. New York: Lancer Books, 1970.

MALINOWSKI, B. *Sex, culture and myth*. New York: Harcourt Brace & World, 1962.

MARSHALL, D. S., and SUGGS, R. C. (eds.). Sexual behavior on Mangaia in *Human sexual behavior*. New York: Basic Books, 1971.

MASLOW, A. M. *Toward a psychology of being* (2nd ed.). Princeton: Van Nostrand, 1968.

_____. *Motivation and personality* (2nd ed.). New York: Harper & Row, 1970.

MAY, R. *Psychology and the human dilemma*. Princeton: Van Nostrand, 1967.

_____. *Love and will*. New York: W. W. Norton, 1969.

MCCARTHY, J. R. *America's retreat from victory*. New York: Devin, 1951.

MCLUHAN, M. *Understanding media: The extensions of man*. New York: McGraw-Hill, 1964.

MEAD, G. H. *Mind, self and society*. Chicago: University of Chicago Press, 1934.

MEAD, M. *Coming of age in Samoa*. New York: Morrow, 1928.

MENNINGER, K., with MAYMAN, M., and PRUYSER, P. *The vital balance: The life process in mental health and illness*. New York: Viking Press, 1963.

MESSINGER, J. Sex and repression in an Irish folk community, in MARSHALL, D. S. and SUGGS, R. C. (eds.), *Human sexual behavior*. New York: Basic Books, 1971.

MILGRAM, S. Behavior study of obedience. *J. of Ab. Soc. Psychol.*, 1963, *67*, 371–378.

MILLER, N. E. The frustration-aggression hypothesis. *Psychological Review*, 1941, *38*, 337–342.

MILLS, C. W. *Power, politics, and people*: the collected essays. New York: Oxford University Press, 1963.

MONTAGU, A. M. F. *Anthropology and human nature*. Boston: Porter Sargent, 1957.

_____. *Man observed*. New York: Putnam's 1968.

MORGAN, E. V. *A history of money*. Great Britain: C. Nicholas & Co., 1965.

MORRIS, D. *The naked ape*. New York: McGraw-Hill, 1967.

MOYERS, B. Listening to America. *Harper's* (Dec.), 1970.

NOYES, J. H. *History of American socialisms*. 1870. Reprint. New York: Dover, 1966.

OLIVEN, J. F. *Sexual hygiene and pathology*. Philadelphia: Lippincott, 1965.

O'NEIL, G., and N. *Open marriage, a new life-style for couples*. New York: Evans, 1972.

PACKARD, V. *The status seekers.* New York: David McKay, 1959.

PERLS, F.; HEFFERLINE, R. E.; and GOODMAN, P. *Gestalt Therapy: Excitement and growth in the human personality.* New York: Julian Press, 1951.

PHILLIPS, E. L. *Psychotherapy: A modern theory and practice.* Englewood Cliffs, N.J.: Prentice-Hall, 1956.

REICH, W. *Myth and guilt.* New York: George Braziller Co., 1957.

ROBINSON, D. S. (ed.). *Anthology of modern philosophy.* New York: T. Y. Crowell, 1931. Trans. by O. W. WRIGHT. The thoughts, letters and opuscules of Blaise Pascal. Boston: Houghton Mifflin, 1888.

ROGERS, C. *On becoming a person.* Boston: Houghton Mifflin, 1961.

ROSTEN, R. A. *"Some personality characteristics of compulsive gamblers."* Ph.D. dissertation, University of California, Los Angeles, 1961.

RUSSELL, B. *A history of western philosophy.* New York: Simon and Schuster, 1945.

_____. *Power, a new social analysis.* New York: W. W. Norton, 1938.

SCHACTER, S., and SINGER, J. E. Cognitive social and physiological determinants of emotional states. *Psychological Review,* 1962, *69*, 379–399.

SCHALLER, G. B. *The year of the gorilla.* Chicago: U. Chicago Press, 1964.

SCHUSKY, E. L., and CULBERT, T. P. *Introducing culture.* Englewood Cliffs, N.J.: Prentice-Hall, 1967.

SOLOMON, P.; KUBZANSKY, P. E.; LEIDERMAN, P. H.; MENDELSON, J. H.; TRUMBULL, R.; and WEXLER, D. (eds.). *Sensory deprivation.* A symposium held at Harvard Medical School in 1958. Cambridge, Mass.: Harvard University Press, 1966.

SPINOZA, B. *Ethics.* Trans. by W. H. WHITE; rev. by A. H. S. MILFORD, London: Oxford University Press, 1927.

STEIN, J. *Effective personality: A humanistic approach.* Belmont, Calif.: Brooks-Cole, 1972.

SZASZ, T. S. *The manufacture of madness: A comparative study of the inquisition and the mental health movement.* New York: Harper & Row, 1970.

TEILHARD DE CHARDIN, P. *The phenomenon of man.* Trans. by B. WALL. New York: Harper, 1959.

THEOBALD, R. *Free men and free markets.* New York: Clarkson N. Potter, 1963.

TILLICH, P. *Theology of Culture.* New York: Oxford University Press, 1959.

THIGPEN, C. H., and CLECKLEY, H. A case of multiple personality. *Journal of Abnormal Social Psychology,* 1954, *49*, 135–151.

WALSTER, E., and BERSCHEID, E. Adrenaline makes the heart grow fonder. *Psychology Today* (June), 1971.

WATTS, A. W. *Does it matter?* New York: Random House, 1971.

_____. *Psychotherapy, east and west.* New York: Pantheon, 1961.

WELCH, R. H., JR. *The politician.* Belmont, Mass.: Belmont Publishing Co., 1963.

WOODMAN, J. *How to write for money.* Hollywood: Marcell Rodd Co. 1944.

WYLIE, P. *Generation of vipers.* New York: Holt, Rinehart and Winston, 1942.

index